THE SYSTEMS THINKING APPROACH

TO STRATEGIC PLANNING AND MANAGEMENT

THE SYSTEMS THINKING APPROACH

TO STRATEGIC PLANNING AND MANAGEMENT

Stephen G. Haines

President and Founder
Centre for Strategic Management®
San Diego, California

S^t_L

St. Lucie Press
Boca Raton   London
New York   Washington, D.C.

Library of Congress Cataloging-in-Publication Data

Haines, Stephen G.
    The systems thinking approach to strategic planning and management/ by Stephen G.
    Haines.
      p. cm.
    Includes bibliographical references and index.
    ISBN 1-57444-278-3
    1. Strategic planning. 2. System analysis. 3. Management. I. Title.

HD30.28 .H3338 2000
658.4′.012—dc21
                                          00-027845
                                              CIP

© 2000 by CRC Press LLC
St. Lucie Press is an imprint of CRC Press LLC

No claim to original U.S. Government works
International Standard Book Number 1-57444-278-3
Library of Congress Card Number 00-027845
Printed in the United States of America 1 2 3 4 5 6 7 8 9 0
Printed on acid-free paper

Preface

Welcome to *The Systems Thinking Approach^SM to Strategic Planning and Management* — our revolutionary new approach to designing, building, and sustaining customer-focused high performance learning organizations that can thrive in the dynamically changing 21st century.

In the mid-1990s, I was at the annual conference of what was then the International Planning Forum in New York City. The Planning Forum, as many of you know, was the premier association in western society focused on improving the practice of **Strategic Management (strategic** planning and strategic change **management)**. While this book claims to have "reinvented" strategic planning, I had wondered if that claim was just so much hype. However, after attending this conference. I was more convinced than ever that we have actually invented a new paradigm for managing strategically. You can't separate planning from management, as it is the first function of management; thus our first premise is that *planning and change are the primary responsibility of senior management.*

Unfortunately, this "state-of-the-art" conference featured numerous well-known concurrent session speakers, each armed with 35-mm color slides, big screens, darkened rooms, and the latest jargon piece of strategic management. **BORING!**

Typically, when the lights were raised at the end of one hour of one-way, passive communications, and questions were finally invited, it was too late. People rarely had much to ask about or comment on. Instead, many had left the sessions prior to this late attempt by the speakers to be "participative" and meet their "customers'" needs.

I thought by 1999 that this old way of thinking about strategic planning was gone along with the Planning Forum (now struggling as the Strategic Leadership Forum). However, 3 months ago I was invited to meet with the CEO and Executive VP of a medium-size, yet well-known company to discuss how I could help them with strategic planning. It took me all of 5 minutes to uncover the fact that they had been spending many days and hours defining their current state (the old SWOT [strengths, weaknesses, opportunities, threats] assessment). However, they were unhappy with their process, so I quickly pointed out that they had no future-oriented vision (or purpose/goals). You'd have thought I discovered the atom, such was their immediate recognition of what they had been doing wrong.

Sadly, this old way of planning by starting with today and extrapolating forward is still alive and well today. Part of my reason for writing this book is to help stamp out this outmoded way of planning, which no longer works in today's dynamic world. Instead, our research found three main premises that form the foundation for this book and our consulting practices, using these same materials.

Our first main premise is that there is no "Holy Grail" to be found in strategic management, only an understanding that *planning and change are the responsibility of senior management*. In fact, it is now their *primary* job in today's world of constant change. Excellent organizations don't just have a budgeting cycle each year; they have a "strategic management" cycle led by senior management as they work *on* the organization, rather than just *in* the organization. As planning is just the first function of management, and strategic planning is just the highest order of planning and the purview of senior management, then every company has three basic goals:

1. Develop strategic and operational plans.
2. Ensure their successful implementation and change.
3. Build and sustain high performance over the long term.

Our second main premise to planning and implementation is a basic truism that *people support what they help create*, thus requiring extensive interactions, dialogue, debate, facilitation, and participation with all the key organizational stakeholders (and especially customers).

Our third main premise in writing this book and in our consulting practice with CEOs is the need for a *systems methodology and structure* in which to build the planning and change management process. Hence, our Systems Thinking Approach to Strategic Management explained in Chapter 3. And our number one systems question is "What is your purpose, goal, end product or even, in planning terms, Vision." Needless to say, that medium-size company mentioned earlier now has reinvented its strategic planning process with our help. They are well on the way to effective implementation of some badly needed and long delayed strategies as a way to achieve their new vision.

Unfortunately, we continue to find conferences, books, and companies similar in many ways to those described above. The same has been true in our extensive literature research of 14 different and popular strategic planning models. We continue to see that every one of the popular planning models in use is an analytic solution to a systems problem.

You see, organizations *are* systems, no matter how good or how poorly they function. Peter Senge and his book, *The Fifth Discipline* was right. His fifth discipline is systems thinking — and as a Western business society we have yet to understand, embrace, and develop skills in this type of thinking.

While the awareness of systems thinking is growing, it seems hard to grasp the basic concepts and specific tools, according to Linkage, Inc. conference planner Robin Pedrelli. She is leading the development of the first independent Systems Thinking Conference in response to constant and growing feedback about the problems with systems thinking. This is not surprising to me, since most of us were brought up and educated in scientific (analytic) disciplines such as engineering (myself), law, accounting, computers, medicine, etc.

Out of 14 models we researched to come up with our Ten Step Reinventing Strategic Management (Planning and Change) Model, there were four key steps no one else had addressed: our Parallel Process, our Plan-to-Implement step, our In-Depth Change Management step, and our Annual Strategic Review and Update.

In addition, only 4 models had a beginning "educating and organizing" step we call "Plan-to-Plan," and only 2 out of 14 had a measurement step (our Step 3, Key

Success Factors). Worse yet, only 4 of 14 tied strategic planning to business unit planning and only 7 of 14 further tied it to annual planning and budgets.

Again, these other popular models are analytic approaches to the systems problem of getting the entire organization to link and function together synergistically in support of the customer. And we wonder why Henry Minzberg, one of the most respected professors in the field of strategic management, published a book in 1994 on *The Rise and Fall of Strategic Planning*.

Even worse, Minzberg also later published a brilliant critique of ten schools of strategic planning entitled *Strategy Safari*. I say "even worse" because when the most astute person in the strategic management field never even mentions systems thinking or our approach as one of the ten, he shows himself to be bound by the world of traditional analytic thinking (not systems thinking). He even says that "we are blind people and strategy formulation is our elephant" from the old story of ten people touching different parts of the elephant in order to identify it and coming to ten different answers, all of which were wrong.

His only concession to systems thinking in the book is that "the field of strategic management may itself be moving toward synthesis" vs. these ten different views. This book is, of course, all about the synthesis of these ten models (and more) within the framework of systems thinking.

My experiences and my observations of this field have clearly shown why planners are an endangered species, while at the same time, the amount of strategic planning in companies is increasing dramatically. Planners and their theories are obsolete.

The increasing rate of change in the business world has caused a corresponding increase in the rate of strategic planning as CEOs try to figure out ways to survive and thrive in this uncertain environment. However, too much of strategic planning has been inadequate, causing what we term the "SPOTS syndrome": Strategic Plans On Top Shelves ... gathering dust! We have reinvented the field of strategic planning into Strategic Management (Planning and Change) using our copyrighted Systems Thinking Approach[SM] in this book.

Further, this is a book about carefully researched "best practices," not only of a successful process on "how to" do strategic planning and strategic change, but also of the selection of successful strategies that give companies a competitive advantage over the long term.

Yes, there are some right answers — just not singular, analytic ones — in today's global, integrated, ever-changing world. We predict that systems thinking will become the norm sometime in the first decade of the 21st century.

About the Author

CEO, Strategist, and Entrepreneur ...
Facilitator, Systems Thinker, and Author

Stephen G. Haines represents a new breed of strategic planning expert: one who places equal importance on both the vision, strategies, and *content* of strategic planning, as well as the *process* of strategic planning and change management. He has worked not only as a strategist from a CEO and senior line management perspective, but also as a change management process expert at the most senior level.

Steve has over 30 years of international and senior executive experience leading planning and change efforts in a wide variety of private and public applications:

- As a senior corporate executive for over 20 years in the areas of managing turnarounds and high-growth changes in organizations.
- As a member of eight top management teams — both in the U.S. and internationally — with corporate responsibilities for all aspects of organization functioning, including planning, operations, marketing, PR and communications, finance, HR, training, and facilities.
- As chief planning executive and strategist for two major U.S. corporations.
- As part-owner and president of University Associates Consulting & Training Services, a well-known and widely respected international firm specializing in strategic planning, change management, and experiential learning, as well as training and development.
- As an entrepreneur, president, and founder of the Centre for Strategic Management, an alliance of experienced professionals who share a strong business orientation that incorporates humanistic values and systems thinking, with ten offices in North America and eight internationally.
- As an external strategic planning consultant applying the lessons, frameworks, and theories learned from the leading practitioners of the recent past:
  1. Michael Kami, Chief Planning Executive at IBM and Xerox
  2. Russell Ackoff, professor (and Renaissance Man), at University of Pennsylvania
  3. J. William Pfeiffer, Founder and President of University Associates
  4. Henry Migliore, Dean of the Business School for 17 years at Oral Roberts University.
- As a 1968 engineering graduate of the U.S. Naval Academy, a Department of Defense Human Goals Institute graduate, Navy jet pilot, shipboard officer, and naval advisor in Vietnam.

He is also a prolific author, having written and published seven previous books. Combining those books with his eight tool kits and reference guides and six executive briefing booklets at the Centre, Steve has over 7000 pages in print. He has also taught over 60 different seminars, served on a number of boards, including chairman of the board for a credit union, and is in demand as a keynote speaker on CEO and board of directors issues.

Acknowledgments

Any time a book is written, there are many people involved in its production. In this case, there are two groups of people to acknowledge who have had no involvement in the actual writing of this book, but who have been instrumental in its formulation.

First, I would like to acknowledge all of my partners at the Centre for Strategic Management who have also used this Systems Thinking Approach over the last 10 years. They have helped to refine this book over and over again as they struggled to learn and perfect their consulting practices.

Specifically, my Canadian Managing Partner, Jim McKinlay of Canmore, Alberta, was the first person willing to try out my radically different ideas on Strategic Management (Planning and Change). At the time, Jim was Staff Development Director for the Province of Saskatchewan and was willing to pilot this process. He soon became my partner and has been involved with the evolution and refinement of this reinventing model ever since.

In the U.S., my partner, Charlie Hoffman of Tucson, Arizona, has been deeply introspective regarding our work and model over the past few years. As a result, many of the latest and best new ideas in the book are a result of the discussions we have had while working with Sundt Corp. of Tucson and Giant Industries of Phoenix. However, since "transparency" is part of the Centre's values, I must admit that most of these good ideas actually showed up about 10 P.M. in a hotel's hot tub while discussing the events of the day.

Secondly, I would like to thank my many strategic planning clients over the past 10 years who have shown a tremendous willingness to experiment with infinite variations in planning and change — to boldly go where no man has gone before — thus teaching me far more than can possibly be measured. Their practical planning and implementation of solutions to problems that we grappled with together were the genesis for the many, many linkages in our systems thinking approach to strategic management. We also jointly discovered most of our "Fail-Safe Mechanisms for Implementation Success" that are detailed throughout this book. They have helped to make this the most practical, common-sense "how-to" book on strategic planning and strategic change management possible.

Lastly, my wife Jayne, the love of my life since high school, has been so supportive and helpful in so many ways and in so many roles that it is hard for me to put it into words. Without her, not only would this book not have been written, cleaned up, and properly edited, but I would also be lost in my work and in my life.

Stephen G. Haines

Table of Contents

Introduction

REVOLUTIONARY CHANGE

Business as usual just won't cut it anymore.

When we try to imagine what business will be like in the new millennium, it seems that the only constant we can count on is change. When we consider the fluctuating, competitive global markets and governments, telecommunications and the Internet, high-technology industries continuing their exponential gains, recessionary cost-cutting, shorter life cycles for products and services juxtaposed with higher consumer quality and service expectations — revolutionary change, in fact, *is* our new daily reality.

These revolutionary changes present us with business challenges that test our creativity and endurance. What business and organizational strategies can we come up with that will help us respond to these challenges? Will it be possible to lead and manage our way through these turbulent times to future successes? Most importantly, can we determine what the right answers are for us and then adjust along the best path to follow amid this revolution?

PAST PRACTICES/FUTURE SUCCESSES

One thing is certain today. "Business as usual" really *won't* cut it anymore. It won't cut it in private industry anywhere, or in government, the military, or any not-for-profit. In these tumultuous times it is tempting to look for answers among solutions that worked for us in the past. Tempting, but perhaps not wise.

The best advice we've heard recently is what Jack Welch, the CEO and Chairman of General Electric, is reputed to have said, "If you are still doing things now the same way you did them five years ago, you are probably doing something wrong."

Applying past practices to current problems will only confuse our need for a future direction or innovative strategies. It is impractical to expect any *single trend* from today's popular lineup — such as value-chain-management, the learning organization, knowledge management, best value, empowerment, service management, cost-competitive, benchmarking, or the balanced scorecard — to act as a general cure-all. There is a continuous stream of books available on every conceivable type of management topic, each one focusing on a different topic, slant, fad, or trend. With each of these trends, it's easy to believe that we've found salvation, when in truth we're only adding to the confusion. Searching for a universal solution just isn't realistic.

During my 30 years of active participation in organizations, I have observed a growing dissatisfaction with the way organizations are managed and led. Playing a variety of executive roles in a diverse range of public and private institutions has convinced me that *there is no one best solution* to the issues that confront organizations today. I believe, however, that there are "right answers" available to us. If it is truly our desire to build and lead a customer-focused, high-performance learning organization in our future, we must completely rethink, reinvent, and replan the way we position, define, and run our businesses.

Throughout my years of work, I have often found strategic plans falling victim to the dreaded SPOTS (Strategic Plans on Top Shelves ... gathering dust) syndrome. Even where de facto strategic plans already exist, I have found that they are often based on simplistic premises, such as purely financial or quality considerations, with no provision for other, complementary and necessary strategies, activities, and implementation of change.

If we tried to sail a boat the way we run organizations, the boats would all sink. Boats have to have *"watertight integrity."* In contrast, for many reasons, organizations don't have an integrated fit, synergy, and commitment to the overall vision. Think about this. Why do CEOs allow this to happen?

Given the current state of global, revolutionary change, planning is needed more than ever before. So is the strategic change aspect of following up, tracking, adjusting, and correcting the plan, which begins to become obsolete soon after the ink is dry. Unfortunately, it seems we have abandoned disciplined thinking, planning, and the difficult job of strategic change for the empty rhetoric of vision or value statements along with short-term communications and training as the way to achieve results.

In short, while the number of planners has dwindled drastically, strategic management (planning and change) is increasing dramatically. Without a multilevel, disciplined, systems approach, however, the "plan" is not worth much more than the paper it's printed on.

MY REASONS FOR WRITING THIS BOOK

My reasons for writing this book grew out of my conviction that these observations are part of a continuing pattern, not just isolated events. Mintzberg's recent book continues to substantiate my views. Prior to developing the Reinventing Strategic Management (Planning and Change) Model that serves as the basis for this book, I observed and participated in a wide variety of planning processes. In addition to this, I researched and analyzed 14 other planning models and 13 more change models that are well known and currently in use throughout North America. However, each one presented only a piecemeal solution to the multilevel need of focusing on the customer from an organization-wide, strategic perspective in our rapidly changing environment.

It became clear to me over time that there were actually three "seemingly simple elements" that failed to appear in most strategic planning processes. As a result, these plans rarely got off the ground. I say "seemingly" simple because, while these elements are easy to pinpoint, in retrospect they actually embrace a complex body of thought and action.

Seemingly Simple Element #1: *Planning and Change are* **THE PRIMARY** *Responsibility of Management and Leadership*

The first seemingly simple element suggests that planning in today's organization is often not viewed as an inherent part of top management's leading or managing role. In fact, the actual planning process often dwindles to nothing more than an activity to be completed quickly, so executives can get back to their real job of managing.

Worse, they abdicate planning to that endangered species — planners — who are then expected to write a doctoral-sized thesis that is then destined for SPOTS. Or, even worse, they listen to organization development consultants who convince them that they simply need a clear and shared vision and values for the organization to self-organize.

This failure to see planning and change now as the primary responsibility of the senior management and leadership has caused us to lose sight of the three common-sense goals in every effective strategic planning and strategic change management process. These three goals are needed by virtually every organization everywhere, and in every sector and country.

So, Mr. and Ms. CEO, below is your set of yearly goals. For you HR executives looking for the core competencies of your organization, strategic management (the competencies of understanding and achieving these three goals) is the number one core competency of every organization.

Goal #1: Develop the strategic and annual plans and documents.
Goal #2: Ensure their successful rollout, implementation, and change.
Goal #3: Build and sustain high performance over the long term.

Most plans that fail do so because there is no provision or focus on Goal #2 (implementation and change) from the beginning of the planning process. Instead, the plan with all its associated documents is seen as an end in itself. In most traditional approaches to strategic planning, planners and CEOs tend to minimize the number of strategic changes and paradigm shifts that will need to be made as the strategic plan is implemented. Thus, they neglect to insert fail-safe mechanisms and structures for successful strategic change management into each step of the strategic management process itself.

Thus, the Right Answer #1 (and our number one absolute for success) is that it is essential to set up an organized *strategic change leadership steering committee* to guide the successful implementation of the strategic plan (Goal #2). To combat this, our Reinventing Strategic Management Model was developed with 44 change management structures and fail-safe mechanisms incorporated throughout the strategic management process. We have our clients to thank for these fail-safe mechanisms as they have consistently worked with us to develop these structures and systems that guarantee success.

SEEMINGLY SIMPLE ELEMENT #2: *PEOPLE SUPPORT WHAT THEY HELP CREATE*

It is critical for successful strategic planning and change management implementation that a complete, committed *"buy-in"* be obtained from the collective leadership of the organization, as well as from all key stakeholders responsible for implementing the plan. Beyond that, the important issue of maintaining the "stay-in" of all those key stakeholders will be a later issue. "Stay-in" is even more crucial over the long term, due to the natural property of all living systems to run down and die over time (i.e, entropy).

We all know that the traditional boss–subordinate relationships prevalent in most organizations 20 years ago have pretty much disappeared. In today's successful organizations, employees are seeking more learning, growth, and empowerment. This requires more of a leader–follower relationship. It introduces a nonfear-based, more proactive or voluntary aspect into the work environment. This in turn raises motivation, productivity, and trust.

Employees today demand participation and respect within the organization, especially (but not only) white collar workers. People need to know that their ideas count, that they have some say in decisions that will affect them, and that they are empowered to use their minds and their ideas. Without this involvement, even the best provisions for implementation of the organizational plan will fall by the wayside. The NIH (Not Invented Here) syndrome wins again. In other words, people naturally want input into decisions that affect them prior to the decision being finalized.

Bringing all the collective leadership and key stakeholders into the development and implementation of a strategic plan presents one of the first tough choices you will face as you think through this process. This is where you must engineer success, up front, prior to beginning the planning process. In selecting who will comprise your core strategic planning team, it is normally important to keep the size of the team to six to eight individuals. From a group dynamics viewpoint, this is the ideal size to do productive planning work although our experience shows it is possible to double this number up to 15 and still be productive in planning.

However, there are still many more individuals throughout the organization and its environment who will be the key stakeholders in implementing the plan — namely, middle managers, frontline employees, customers, vendors, etc. The problem then becomes, how do you get buy-in and commitment from all the key stakeholders who did not participate in creating the plan? This dilemma is usually handled very differently in public and private organizations; however, neither group has been particularly successful.

In the public sector, with its need for openness and public consultation, the conventional response is that the leadership delegates the planning to task forces in the name of participation. The frequent result, however, is that senior leadership actually ends up abdicating their responsibilities; i.e., there is no sense of ownership by the collective leadership. The result is barely a SPOTS syndrome, and fulfills only part of Goal #1 (creating the document).

The private sector, with its competitive and confidential leanings, is just the opposite. The number of people involved in any planning or decision-making process is usually so small that there is no ownership or understanding of the plan outside of a few select executives. As in the public sector, this breeds lack of commitment to a plan in which most of the organizational members had no participation. These examples point out, again and again, why the seemingly simple element of getting committed buy-in of key stakeholders, along with a critical mass for change from everyone involved, is really quite complex.

This Reinventing Strategic Planning Model uses what I call a "Parallel Process" to address this issue. This Parallel Process identifies the specific key stakeholders and collective leadership that can either block or assist effective implementation. In Chapter 6 we will deal with this fact and the tough choices involved in the Parallel Process.

In sum, this leads us to Right Answer #2 in Reinventing Strategic Management (Planning and Change), the development of professional management and leadership skills and practices in order to involve and empower employees in pursuit of your mission. This critical, but often-overlooked element is business' *only* true competitive advantage over the long term.

SEEMINGLY SIMPLE ELEMENT #3: *THE SYSTEMS THINKING APPROACH*[SM]

> *Problems that are created by our current level of thinking can't be solved by that same level of thinking.*
>
> *-Albert Einstein*

The third seemingly simple element is one that embraces a common-sense way of looking at the organization as a whole *system.*

System (sis'tem) n. a set of components that work together for the overall objective of the whole. (From the General Systems Theory (GST) developed during the study of biology in the 1940s through the 1970s.)

By definition, the piecemeal approach of solving only one problem at a time, then moving on to the next, cannot succeed in our interactive, living systems world. However, most of the 14 other planning models I researched had the following worn-out analytical approach to planning:

1. Analyze today's issues as our starting point
2. Problem-solve those issues
3. Conduct long-range forecasting and planning by projecting into the future.

In my experience, this methodical approach produces plans that are unveiled and then sit collecting dust and are never looked at again.

Though this "one-foot-in-front-of-the-other" approach may have worked in a relatively constant environment, it won't work in today's ever-changing business environment. Rather, we must make a fundamental shift to systems thinking, where our focus is consistently on outcomes and adjusting the relationships among the parts as necessary to keep on track.

This focusing on the outcomes compels us to practice what I call *"backwards thinking."* In backwards thinking, we focus on what we perceive as the ideal future vision and outcomes for our organization and then think backward to our present state. We then look for ways to bridge the gap between the two.

Or, as Stephen Covey says, "We must begin with the end in mind." Only then can we determine how to fit all our activities together into an integrated and aligned system of managing strategically (i.e., a strategic management system). This is a fundamental building block for achieving your ideal future vision as a customer-focused, high-performance, learning organization.

This systems thinking, in essence, equals the third building block or Right Answer: focusing on outcomes and serving the customer. It's just common sense that the primary outcome and reason for existence of any organization is serving the customer.

We have incorporated each of these three seemingly simple elements into the Reinventing Strategic Management (Planning and Change) model. To summarize:

1. Planning and change are *the* primary function of management and leadership. A strategic management structure and system is needed for this to become a reality.
2. People support what they helped create through skilled management and leadership practices to ensure committed buy-in from all key stakeholders.
3. The use of systems — or backwards — thinking is required to become outcome- and customer-focused.

This has led to a number of interesting outcomes. The first outcome is that the strategic planning process ceases to be an activity or duty that is soon forgotten. Instead, planning becomes a normal part of leading and managing daily organizational work life from a strategic, integrated systems perspective. And, after the strategic planning (Goal #1) is completed and implementation (Goal #2) has occurred, the results have been both measurable and dramatic. This is especially true for our clients beginning in their second year of implementation once Goal #3 (Annual Strategic Review) is executed, which keeps up the pace of change and deals with the ongoing emergent strategies Mintzberg articulates.

Lastly, I've discovered that, when organizations center their approach to strategic management around these three seemingly simple elements, they achieve the flexibility to fit their plans to virtually any organizational application, public or private, large or small, professional, or even personal.

THE ABCs OF THIS SYSTEMS THINKING APPROACH

At first glance, the idea of reinventing the way we plan, lead, and manage our organizations on a day-to-day basis seems to be a formidable one. To prevent us from straying too far from this fundamental systems framework, it is critical to put the strategic planning and change management process into simple, memorable language. It was for this reason I developed concrete phases to frame any strategic planning that falls into General Systems Theory (GST) and its systems thinking—what I refer to as the "ABCs" of strategic management (actually, A, B, C, D, and E):

- **Phase A — Output:** Creating Your Ideal Future. This is the magnet that pulls you toward the future, toward focusing on your desired outcomes and envisioning the year 2010 as if it were today.
- **Phase B — Feedback Loop:** Measurements of Success. Creating quantifiable outcome measures of success: How will you measure the success of Phase A on a year-to-year basis? What are your measurable goals?
- **Phase C — Input into Action:** Converting Strategies to Operations. Developing the strategies you need to close the gap between today's status and your desired future vision (with the specific actions and priorities necessary to support them).
- **Phase D — Throughput/Actions:** Successful systems. Putting your plans into motion as well as tracking, monitoring, and adjusting as necessary.
- **Phase E — Environmental Scanning:** Observing and acting on the environmental changes. Ensure that there are no external barriers to success.

Again, these phases and crucial landmarks from General Systems Theory may seem obvious and simple, but they are a fundamentally different paradigm and way of thinking. By following these phases as initial points of departure for systems thinking and planning, you can create:

1. A comprehensive strategic plan for a large organization.
2. A quick, but meaningful plan for smaller organizations.
3. A large organization's definitive plan for a specific business unit, division, department, or project.
4. A strategic plan for an entrepreneurial or family-owned business.
5. A strategic life plan for yourself or your family.

In fact, I have worked with individuals and families (including my own) who have successfully applied these same phases to building a strategic life plan for their personal life goals. (A complimentary sample copy is available by writing to the Centre *for* Strategic Management®, 1420 Monitor Road, San Diego, CA 92110-1545; telephone, (619) 275-6528; fax, (619) 275-0324; or E-mail, csmintl@san.rr.com.)

The results of our centre's work within diverse public and private organizations all across North America have proven that you can navigate the turbulent organizational waters successfully. With a common-sense planning and change management system in place, you will not only survive, but also thrive in the new millennium. Yes, it will require patience and persistence. It can be accomplished, however, with great satisfaction, pride, and financial rewards.

It begins with each organization and its leadership recognizing that strategic planning is a vital part of management and leadership. Then, our visions, values, and core strategies become the drivers of managing continuous change in an integrated, participative, aligned, and systems fashion.

A WRITER'S ARROGANCE — THE ABCs PARADIGM SHIFT

It would be pure arrogance to presume that I — or any one individual — could set down the one, complete, perfect method for reinventing strategic planning and change management. Indeed, if there is anything in my Reinventing Strategic Management Model that comes close, it is the common, logical, A, B, C, D, E systems framework of General Systems Theory. It is a new paradigm, a Systems Thinking Approach to leading planning and change in an organization for the better in a strategic and holistic fashion.

When I view the glut of management books, I believe that the only way to create a cohesive whole is by looking at everything we do within the framework of systems thinking. If you agree that this systems thinking framework is the key to planning and progress, then the most important thing to take away from our Reinventing Strategic Management Model is not its details. What's most important is that it gives you a simple, yet comprehensive way to strategically plan and manage your entire organization as a system, using the A, B, C, D, E phases as your guide.

IN SUMMARY: STARTING WITH THE RIGHT ANSWERS

The changes that have beset countries, organizations, and individuals in the past 10 years have been staggering, to say the least. If you are to survive these changes, along with those that will surely come in the next 10 years, you must now begin to plan for and apply the answers we know to be "right." It's not enough to wait for the perfect answer; it will never come. You need to take those systems thinking elements that we've observed, researched, read, and heard about as being successful and use them to the very best of your abilities.

Reinventing Strategic Management isn't simply a catch phrase; it's something we all must do in order to effectively integrate our organizations into the new global village that our instantaneous Internet communications is creating. As telecommunications and technology continue to explode, so too does our political and socioeconomic world. It is a world in which a hierarchical, analytical approach is fast becoming extinct. Instead it is being replaced by the Systems Thinking Approach, where every action has a reaction, and each part must be considered in light of the whole organization, focusing on the customer.

In the early 1970s, as a part of my Master's of Science and Administration degree at George Washington University, I was required to take a comprehensive course on General Systems Theory (GST). GST was derived in the 1920s from biology. At the time, I felt it to be a somewhat arcane, even wasted, subject.

About 5 years later, however, it ultimately became the turning point of my professional life. I was working at Sunoco, and had an opportunity to hear Russ Ackoff — a professor at the University of Pennsylvania, and a renowned strategic planning expert — deliver a presentation. It was his belief that systems thinking, and General Systems Theory, was the most practical approach to any life effort.

A light went on in my mind. I went back to my old course papers and reevaluated my thinking from beginning to end. It dawned on me that this theory, this systems-thinking approach, was one that could be applied to virtually everything in our lives.

My advisor at George Washington, Jerry Harvey, often told me "there is nothing so practical as a good theory." At the time, I never believed it, but now I do. Thanks, Jerry and Russ.

What tipped the scale for me was the realization that systems thinking could not only be used in any application, but that it could be successfully applied to any time and any area of our lives. No matter what period of time we exist in, systems thinking will always work for us. As long as there exists a human society, there will be systems at every level that can potentially work together for mutual benefit. It is in identifying and analyzing those systems, and then working on and within them, that we can choose and achieve the outcomes we desire.

Reinventing Strategic Management, then, is all about becoming customer-focused by incorporating the systems approach into everything that goes on inside our organizations. We must create a systems framework in which each process, action, and reaction is analyzed and fits our ultimate goal of a customer-focused, high-performance learning organization.

Shaping and implementing a strategic plan successfully is your organization's biggest challenge in this global, instantaneous, and revolutionary marketplace. If you do it well, and tend to it with disciplined thinking and persistence (i.e., "water-tight integrity"), you can achieve a high level of performance despite this rapid change. You can design, build, and sustain the kind of organization that will allow you to reach and satisfy every customer.

Part 1

Reinventing Strategic Management: An Overview

1 Revolutionary Change: Its Implications for Organizations

The end of one century, and the beginning of another, ushers in a fundamental period of transition, a time in which we all must reshape our mental maps of the world.

One thing is certain — having ushered out the 20th century and embarked on the third millennium, we are vulnerable to more multifaceted, simultaneous changes than ever before. The revolutionary change we experienced in the last part of the twentieth century presents some harsh realities against a backdrop of promising horizons.

This change continues to rush at us with mind-numbing speed, affecting our personal lives, our choice of careers, our workplace, our communications, our governing bodies, our natural environment, our entire world. To fully understand how it will affect us and what will be required to deal with it, we must examine the nature and extent of this change.

ASTONISHING CHANGES IN THE LAST 10 YEARS

First, it is important to understand that literally everything that impacts our daily lives is in a transition because of change: countries, governments, companies, technologies, industries, the workplace. It would be difficult to imagine a more revolutionary period of change in both the geopolitical and business environments. Over the last decade, this unprecedented change has caused deep structural uprootings on a global basis.

There have been astonishing changes in the past 10 years: the fall of the Berlin Wall, the reunification of Germany, the formation of the European Common Market and introduction of the Euro, and the toppling of communism throughout eastern Europe and the former Soviet Union. At the same time, the "Asian Tiger" countries and China's Communist mandarins appear to be mounting a campaign toward free markets as they restructure their economies and debt loads.

All of this and more, has a direct impact on the world economy. Former eastern bloc countries are selling more manufactured goods to nations that were previously considered enemies, foreign investments in emerging Third World countries are causing rapid expansion of their economies, and Latin American dictatorships are veering toward the free market mind-set. Argentina even ties its currency to the U.S. dollar.

1-57444-278-3/00/$0.00+$.50
© 2000 by CRC Press LLC

The fiber of global business and industry has also changed dramatically. The breakup of AT&T, once a monopoly that virtually owned the U.S. communications business, gave rise to a number of smaller (but now larger, merged) competitors that are in it for the long haul. The introductions of fax machines, E-mail, the Internet, and cellular telephones have greatly expanded the time and space range of our interpersonal communications and the communications industry. Fiberoptic cables positioned beneath the ocean floor and satellites in outer space have overcome previous limitations to provide us with instantaneous global communications.

The rise of the Internet economy needs special mention, as it is coming to us at breakneck speed. By the time the U.S. government's lawsuit against Microsoft is finalized, many of the issues will probably have become moot points. The economic landscape and E-commerce keep reinventing themselves over and over. The innovations are limitless.

And during the past 10 years, who would have predicted innovations in the personal computer, Direct TV, and Web TV markets? For all of these industrial and commercial innovations, however, there are just as many changes in the workforce itself that must be acknowledged.

Corporations around the globe have had to address cultural diversity, communication, and training barriers as they manage a more diverse workforce. Immigrants, racial minorities, women, and disabled workers, who were once a relatively small part of the workforce, are now entering the workplace in burgeoning numbers. Other members that are being heard from more and more are the seniors in the workplace. Older workers who once chose early or mid-60s retirement are demanding more flexible work options or part-time reentry into the workplace.

The phenomenon of the Boom, Bust, and now Echo generations deserves special mention. The Echo generation (born between roughly 1975 and 1995) is almost as large (60 million in the U.S. alone) as the Baby Boom generation (66 million now), and will obviously eclipse it soon as Boomers age and die. The Echo demographics must be studied closely for all the differences they will soon (and are now) bringing to society and business.

In addition to the changing demographics of the workforce, organizations are also facing radical paradigm shifts in employee values and expectations. As the hierarchical structure of organizations gives way to a more democratized workplace, employees have become more empowered and are seeking more active participation in the outcomes of their organizations. Teamwork has become a standard part of organizational frameworks, which has led to an increase in individual creativity and autonomy.

Jobs themselves are changing as organizations downsize and rightsize, creating more and more telecommuting jobs and consulting needs to fill in the gaps caused by permanent layoffs, even in middle-management jobs that are now obsolete and have been eliminated. Organizations now have to think of their resources in three ways: (1) employees, (2) contingent and contract workers, and (3) external alliances and partnerships.

Further, the spiritual and religious profile of the U.S. is undergoing a massive face lift away from traditional or mainstream religion. Nuns and agnostics are now on the board of the National Conference of Christians and Jews, and Hindus, Buddhists, and Muslims take their new place as mainstream.

The public sector has also been in a state of metamorphosis over the past 10 years. Public resources are maxed out (or are perceived to be) as global economies decline or integrate, yet the demands of society steadily increase. Also, as more and more governing bodies once based on socialism, turn toward privatization and free enterprise, the lines between public and private organizations are becoming blurred. As a result, the public sector finds itself reorganizing its services for greater efficiency and accountability.

This environment is also requiring the public and not-for-profit sectors to employ more business and market approaches. In effect, these sectors are undergoing an entrepreneurial renaissance, in which such tactics as user pay, competition, privatization, and site-based management are the standard rather than the exception.

It is truly a renaissance whose time has come, as witnessed by the growing trends of decentralized authority, market-based incentives, preventing problems vs. curing crises, customer focus, and empowering communities to be proactive in solving their own problems.

This is also a time in which the workplace employees are realizing enormous, life-altering changes. In addition to the influence of corporate mergers and acquisitions so prevalent today, organizations now face enormous global competition in production and financing. We are all learning how to function in a much more deregulated, fiercely competitive global and Internet environment.

SOME ANTICIPATED CHANGES IN THE NEXT 10 YEARS

It is unrelentingly clear that the last 10 years have produced fundamental upheavals in global leadership, marketplaces, and individual values. What is also becoming alarmingly clear is that the next 10 years will bring even more change than the past 10 years. Not only is our environment experiencing tremendous change; the rate of that change has virtually doubled. The changes we're dealing with today are happening at such a high level of speed that the changes of the past 10 years are essentially the equivalent of the previous 20 years ... a disquieting thought, at best.

The rapid waning of Socialism and the rise of the Internet around the globe will continue to bring a steady stream of change to the world economy. And, as more and more borders open up — from Eastern Europe to Mexico to China — numerous free trading blocs exist. The North American Free Trade Agreement (NAFTA) between Mexico and the U.S. is dramatically impacting future trade and creating social change within North and South America as well.

Previously unheard of regional affiliations are also entering the global trade market, particularly in Latin America, where groups such as Mercosur (a common market between Argentina, Brazil, Paraguay, and Uruguay), the Andean Group, the Central American Common Market, the Mexico–Chile Free Trade Agreement, and the G3 Agreement between Mexico, Colombia, and Venezuela have rapidly gained strength. In all, the overriding trend for trade is from nationalism to regionalization (including the GCC, the Gulf Coordinating Council in the six Persian Gulf more prowestern states) and eventually, globalization.

Unfortunately, nationalism and fragmentation are on the rise in countries all over the globe. In North America, Quebec continues to seriously push for a form of secession from Canada. Ex-Soviet Union republics are all struggling with their futures. Ex-Yugoslavian (Bosnia, Kosovo, etc.) and Czech-Slovakia are experiencing ongoing chaos. And with their combustible nationalism, Southeast Asia and the Middle East aren't doing much better. Africa's turbulent politics of the past several decades show no sign of resolution. Only in places like Northern Ireland and South Africa are real change toward peace and equality occurring.

Most futurists agree that technology is often the driving force of change. The next 10 years of technological growth won't do anything to disprove that theory. Continuing changes in robotics, automation, mechatronics (microprocessing within products), computer-assisted design (CAD), computer-assisted manufacturing (CAM), computer-integrated manufacturing (CIM), microelectro-mechanical systems (MEMS), and graphical user interface (GUI) are expected to redefine industrialized manufacturing.

In addition, massively parallel processing (MPP) machines, with their ability to receive and transmit data at practically unlimited speeds, represent a phenomenal new growth market for just about everything from oil and biotech companies to banks, retail chains, and automobile manufacturers.

The seemingly innumerable uses for CD-ROMs in retail and consumer interactive applications, especially with their massive storage capabilities, will assist in this redefining. With all this new technology, mass customization is fast becoming a new reality.

The explosions in biotechnology and gene-testing promise massive changes in science, health, and manufacturing at which we can only guess. The mapping of the human genome with its 100,000 genetic codes will be completed within the next few years. Cloning is already occurring with animals. Also, computer programs such as *Inventon* can literally invent new molecules, proffering an unimaginable boon for chemical and pharmaceutical companies.

The Internet and cyberspace along with all kinds of information technology and telecommunications will also continue to be big winners. E-commerce will be huge in the next 5 to 10 years. Further applications will grow dramatically in miniaturization, fiberoptics, expert systems imaging, digital cellular communications, super computer networks, personal communications systems (PCS) and computer bulletin-board inter- and intra-networks, as well pocket phones, cellular-projected electronic E-mail, wireless computer networks, and video conferencing, to name a few.

Satellite systems such as NAVSTAR (a 24-satellite global positioning system), TIROS (for meteorology), SKYNET IV (for submarine communications), Motorola's planned IRIDIUM network of 66 satellites (or its successor due to its economic woes), or Teledesic's global network goal of 840 satellites are almost too far-reaching to imagine their ultimate effects on us. Geo positioning satellites (GPS) already help us understand and predict the weather and fly commercial aircraft over the poles.

Already making itself known in telecommunications is "infotainment," a radical new megaindustry that brings together (1) telephone communications, (2) network and cable television, (3) the publishing and computer industries, (4) retail and video stores, and (5) the multibillion dollar entertainment industry. The home shopping television networks, already a $2-billion-plus industry and growing at approximately 20% each year, are but one example of this merger. Virtual reality — stereoscopic visual effects that project a 3-D image, making it seem real — is another phenomenon already making waves that is expected to explode within the next 5 years. Even imaging technology that will make information systems more user-friendly and artificial intelligence (AI) continue to grow into real possibilities.

Space-age designer materials will continue to grow. Graphite and other materials are being tested as conductors of electrical energy. Heat and resistance-free graphite could eventually greatly reduce the cost of energy transmission. Wood ceramic (sawdust injected with phenol resin) efficiently absorbs electromagnetic radiation, creating a wealth of potential uses in heat and electrical elements, as well as an effective shield for computers and electronic devices.

Answers are still being sought to counteract the relentless global warming, and the next decade is already spawning an entire industry dedicated to this and other environmental sciences. In its earlier days, organizations complied with the environmental protection movement's "3 R's" — reduce, reuse, recycle — largely as a response to governmental mandates. In fact, the business community has often been at odds with governmental regulations, seeing them as an obstruction to doing business.

Though political intervention has created an initially negative reaction on the part of manufacturing, there is currently a surprising about-face in the environmental vs. manufacturing evolution. What is happening is that organizations are discovering significant, ongoing cost and time savings in their environmentally regulated operating and manufacturing activities. As a result, they are now realizing that environmental protection is just good business, and are exploiting more and more environmentally friendly methods of operation.

The next 10 years will almost certainly create many new industries and expand several more, some of which are obvious, while others are still emerging. A consensus list, derived from my own experiences, publications of the World Future Society, the Deutsche Bank (Germany), MITI (Japan), and others shows targeted new industries for the 21st century:

- Microelectronics
- Robotics/machine tools
- Telecommunications
- Environmental protection
- Space-age metallurgy/ "designer" materials

- Biotechnology
- Computers/software
- Infotainment
- Civil aviation
- Cottage industries

The cottage industry boom promises to be an interesting one. The "think globally, act locally" catch phrase was definitely at work in the 1990s. Originally perceived as a 1980s expansion industry, cottage industries of every description are just now starting to realize substantial growth, with no sign of slowing any time soon. One only need look at the explosion of E-mail, fax, and secretarial service franchises, such as Mail Boxes, Etc., as well as the huge spurt of growth in ergonomic computer furniture for the home office, to recognize that this particular wave will continue.

QUESTIONS TO PONDER

- What changes are happening in the environment of your particular industry? How is your industry changing? How has the Internet affected it? How will it?
- Do you believe your organization has recognized it is in the midst of revolutionary change? What is it doing about it?
- What are your organization's global opportunities and threats?
- Do you know who your future competitors are and where they are located?
- Does your organization formally scan the environment at least every quarter to stay abreast of the ongoing changes in technology, social values, telecommunications, etc.?

IMPLICATIONS FOR ORGANIZATIONS OF ALL TYPES — PUBLIC AND PRIVATE

There's no doubt about it: everything is undergoing fundamental change. Indeed, organizational megamergers continue and the jobless rate is very low across North America. Companies are trying not to hire people if possible. They're concentrating on increasing productivity and lowering fixed costs, while making do with a streamlined permanent workforce supplemented by the contingent workforce and alliances.

Overall, the leading socioeconomic indicators show a tremendous U.S. global cycle of growth. However, despite the stock market being at historical highs, the rest of the globe is not doing nearly as well. Even in the U.S., we have overconsumed and underinvested, which combine to present us with many questions, great opportunities, and few answers.

Nothing seems to be immune from the need for change including entire nations, corporations, and their leaders. While it's important not to surrender to the complexity, chaos, and speed of life, it is necessary to understand that without thought and careful planning, anyone is subject to a crash landing.

Change, by its very nature, brings with it fear and uncertainty as well as opportunity. Rules and boundaries change with no clear rationale; our paradigms shift, change, even disappear. In order to enter the third millennium with a sure step, we will need to reshape our mental maps of the world.

Einstein's great quote bears repeating here: "Problems that are created by our current level of thinking can't be solved by that same level of thinking." We must find ways to reinvent ourselves in order to survive, grow, and move on to future growth cycles. And, in doing so, we must remember not to let the limits of our mind shape the limits of our world.

Paradigms = Limits of our minds
Paradigm: n. 1. sets rules; 2. establishes boundaries

Paradigm shift: 1. adapting new or revised frameworks and ways of thinking; 2. establishing new rules and boundaries

By shifting our mind-sets and our paradigms, it is possible to move on to a new cycle of growth, in our nations and in our organizations. In fact, there are many examples of these new cycles across the globe, again and again.

Germany has had innumerable paradigm shifts in its reunification efforts, which are taking hold. So, too, have South Africa and Poland. Even Russia and other former Eastern European communist countries are starting to take halting steps toward private enterprise within a free market economy.

Doing nothing, remaining static, or merely shifting resources and programs, however, changes nothing, as witnessed in Japan, where the same political party and philosophy has been in place for more than 40 years with almost no change.

The question, then, is how do we objectively step outside our organizations, reshape our paradigms, and regain our focus? How can we possibly know how to plan for future successes when we don't completely understand the changes that are occurring in the present? Are there any organizations out there that are doing it right? Are there, in fact, any "right answers?"

YES ... THERE *ARE* RIGHT ANSWERS

The best way to guarantee your future is to create it yourself.

Fortunately, the answer to the crucial question posed above is a resounding "yes." There *are* right answers; in fact, there are three right answers. The plain truth, however, is that no organization can survive to implement these right answers unless it persistently, and with focused discipline, addresses the harsh realities of today's social changes and competitive marketplace, and is willing to shift its paradigms in response to change. To make these changes, every organization must have an honest and realistic picture of where it is now. (Honesty really *is* Job #1, folks!)

My careers have taken me through many, many public and private organizations, and a wide variety of large-scale change projects. They have given me the opportunity to see what works and what doesn't.

Over and over again, three *Right Answers* have presented themselves as a recurring pattern for organizational success.

For the most part, these right answers are simple, straightforward steps that follow common sense and logic. None of them alone is ideal. Together, however, each one becomes absolutely critical to the long-term success and viability of any organization, public or private.

OVERVIEW OF THREE RIGHT ANSWERS

First, let me give you an overview of these three Right Answers; then, I'll proceed to discuss them in greater length in the next chapter. It's significant to note, however, how all three are interrelated and lead to the synergy (i.e., 2 + 2 = 5) needed for organizational success.

Right Answer #1: Structure — Institutionalize a Strategic Management System

Highly successful corporations continuously re*structure* their organizations into an integrated systems framework. The function of this framework is for all parts of the organization to be strategically aligned and attuned so as to be led and managed as a system. This watertight integrity is crucial in order to focus on its main purpose or outcome of satisfying the customer.

Hence, there is a need to institutionalize a Strategic Management System. Designing, building, and sustaining a Strategic Management System (SMS) as the new way to run your business day-to-day is essential for success. This flows directly from Seemingly Simple Element #1 (see Introduction): *Planning and change are the primary responsibility of management and leadership.*

Right Answer #2: Process — Create Professional Management and Leadership Practices Organization-Wide

This is the *process* — the part where "the rubber meets the road," and eventually separates the winners from the losers. Over the long term, the only difference — and the ultimate competitive advantage — in any organization is the leadership of its managers: their mind-sets, paradigms, and behaviors.

All of the talk about employees as your competitive advantage misses the point that management's actions are the competitive advantage that leads to creative and innovative employees; employees who are free to use their hearts and minds, as well as their hands. This flows directly from Seemingly Simple Element #2: *People support what they help create.*

Right Answer #3: Content — Focus on Outcomes, Serve the Customer

This should be the focus — the *content* — of every core strategy you create, and every system you set in place. It's obvious, but true, that the key task of each organization is to determine the needs and wants of its customers/markets, and to adapt its products and services to delivering the desired satisfactions more effectively and efficiently than its competitors (i.e., unsurpassed customer satisfaction). This flows directly from Seemingly Simple Element #3: *Our Systems Thinking Approach to strategic management,* focusing on the key outcome of serving the customer.

Without exception, experience and research have shown me that successful organizations have leaders who commit to these right answers for addressing change and moving forward to achieve their vision. Also, I have found that success most often has much to do with common sense and persistence. There really is no magic solution.

The closest I can come to an ideal formula for success is when each of these three Right Answers folds into the overall organization as a system; a system with fit, alignment, attunement, and integrity to focus on the customers' wants and needs.

Even if that blend exists, however, it won't progress without persistence — disciplined persistence of management and leadership organization-wide.

In our view, when all else fails, use common sense (which is what this book is based on — common sense about what we know, what is proven, and what works, Figure 1.1).

"IF NOTHING ELSE WORKS, THIS MAY BE A PERFECT
OPPORTUNITY TO USE COMMON SENSE."

FIGURE 1.1 Reprinted courtesy of Bunny Hoest and *Parade* Magazine, ©1999. With permission.

There are many examples of businesses today that are moving forward in spite of daily struggles and apprehension about the future: organizations such as General Electric, Wal-Mart, Bell of Canada, Ford, Walt Disney, Poway Unified School District, and the San Diego Zoo; the cities of Saskatoon, Sunnyvale, CA, and Indianapolis, IN; the Marriott Corp., the State of Oregon, the U.S. Postal Service, the State of West Virginia, the Province of Alberta and the Province of British Columbia, and the Department of Agriculture in Alberta.

Today's number one management guru, Tom Peters includes these and more highly successful corporations, both big and small, in his works and presentations. None of them is perfect, but they are surviving — and thriving — through these tough times.

This, then, is the summary outline of these three Right Answers. Over the last two decades of my work within organizations, I have discovered ingredients, along with some common-sense basics, that go hand in hand with these answers and make them work for virtually any organization.

RECAP OF KEY CONTENT POINTS

- In the last 10 years, countries have divided and are restructuring, world leaders were voted out of office, and the beginning of a world economy was introduced.
- Technological breakthroughs, the Internet, and other advances in global communications, manufacturing, and space age metallurgy, etc., have been the driving force behind change, causing paradigm shifts in market-places, organizational structures, and individual values.
- In the midst of deregulation and a soft economy, once-strong corporations failed or underwent extensive restructuring; many corporate leaders were fired.
- Increasingly diverse workforces and changing social values challenge traditional hierarchies as the route to success. The Echo generation is coming to the fore.
- Public disenchantment with public services is forcing the public and not-for-profit sectors to examine more market-like approaches.
- The next decade will see an increase in wars, nationalism, fragmentation, and regionalism, further affecting world trade and the global economy.
- Technological breakthroughs will continue, such as CAD/CAM/CASE/MEMS, artificially produced "designer" materials, the Internet, super-computers, cloning, artificial intelligence, virtual reality, multimedia optical, graphical user interface, open systems architecture, and more.
- New and recent industries will continue to expand and develop in such areas as microelectronics, biotechnology, telecommunications, civil aviation, space age metallurgy, robotics, and computers.
- Infotainment — a combination of telecommunications, the computer industry, network and cable television, telephone communications, publishing, video and retail stores, and the entertainment industry — will become a new megaindustry.

2 Yes...There *Are* Right Answers

It's simple common sense, but it's true ... without prompt,
consistent action, no change can occur.

In order to plan for future success, we must put the Right Answers from Chapter 1 in place right now. We must step back and reassess our current state, with the objective of building a healthy foundation that will carry us into a new age. But first, it is important to more fully understand the dynamics of these three Right Answers.

RIGHT ANSWER #1: INSTITUTIONALIZE A STRATEGIC MANAGEMENT SYSTEM
(as a new way to run your business day to day)

From the very beginning of strategic planning, you are actually creating the structure, or framework, within which you will implement your strategic plan. Without a structure that is systematically developed and institutionalized, your vision of a customer-focused, high-performance organization won't be implemented, and all your careful planning will indeed fall victim to the SPOTS syndrome.

In order to implement your strategic plan successfully, it's best to look at planning as one part of an overall, three-part/three-goal structure that is our Strategic Management System (see Figure 2.1). This system is crucial to designing, building, and sustaining a customer-focused, high-performance learning organization for the 21st century. Review Figure 2.1 through the lens of our three goals, described below.

GOAL #1: STRATEGIC PLAN DEVELOPMENT

What often happens is that when Goal #1 (development of the strategic plan) is finished, the planning process ends. Executives breathe a sigh of relief and move on to the next project, not realizing that we are talking about a new way to run the business day to day. Thus, they miss the point that the persistence that is so important in Goals #2 and #3 is just beginning.

GOAL #2: SUCCESSFUL CHANGE

As you can see in the more detailed illustration in Figure 2.1, to kick off the achievement of Goal #2, the Plan-to-Implement step (Step #8) is critical. It provides a way for your organization to bridge the gap from Goal #1 (the strategic plan document) to Goal #2 (successful implementation of the plan).

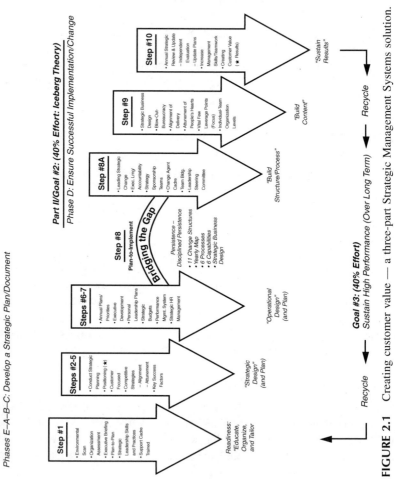

FIGURE 2.1   Creating customer value — a three-part Strategic Management Systems solution.

Designing and building a Strategic Change Leadership Steering Committee (SCLSC) of your collective leadership is also vital to this process. It provides the organization with a structure for managing, leading, and guiding change, and a resource of real people who are accountable for tracking the strategies from words on paper to successful results and outcomes.

GOAL #3: ANNUAL STRATEGIC REVIEW AND UPDATE

If the plan is beginning to become obsolete as soon as the ink is dry, and you need regular Leadership Steering Committee meetings throughout the year, what do you need by the end of each year? You need to conduct an Annual Strategic Review and Update, beginning with an independent *strategic* audit, just as we are required by law to do an annual financial audit.

In this annual review, extend your strategic plan one year further as you set actions, priorities, and budgets for the next year. However, don't just make it an operational update; instead take a blank sheet approach to strategically planning all over again, even if just to reconfirm that you made the correct strategic decisions a year ago.

STRATEGIC MANAGEMENT REALITY CHECK

If you're thinking that all this theory is fine, but how much of it makes a difference in the real world, think about this. In an Oechsli Institute survey of over 500 small and mid-sized companies, published in *Inc.* magazine, a whopping 97% of management and 77% of sales or frontline employees answered "yes" when asked if their company had a clear, written mission statement.

Those statistics fell to 54% management and 55% sales/frontline employees when asked if that statement was supported by management's actions. It slipped again considerably, with only 46% management and 38% sales/frontline employees stating that each employee understood what was expected in terms of performance. Finally, a meager 21% management and 22% sales/frontline employees answered affirmatively when asked if all employees were held accountable for their daily performance.

What this says to me is that talk is cheap. We all want to sound good when asked the tough questions, but unless we find ways to back up our intentions with solid, disciplined, and persistent management systems, we just plain won't survive. However, designing, building, and sustaining a customer-focused, high-performance organization takes incredible discipline and persistence over a period of years.

Setting a Strategic Management System in place as outlined in Figure 2.1 is the only way I know to make an organization a long-term winner. It includes defining your shared direction, creating core strategies that will help you build toward your vision and desired customer-focused outcomes, implementing your strategic plan and adjusting it regularly throughout the year, and performing an Annual Strategic Review (and Update). This is what we mean when we state Seemingly Simple Element #1 (see Introduction): planning and change are the primary part of management and leadership. It is your job to carefully design, build, create, and sustain this Strategic Management System and yearly cycle.

RIGHT ANSWER #2: CENTERING YOUR LEADERSHIP PRACTICES
(the only true competitive business advantage)

Like all else facing us in the 21st century, organizational management and leadership practices are undergoing fundamental change. Traditionally accepted managerial roles that developed out of the Industrial Age consisted of approximately 5% strategizing, 15% coaching, developing, supporting, and building, and 80% directing and maintaining.

The Information Age, however, is transforming the role of the manager into quite a different equation that seems to be: 20% strategy selection and shared ownership (different way to control), 60% coaching, developing, supporting, learning, and building, and 20% directing, maintaining, and controlling.

This newer definition of the managerial role results in a much greater emphasis on such interactive skills as coaching, facilitating, and developing staff and teams. In order for people to support what they help create, these types of new leadership and management practices and skills are essential, hence Right Answer #2.

In order to steer your organization through the revolutionary changes that will continue in the 21st century, you must be willing to act as a visionary and leader of change, with the skills of a coach, trainer, and facilitator.

> The routine manager tends to accept things the way they are. Leaders seek to revise processes, directions, cultures, and structures to reflect changing realities.

Additionally, the best leaders know that people support what they help create. To implement strategies successfully, the best leaders recognize the wisdom of soliciting commitment at all levels of the organization. At the risk of being redundant, you'll hear me say this over and over again, because getting committed buy-in, and later, stay-in, from all organizational members is the one element that can literally make or break successful implementation of any strategic plan.

Without this element, no organization can ever hope to gain a competitive business advantage. You only need to glance at a list of successful organizational leaders over the past 20–30 years — Ray Kroc (McDonald's), Sam Walton (Wal-Mart), J. W. Marriott, Sr. and Jr. (Marriott Corp.), Jack Welch (General Electric), Bill Gates (Microsoft), Walt Disney (Walt Disney Corp.), Lee Iacocca (Chrysler), and John Watson, Sr. and now Louis Gerstner (IBM) — to recognize the underlying truth of this premise. Each of these organizational winners was a strong, proactive leader who valued customers and introduced a philosophy of committed buy-in from all organization members.

In order to better understand what the core competencies of leaders should be, the Centre did its usual research into all the existing leadership authors. However, first we had to find a Systems Thinking Approach to uncover the natural leadership core competencies that exist on earth. None of the 27 authors addressed this. Thus, we had to become interpreters and translators of the research of those authors within the seven levels of living systems on earth.

SEVEN LEVELS OF LIVING SYSTEMS

In addition to the previously stated definition of systems as a set of components that work together for the overall objective of the whole, the biologist James G. Miller contributed a second key concept about systems that's often overlooked in organizations today. He identified seven levels of systems in his classic book, *Living Systems*:

1. Cell (as in the cells that make up our physical bodies)
2. Organ (lungs, heart, kidneys, etc.)
3. Organism (humans, animals, fish, birds, etc.)
4. Group (teams, department, strategic business units)
5. Organization (private, public, not-for-profit)
6. Society (German, French, American, Indonesian, etc.)
7. Supranational (Western, Asian, Communist, global, etc.)

In considering these seven levels of living systems, we see that each system impacts every other system, and that there is a natural hierarchy of systems within systems. What is a system or a department or category to you is only a piece of an organizational system. We also see what is probably the single most important feature of any system: that its performance as a whole is affected by every one of its parts. When looked at from an organizational perspective, the concept of a systems framework really does constitute a total reinvention of the ways in which we think and do business. It literally creates an environment in which all systems and subsystems are linked together to achieve the overall organizational goals (or vision).

Thus, to build our *Centering Your Leadership*^{SM} systems framework for leadership core competencies (which will be detailed in the following section), we obviously used Levels 3, 4, 5 and 6 of the seven levels (individuals, department, teams, organizations and society). Most of you will recognize these levels and see nothing new about them. They are the basic building blocks of organizations.

However, the issue is more complex than that. Each living system also interacts, collides, or interfaces with all other living systems at the same level. In other words,

- Each employee (Level 3) interacts with all the other employees at a one-to-one level.
- The same thing is true at the department team level 4 — each team interacts with other cross-functional teams or departments.
- At the organization-wide level 5, each organization interacts with all the other systems in its environment — customers, competitors, regulators, etc.

Examining these collisions/interactions of living (human) systems reveals that there are six natural levels of human functioning in which leaders must be competent:

1. Individual
2. One-to-one
3. Teams
4. Cross-functional teams
5. Organization-wide
6. Organization–environment interfaces

CENTERING YOUR LEADERSHIP^{SM}

Building on the six levels of human functioning, the Centre for Strategic Management's leadership framework is The Systems Thinking Approach supported visually by our model (Figure 2.2) on the Six Natural Leadership Competencies.

Our model is the result of many years of experience working as leaders, with leaders, and for leaders, plus a literature review of 27 leadership authors that was centered on our understanding of the *Seven Levels of Living Systems* (specifically, the individual, team, and organizational levels). It reveals that by focusing on these three systems levels, and the three places where systems interface, we can see the six areas where leadership naturally occurs. In reviewing these 27 authors, only 3

FIGURE 2.2   Centering Your Leadership^{SM} — a systems approach to six leadership competencies.

dealt with 4 of our 6 core competencies — the remaining 24 dealt with 3 or less. They keep looking for the one best answer, and it doesn't exist.

Thus, our approach to the development of leaders views the six competencies described below as the natural way we live and work.

SIX NATURAL LEVELS OF LEADERSHIP COMPETENCIES

I. Basic Leadership Competency Levels

Level #1.   Enhancing Self-Mastery
Level #2.   Building Interpersonal Relationships
Level #3.   Facilitating Empowered Teams

II. Advanced Leadership Competency Levels

Level #4.   Collaborating Across Functions
Level #5.   Integrating Organizational Outcomes
Level #6.   Creating Strategic Alliances/Positioning

Under each of these six levels of competencies were five skills our research showed were the primary (or core) leadership skills for each level. With the self as core, you progress around our Centering Your Leadership model until you are capable of exercising your basic leadership competency levels in much more advanced, complex, changing, and global environments. Senior management, in particular, needs a very high level of these skills and competencies to deal with their role complexity. (For a full list of these 30 skills, call the Centre at (619) 275-6528.)

Most people will agree with the competencies and skills listed in the model, but the real power of the model is that it also considers a leader's mind-set. We put forth the notion that leaders must be self-aware to achieve their goals and they must truly value service if they are to focus on customers. Effective leaders know that shared values and vision are the keys to adding customer value and that synergy is required to be globally competitive today. These mind-sets or beliefs are called "energizing forces" because they are internal forces that drive personal action.

The competency building shown in Table 2.1 is absolutely essential for the leadership of an organization. Think about this truism: Leadership is the *only* thing that really differentiates successful organizations from others over the long term.

Again, the only true competitive business advantage that will help your organization thrive in the new millennium is strong, professional leadership and management at all levels. You will need to go beyond lip service and "walk the talk," starting with top management.

TABLE 2.1
Centering Your Leadership^{SM}

Living Systems (Five Areas)	Six Energizing Forces	Lead to 6 Competencies (and 30 Skills)	That Yield These Outcomes
		Basic Leadership Competency Levels	
1. Self	1. Awareness	1. Enhancing Self Mastery	1. Balanced Life
2. One-to-One	2. Integrity	2. Building Interpersonal Relationships	2. Trust
3. Teams	3. Interdependence	3. Facilitating Empowered	3. Mission Attainment
		Advanced Leadership Competency Levels	
4. Team-to-Team	4. Valuing Service	4. Collaborating Across Functions	4. Customer Focus
5. Organization	5. Shared Vision and Values	5. Integrating Organizational Outcomes	5. Added Customer Value
6. Organization-to-Environment	6. Synergy	6. Creating Strategic Positioning	6. Globally Competitive

QUESTIONS TO PONDER

- Have you shaped a strategic management structure and system that will help you bridge the gap from Goal #1 (the strategic plan document) to Goal #2 (successful implementation of the plan)?
- Does the managerial role in your organization generally follow the 20% strategy development, 60% coaching and development, 20% directing formula?
- Do the leaders in your organization actively seek commitment and buy-in from all their organizational members?
- Do you have an organization-wide action plan to focus on the number one core competency of any organization — the six natural levels of leadership core competencies and 30 associated skills?
- Is the continuous development of your own management and leadership skills your top personal priority?

RIGHT ANSWER #3: FOCUS ON OUTCOMES: SERVING THE CUSTOMER

(as the *only* reason for our existence)

Almost every organization says it is customer-driven, but the reality is, few are — they just talk a good game. What they've really got is an analytic approach to an organization as a system, and they rarely use systems thinking throughout the organization (Seemingly Simple Element #3).

In fact, most organizations today have become so distracted by more visible, immediate, or urgent issues such as regulatory considerations, day-to-day internal operations, profits, product development, or employees, that they actually become enslaved to obsolete activities as ends to themselves. They only focus on finding one solution at a time, thereby losing any sense of an organization-wide *systems* focus, much less making the customer the focal point.

The problem is, that no matter how much they concentrate on all these other issues, without a central, organization-wide focus on meeting the customer's needs and wants, no organization can stay in business over the long-term. This is true for organizations in both the public and private sectors.

Figure 2.3 illustrates the evolution of the driving forces of organizations over a period of time. In earlier eras, when more business monopolies were prevalent, for instance, organizations were mainly driven by regulatory issues. In a marketplace with no competition, that worked fairly well. Earlier eras also saw organizations driven by the Better Mousetrap Theory: organizations were able to keep their doors open as long as they came up with the best product or service.

CUSTOMER-FOCUSED ORGANIZATIONS

What does it take to "design, build, and sustain" a customer-focused, high-performance organization for the 21st century?

Today's marketplace has enormous, global competition and a more sophisticated customer. In such a marketplace, most of the answers to "how driven are you," shown in Figure 2.3, will not cause an organization to be successful. Of course, most of these issues are present and an ongoing concern in the day-to-day business of any organization.

However, every one of these methods for driving your organization must ultimately be evaluated in terms of how they fit into the overall focus of meeting the customer's needs and wants. A broad, customer-driven orientation must be the outcome that sets the framework for all your core strategies and priorities. Richard Hoskin stated it most eloquently in his *Training & Development Magazine* article, "Decision MAPping™: Managing to Win":

> We can restructure, reorganize, redeploy, redesign, and refinance. We can acquire; we can divest; we can go public, go private, swap debt for equity. We can redefine our statements of vision, mission, and objectives throughout every business unit in our organization. We can rethink our strategic plan, rewrite our five-year business plan, adopt the habits of highly successful people and embrace total quality. **But it won't amount to a hill of beans if our customers don't buy**.

I can't stress this enough: any organization — public or private — that fails to focus on, or be driven by, the customer as its primary outcome and reason for existence will not survive the current decade, much less the rest of the millennium.

Following this basic fact of organizational life, I've researched both the literature and successful customer-focused organizations to develop the following Key Com-

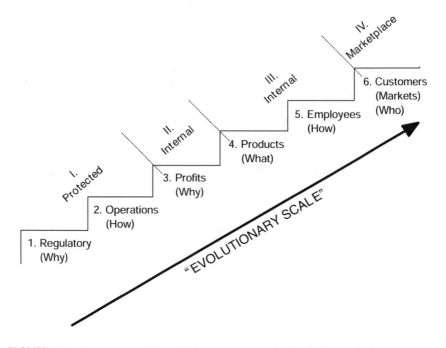

FIGURE 2.3   How are you driven? Where are you on the Evolutionary Scale?

mandments of Customer-Focused Organizations. It can help you quickly determine if your organization really is customer-driven.

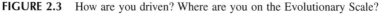

KEY COMMANDMENTS OF
CUSTOMER-FOCUSED ORGANIZATIONS

1. Be close to the customer. This is especially important for senior executives (i.e., see, touch, feel, meet, and speak with them face-to-face on a regular basis out in the marketplace).
2. Include the customers in executive decisions, focus groups, meetings, planning, and deliberations.
3. Know and anticipate the customers' needs, wants, and desires continually, as they change.
4. Surpass customer needs. This should be the driving force of the entire organization.
5. Survey the customers' satisfaction with the organization's products and services on a regular basis.
6. Have a clear "positioning" in the marketplace vs. the competition in the eyes of the customer.

7. Focus on creating customer value — i.e., "value-added" benefits to the customer through our Star Results Model presented later in the book (quality products and services, customer choice, responsiveness, delivery, speed, service vs. total cost of doing business with you).

8. Set quality customer-service standards — expectations that are specific and measurable for each department.

9. Base customer service standards on customer input and focus groups.

10. Require everyone in the organization to experience moments of truth by meeting and serving the customer directly — at least one day every year.

11. Focus and reengineer the business processes based on the customer's needs and perceptions, and do it across all functions.

12. Focus the organization structure based on the marketplace, i.e., structure the organization by customer markets (1 customer = 1 representative).

13. Reward customer-focused behaviors (especially cross-functional teams that work together to serve the customer).

14. Have a clear policy on service... and the heavy use of Customer Recovery Strategies (CRS) to surpass customer expectations when you make a mistake and must recover.

15. Hire and promote customer friendly people.

Once your organization has a clear vision of its ideal, customer-focused vision, you'll then have two key needs to align and achieve with this vision:

1. **Determine what the desired outcome measurements of its vision will be.** It is crucial at this point to develop methods by which your organization can measure these outcomes in a specific and quantifiable way. I call these measures the Key Success Measures/Goals or KSMs. Organizations should develop KSMs to suit their own unique needs, as long as they end up with something that can quantitatively or qualitatively measure the organization's desired outcomes with the customer.

2. **Develop a focused set of core strategies as the main method for ensuring your entire organization is focused on the customer.** Probably the most critical step in achieving a customer-focused vision for your organization is in the development of these primary (focused) means or core strategies. Some organizations name these core strategies "goals" or "objectives"; it doesn't matter what you call them as long as you, and everyone involved, are clear on what they are.

It is also essential that your core strategies be few and focused in number. To successfully achieve the outcome of focusing on the customer, organizations should limit their core strategies to a maximum of three or four. Less is more.

Given the present dynamic environment in which many paradigms are changing, it will be difficult to resist the temptation of developing 6, 10, or even 20 of these strategies. Resist it you must, however, because implementing and coordinating more than three or four will quickly become overwhelming and unmanageable. Then, the temptation is to put all of it aside, and all your hard work will be for naught. Trying to be all things to all people is the single most common strategic planning failure.

BOARD OF DIRECTORS' KEY ROLES

There are also certain expectations regarding the board of directors' role in leading and managing the three goals of your strategic management system. For Goal #1 (developing a strategic planning document) your board of directors should

- Be actively involved in the development of your vision/mission/values only. Then allow managers to figure out the strategies that are their responsibilities.
- Assist with the parallel process of these three documents with other key stakeholders.
- Formally approve the vision/mission/values and positioning as a guide to management's finalizing the rest of the strategic plan. (Optional: some senior executives may also want one or two board representatives to remain with the core planning team for these steps to provide a crucial board/management link.)
- Formally approve the final strategic planning document after a full examination and debate including approval of Key Success Factors (outcome measures of success) as they are developed and tied to executive-level bonus programs.

For Goal #2, ensuring the successful implementation of your strategic plan, your Board will need to

- Actively support the strategic plan and management's implementation of it.
- Use the plan as a template for all items and actions that come before the board and have it present in all board meetings, especially as it pertains to yearly budgeting (so it becomes "strategic budgeting").
- Become leader-sponsors of the plan, as well as challenge-advocates for all its changes.
- Use the plan as a guide in all board committees.
- Use the plan actively in any public speaking roles within the company, with investors, or within the community.
- Challenge parts of the plan that are unclear, confusing, or in need of adjustment over time (due to environmental changes).
- Have management formally report on the plan to the board each quarter.

As for Goal #3, the Annual Strategic Review, the board has to play the same roles as in Goal #1 above.

PERSISTENCE, DISCIPLINED PERSISTENCE

A final element of Right Answer #3 that must be a key ingredient of your organizational leadership is good old, *uncommon,* everyday perseverance. Persevering is probably the single most significant concept in each step of your envisioning, planning, and implementation. Bringing persistence and discipline to your organization's vision seems like a simple enough thing to remember, yet without it, the chances of seeing your strategies acted upon and your vision take shape are less than none. As Bobby Ross, the former coach of the San Diego Chargers and Detroit Lions football teams, put it,

> I went through almost two years at Georgia Tech [before winning]. I hope it's not that long [before we win]. I'm not going to all of a sudden in midstream change the offense or change the defense. I'm going to persevere. I have a plan that I'm going to stick to, and I'm not going to back off it. *I'm* going to be stubborn as hell.

Regarding discipline, Ross went on to say

> I'm going to be pretty demanding, but not in the sense of beating on guys. I'm going to be demanding in the sense of doing things right. I've [written] a philosophy on our football team which is in our players' playbook, and one of the things is *discipline.* I made the statement that if discipline is doing things right, then that's what we're going to do. Discipline is not harassing someone or wearing your shoes a certain way; *it's just doing things right.*

When you think about this, it makes perfect sense. After all, one of the main reasons so many of us are searching for the "right" answers is that we're not certain how to press on and persevere in the face of continuing and enormous change. Among all of the strategic planning efforts I've participated in, without exception the organizations that succeed and reach their goals are the ones that persevere and patiently persist in being loyal to their plans.

Yet, these organizations are also flexible enough to adjust and to manage the roller coaster of change we're all on these days. This is what I call having *strategic consistency, yet operational flexibility.* You'll hear me refer to this often, as it is the key to persistence, disciplined persistence in good leaders.

As you persevere, keep in mind some more common-sense findings from an extensive statistical survey (conducted by the American Quality Foundation, along with Ernst & Young) of over 580 organizations in the U.S., Canada, Germany, and Japan in the automotive, banking, computer, and health care industries. This survey presumed that the overall objective of the organizations studied was profit from serving the customer. It found that — regardless of the starting position — only these three universal practices had a significant impact on organizational performance:

1. Strategic planning and implementation
2. Business process improvement methods (based on customer needs)
3. Continually broadening the overall range and depth of management practices

These three practices directly tie in with our three Right Answers:

1. Strategic planning and implementation ties into Right Answer #1 — *institutionalize an organization-wide strategic management system.*
2. Business process improvement methods are linked to Right Answer #3 — *focus on the customer.* After all, a fundamental aspect of focusing on the customer is the practice of business process reengineering, working backward to reengineer and refocus your processes better and more simply on the customer.
3. Finally, continually broadening and deepening the overall range of management practices ties directly to Right Answer #2 — *professional management and leadership practices.*

Together, these three Right Answers are absolutely essential for your organization to reinvent (i.e., design, build, and sustain) itself as a customer-focused, high-performance learning organization for the new millennium.

QUESTIONS TO PONDER

- Is your organization's Ideal Future Vision customer-focused? How do you know?
- Have you defined your outcome measures of success (Key Success Factors)?
- Have you established a focused set of core strategies so that your organization can achieve its desired outcomes?
- Do your organization's core strategies include customer-focused strategies — especially Customer Recovery Strategies (CRS)?
- Do you follow all of the Key Commandments of Customer-Focused Organizations?
- Does your board of directors take an active role in leading and managing the three goals of your Strategic Management System?
- Do you incorporate persistence and discipline into your leadership style?
- Are you incorporating all three Right Answers into designing, building, and sustaining a customer-focused, high performance learning organization?

"HOW TO" — ACTION CHECKLIST

1. Be willing to face up to the harsh realities of today's revolutionary changes, and make an honest commitment to an organization-wide planning and change effort. Honesty really *is* Job 1!

2. There *are* right answers:
    1. Focus on the outcome (serving the customer),
    2. Institutionalize a Strategic Management System/cycle and structure, and
    3. Create organization-wide professional management and leadership practices and development.
3. Be sure your organization is following the Key Commandments of the Customer-Focused Organization.
4. The only true competitive advantage for organizations in the long run lies in strong, professional management and leadership practices.
5. In order to be successful, a Strategic Management System must have three goals: (1) create a strategic plan, (2) ensure its successful implementation, and (3) build and sustain high performance over the long term.
6. Establish key human resource programs to support the attraction, development, and retention of a professional, customer-friendly staff.
7. Finally, remember what coach Bobby Ross said so well: persistence, *disciplined* persistence, is the key to all success.

3 The Organization: A Living, Breathing System

*The great successful men [and women] of the world have
used their imagination ... They think ahead and create their
mental picture, and then go to work materializing that picture in all its details, filling in here, adding a little there,
altering this a bit and that a bit, but steadily building —
steadily building.*

-Robert Collier

THINKING BACKWARDS TO THE FUTURE

If you think about it, the whole reason behind reinventing the way you do day-to-
day business is that you want to exercise better control over achieving your organization's future. You want to be proactive in seeing that your organization realizes
your desired vision and outcomes. To do this, you'll need to practice what I call
"backward" (or systems) thinking.

This calls for starting with your Ideal Future Vision, then thinking backwards
to where your organization is right now. From there, you have to determine how to
bridge the gap between today's current state of operations and that vision you want
to achieve.

If your organization is indeed customer-focused, it is already performing the
most crucial survival task — focusing on its outcomes. This is Right Answer #3,
and it tells us *what* we must do to reinvent our organizations to withstand all the
changes, present *and* future, that rock our global marketplace.

Right Answers #1 and #2, discussed earlier, provide the *how* — by thinking
backwards in order to

1. Build an organization-wide strategic management system, and then
2. Instill commitment throughout the organization by creating professional
   management and leadership practices.

Introducing these concepts, clarifying your terminology, and getting it all organized may seem like a lot of prework, and not really related to the planning process.
However, it's actually a *part* of the planning process; it's a way to fold each of the
three Right Answers into the overall organization as a system with the fit, alignment,
attunement, and integrity necessary to focus on the customers' needs.

After all, the main reason you do strategic planning is because you want your
organization to change and grow in some way. This implies continuous progress.

By maintaining a permanent mind-set of strategic thinking, you get into the habit of thinking with clarity, meaning, focus, and direction. Skipping this process is the surest way I know to create one more strategic plan that falls by the wayside.

These concepts, and the system and structure in which they exist, are essential because they serve as tools for moving your plans into an integrated and successful implementation. This is especially true in the face of the revolutionary change that faces us now and will continue well into the 21st century.

STRATEGIC PLANNING DEFINED

> *If you do not look at things on a large scale, it will be difficult*
> *for you to master strategy. If you learn and attain this strat-*
> *egy, you will never lose, even to twenty or thirty enemies.*
> *More than anything ... you must set your heart on strategy*
> *and earnestly stick to the Way.*
>
> *-Miyamoto Musashi (1643 A.D.)*

I'll say it again: if you don't know where you're going, any road will take you there. Avoiding dead ends, and instead, developing a shared vision or road map that becomes a reality, is what strategic planning is all about.

Strategic planning is a dynamic, backward thinking process by the collective leadership of an organization that:

- first defines the Ideal Future Vision and then the appropriate core directional statements (strategies) in order to
- establish consistent, meaningful annual operating plans and budgets that
- drive the measurement and achievement of this future vision.

Your organization's strategic plan should serve as a blueprint, with the annual plans and budgets that result from it providing the specific, necessary yearly details.

Once this plan has been put to paper, however, many organizations run into trouble. Having a sleek, sophisticated plan on paper is one thing; getting it implemented can be quite another. In order to use strategic management as an ongoing way to grow your business into the 21st century, you must refocus your mind and mental map on Right Answer #1: moving from strategic planning to establish a comprehensive, strategic management system (from planning to management).

Strategic *Planning* vs. Strategic *Management*

To be successful, your strategic plan needs to be built into a structure that is designed to lead and manage your organization as it continues to grow, develop, and change. Simply developing a plan on paper won't carry your organization forward; the plan must be implemented and it must be led and managed day to day.

Thus, you'll need a process in which strategic *planning* is only one part, albeit in the lead position. The overall process — strategic *management* — is a field of management that is rapidly gaining in popularity. You'll hear me (and, increasingly, others in the field) refer to it often. It's an integral part of Seemingly Simple Element #1: *planning is a part of management.*

Most organizational planners make the mistake of looking at *strategic planning* as an event or a process that is an end in itself. Once it's been developed, that's the end of it.

Strategic management, on the other hand, is a new way to run your business *day-to-day.* It incorporates strategic planning and thinking into the everyday, ongoing progress of the organization, making it the backbone and focus of every organizational activity.

Going beyond strategic planning into strategic management means making a commitment throughout your organization to ongoing strategic (backwards) thinking and continuous improvement. It means accepting that no one plan can possibly anticipate or resolve every need, that the organization must have in place a strategic management *system* for planning and dealing with all organizational change and growth, now and in the future, and at all levels of management.

Where strategic planning once was mostly staff driven, strategic management is driven by senior line management leadership that aggressively pursues the commitment of all key stakeholders. As exhibited in the following comparison, strategic management also goes far beyond the "warm fuzzies" that sound so nice in the organization's mission statement. It lays out clearly what specific actions and tasks must take place for the plan to be successful. Then, it sets up concise, practical ways to lead, monitor, and measure its progress. It also incorporates the specific Annual Strategic Review (and Update) to keep the organization on track (much like a yearly independent financial audit).

Strategic Planning vs. Strategic Management

Analytic Thinking Traditional Strategic Planning "A Project"	vs.	Systems Thinking Strategic Management System "A New Way to Run the Business"
1. Project	vs.	1. Continuous/ongoing process with yearly Strategic Management System cycle/review to stay "on track"
2. Staff written	vs.	2. Line leadership driven/staff supported
3. Focus on today/extrapolation	vs.	3. Start with Future Ideal and work backward
4. "Motherhood/apple pie" words	vs.	4. Outcome measures and action plans set and accountability tracked
5. Big strategic planning document as end	vs.	5. Execution/change management/ customer focus is the goal; small document
6. Senior leadership/planning department answers only (we/they)	vs.	6. Key stakeholder feedback and commitment also (Parallel Process)
7. Weekend retreat	vs.	7. Strategic change in our roles/behaviors day to day
8. Strategic level only	vs.	8. Integrated into business units' annual and daily decision making levels, too

9. Individual change projects (TQM, service, empowerment, value-chain, etc.)	vs.	9. Customer-focused positioning and value-added delivery
10. Single event — one time only	vs.	10. Annual Strategic Review (and Update) each year
11. Environmental scan of today only	vs.	11. Future environmental scan/quarterly reviews
12. Analytical tools/analysis focus	vs.	12. Focus on strategy, commitment, and buy-in
13. Units/departments/silo mentality	vs.	13. Shared strategies as the glue and organizing forces
14. Hierarchy/controls	vs.	14. Customer-focused and values-driven empowerment
15. Organization structure remains the same	vs.	15. Strategic business redesign (watertight integrity)

The reason for reinventing the way we do business is the overwhelming change occurring within our environment and organizations today. Therefore, successful strategic management *must include mechanisms that address ongoing change.* And structuring strategic management so that it integrates ongoing change mechanisms requires Right Answer #1 — institutionalizing a three-part/three-goal strategic management system.

Though thinking, planning, and managing strategically are all essential, establishing a system within which to manage the myriad of changes is the only way to ensure continuous implementation of your core strategies. That's why the Strategic Change Leadership Steering Committee is the first absolute for success. Otherwise, change and good intentions always lose out to the day-to-day crises.

Strategic management system — A comprehensive, interactive, and participative system that leads, manages, and changes the total organization in a conscious, well-planned, and integrated (watertight integrity) fashion based on core strategies; such a system uses proven research that works to develop and successfully achieve the ideal future vision.

"SYSTEMS" — AN OVERUSED, MISUNDERSTOOD TERM

> *In one way or another, we are forced to deal with complexities, with "wholes" or "systems" in all fields of knowledge. This implies a basic re-orientation in scientific thinking.*
>
> *-Ludwig Von Bertalanffy*
> *(father of Systems Thinking)*

In spite of the fact that we're inundated with an infinite variety of business management trends these days, the idea of incorporating a systems framework into our organizations is not just another fad. Far from it. In fact, I consider it to be a critical element that can make the difference between organizational success and organizational failure.

Because the term "system" is frequently applied to a veritable cornucopia of organizational concepts, however, I'd like to first address the actual definitions of a system. Then, let's discuss how they can be used as a way to think backwards to your ideal future.

During the 1940s, the field of biology, with Ludwig Von Bertalanffy leading the way, brought forth a new way to look at the structure of all life — the system. In defining a system as *a set of components that work together for the overall objective of the whole*, scientists began to look at life and the elements that support it from a totally different perspective, ultimately ending up with a new theory called the General Systems Theory (GST).

In describing this theory, author Geoffrey Vickers wrote

> The words "general systems theory" imply that some things can usefully be said about (living) systems in general, despite the immense diversity of their specific forms. One of these things should be a scheme of classification. Every science begins by classifying its subject matter, if only descriptively, and learns a lot about it in the process; and systems especially need this attention, because an adequate classification cuts across familiar boundaries and at the same time draws valid and important distinctions which have previously been sensed but not defined.
>
> In short, the task of GST is to find the most general conceptual framework in which a scientific theory or a technological problem can be placed without losing the essential features of the theory or the problem.

Our Centre utilizes General Systems Theory and The Systems Thinking Approach as our foundation and new orientation to life, and to all our work, learning, and effectiveness with clients. Why?

Systems thinking is a heavily researched methodology and rigorous macroscientific theory with its roots in the universal laws of living systems on earth and in ecology and biology. It has been a recent focus of Dr. Russell Ackoff (renaissance professor emeritus at the University of Pennsylvania) and Jay Forrester at MIT, among others. In fact, we have identified over 25 other scientific disciplines such as electronics, architecture, complexity and chaos theory, project management, etc. whose leading thinkers and writers are moving in this direction. Four superstars founded the interdisciplinary society for General Systems research — one in economics, one in physiology, one in physics, and Von Bertalanffy from biology. They searched for a unity of science that encompassed all living things on earth.

The ultimate outcome of this discovery was that theorists began to apply this reasoning to all forms of social structure, including sociopolitical and socioeconomic focuses.

By 1979, *Business Week* magazine noted that "Nobel Laureate Wasily Leontief's 'Input-Output Analysis' has long been considered an ideal framework for economic planning."

The point is, this systems thinking and structure has a permanence and a flexibility that permits it to readily adapt to all the variations and complexities of our dynamically changing organizational environment. That's why it's called a *General Systems Theory*! It's the natural way that living things exist on earth.

In short, systems thinking is an old/new *orientation to life*. It is a better, more natural, and holistic view of living systems, such as individuals, teams, and organizations as they try to survive and thrive in today's dynamic environment.

This holistic and more purposeful outcome-oriented approach distinguishes the Centre from other consultants who have a sole focus on the components or separate functions of an organization (a more narrow, piecemeal, and fragmented analytical approach).

In the traditional analytic approach to planning, organizations start with today's problems, breaking them out into separate parts, analyzing and resolving one area at a time, then moving on to the next.

Systems thinking practices the exact opposite of this analytic approach. Systems thinking studies the organization as a whole in its interaction with its environment. Then, it works backwards to understand how each part of that whole works in relation to, and support of, the entire system's objectives. Only then can the core strategies be formulated.

In fact, it takes a higher, more integrated intellect and maturity to fully utilize this different worldview. It gives you a new way to think.

To use General Systems Theory in your own thinking, start thinking about:

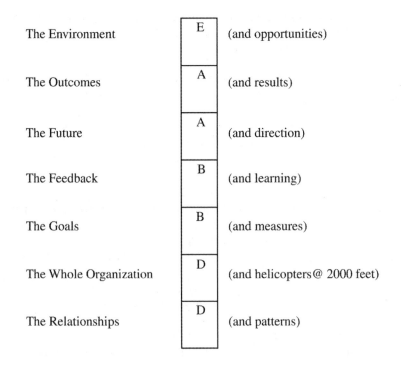

The Environment	E	(and opportunities)
The Outcomes	A	(and results)
The Future	A	(and direction)
The Feedback	B	(and learning)
The Goals	B	(and measures)
The Whole Organization	D	(and helicopters @ 2000 feet)
The Relationships	D	(and patterns)

How we think ... is how we act ... is how we are.

How is the systems concept best described? As you can see in the General Systems Theory chart (Figure 3.1), a system is described as an actual process with some key elements: in the system process, there is a series of *inputs* to *throughputs* (or actions), resulting in *outputs* into the system's environment. A system also contains a *feedback loop* for monitoring and evaluating the system's input, through-put, and output. Every living system also openly interacts with its own *environment*. Stop thinking about:

1. Issues and Problems
2. Parts and Events
3. Boxes/Silos
4. Single Activities of Change
5. Defensiveness
6. Inputs and Resources
7. Separateness

General Systems Theory has four main concepts of which the phases A, B, C, D, E shown in Figure 3.1 are one. These concepts will be explained below.

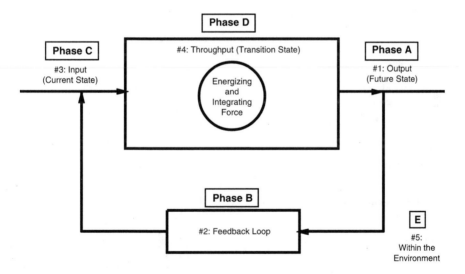

Systems: Systems are made up of a set of components that work together for the overall objective of the whole (output).

FIGURE 3.1 Systems Thinking: five key elements — from theory to practice.

FOUR MAIN CONCEPTS OF GENERAL SYSTEMS THEORY

CONCEPT #1: STANDARD SYSTEM DYNAMICS

The following table shows the 12 characteristics of General Systems Theory.

Natural Laws/Desired State vs. Experienced Dynamics

Part I: The Whole System		
Holism — Overall purpose-focused synergy/transformational	vs.	Parts/activity focused/suboptimal results
Open Systems — Open to environment	vs.	Closed systems/low environmental scan
Boundaries — Integrated/collaborative	vs.	Fragmented/turf battles/separate/parochial
Input/Output — How natural systems operate	vs.	Piecemeal/analytic/sequential and narrow view
Feedback — On effectiveness/root causes	vs.	Low feedback/financial only
Multiple Outcomes — Goals	vs.	Artificial either/or thinking
Part II: The Inner Workings		
Equifinality — Flexibility and agility	vs.	Direct cause-effect/one best way
Entropy — Follow-up/inputs of energy/renewal	vs.	Decline/rigidity/obsolete/death
Hierarchy — Flatter organization/self-organizing structures/infrastructures	vs.	Bureaucracy/command and control
Interrelated Parts — Relationships/involvement and participation	vs.	Separate parts/components/entities/silos
Dynamic Equilibrium — Stability and balance/culture	vs.	Short-term myopic view/ruts/resistance to change
Internal Elaboration — Details and sophistication	vs.	Complexity and confusion/need for KISS (keep it simple)

CONCEPT #2: SEVEN LEVELS OF LIVING SYSTEMS

All systems are actually subsystems of larger and larger systems in their environment. There is an actual hierarchy of interrelated systems, i.e.,

1. cell
2. organ
3. individual
4. group/team
5. organization/community
6. society/nation
7. earth/world/continent
8. solar system/universe?

Concept #3: Basic Systems Model

(This model is part of the 12 characteristics described in Concept #1.) There are many applications of the basic systems model.

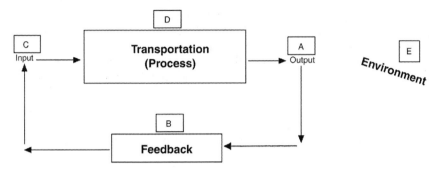

Concept #4: Historical/Natural Cycles of Change

- The Rollercoaster of Change[SM] depicts how all types of change occur naturally in life.

The Benefits of Systems Thinking

The benefits of systems thinking are tremendous and include

1. A way of thinking more effectively about any system:
   - Its purposes
   - Its environment
   - Its components.
2. A framework and way to make sense out of life's complexities, since all living things are systems.
3. A way to learn new things easier, as the basic rules stay the same from system to system.
4. A framework for diagnosing, analyzing, problem solving, and decision making in the system. A clearer way to see and understand what is going on in an organization — or in any system. Complex problems become easier to understand, as do the interrelationships of parts and the multiple cause/effect cycles.
5. A way to manage in the complex "systems age," i.e., focusing on the whole, its components, and the *interrelationships* of the components. A better way to integrate new ideas within the systems context.
6. A way to see the big picture as well as the details.
7. A view of the long-term and the short-term consequences.
8. A new and better way to create strategies, solve problems, find leverage points, keeping the outcome/vision goal in mind at all times. It uncovers points of leverage for change that might otherwise be ignored.

9. A method of understanding the relationship, patterns, and themes between issues and events.
10. A method for identifying the root causes of a current problem. It engages teams and people in a deeper thought process/analysis and definition of more root causes that provide longer-lasting results.
11. It helps get at the deeper structure and relationship/process issues that aren't obvious with a "quick fix" mentality.
12. A framework for focusing on the customer and your external environment.
13. A forward-looking, solution-seeking perspective instead of simply problem-solving today's issues.
14. A common language with a better way to communicate and collaborate.

In summary: Systems thinking leads to a new and better orientation to success in life.

SYSTEMS ("BACKWARDS") THINKING: AN ORIENTATION TO LIFE

Everything everywhere now truly affects everything else.

-Ian Mitroff

I refer to systems thinking as a "new orientation to life" because of its use in thinking differently and better about everything we do. It's about thinking backward from your desired outcome, determining where you are now, and then finding the core strategies or actions that will take you from today to your desired outcome. Backwards — or true systems thinking — employs what I call the A, B, C, D, E guideposts (introduced in Figure 3.1): five critical questions or phases that serve as locator points to clarify this thought process beginning at Phase A.

Phase A: Where do we want to be? (i.e., our ends, outcomes, purposes, goals, holistic vision)
Phase B   How will we know when we get there? (i.e., the customers' needs and wants connected into a quantifiable feedback system)
Phase C: Where are we now? (i.e., today's issues and problems)
Phase D: How do we get there? (i.e., close the gap from C → A in a complete, holistic way)
Phase E: What will/may change in our environment in the future? (This is an ongoing question.)

Pretty simple, right? In a sense, it truly is a simple, common-sense approach. That's why I've incorporated it as one of the three Seemingly Simple Elements. Before deciding it is *simplistic*, however, let's see how this changed orientation points to a new paradigm of how to lead and manage complex organizations.

Figure 3.2 shows that these five A, B, C, D, E questions relate directly to the phases of our systems model. They set up the holistic approach to strategic management.

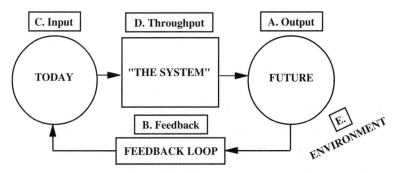

Systems: Systems are made up of a set of components that work together for the overall objective of the whole (output).

FIGURE 3.2 Systems Thinking: five key elements — from complexity to simplicity.

Phase A: Concentrate on defining outcomes first.
Phase B: Establish a quantifiable feedback system by which your organization will specifically measure its progress.
Phase C: Determine where you are now.
Phase D: Figure out what actions you need to take to reach your vision.
Phase E: All the while, continuously scan the environment.

Systems thinking clarifies the overall objectives of the whole, starting at Phase A. It simplifies the process and makes sure all those pieces fit together in a continuous, growth-oriented system that focuses on outcome. In systems thinking, the whole is primary and the parts are secondary (not vice versa).

The holism of systems thinking is in stark contrast with the fragmentation of analytic thinking, which

1. Starts with today and the current state, issues, and problems.
2. Breaks the issues and/or problems into their smallest components.
3. Solves each component separately (i.e., maximizes the solution).
4. Has no far-reaching vision or goal (beyond the mere absence of the problem).

If you don't know where you're going,
any road will get you there.

QUESTIONS TO PONDER

- Are you clear on the difference between systems and analytical thinking — and why both are used within the systems framework?

- Does your strategic plan incorporate the four elements of a true system: input, output, throughput, and feedback within the environment?
- Are you clear on the difference between strategic planning and strategic management? Which do you practice?
- Does your organization view strategic planning as an isolated event or process, or has it created an ongoing, three-part strategic management system for achieving its ideal future vision?

EXACTLY WHAT *ARE* THE PROPERTIES OF A SYSTEM?

The most distinctive feature of any system is that *each and every part influences and affects every other part of that same system.* Ideally, all parts of a system fit and work together synergistically. By definition, no individual part can be independent. The following list identifies most of the properties of a true system:

1. **The Whole Is Primary** — The whole is primary and the parts are secondary. Focusing on maximizing the parts leads to suboptimizing the whole.
2. **Systems Must Be Viewed Holistically in Their Environment** — Systems, and organizations as systems, can only be understood holistically. Try to understand the system and its environment first. Organizations are open systems and, as such, are viable only in interaction with and adaptation to the changing environment.
3. **Each System Functions Uniquely** — Every system has properties/functions that none of its parts can do individually.
4. **System Purposes First** — The place to start is with the whole and its purposes within its environment. The parts and their relationships evolve from this.
5. **Parts Support the Whole** — Parts play their role in light of the purpose for which the whole exists. Focus on the desired outcomes, not just the problems of the parts.
6. **All Parts Are Interdependent** — Parts, elements, subsystems are interdependent ... a web of relationships. Therefore, yesterday's great solutions may lead to today's issues. Systems cannot be subdivided into independent parts; a system as a whole cannot function effectively when it loses a part.
7. **Small Changes Produce Big Results** — Change in any element of a system affects the whole as well as the other elements, or subsystems. The small changes can produce big results if the leverage points are clear.
8. **Maximizing Parts Suboptimizes the Whole** — Exclusive focus on one element or subsystem without simultaneous attention to other subsystems leads to suboptimal results and new disturbances. The solution or simple cure can often be worse than the real disease.

9. **Causes and Effects Are Not Closely Related** — Time delay and delayed reactions (or cause and effect being not closely related in time and space) cause inaccurate diagnoses and solutions. Direct cause and effect is an environmentally free concept.
10. **Faster Is Ultimately Slower** — Systems have a natural pace to them. Sometimes trying to go faster is ultimately slower.
11. **Feedback and Boundaries** — Systems are more "open" and likely to sustain their existence longer and more effectively, the more feedback they receive from the environment through all aspects of their boundaries.
12. **Multiple Goals** — All social systems have multiple goals; building consensus on them first is the key to successful teamwork and achieving these goals.
13. **Equifinality and Flexibility** — People can achieve their goals and outcomes in many different styles/ways. Thus the CSM "strategic consistency — operational flexibility" concept of the 1990s.
14. **Hierarchy Is Natural** — Despite some recent "political correctness" issues against hierarchies, all systems have a natural hierarchy; find it, minimize it, and make it work for you.
15. **Entropy and Tendency to Run Down** — All systems have a tendency toward maximum entropy, disorder, and death. Importing resources from the environment is key to long-term viability; closed systems move toward this disorganization faster than open systems.

In the previous section, we looked at the differences between analytic and systems thinking. It's important at this point to mention that neither thought process is bad, nor do they automatically exclude one another. There will be times in our organizational environment when an analytical approach is called for. It's critical, however, that when we apply it to a problem, we're applying it within the context of an overall, integrated systems thinking framework.

A good way to summarize the notion that every part of a system interacts with and depends upon every other part is to review some of the things that took place in the financial marketplace during one month in 1984. On March 4, 1984, a small Florida securities dealer known as E.S.M. collapsed. Home State Savings Bank in Cincinnati, Ohio, having one third of its loan portfolio in E.S.M. securities, then closed its doors.

Following this, there was a run on savings and loans throughout Ohio, which were then taken over by the Federal Home Loan Bank Board (FHLBB), the old Savings and Loan Insurance Corp. Understandably, this caused some major jitters on the already deficit-ridden financial system and market of that time. During March 18th through 20th, only 2 weeks later, the U.S. dollar fell 6% against the British pound, one of the largest drops in history. Finally, British oil assets took a severe beating because they were measured and traded in U.S. dollars.

This is a perfect example of systems theory in action. It shows us clearly that not only are all the parts of any given system (in this case, our global economic system) dependent on one another, but that every system affects every other system in our globally interconnected world.

ORGANIZATIONS AS SYSTEMS — BACKWARDS THINKING SYSTEMS

One of the primary reasons I began to research a systems approach to strategic management was the surfeit of organizational trends I kept running into throughout my years in senior management. Between management-by-objective, quality circles, TQM, restructuring, downsizing, coaching, mentoring, benchmarking, business re-engineering, and more, I had a lot of headaches — but no real problems resolved. It was becoming obvious to me that this analytical approach to problem solving was somewhat like trying to build the world's greatest car.

Picture yourself building the premier car in the world. You have access to every automobile ever made. First, you examine them for which one has the undisputed best engine. Next, you select a distributor from a different car, one which you know has the very best in distributors. Now it's time to select the best, most reliable carburetor — which of course comes from another, totally different car.

One by one, you gather these "best parts" until you have every part necessary for making the world's best car. Once you've tried to put them all together, however, just what is it exactly that you have? One thing's for sure: you don't have the world's greatest car — you don't even have a car, *because the parts don't fit!*

Though you have in your possession all of the parts necessary for building a car, none of those individual parts was designed to fit with the others. They're all from different systems, and used independently of their systems, they're worth nothing.

After talking to hundreds of other business executives — who were also trying to build "the world's greatest car" within their own organizations and who felt the same sense of frustration and confusion that I did — I began to wonder how in the world any of us could take all of the intricate components that exist (in infinite variations) within every organization, match them to whatever trend was the "flavor of the day," and make sense out of it all, much less come up with any answers that would truly serve our customers?

It was at this point that I realized my earlier work on the General Systems Theory should serve as an overall framework that would accommodate all of the intricacies presented by a typical organization. In viewing the organization as a living system, we see it as an intricate puzzle, a network of inputs, processes, outputs, feedback from suppliers, employees, customers, and other key stakeholders in the environment.

Every part of this system depends on every other part working as it should. To successfully lead and manage this requires a specific and complex set of concepts, tools, and skills for wiring and aligning these components together for the overall objective of the whole, i.e., focusing on the outcome of serving the customer. And, the customer has a complex set of expectations for quality products, high-level service, prompt delivery, and reasonable cost.

What all my peers and I had been trying to do was to apply an issue-by-issue, analytical solution to a systems problem. No wonder it wasn't working! No wonder it is so difficult to lead and manage today's organizations.

Some of the attributes one could expect to find in a systems-oriented organization that might not exist in a more hierarchical one include

- A shared vision of the overall organization's future.
- Better horizontal, cross-functional communication and cooperation to serve the customer.
- Teamwork within and across functions.
- Cross-functional task forces and project teams.
- Integrity of the various parts and departments of the organization fitting and working together for the good of the whole.
- An alignment of work processes horizontally across the organization that meet the needs of the external customers.
- Focus on system-wide core strategies rather than functional or department goals.
- Fewer levels of hierarchy and management; greater operational flexibility and empowerment.

The best place to begin establishing a true strategic management system in your organization is to set up the A, B, C, D, E Phases I referred to in the previous section. Applying them as an organization-wide systems or backwards thinking process enables you to chart a clear course for developing and putting your vision/mission/values into practice.

- **Phase A — "Where do we want to be?"** This is the place to begin replacing the traditional analytic approach with backwards thinking. It's actually the starting point for putting your systems framework into place by focusing on the outcomes you desire for your organization, envisioning the future as if it were today, and then working backward to the present.
- **Phase B — "How will we know when we get there?"** It's crucial to develop concrete feedback; you need to define your outcome measures of success, both organization-wide and unit by unit. This is how you'll be able to gauge whether the implementation of your core strategies is progressing successfully; it's where you will determine the success of Point A on a year-to-year basis.
- **Phase C — "Where are we right now?"** This is the step in which you design strategies and actions for closing the gap between your organization's current state and its desired future vision, with the specific action priorities necessary to support them.
- **Phase D — "How do we get there from here?"** It is at this point that you further develop the systems framework that will include detailed considerations on how to implement and manage change throughout your organization. Integrate your change management techniques into an organization-wide system and put your plans into motion — tracking, monitoring, reporting, and adjusting as necessary.

- **Phase E** — **"What is changing in the environment that we need to take into account?"**

Six Uses of the A, B, C, D, E Framework

As you can see, this A, B, C, D, E framework aligns directly with the five phases of a system: (1) output, (2) feedback loop, (3) input, and (4) throughput/actions (5) within the dynamic and changing environment. By addressing the five phases, starting with Phase A, and then following through with the implementation of the five phases of a systems framework, you lay the groundwork for a common-sense, practical strategic management system that helps you focus on the changes you want to accomplish.

The real beauty of working within a systems framework is that you can be quite flexible in how you apply it. Remember, the General Systems Theory provides a generic, universal framework to which literally any set of requirements can be adapted. Depending upon your specific needs or situation, you can adapt this framework in numerous ways. You should always use the same A, B, C, D, E phases in sequence and in conjunction with backwards thinking. It's just applied in different time frames, depending on the use to which it is put. Six uses of the A, B, C, D, E framework include the following:

1. **A Comprehensive Strategic Plan.** For a large organization, this is a process in which your collective leadership develops a comprehensive plan that encompasses the entire organization. Your investment in time will depend on whether you are starting from scratch or tailoring and filling in the missing pieces of your organizational systems framework to get synergistic implementation. Expect to spend anywhere from 8 to 16 days off-site over a 4- to 6-month time frame.
2. **Strategic Planning Quick.** This allows you to conduct a less comprehensive version of strategic planning for a smaller to mid-sized organization. It requires approximately 5 to 7 days off-site, over 2 to 4 months.
3. **Three-Year Business Planning.** If you need to create a strategic plan for a specific business unit — or a major support function, section, or program for a larger organization — you can complete a shortened 3-year business planning process in about 3 to 5 days off-site, over 2 to 4 months.
4. **Microstrategic Planning.** Even if your organization is very small, you still need to create a strategic plan for it. This "micro" process enables you to develop a strategic plan in only 2 days off-site, over 2 months, and complete the rest without off-site meetings. However, it does require immediate implementation through a Strategic Change Steering Committee to keep up the momentum started and to finish any planning pieces missed due to the short time frame.

5. **Project Planning and Strategic Changes.** You can apply this A, B, C, D, E system to a major project or change effort, such as TQM, customer service, business process reengineering, empowerment, partnerships/teamwork, and technology, etc. Even if you are going to go after change in this piecemeal fashion, use systems thinking to leverage your effectiveness and success in this project. Remember, always differentiate between analytical and systems thinking; when you need to apply analytical thinking, do it within a systems framework and context.

6. **Strategic Life Plan.** Your personal life is even more important than your business life. This A, B, C, D, E systems framework can be used to conduct a personal (person, family, couple) life plan. My wife and I, along with numerous other personal and professional acquaintances, have developed a life plan with very satisfying results.

Keep in mind, the systems or backward thinking framework can be applied to virtually any professional or personal situation. No matter what the particular requirement may be, as long as you stay focused on the A, B, C, D, E phases in the proper sequence, they will work for you. Remember, systems thinking is a better way to think, and to act, as a new orientation to life.

Strategic Management Comparisons — Ten Unique Concepts and Paradigm Changes: The Systems Thinking Approach

Analytical Planning Model	vs.	Reinventing Strategic Management (Systems Model)
1. Focus on plan content only.	vs.	1. Team building and leadership development (skills of trainer/coach/facilitator) are an integral part of this, including senior management personal life visions and personal values.
2. Preset steps/actions.	vs.	2. Plan-to-plan and team building first to build in and engineer success up front (educate and organize).
3. Current state emphasis (starts with today's problems).	vs.	3. Ideal Future Vision (vision — mission — values) as the place to start. The use of backwards thinking to redirect the status of today toward a future vision of total customer-focus on their wants/needs and product/services and their benefits.
4. Total community participation.	vs.	4. Involvement of many stakeholders through the use of a Parallel Process. (People support what they help create.)
5. Written in platitudes (high level only).	vs.	5. Quantifiable outcome measures of success developed as a year-to-year score board.

6. Smooth over conflict and disagreements with words.	vs.	6. Making/forcing tough choices. Focusing your business with priority setting (mission, driving force, outcome measures, core strategies, annual action priorities at a number of levels).
7. Discrete and separate/planning projects and goal-setting process (department/ individual annual budgets).	vs.	7. A "Cascade of Planning" to link strategic planning with business unit plans, with functional/department plans, with individual goal setting/rewards, and day-to-day decision-making empowerment within a framework.
8. Set budgets first; work within them to plan.	vs.	8. Strategic budgeting that includes ten different ways to force your annual resource allocation to become based on your strategic plan's priorities/focus.
9. Focus on the Strategic Planning document.	vs.	9. Both a "Plan-to-Implement" day with a Yearly Comprehensive Map, and a Strategic Change Leadership Steering Committee to bridge the gap between planning and implementing and to build a team with the skills to manage change.
10. Plan on left, manage on the right — "structure" is not important.		10. The last step is an Annual Strategic Review and Update — like an independent financial audit to recycle your annual priorities and recommit to your revised plans.

MACRO LEVEL – Systems Thinking Approach

11. Didactic (tell client the answers, meaning outside client).		11. Facilitator role of planner and staff to help the client find and own the answers. Experiential, with meaning developed internal to client. Line executives are in charge as part of their management responsibility. Take the time for in-depth discussions/full buy-in and understanding. (Two steps forward; one step back.) Focus on the Systems Thinking Approach throughout (i.e., a strategic management system).

QUESTIONS TO PONDER

- Do you understand why it's crucial to start at Phase A — the future outcomes you desire — rather than starting with the present?
- Do you know and understand what the five key properties of a system are?
- Are you clear on some of the key attributes of a systems-oriented organization vs. a hierarchical one?

- Which of the six possible uses for the Reinventing Strategic Management Model do you and your organization need?

  1. A Comprehensive Strategic Plan
  2. Strategic Planning Quick
  3. Three-year Business Planning
  4. "Microstrategic" Planning
  5. Project Planning and Strategic Changes
  6. Strategic Life Plan

IN SUMMARY

It is abundantly clear to most of us in business these days that what worked before won't work now. The traditional, time-consuming method of analyzing and solving one problem at a time has given way to the sweeping and sometimes obliterating winds of revolutionary change. A fresh new approach is called for, one that can set in place a framework sturdy enough to withstand the ongoing complexities of continuous change and organizational dynamics.

From extensive experience, I have come deeply to believe that long-term success can only come from a systems thinking approach. In this chapter I have tried to explain the "why" behind that approach. It begins with an obscure scientific discipline called General Systems Theory. In the next chapter, I'll present the "how" by using the systems framework to conduct successful strategic management. The following chapter also discusses some common mistakes and benefits through using our Reinventing Strategic Management (Planning and Change) Model.

The Systems Thinking Approach is an absolute necessity to make sense of and succeed in today's complex world.

If life on earth is governed by the natural laws of living systems, then a successful participant should learn the concepts and principles.

-Stephen G. Haines, 1998

RECAP OF KEY CONTENT POINTS

- Focus on systems thinking in your strategic management.
- Start with your Ideal Future Vision and then work backward to determine the core strategies you'll need to achieve this.
- Goal #2 — ensuring successful implementation — is the key to strategic planning, *not* the document.

- Simply developing a strategic plan on paper won't work; you must incorporate a three-part strategic management system to ensure continuous improvement.
- Where strategic planning is mostly staff-driven, strategic management is driven by line management leadership and aggressively pursues the commitment of all key stakeholders.
- Any system can be described as an actual process, with inputs, throughputs, outputs, and feedback within a dynamic and rapidly changing environment.
- In traditional analytic thinking, issues are broken out and resolved one at a time. Systems thinking is the opposite; it studies the organization as a whole and the achievement of its objectives as it interacts with its environment.
- A systems framework sets up an A, B, C, D, E sequential, five-phase approach to strategic management: (A) concentrating on outcomes first, (B) establishing a quantifiable feedback system for measuring progress, (C) determining where you are now, and (D) how you'll reach your ultimate vision within (E) a rapidly changing environment.

4 Reinventing Strategic Management (Planning and Change)

Every moment spent planning saves three or four in execution.
-Crawford Greenwalt, President, DuPont

Though most of the ideas presented in previous chapters may seem like plain, old-fashioned common sense, your strategic plan will never see the light of day without a lot of elbow grease and commitment. In my experience, the organizations that are successful are those that are willing to educate and organize themselves, tailor the process, create a clear plan, make the tough choices, and then get on with the process of change.

The plans that fail are often just as good as those that succeed; the difference lies in the organization's disciplined persistence and commitment to implementation and its ability to keep the ball rolling over the long term.

Once you're clear on how to use a systems framework for planning, implementing, and updating your organization's core strategies, you're ready to begin the actual shaping of your plan.

REINVENTING STRATEGIC MANAGEMENT

Following the A, B, C, D, E phases in this Reinventing Strategic Management Model provides us with a customer-focused systems solution for creating your own high-performance organization. It consists of the five phases outlined in Chapter 3, within which there are ten clear, practical steps (Figure 4.1).

PHASE A — OUTPUT: IDEAL FUTURE VISION

Step #1: Plan-to-Plan

This is the step that assesses, educates, organizes, and tailors the strategic planning process to your organization's specific needs. It includes setting up your core planning team and the concept of a Parallel Process that involves key stakeholders (remember that people support what they help create). It also clarifies top management's role in leading, developing, and owning their strategic plan.

Example: During their Plan-to-Plan step, the Hayward Unified School District in California established a planning team of 15 people. However, because of the district's broad impact on the lives of thousands of families, its Parallel Process with key stakeholders included over 100 meetings involving more than 2000 people.

1-57444-278-3/00/$0.00+$.50
© 2000 by CRC Press LLC

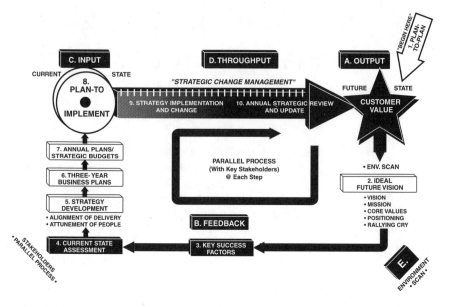

FIGURE 4.1   Reinventing Strategic Management (Planning and Change) — a Systems Thinking approach to crating your competitive edge. Courtesy of the Centre for Strategic Management, San Diego, CA, 1997 Revised. With permission.

As part of the Plan-to-Plan (Step #1), each organization needs to conduct Phase E — Environmental Scanning. While the letter "E" doesn't normally follow sequentially from A, the process of scanning the environment is too important to wait for completion of the other phases; it must be undertaken at the beginning. For this reason, we will cover the environmental scanning process in greater detail in Chapter 6.

Step #2: Ideal Future Vision

This step concerns itself with formulating a vision and dreams that are worth believing in and fighting for. This is where you should focus on your desired outcomes (customer). You also need to define your mission (reason for being), core values (desired culture), and positioning in the marketplace with your customers vs. the competition.

Example: When you put it all together, you need, in eight words or less, an internally motivating "essence" of your Ideal Future; a rallying cry. Ford's *Quality is Job 1*™ is still the most well-known rallying cry today, and is even used liberally throughout their advertising.

PHASE B — FEEDBACK: KEY SUCCESS MEASURES OR GOALS

Step #3: Key Success Measures (KSMs) or Goals

It is at this point that you must begin developing ways in which to measure your organization's outcome measures of success toward its vision, mission, and core values.

Example: Some typical KSMs in the private sector include: (1) customer satisfaction (quality, service, customer-responsiveness), (2) employee satisfaction, (3) financial success (revenue, return on investment, profits, etc.), and (4) competitive edge vs. the competition (market share, etc.).

PHASE C — INPUT: TODAY'S ASSESSMENT AND STRATEGY DEVELOPMENT

Step #4: Current State Assessment

In this step, you'll analyze the organization's strengths, weaknesses, opportunities, and threats, and contrast them against your vision. There are numerous sophisticated techniques to do this; we'll cover them in the chapter on Current State Assessment. This is where planners have historically spent their time: analyzing today only.

Example: The Palomar Pomerado Health System in California did a thorough analysis of each major health care system in its marketplace. These analyses were crucial in its deliberations on how to compete in an industry of shrinking margins, tougher competition, and calls for government to reform health care.

Step #5: Strategy Development

This step develops the core strategies — or major means and efforts — you'll need to bridge the gap between where you want to be in your Ideal Future Vision (Step #2) and your Current State Assessment (Step #4).

Example: It's important in developing your strategies to remember that less is more. In my doctoral research of 200 financial services firms, the top financial performers had 40% fewer core strategies than the poorer performers. As a result of having fewer, more highly defined core strategies, the top performers remained more continually focused, which resulted in more successful implementation and healthy financial results.

Step #6: Business Units and Three-Year Business Planning

At this point, the strategic business units (SBUs) in the private sector — or major program areas (MPAs) in the government and not-for-profit sector — that comprise your organization's overall business portfolio are identified and prioritized according to their contribution to your future growth, profitability, and direction. Ideally, three-year business plans for each of these need to be developed, along with overall pro forma financial statements on revenue/growth/expenditures/profits, etc.

Example: General Motors is generally criticized for having too many automobile SBUs: Cadillac, Buick, Pontiac, Chevrolet, Oldsmobile (frequently rumored to be closing), and their newest SBU, Saturn Corp. They often overlap, duplicate, and compete with one another.

Step #7: Annual Plans and Strategic Budgets

This is where the rubber meets the road — where you develop unit/department annual plans with prioritized tasks and then provide the resources to actually implement your core strategies. *Planning should lead to budgeting, not vice versa.*

Example: The city of Yuma, Arizona now has all city departments with annual plans based on the corporate strategic plan (and organized by core strategies).

PHASE D — THROUGHPUT: ACTIONS, IMPLEMENTATION, AND CHANGE

Step #8: Plan-to-Implement

This step serves as a crucial bridge between Goal #1 (developing a strategic plan) and Goal #2 (ensuring the successful implementation of strategic change). Similar to Plan-to-Plan (Step #1), it also educates and organizes senior management for the change management process. It establishes a Strategic Change Leadership Steering Committee (SCLSC) and a yearly comprehensive map (i.e., project plan) to guide the changes dictated by the strategic plan. It also develops a rollout and communications plan for the newly developed strategic plan.

Example: At a large suburban school district in central California, the superintendent resigned at the end of strategic planning. However, because they had completed step #8, Plan-to-Implement, the district retained a critical mass of both board members and management that remained strongly committed to successful implementation.

Step #9: Strategy Implementation (and Change)

The goal of this step is to transform the strategic plan into all the hundreds of necessary individual plans, programs, and efforts, and to tie a rewards system to it.

Example: In British Columbia, Canada, the Environmental Protection Division holds quarterly Strategic Change Steering Committee meetings. It has been highly successful in implementing its strategic plan, through strong leadership. Even in a difficult government setting, strategic planning has a wide reputation for excellence.

Step #10: Annual Strategic Review (and Update)

A formal Annual Strategic Review and Update of the strategic management systems' results and process needs to be conducted, much like a yearly independent financial audit. In this way, you persistently keep your implementation up and running year after year as a strategic management system — even after the newness has worn off.

Example: Eagle Creek Travel Outfitters never misses this yearly update — hence its continuing financial, organizational, and human successes and growth.

MAKING IT WORK

As you would expect, achieving the goal of fitting all the parts of your organization together with "watertight integrity" in support of your vision is extremely difficult. As you can see above, each of the various steps in this planning model incorporates actions and accountability on the part of many different individuals throughout the organization. For example:

Strategic Management Step	Typical Accountability
Plan-to-plan	Planning/CEO
Vision/mission/values	OD/Training
Business plans	Business Units or Business Development/Planning
Current state assessment	Planning/Business Development
Department plans	Department heads
Strategic budgets	Finance
Compensation/staffing	Human Resources
Annual Strategic Review	Finance

Looking at this, it's easy to see why the need for a systems framework is so great. *Strategic management* requires all of the various organizational departments to work together as efficiently as possible. After years of experience in trying to "build the world's greatest car" — only to fail — it has become obvious that the traditional paradigm of analytical thinking alone wasn't working, and won't work. It has no watertight integrity.

SOME PROGRESS: PARTIAL SYSTEMS SOLUTIONS

For a long time, organizations got away with approaching the future from an analytical perspective. Problem solving of current issues was typically handled by analyzing problems, breaking down each part, solving it separately, then moving on to the next one. Analytical thinking also put the current state of affairs above all other considerations: "handle today's issues, and deal with tomorrow when it gets here." Strategic planning from the analytical approach mostly extrapolated and projected today's issues into the future. Some businesses are still working this way today and surviving, but not for long.

Today, when just about every existing organizational paradigm has flown out the window, organizations are beginning to respond with what I call *partial systems thinking*. This seems to be a beginning stage in moving away from the traditional analytic approach and thinking. Organizations are attempting to find integrated answers for individual problems, rather than the earlier way of applying a one-time only solution to a problem that had ongoing implications (see Figure 4.2).

It is because of this kind of thinking that we're seeing such an abundance of organizational change trends such as value-chain management, cultural change, systems change, TQM, business process reengineering, empowerment, and restructuring, to name a few. It's an attempt to begin combining parts of problems into more complete and integrated solutions.

I.   Analytic thinking (scientific thinking)

Break it down into individual parts – *problem-solve each part separately.*

Typical individual consultant/trainer projects – *however, a system cannot be*

subdivided into independent parts.

II.   Begin to combine parts into solutions (partial systems thinking)

Eclectic list of parts/models, today's fads/models and consultant

broader projects – *"what you see depends on where you sit."*

Suboptimal results and new disturbances as unintended by-products.

III.   "True" systems thinking – systems fit, alignment, and integrity

(General Systems Theory)

A system cannot be understood by analysis, but by synthesis, looking at it as a whole

within its environment.

You must become a *customer-focused, market-driven* organization with a systems

model to visualize, understand, and change as necessary.

FIGURE 4.2   Partial systems solutions — a beginning reversal of analytic thinking.

STRATEGIC PLANNING LEADS THE WAY

The problem with this partial systems approach is that it creates a "what you see depends on where you sit" environment. As in the "world's greatest car" example, some things get fixed or improved along the way. However, no provisions are made for questions that arise as a result of changing one area and leaving others as they were.

True systems thinking, on the other hand, studies each problem as it relates to the organization's objectives and interaction with its entire environment, looking at it as a whole within its universe. Taking your organization from a partial systems to a true systems state requires effective strategic management and backward thinking.

As you'll see in the following listing, it is the most important tool you can use for creating the necessary changes organization-wide while tying together all the fads and concepts of others into one framework. Otherwise, how can you understand, much less keep track of, all the brilliant solutions being bandied about today? Some of these popular solutions include TQM, customer service, business process reengineering, empowerment, leadership, visioning, teamwork, self-directed work teams, and more. Each of these solutions is correct and effective in its own right.

However, when viewed in a systems context, they are only partial solutions and therefore are only partially successful for the organizations that use them. On the other hand, if they're looked at as a part of the overall strategic plan, then the plan can lead the way to a fully successful implementation.

STRATEGIC PLANNING, MANAGEMENT, AND LEADERSHIP LEAD THE WAY

Strategic planning is the major organizational intervention to develop a shared vision of your future and the values, culture, and business strategies needed to be implemented and managed to get you there.

It is a way to

- Accelerate/advance the changes you want to make.
- Tie in and increase the importance of other major changes that should be (but usually aren't) corporate strategies with total buy-in/ownership by the organization.

The following outlines details of the system approach to strategic planning for TQM.

- *Plan-to-Plan* — Step #1: Get educated and organized and tailor the process to your needs
- *Environment (Phase E)* — Ongoing: Environmental Scanning/Best Practices Research
    1. Why: stockholders, stakeholders, customers, society
- *Outputs (Phase A)* — Step #2: Vision and Mission
    2. Who: customer focus
    3. What: quality, service, response, cost, profitability
- *Outputs (Phase A)* — Step #2 (also): Core Values
    4. Self-directed work teams
    5. Employee empowerment/creativity
    6. Continuous improvement

> 7. GE's Workout (blowout bureaucracy); reinvent government
> 8. Communications effectiveness; drive out fear

- **Feedback (Phase B)** — Step #3: Key Success Measures/Goals
  > 9. Benchmarking/measurement systems (world-class comparisons)
  > 10. Employee and customer satisfaction surveys
  > 11. Market research
  > 12. Executive compensation and other rewards practices
- **Inputs (Phase C)** — Step #4: Core Strategies
  > 13. TQM/TQL — some of Deming's 14 Points
  > 14. Service management/quality service
  > 15. Speed and response time
  > 16. Business process improvement/reengineering
  > 17. Improved sales and market-driven culture
  > 18. Cost efficiencies, reductions, and productivity improvements
  > 19. Delayering
  > 20. People as our competitive business advantage
  > 21. Culture change
  > 22. Organization structure/design
- **Throughputs (Phase D)** — Steps #6–10: Operational Planning and Implementation
  > 23. Annual/operations/tactical planning
  > 24. Annual budgeting
  > 25. Performance management/evaluation system
  > 26. Strategic Change Steering Committee/transition management/Q.M.B.S.–P.A.T.s
  > 27. Annual strategic reviews and updates, management meetings

This is what systems thinking is all about: the idea of building an organization in which each piece, and partial solution of the organization has the fit, alignment, and integrity with your overall organization as a system, and its outcome of serving the customer.

Seven Levels of Living Systems (A Quick Review)

In Chapter 2 we discussed the key Systems Thinking concept of the Seven Levels of Living Systems. These seven levels demonstrate that each system impacts every other system, and that there is a hierarchy of "systems within systems." When looked at from a strategic management perspective, the concept of the different levels really does present a challenge to implementation that planners rarely consider and to which we found no solutions in the literature.

We had to literally invent a way in which we think and do business down through the entire organization. Such a model had to create an environment in which all systems and subsystems are linked together to achieve the overall organizational system (or vision).

CASCADE OF PLANNING

Once your organization has a strategic plan in place, how do you keep it going successfully? How do you keep up your plan's energy, momentum, and focus throughout all the multiple systems levels that make up your organization?

In light of the Seven Levels of Living Systems, this is a crucial question. One of the General Systems Theory's principles is that the minute a system is born (or set in place), it begins to die: there exists the natural phenomenon of incremental degradation, which eventually causes every system to slowly run down. This is the principle of *entropy*, and it's in direct opposition to the principle of continuous improvement.

This is where the "Cascade of Planning" (Figure 4.3) comes in. By designing a framework for your strategic plan that automatically includes every level of your organization, you have a built-in protection against entropy. Visualize your organization as having at least three levels of the living systems: individual, group, and organization. This requires you to *"cascade"* your planning and change down *through each level*. It's the only way your strategic management system can continue to move the plan forward and perpetuate its success.

If you recognize that all the levels of your organization (departments, units, and people) must work together to align the system's output of serving the customer, you are well on your way to success. In addition to this, the Cascade of Planning mandates that planning be conducted for every part of the organization on two levels: (1) the strategic planning level, and (2) the annual planning level.

1. **Strategic Planning Levels**
   - *Organization-wide strategic planning:* You need an organization-wide, 3, 5, or 10-year strategic plan, defining the organization's vision, mission, core values, and Key Success Measures, along with the core strategies for achieving them (the organizational level is the fifth of the Seven Levels of Living Systems).
   - *Business unit strategic planning* often called business plans. Three-year business plans are needed for each business unit, major program area, and major support department within the organization (this is the fourth level of the Seven Levels of Living Systems).

2. **Annual Planning Levels**
   - *Annual plans* for all departments/functional units: Annual operating plans are needed over the next 12 months (and budgets, too) for all parts of the entire organization (this is also the fourth of the Seven Levels of Living Systems).
   - *Individual plans, goals, and objectives:* Individual plans are needed to show how each employee intends to accomplish the goals they must meet in order to carry out the organization-wide strategic plan. You

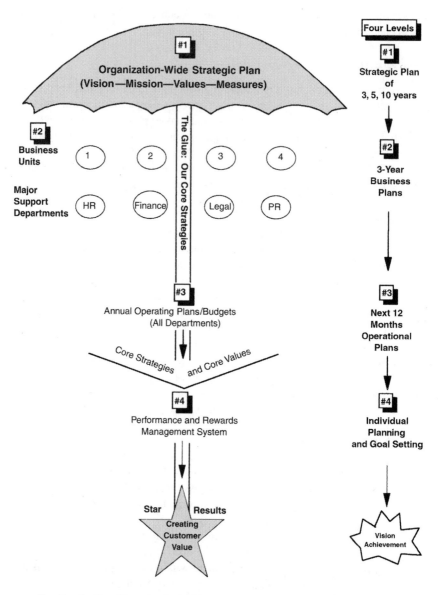

Key: Use the Core Strategies as the "Organization Principles" at all levels.

FIGURE 4.3   Cascade of Planning: shared strategies — strategic consistency yet operational flexibility.

also need to revise your performance appraisals, basing them on core strategies (results) and core values (behaviors) (this is the individual level; level three of the Seven Levels of Living Systems).

The Cascade of Planning also takes into account the fit that must exist between each of the interacting levels of the system that make up the organization. It does this by using the organization-wide core strategies as the glue — or organizing principles — for the two levels of systems (group and individual). This helps establish the mind-set of the organization to thinking about the core strategies as the "shared strategies" needed to successfully carry out the plan. This, in turn, creates a critical mass for the desired change.

QUESTIONS TO PONDER

- Have you used the four systems elements as your A, B, C, D, E phases to first define your Ideal Future Vision (or outcomes of serving the customer)? Have you completed the rest of the five phases?
- Are you clear on the specific steps in strategic planning, as well as on how they relate to the systems model?
- Have you included the Cascade of Planning as a part of your Strategic Management process to ensure that it is cascaded down from the organizational level to 3-year plans for business units and major staff support units? Also, do you have 12-month annual departmental plans and individual goal setting?
- Are you clear on what planning documents and performance appraisal format you need to tie it into the strategic plan as well?

15 COMMON MISTAKES IN STRATEGIC MANAGEMENT (PROVEN WORST PRACTICES)

My experience has been that even the most dedicated, organized, or systems- oriented CEO is susceptible to mistakes. Even if your strategic plan is based on well-defined, common-sense systems or backwards thinking, the processes involved in planning and implementation are complex and rarely straightforward. Some of the typical areas that I've researched as well as observed myself to be particularly vulnerable to mistakes include the following "Proven Worst Practices."

MISTAKE #1: FAILING TO INTEGRATE PLANNING INTO ALL THREE LEVELS

Throughout my years in Strategic Management, I've lost count of the times I have gone into a situation where no previous plans included this type of integration. Whether or not your organization has a concise, well-thought-out strategic plan, you will almost always fail to cascade the plan down to the three levels (and four necessary documents) previously mentioned. If you want an easy business advantage over your competition, just do this and you'll have one!

MISTAKE #2: KEEPING PLANNING SEPARATE FROM DAY-TO-DAY MANAGEMENT

The most common mistake I see in public and private organizations alike, is that people treat strategic planning as a process separate from daily management, not as a way to reinvent the way we do business day to day. If it's done in your organization at all, it is treated primarily as an "exercise in planning," something to get over with so you can get back to your "real work." Entrepreneurial companies are especially susceptible to this mistake.

Instead, your planning (and Strategic Management) system should be designed organization-wide so it is self-renewing and self-perpetuating. One of its most critical characteristics should be the ability of the plan and its implementation to address change. Change is a given today, and your organization needs to prepare for that, creating a permanent environment of transition and change management.

MISTAKE #3: CONDUCTING LONG-RANGE FORECASTING ONLY

Another extremely common mistake that almost always results in strategic planning failure is that of long-range financial forecasting. This is where you begin with the present and project a straight line out into the long-term future. Though some people view this as viable strategic planning, it truly is nothing more than budget projections. Think about it — if you only examine today's picture, how can you plan for the future, much less have a clear idea of what that future should be?

Oil companies suffered from this immensely in the 1970s, when everyone thought a barrel of crude oil would go from $32 to $80 per barrel. It never did.

MISTAKE #4: TAKING A "SCATTERSHOT" APPROACH

This mistake encompasses a failure to educate and organize yourself first; running off before you know how to successfully complete and implement the plan.

Action-oriented firms often make this error. Remember, never mistake *activities* for *progress!*

MISTAKE #5: DEVELOPING VISION/MISSION/VALUES STATEMENTS THAT ARE LITTLE MORE THAN "FLUFF"

Another common failure is the development of vision, mission, and values statements that are unconnected to the organizational business plans and evaluation systems. Many organizational development practitioners and planners have helped CEOs see the need for these documents. However, they don't know how to help them go any further and actually use the documents.

If you, as an executive, really want to lose all your credibility with your employees, this is an excellent way to do it. Making up the statements and putting them out for all to see but failing to take them seriously will make you look foolish in the eyes of your staff.

Unsophisticated executives who merely follow the current "fads" are uniquely prone to this. So are the majority of organizations whose leaders don't really think strategically and define their unique positioning in the marketplace.

Positioning is an issue so daunting that we call it an advanced degree topic in strategic planning and one that is the $64,000 question (or today, the $64 million dollar question). In Chapter 7 we will cover positioning in detail.

MISTAKE #6: HAVING YEARLY WEEKEND RETREATS ONLY

In the past, your typical board and organizational approach to planning might have been to set aside a yearly weekend retreat in some luxury resort area for top management and/or board members. During this retreat — which includes extensive and expensive social time — organizational leaders and planners will more often than not present a slick, sophisticated planning document. It will have all the requisite warm and positive mission and value statements and a detailed analysis of the organizations's current state, accompanied by numerous detailed and brainstormed lists of the actions you'll need. This is not a plan designed to be implemented — it just has to look good. It's all form and no substance.

I saw quite a bit of this in the 1980s, with the Federal Home Loan Bank Board (FHLBB) and others — and we all know the result of the savings and loan debacle. It still goes on today in many credit unions and other not-for-profits, as it seems the primary purpose is to reward the volunteer board members with a resort weekend.

MISTAKE #7: FAILING TO COMPLETE AN EFFECTIVE IMPLEMENTATION PROCESS

A problem often arrives at the implementation stage, after the organization develops an excellent strategic planning document, with key stakeholders and the KISS philosophy. Many organizations fail to set in place a Strategic Change Leadership Steering Committee of the collective leadership, responsible for initiating and maintaining the plan's implementation.

Organizations in the not-for-profit sector, such as schools and governmental agencies, need to be especially aware of this potential pitfall. Our experience with school districts is, unfortunately, that they plan like crazy and implement like nothing.

MISTAKE #8: VIOLATING THE "PEOPLE SUPPORT WHAT THEY HELP CREATE" PRINCIPLE

Another problem arises when the planning process neglects the necessary involvement of key stakeholders (other than top management). This leaves the key stakeholders with a "not-invented-here" mentality and no real understanding of the plan. Therefore, they have no comprehension of what's expected of them in the implementation of the plan. Worse still, inadequate involvement by line and staff personnel creates a closed and secretive environment in which the organization's strategic plan is developed in a vacuum. It's as far removed as you can get from those who know your customer the best — your frontline troops.

This is a mistake often found in private sector organizations that have control-oriented CEOs.

MISTAKE #9: CONDUCTING BUSINESS AS USUAL

One of the most common failures I've seen in strategic planning occurs when the planning team approaches it with a "business as usual" mentality, basing the entire plan strictly on how the organizations does business today. The team isn't willing to identify, much less implement, the change efforts needed in our rapidly changing environment. This is often the result of starting strategic planning at Phase C, the Input side of the system rather than at Phase A, the Output side.

Larger, established bureaucratic organizations often fall victim to this error. This results in the all-too-familiar SPOTS syndrome.

MISTAKE #10: FAILING TO MAKE THE TOUGH CHOICES

This begins with planners taking a "tell 'em what they wanna hear" approach, and often leads organizations straight into another typical planning trap: failure to take a stand and make the tough choices.

Some executives would rather be polite to each other than be effective through real dialogue and give-and-take. It's conflict avoidance at it's worst. The whole reason you're doing strategic planning in the first place is to firmly steer your organization into new and different actions and directions. This literally cannot take place unless you face and deal honestly with whatever problems or disagreements stand in the way of progress.

Some of our nicest, and largest bureaucratic organizations and good corporate citizens are especially prone to this error — being *too* polite. The key is focus, focus, focus.

MISTAKE #11: LACKING A SCOREBOARD

If your methods for measuring organizational success aren't clearly defined up front, its progress will be virtually impossible to determine. Unless you establish Key Success Measures or goals (beyond financials), your plan isn't worth the paper it was printed on. You'll often be tempted to measure what's easy — your activities — instead of what's important — your outcomes. For example: Do you have regular, ongoing surveys of customer and employee satisfaction?

Companies that aren't customer-focused often fail to see the importance of a scoreboard with anything on it except financial numbers. This is especially true when the planning team is made up mostly of insiders who focus on operations rather than employees with customer- or service-oriented jobs. The way most organizations are functionally organized tends to reinforce this problem, since usually there is only one member of senior management with customer/marketing responsibility.

MISTAKE #12: FAILING TO DEFINE BUSINESS UNITS OR MAJOR PROGRAM AREAS IN A MEANINGFUL WAY

Many organizations either fail to define their strategic business units in a meaningful way, or they initially gloss over this task, thinking they can always come back to it later. They never do; it's a losing proposition from the very beginning. Failure to differentiate between what your business or reason for existence is, as opposed to what your staff support areas are, results in conflict and turf battles.

I continue to find far too many organizations structured in such a hodge-podge way that the focus on the business (and the customer) is almost impossible to find, much less maintain.

MISTAKE #13: NEGLECTING TO BENCHMARK YOURSELF VS. THE COMPETITION

One of the most common mistakes in strategic planning — and one of the easiest to correct — is in isolating your organization from its competitive environment. Without a specific sense of your competitors' best practices and market share, as well as strengths and weaknesses, it's impossible to know what to strive for, or what your own competitive business advantage is. If you continually fail to be open and learn from others, your organization will soon fall victim to the "know-it-all" syndrome.

The arrogance and ignorance some private sector executives show in disregarding this key area continues to astound me. Learning is a life-long process; it should never be curtailed just because you have obtained a certain level of stature within the organization.

MISTAKE #14: SEEING THE PLANNING DOCUMENT AS AN END IN ITSELF

Remember, the document isn't the objective; it's only Goal #1. If this is a problem in your organization, you need to get Goal #2, implementation of the strategic plan, back into your realm of thinking.

Until recently, Goal #2 and Goal #3 haven't even been in the planning literature that most executives read. You'll need to put them on your own radar scope, and view Goals #2 and #3 as the only true goals.

MISTAKE #15: USING UNCLEAR OR CONFUSING TERMINOLOGY AND LANGUAGE

While we mentioned this in previous chapters, it needs repeating here. Sometimes the English language tends to confuse rather than clarify. In strategic planning, you may experience difficulty in understanding the difference between *means* and *ends*. As you attempt to establish a hierarchy of terms in your organization, the real meaning and level of importance in these concepts can be obscured by the use of similar descriptors such as "goals" or "objectives." (For instance, just by looking at them, can you determine which of these descriptors is the higher order?)

Well-read private sector executives are especially prone to picking up the latest fads or terminology, and using them independently without regard to how they integrate or fit into the overall organizational system. Just by reducing the number of terms for the different levels of planning can make your organization much more effective. In analyzing where companies are with terminology when we meet them, just looking at the large number of terms used is a 100% accurate indicator of failure. Keep it simple.

As you can see in Figure 4.4, using the A, B, C, D framework (E doesn't seem to have much of a terminology issue) is much more effective in making it clear that "vision" and "mission" will be your ultimate end, or your desired outcomes. Your primary means to that end will be your core (or shared) strategies. Your Key Success Measures/Goals will be the quantifiable way by which you measure your performance against your goals.

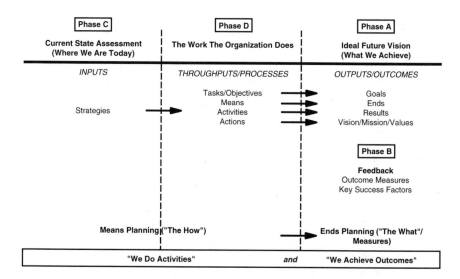

FIGURE 4.4   Systems Thinking: focus on outcomes. Systems Thinking is what creates a successful customer-focused organization.

In Summary

In reinventing the way we do business day to day, it's easy to get lost in strategic planning as an activity, event, or process in and of itself. The point is to be aware of and alert to the pitfalls and all other "red flags" described above. It's a given that you'll make some mistakes — we all do. Keep in mind, however, that much about conducting successful strategic management stems from an ability to face reality (even when it's tough), and to "cut to the chase" with good old common-sense. The benefits are worth it.

15 KEY BENEFITS OF A STRATEGIC MANAGEMENT SYSTEM

Many of the organizations with which I've worked have followed through in an excellent fashion by implementing their strategic planning successfully. They've given me specific examples of the benefits they've experienced. Those that have fully implemented their strategic plan have uniformly seen vast improvement in the achievement of their primary outcomes as measured by their Key Success Measures:

1. Increased market share
2. Dramatic increase in stock price
3. Improved profitability and cash flow
4. Much more satisfied customers as a result of added value (quality, service, responsiveness, etc.)
5. Increased employee satisfaction

In addition to these primary, "bottom line" outcomes, the following lists other key benefits culled from their responses over a period of time.

- **Benefit #1:** *Taking a proactive approach to your future.* Having a strategic management system in place enables you to adapt proactively to a changing global world, marketplace, and turbulent business environment, increasing the probability of both the healthy, long-term viability of the organization and job security for your executives, managers, and employees.
- **Benefit #2:** *Building an executive team.* Strategic planning and strategic management enable your executive team to learn to function as a highly effective team in their own right, as well as in building and supporting your strategic plan. This modeling of cross-functional and horizontal teamwork is key to successful implementation.
- **Benefit #3:** *Having an intensive executive development experience.* Strategic planning is also one of the most intense and best executive development and strategic thinking processes a new or aspiring executive could ever have.
- **Benefit #4:** *Defining focused, quantifiable outcome measures of success.* Phase B (Key Success Measures) enables your organization to develop a focused set of specific and quantifiable outcome measures of success, including customer and employee satisfaction. These become the way to focus on measuring and dramatically increasing your success year after year.
- **Benefit # 5:** *Making intelligent strategic budgeting decisions.* Implementing your strategic plan in an organization-wide systems framework encourages organizational focus and priority-setting to determine precision (i.e., strategic) budget cuts during tough economic times.

- **Benefit #6:** *Clarifying and achieving your competitive advantage.* Advanced-level strategic planning and clear positioning enable you to stay ahead of the competition. They help you clarify your competitive business advantage by providing a more thorough analysis of success factors, environmental influences, and core strategies than conventional, incremental annual planning and forecasting.
- **Benefit #7:** *Reducing conflict; empowering the organization.* A strategic management system motivates and empowers employees, as well as reduces or focuses conflict by providing a clear sense of direction with all parts of your organization as a system working together and focusing on the customer.
- **Benefit #8:** *Providing clear guidelines for day-to-day decision making.* A constructive, visionary basis is provided for day-to-day decision making throughout your organization, making it easier to set priorities about what to do and what not to do.
- **Benefit #9:** *Creating a critical mass for change.* Everyone involved as a key stakeholder has a shot at helping to create your organization's future, rather than being overwhelmed by the uncertainties of change. Remember that people support what they help create.
- **Benefit #10:** *"Singing from the same hymnal."* In a strategic management system, a process is provided whereby your leadership can communicate organizational goals and core values in a simple language to everyone affected by them. It enables everyone to "get on the same wavelength," aligning their personal values and professional goals with the direction of your organization as a whole. In today's society, this is essential for every firm to do, as employees have a great ability to provide or withhold their "discretionary effort."
- **Benefit #11:** *Simplifying the barrage of management techniques.* Strategic management enables you, other senior executives, and employees alike to make sense out of the confusion resulting from so many different ideas and solutions coming from the proliferation of management writers today. While many of these writers are convinced that they are providing the best answers for you, some of these answers are in conflict. This only adds to the Chaos that Tom Peters wants us to thrive on! Only an integrated Systems Thinking Approach pulls all of this together.
- **Benefit #12:** *Empowering middle managers.* The A, B, C, D, E systems framework enables middle managers to conduct this process successfully within their own departments, even in organizations where no strategic planning is taking place (see the Environmental Protection Division example earlier in the chapter).
- **Benefit #13:** *Focus, focus, focus.* When everything your organization does fits strategically within the same overall framework, employees are able to continually focus on the desired outcome and set their day-to-day priorities accordingly. In today's Internet and "Dot Com" society of limitless opportunities, this benefit is tremendous if you can be disciplined enough to focus.

- **Benefit #14:** *Speeding up implementation.* The ability to clarify and simplify strategic management within the systems framework will always speed up the actual implementation of your core strategies. It becomes easier for you to identify problem areas, focus on dealing with them, and then take action.
- **Benefit #15:** *Providing tools for dealing better with the stress of change.* When a strategic management system is firmly in place, your organization can give your employees the necessary tools to battle the stress of ongoing, revolutionary change. Everyone in your organization will feel better equipped to focus, understand, and address issues within the overall context of your strategic plan.

In Summary

It is now abundantly clear to anyone still in business these days that Jack Welch was right when he said that what worked before won't work now. The traditional, time-consuming method of analyzing and solving one problem at a time has been overpowered by the sweeping and sometimes obliterating winds of revolutionary change. A fresh new approach is called for, one that can set in place a framework sturdy enough to withstand the ongoing complexities and chaos of change.

During these incredible times of global restructuring, fierce world and national competition, increasing local pluralism, fragmentation and nationalism, and faster technology obsolescence, every organization will need new visions, strategies, programs, and actions.

From extensive experience, I have come to believe deeply that long-term success can only come from a systems approach: it alleviates most common mistakes and provides many, many benefits. In the coming chapters, I will take you through Strategic Management step by step within a systems thinking framework, beginning with Step #1, Plan-to-Plan.

RECAP OF KEY CONTENT POINTS

- Looking at your organization as having at least three levels — individual, group, and organization — you'll need to "cascade" your planning and change management down to all levels.
- Strategic planning should lead the way in integrating many of today's organizational change fads and concepts, such as TQM, business process reengineering, empowerment, customer service.
- Which of the 15 Strategic Management mistakes have you made?

  1. Failing to integrate planning at all levels.
  2. Keeping planning separate from day-to-day management.
  3. Conducting long-range forecasting only.

4. Having a scattershot approach to planning.
5. Developing vision, mission, and value statements that are little more than fluff.
6. Having yearly weekend retreats as your only planning activity.
7. Failing to complete an effective implementation process.
8. Violating the "people support what they help create" principle.
9. Conducting business as usual after strategic planning.
10. Failing to make the "tough choices."
11. Lacking a scoreboard. Measuring what's easy, not what's important.
12. Failing to define Strategic Business Units in a meaningful way.
13. Neglecting to benchmark yourself against the competition.
14. Seeing the planning document as an end in itself.
15. Having confusing terminology and language.

- Which of these benefits are still missing in your organization?

  1. Having an organization-wide, proactive approach to a changing global world.
  2. Building an executive team that serves as a model of cross-functional or horizontal teamwork.
  3. Having an intense executive development and orientation process.
  4. Defining focused, quantifiable outcome measures of success.
  5. Making intelligent budgeting decisions.
  6. Clarifying your competitive advantage.
  7. Reducing conflict; empowering the organization.
  8. Providing clear guidelines for day-to-day decision making.
  9. Creating a critical mass for change.
  10. "Singing from the same hymnal" in communicating throughout.
  11. Clarifying and simplifying the broad range of management techniques.
  12. Empowering middle managers.
  13. Focusing everyone in the organization on the same overall priorities.
  14. Speeding up implementation of your core strategies as shared strategies organization-wide.
  15. Providing tangible tools for dealing with the stress of change.

Part 2

Developing a Strategic Plan: Step by Step

5 The Plan-to-Plan Day (Step #1)

We never have time to do it right the first time, but we always have time to do it over.

PLAN-TO-PLAN: ASSESSING, EDUCATING, ORGANIZING, AND TAILORING

The maxim above is never truer than when applied to the art and science of strategic planning. Because the purpose of strategic planning is to develop and implement a strategic plan through a strategic change management system that will cause your organization to grow and profit, it's something you definitely want to get right the first time. In my experience, if you don't do it right the first time, you've polluted the organizational environment for good planning and management to the extent that it is usually years before it is ever attempted again.

In our Reinventing Strategic Management Model, getting it right the first time is what Step #1 — Plan-to-Plan — is all about. Another old maxim that perfectly describes this step is "look before you leap." As we saw in the last chapter, one of the most common mistakes planners make is that of running off to make the plan before educating and organizing themselves on precisely what needs and issues are critical to their organization and before properly organizing the effort. In failing to "engineer" the success of the planning and implementing up front (*before* you begin), you've set yourself up for failure before even starting.

ENGINEERING SUCCESS UP FRONT

The Plan-to-Plan Day includes setting up your core planning team, along with a Parallel Process that involves key stakeholders. It also clarifies top management's role in leading, developing, and owning their strategic plan. It forces you to focus on your core strategic issues, then find ways to fit them into an overall systems framework.

Example: A good example of this was an initial meeting on strategic planning to implement the strategic plan — called the Quality Network — for a $1 billion division of General Motors. (The Quality Network is a total quality process developed organization-wide at General Motors.)

In the middle of the meeting, the facilitator got so angry and frustrated with the various disagreements among joint union-management executives, he threw up his hands and quit, leaving the meeting. Needless to say, the meeting quickly deteriorated, and was soon called to a halt. It was more than 4 years before that same collective leadership got together to finally begin their Plan-to-Plan step and implement their strategic plan.

Avoiding this pitfall is what the Plan-to-Plan step is all about. There are a number of specific tasks, (covered below), that you can follow to successfully complete this step. By carefully evaluating what your future should look like, and how you can realistically take your organization into that future, you'll not only come up with a strategic plan that works, you'll end up with benefits that will grow and strengthen your organization throughout the life of the plan.

The *Plan-to-Plan Day* is the step in which you answer these questions. Since it's also Phase A of the A, B, C, D, E guideposts, it is also where you begin replacing the traditional analytical approach with outcome-oriented systems — or "backwards" thinking.

SOME INITIAL PREWORK FOR THE PLAN-TO-PLAN STEP

The Plan-to-Plan step is really pretty straightforward once you know how and where to get started. Following are several prework steps that can be helpful prior to initiating this Plan-to-Plan Day.

CONDUCT A STRATEGIC/ORGANIZATIONAL ASSESSMENT

Prior to the Plan-to-Plan day, conduct an overall assessment of your entire organization and where it stands currently. What kind of strategies (if any) are you currently following? Are they still valid or do they need to be reassessed and worked into your new strategic plan? Try to get the most realistic overview possible of how your organization has been running so far, and what needs to change.

ESTABLISH YOUR INTERNAL SUPPORT CADRE

This is where something I call "capacity building" comes in. Keep in mind that no matter what your strategic plan entails, you'll need to engineer your organization's capacity for support, persistence, and coordination by real people over a long period of time. Think this facet through and select and assign those individuals who will be accountable for this process. Select these folks at the very beginning so they can get up to speed themselves. This includes assigning someone with a laptop at the meetings so they can take down the notes on the flip charts in realtime.

CONDUCT AN EXECUTIVE TEAM-BUILDING AND VISIONARY LEADERSHIP PRACTICES WORKSHOP

Even before the capacity building just mentioned, however, you should conduct a leadership assessment/workshop to build motivation within your executives. This leadership skills issue is absolutely essential to any organization's success in strategic management. For this reason, there will be more to say on leadership in the Current State Assessment step (Chapter 9), and the Core Strategy Development step (Chapter 10). However, there has been a quantum change in the roles of executives that began in the 1990s. We covered this in Chapter 2 in discussing Right Answer #2; our systems thinking approach to Centering Your Leadership and the six natural core leadership competencies.

However, in order to boil all this down to a quick and useful leadership skills program, consider three skills: *"trainer," "coach,"* and *"facilitator."* The key here is not knowledge alone, although that is important. The key is the skills and attitudes of today's leaders: their willingness to learn, to be open to feedback and the acceptance of responsibility and, above all, to change.

We could (and probably should) do a whole book on this Leadership Development area, based on our systems perspective. The key is to set up a structured leadership skills development process right away — even before strategic planning. You must build the capacity of the organization's senior management to successfully implement the strategic plans they design.

Once the prework is out of the way, then the actual off-site day is needed.

PLAN-TO-PLAN OFF-SITE DAY

MORNING: EXECUTIVE BRIEFING — THE EDUCATING TASK

The Plan-to-Plan off-site day prepares your organization for Goal #1 — developing your strategic plan and document. The first stage in the Plan-to-Plan off-site is an executive briefing for senior management and other key stakeholders. This is a crucial part of the process, because it's one in which your organization's CEO, executive directors, and senior management learn more fully about Strategic Management and all its pitfalls, mistakes, and benefits. It is also where the systems model for Reinventing Strategic Management is explained, discussed, and accepted as a practical, common-sense approach to success. Lastly, within the system's A, B, C, D, E framework, the terminology for strategic management is clarified and simplified.

The executive briefing generally requires half a day. Depending on the complexities of your particular issues, however, you may feel you need more or less time. Whatever period of time you require, just be sure you do it. This is probably the first critical step of the entire planning process.

Prior to the executive briefing, it's a good idea to distribute a brief questionnaire, such as the one below, with key points to think about. Make sure your executives and key stakeholders understand that their opinions will be sought in these areas, and that they will be an ongoing part of the strategic planning and implementation process.

PREBRIEFING QUESTIONNAIRE

1. What is your vision for the organization in the year 2010?
2. What are the values/beliefs and principles that you believe are key to achieving this vision?

3. What business should we be in the year 2010? Why do we exist?
4. Who is our customer?
5. What is our current driving force? How should it change for the year 2010?
6. How would you define the units (elements or programs) that make up our business?
7. Currently, how many top priorities do we have as an organization? List them.
8. What does the above list say about our ability to focus and make tough choices?
9. What are the major, future-oriented core strategies we should adopt to reach our vision for the year 2010? Be specific.
10. How will we measure success for our organization in the year 2010?
11. How should we manage a multiyear, organization-wide change process to ensure the success of our vision?

It is imperative that your organization's CEO be the driving force behind all parts of this planning and implementation process. CEOs, after all, are the individuals vested with overall leadership and responsibility for the development and implementation of their organization's strategic plan (in tandem with the board of directors' consent and veto power). Those CEOs who delegate this responsibility to a planning department or independent task force fail to fundamentally understand their job.

Planning is an inseparable part of management and leadership, and strategic management is the responsibility of senior management and the CEO. Without their leadership, presence, and full commitment to the process, the plan will go nowhere. I've lost count of the number of times I've seen or heard of strategic planning dying because senior management failed to commit themselves to the development and implementation of the plan.

AFTERNOON: THE ORGANIZING AND TAILORING TASK

The Plan-to-Plan off-site also needs to include a half day or so devoted to completing a series of organizing and tailoring tasks to properly set up the planning process. This includes:

- Identifying your key stakeholders.
- Designing a Parallel Process for key stakeholder involvement/commitment.
- Organizing and committing the planning effort and team to its success.
- Feeding back the strategic/organizational assessment to the leadership team.
- Developing a "strategic issues" list to help guide the planning content.
- Examining ongoing communication, leadership, and team-building skills.

- Identifying potential barriers to the planning process.
- Linking your strategic planning sequence to your annual planning/budgeting sequence and to your individual performance management system.
- Defining the level of environmental scanning you'll need to stimulate your strategic planning process properly.

Lastly, this Plan-to-Plan day should include a summary of the day. This is the time for senior management, key stakeholders, and the CEO to get behind the plan — educating, organizing, and committing themselves as the driving force behind the strategic plan and change management system, and making sure they're all singing from the same hymnal. Also, this is the point at which your executive team should have uniquely tailored the strategic plan to fit your particular organization.

QUESTIONS TO PONDER

- Have you conducted an executive briefing so that all top executives in your organization are in sync with the strategic management process?
- Did you undergo a strategic/organizational assessment so that you have the information for later use?
- Is your CEO committed to and actively leading the planning process — or has it been delegated?
- Are key stakeholders in your organization prepared to engineer your plan's success upfront by being active throughout the process?
- Are you willing to take the time to get organized before you begin, or are you tackling a planning activity without thinking it through first?
- Have you begun your capacity building with executive team building/leadership skills development, and with an internal support cadre?

ORGANIZING TASKS FOR PLAN-TO-PLAN

The following sections provide the details of each organizing task.

ORGANIZING TASK #1: DETERMINING THE ENTITY TO PLAN FOR

Following the executive briefing, the first task of the Plan-to-Plan organizing time frame is to determine the *precise* entity you're planning for. While this may seem simple or obvious to many of you in the private sector, failing to do this is an all-too-common mistake in strategic planning. In the public sector, for instance, you'll frequently find people trying to do a strategic plan for curing health care for the entire geographic area or county. This is not realistic.

Instead, it would be better to plan for the county's Department of Health and define what *its* role should be in accounting for that particular area's health system. Don't take responsibility that is far beyond what you can control.

For some of you, the entity to plan for will be obvious. A large corporation, the City of Saskatoon, or an entire school district are good examples of obvious entities. It is also possible, however, to conduct strategic planning for a strategic business unit, such as General Motors' North American operations or its Cadillac division, or a major support area, such as the finance department of a large corporation.

Ideally, this corporation would have its overall strategic plan completed first, but there are many instances in which it is appropriate (though a bit more difficult) to plan for an entity that is a single piece of the larger whole. The key here is to make certain any entity you come up with is specific, with well-defined boundaries.

One last thing before closing on this task: be clear not only about the entity you're planning for, but also about what your specific time frame will be. Will it be a 3-year, 5-year, or even 10-year strategic plan? Whatever makes the most sense for your particular organization is fine; just be clear. For more creative and innovative thinking, using a time frame of 5 years or more is more effective for freeing up one's mind to future possibilities.

Organizing Task #2: Identifying Critical Issues

Plan-to-Plan is a critical step because it's the time you set aside for creative brainstorming before the planning begins. It's a time to identify the critical issues that are pivotal to your organization, and it's important to get input from all your executive stakeholders. You will get many different opinions, and that's exactly what you want at this point. You want everyone who has a stake in your organization's strategic plan to bring his or her own list to the table.

Use all the prework here: (1) the strategic/organizational assessment, (2) the team building you conducted, and (3) the leadership assessment, as input to this step. After this has happened, you may find that you have a pool of as many as 30 to 50 issues on the table. Keep in mind, however, that this is only a brainstorming list to be used as a checklist to keep your strategic plan practical throughout. However, because there are no limits on your executives' imaginations during this part of the process, the resulting lists are often quite enlightening.

Caution: Don't troubleshoot the critical issues list at this time. If you do, your planning will just become a Current State Assessment (Phase C) or an analytical exercise for dealing with today's issues only. Contrast this with the organization as a system problem of defining and achieving a desired ideal future.

Organizing Task #3: Examining Personal Readiness and Concerns

Throughout this chapter, I will continually stress the importance of enthusiasm and commitment on the part of your senior executives. In my experience, this is a critical aspect; in fact, I've never seen a strategic planning and change management process succeed without it being understood and accepted that this is now the primary part of their job.

The top members of your collective leadership must be personally ready and committed to your strategic management process. This task requires them to focus on their personal readiness, and to determine what exactly they want to see happen as a result of this process.

You should start by asking each of your executives to list the three to five most important concerns they personally have about conducting a strategic management process. Then ask them to specifically describe what prework or other actions should be taken to cope with those concerns before beginning the planning process.

It can also be helpful to start this task by requesting that your executives define what it is they might fear about setting this process in motion. In Plan-to-Plan, it's just as important to examine negative impact as it is to address the positive side of Strategic Management.

Tip: Skeptics Are My Best Friends

At this point, don't shy away from resistance from any individual, even if it's negative or skeptical. Over the years that I have been involved in strategic management, I have come to regard skeptics as my best friends. They are more willing to bring up the more unpopular areas that others are either too reserved or conservative to broach.

The end result can be good, even beneficial to your organization. In fact, I've often been in planning processes where skeptics have — sometimes through sheer stubbornness — introduced critical questions that changed the entire scope of the organizational plan for the better. (*Honesty* is Job #1 in strategic management.)

ORGANIZING TASK #4: ADDRESSING POTENTIAL BARRIERS IN THE PLANNING PROCESS

This is where you'll get further organizational problem areas in strategic planning out on the table, with your executives and stakeholders addressing them collectively. In this task, it's important to ask the following questions:

1. What problems have you had in past strategic planning efforts as an organization?
2. What potential barriers do you think exist that will prevent us from doing future strategic planning in an effective way?

We have already listed the "Proven Worst Practices" in Chapter 4. Refer to them if necessary for this task.

Once you've gathered a working list of potential barriers, you can get to work on problem-solving them now, up front — *before* you begin the actual plan — so that they don't come back to bite you, and derail your plan at a later date.

It's also important to assess your organization's current level of effectiveness in strategic planning. In my research and implementation of strategic planning over the years, I have observed 10 levels of planning effectiveness, under three types of organizational cultures: (1) reactive, (2) traditional, and (3) proactive.

As you'll see in Figure 5.1, reactive organizations typically have low levels of planning effectiveness. Such organizations use methods such as (1) survival and

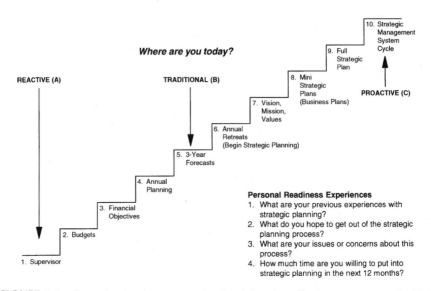

FIGURE 5.1   Strategic planning process: levels of planning effectiveness — toward a high performance organization.

confusion; day-to-day planning only, (2) letting the budget alone drive the plan for the entire organization, (3) planning that is synonymous with financial objectives only, or (4) strategic planning that encompasses 12-month thinking only, with no long-term planning.

The level of planning effectiveness in traditional organizations is a bit better. They develop outcomes as (5) 3-year forecasts, possibly with some business unit planning, (6) longer-term planning that takes place during an annual retreat, (7) the development of vision/mission/values statements alone, or even (8) some beginning or mini-strategic planning for some units or divisions.

The level of planning effectiveness in proactive organizations, on the other hand, is much higher. They often shape a (9) comprehensive strategic plan that is conducted for the organization as a whole.

At their very best (10), they start out right at the beginning with a clearly-defined, organization-wide, shared, and integrated vision. Then, these proactive organizations go on to fully develop a strategic plan in a participatory (i.e., Parallel) process, and become committed to the implementation of a strategic management system as a new way to run their business successfully day to day. In other words, once again, people support what they help create.

Determine where your organization fits into this ten-point scale. If you're too low, that may very well be one of your biggest potential barriers to strategic planning. If so, make sure that the planning team is fully educated and fully committed to the jump you are about to make before you even begin. Conducting full 2 to 3 day strategic planning workshops and reading this type of book on strategic planning may be key. The same holds true for implementation and change. Something more than the Plan-to-Implement Day (Step #8) may be needed.

ORGANIZING TASK #5: ENVIRONMENTAL SCANNING

To make sure you're not trying to create your strategic plan in a vacuum, you will need to conduct an environmental scanning process on a regular basis. For instance, if you're planning out to the year 2010, it will be helpful to scan the environment to see what is and what will potentially be happening over this horizon.

I find it useful to focus on the SKEPTIC acronym when beginning environmental scanning. In general terms, "S" represents sociodemographic scanning, "K" stands for your (k) competitors, "E" stands for scanning both the economic and natural environments, "P" is for political, "T" represents technology (not just computers/tele-communications), "I" is for industry, and "C" represents the customers.

Whether they choose the SKEPTIC formula as a general guideline or create their own unique environmental scanning formula, the planning team should examine what the future might hold, especially in an environment of such dynamic and revolutionary change as we find today and will continue to find in the future.

Remember, if you try to create a strategic plan in a vacuum, with no real facts and figures on the environmental changes you can expect, you will end up with just one more strategic plan that's worth nothing more than the paper it's printed on.

ORGANIZING TASK #6: LINKING STRATEGIC PLANNING TO YOUR BUDGET

This is simple, obvious logic, right? Your organization's vision and the strategic plan are what drive your budget, not vice versa. Right? You would be amazed at how few organizations really get this concept; how many actually let the budget set their planning boundaries. This is one of the ways that business as usual is perpetuated.

Of course, all organizations have to be realistic about their financial limitations; it would be organizational suicide not to take financial resources into consideration. If you allow all your planning decisions to be dictated solely by budget, however, I can guarantee you won't have to concern yourself with your organization's future.

In my view, one of the key reasons for strategic planning is to create a tension and conflict between your future vision and the resources you need to complete key tasks to achieve it, versus your current way of allocating your budget. This tension and gap between resources is what can motivate you to make the hard choices of how you spend your budget; either on past, obsolete activities or on future-oriented priorities.

Another critical mistake many organizations make at this point is not allowing an appropriate amount of time for both the planning process and the integration of planning into budgeting. They rush too fast into budgeting, thus doing a poor job of planning.

Tip: Long-Term Effort

Putting your strategic management system in place is a long-term effort. Looking at it realistically, it will often require as much as two annual planning and budgeting cycles before it is fully coordinated and implemented.

The executive members of the planning team need to lay out a specific time line for when and how the strategic plan will be linked to the budget. Without it, any strategic management system you incorporate will not have the fit, alignment, and integrity needed to see it through to completion.

ORGANIZING TASK #7: IDENTIFYING KEY STAKEHOLDERS

This is one of the key tasks in the Plan-to-Plan step. If purposely utilized, your key stakeholders will actually become another group of supporters and cheerleaders for the implementation of your strategic management system on an ongoing basis. A stakeholder is defined as "any group or individual that affects, or is affected by, the organization's strategic plan."

Most organizations make the mistake of assuming only top management can perform as their strategic plan's stakeholders. Because organizations exist in a complex system, however, it's virtually impossible for senior executives to monitor what's happening at every level. In order to implement the organization's strategic plan at every level, therefore, you'll need to involve stakeholders both inside and outside the organization that bring different vantage points to the table.

Members of middle management absolutely need to be involved as the first key group of stakeholders in a Parallel Process each time. However, it is crucial to involve the employee's point of view also, as well as customers, union representatives, and even suppliers. In some instances, it may be important to include members of special interest groups (SIGs), as well. Once you've selected your list of stakeholders, then decide who are the top five to seven stakeholders in terms of importance to the success of your plan, and discuss how to fully involve them in the planning and change processes.

Tip: Consider Internal and External People

Again, whenever we look at the organization as a system, it's important to consider both its internal and external environments. If you have only individuals from your organization's internal, immediate environment involved in the planning and implementation process, you drastically limit the quality of your thinking and the possibility of successfully completing the plan. You also cut yourself off from gaining a greater understanding of how your organizational system interacts within other systems and the environment that surrounds it.

ORGANIZING TASK #8: PLANNING TEAM MEMBERSHIP

Once you've identified the key stakeholders for your strategic plan, you're ready to build the planning team. At this point, keep in mind that people support what they help create. The first, most obvious group of people that have to support implementation is the top management team. They will form the core of the planning team.

Next, you'll have to consider the size of the planning team. A typical top management team in a medium-sized organization may consist of 6 to 8 executives. Though research on effective group dynamics says that keeping the total group at

6 to 8 members is best, our experience has shown that you can double that size to around 14 or 15, and still have a reasonably effective team. Beyond 15, however, you don't have a planning team — you have a mob.

So, if you have eight people on the top management team, you could conceivably seed the rest of the team membership with an additional six or seven from your key stakeholder list. You may want to select an up-and-coming middle manager and use this as an executive development experience. You could also select a key worker and informal leader who is strongly committed to the plan's implementation, or someone more on the fringe who can act as a stimulating resource and bring a different perspective into the mix. You could also choose a union leader, a retired businessperson, an external content expert/consultant, a supplier or vendor, or even a customer. Another thing to keep in mind is that, in addition to their peer members, these executives must feel comfortable with every other member of the planning team as well.

Again, I would strongly caution against going beyond 12 to 15 members. If the group gets too large, it will soon degenerate into nothing more than a crowd control activity for the facilitator. However, be sure you have enough externally oriented sales, marketing, and customer-focused members to ensure that it is a strategic, not operational, plan.

INVOLVEMENT ISSUES IN STRATEGIC PLANNING

1. Core Planning Team Composition
   - Sense of clear direction
   - Ownership and commitment: senior level/middle management
   - Data reality — key players
   - Stakeholders — key to broad perspective; external/customer focus
   - Helps implementation — key players
   - Staff support team — administration/coordination
   - Leader preference/comfort

2. Numbers vs. Group Dynamics Reasonableness
   - 6 to 8 people is the best size for group dynamics/team building
   - 10 to 15 people is an acceptable size (with two or three subgroups)
   - 16+ people is a mess — crowd control becomes the issue

3. Involvement of Others Through a Parallel Process
   - Through data collection homework at Current State Assessment step
   - Through involvement in business/department planning
   - Through asking their opinions/reactions to drafts (two to four times throughout the process)

In any case, this planning team composition and involvement issue is the first place you'll begin to make tough choices. As you can see above, it's important to be selective, not only in terms of the size of the team, but also in terms of conceptual and strategic abilities as well as diversity and commitment to your organization's strategic management system.

Example: You might consider the eligibility of having a union executive on your team. However, unless he or she has full commitment to your organization's strategic plan — rather than an overriding loyalty to the union's mission alone — it might make better sense to include that individual as a key stakeholder and not as a member of the planning team. If you are on the planning team, you are not there as a representative of a constituency, but as a member committed to the organization's overall vision and mission.

ORGANIZING TASK #9: ASSIGNING PLANNING STAFF SUPPORT ROLES

When selecting your planning team, you'll need to keep three things in mind:

1. The organization's leadership team must lead the strategic plan.
2. You will need to involve every key stakeholder — whether or not they're a part of the planning team — in some sort of Parallel Process to ensure their continuing participation in creating the actual documents and in buying in to the changes.
3. Your planning team must also have individuals who can support them, so they can concentrate on the content and strategies of the strategic plan. Generally speaking, these support persons do not count as members of the planning team, since they are expected to focus on the process, not the content. There are instances, however, in which these individuals would also naturally be a part of the planning team anyway.

For many organizations, these support and process roles can make the difference between the strategic plan's success or failure. Yes, line managers are always the ones responsible for managing the *content* of the plan, but you'll still need individuals who are responsible for the myriad of details involved in the planning and change management process, mechanics, and logistics. These individuals are necessary for the following purposes:

1. To ensure the day-to-day planning and change process linkages occur.
2. To develop the internal organizational capability for ongoing development and institutionalization of the strategic management system as the new way to run business day to day.

The planning team will need an administrative assistant in the room who takes care of the logistics of each meeting. That person will type up the minutes (he/she should have a laptop at the meeting), take care of the flip charts and lunches, and distribute the "to do" lists and strategic planning drafts that will be an ongoing result of all the meetings.

A second and critical role that needs to be assigned at this time is that of an internal coordinator/facilitator of the entire strategic management system's process. This should be someone who concerns himself or herself mainly with the process of both the plan and the change management process; not someone who is a member of the senior management team with a high stake in the content of the plan.

The executives in planning, finance, human resources, etc., who are on the senior management team cannot be an objective or effective facilitator of the planning process. This overall support role should include facilitating Parallel Process meetings, coordinating the Strategic Change Steering Committee, developing other internal consultants, and assisting with annual and 3-year departmental and strategic business unit planning.

In addition, the planning team will probably need to call on other individual members for specific support resources. For instance, one of the members of your planning team may be a vice president of finance, so that when you begin to develop the financial data and budgeting based on the strategic plan, you would look to that individual for supporting advice, input, and coordination. One of these people may also be the overall Key Success Measures/Goal Coordinator.

Another need could be filled by your organization's human resources vice president, who is also a part of your core planning team. He or she would also serve as the team's support person in the area of tying in the HR programs to the strategic plan including staffing, personnel appraisals, succession planning, and rewards systems concerns. They often handle communications as well. It is vital that they tailor the performance management/appraisal and incentive programs to the strategic plan.

Tip: Support Rules

Bear in mind that these support roles are not always meant to be full-time jobs. However, they do become permanent parts of the participants' regular jobs. The support roles exist so that the planning team has resources that will help link them to the various parts of the organization.

ORGANIZING TASK #10: SELECTING AN EXTERNAL STRATEGIC PLANNING FACILITATOR

In addition to the internal coordinator/facilitator, you will usually need an external professional strategic planning facilitator to conduct your strategic planning process. The fact is, no matter how skilled or experienced your internal facilitator may be, their ultimate loyalties lay within the confines of the organization. After all, their paycheck comes from you. Their ability to be neutral, to find the courage to challenge and to play devil's advocate with senior management (including their own boss) is usually quite suspect, and to take such a role is often foolhardy and career limiting. They also usually lack the breadth and depth of a professional strategic planning facilitator.

Tip: Facilitating Closure

In fact, most experienced internal or external organizational development consultants can still only facilitate about 75% of the planning process effectively. In my personal experience, I have watched numerous times where these professionals cannot navigate serious business and conflict issues to a consensus and closure among strong-willed and opinionated senior executives. In addition, even if they can do an excellent job with the vision/mission/values step, they get lost beyond that point.

Particularly in the strategic planning phase, you will be dealing with sensitive issues and looking at some very tough choices. The professional strategic planning facilitator has no personal stake in any of these issues, and is trained to keep the process moving, resolve conflict, and methodically help you work through each tough choice. He or she should be equipped to play devil's advocate and push for concrete decisions, directions, and priorities. An external facilitator is better able to challenge you and confront key issues if you back away from your desired outcomes.

In choosing an external strategic planning facilitator, you should look for the following seven qualifications:

1. A strong business, economic, and industry orientation.
2. Expertise in strategic management and project management.
3. An excellent sense of overall organization fit, functioning, and design.
4. Understanding of group dynamics and human behavior.
5. Knowledge of large-scale change and transition management.
6. Consulting steps and facilitator/process/meetings management skills.
7. Strong internal sense of self, ego, and self-esteem when dealing with strong senior executives.

One of the last key reasons for having an external professional strategic planning facilitator is to assist in developing your strong internal staff support team. A good facilitator should be capable of showing your internal team how to facilitate the planning process and actually develop the knowledge and skills to handle the change management process internally.

Tip: External Facilitation Skills

In short, he or she must have the maturity and wisdom to consciously act in a "loose–tight" fashion so as to guide, yet not intrude. And, when deciding on who to choose to assist you, look at it from a system's return on investment (ROI) perspective; not an analytic "cost only" perspective. If the person can really help the CEO and top management team define and execute their strategic plan, the return on their investment is enormous. So don't be penny-wise and pound foolish (as the saying goes).

Organizing Task #11: Initiating a Parallel Process

The key stakeholders you've identified are all a part of your planning community. They do not all play the same role, however. Some are part of the core planning team; others play an adjunct or input role that lies within the Parallel Process. In this process, it becomes obvious why your community of key stakeholders is so essential to the success of the plan.

In the Parallel Process, the planning team sends out each document it drafts for review by the larger key stakeholder community. Invariably, those stakeholders will have recommendations for the inclusion or exclusion of certain points. Once the planning team has incorporated this feedback into the document, it is ready to prepare a final draft. In this way, the key stakeholders act as a sort of "check-and-balance" input to the planning team, reacting from a different perspective.

Depending on the number of planning meetings held by the core planning team, there may be anywhere from two to four Parallel Process rounds of meetings to give feedback on the draft documents in bite-sized increments as they are developed.

If you've ever been part of a planning team, you already know how difficult it can be to retain objectivity and stay focused at all times. Thus, it's easy to see why the Parallel Process is such an invaluable framework for the planning process. The larger key stakeholder community literally provides a devil's advocate/safety net and an input communication/response channel for the smaller planning team.

Tip: The Parallel Process

Each Parallel Process usually needs two planning team members: one to explain the documents and process, and the other to facilitate and write up the feedback on a flip chart. If you don't use a flip chart or some other visual written note taking, people will often become skeptical as to whether you've really heard them.

Another key point is that training needs to be conducted for the planning team members prior to their first Parallel Process — again, engineering success up front. In addition, another kind of Parallel Process is needed at this time as well: training for senior and middle management on today's visionary leadership practices, as well as on the necessary skills to carry out the plan's implementation.

Following each core planning team meeting, it is also critical that one individual be responsible for developing and sending out written communications, *from the CEO,* to all key stakeholders. These communications should be simple memos in a question-and-answer format that highlight the status, what actions have been taken, what still needs to be done, etc. Most importantly, they should update key stakeholders on their role in your strategic planning and change management process, and what specifically is expected of them. There will be more on this Parallel Process in upcoming chapters.

ORGANIZING TASK #12: ESTABLISHING GROUND RULES AND DOCUMENTS

The planning team facilitator is responsible for setting up clear, mutually agreed-upon ground rules for the planning team. This is essential to the success of any planning and large-scale change activity. Considering the amount of change involved in implementing a strategic plan, you'll greatly increase your chances of success if you establish some basic rules or norms of behavior. They should be set around such topics as openness and honesty, keeping in mind that conflict is good, having the persistence to hang in with the process, listening and explaining "why" (the logic or rationale behind a position) rather than being self-serving, consensus decision-making (actively support the decision), substance vs. wordsmithing, and making tough choices right from the start.

Adopting a "win-win" discussion framework is crucial here. The key to true win-win discussions is twofold:

1. To expand your base of information and develop an understanding of the logic, rationale, and criteria behind other points of view.
2. To listen first and exhibit a clear understanding of others' perspectives and logic *before* trying to influence with your point of view.

In every discussion, keep in mind that a fair amount of negotiating and manipulating is going on. Remember, you're either *claiming* value — i.e., defending your "piece of the pie" — or *creating* value — expanding the information available and exploring alternative solutions. Obviously, it's more desirable to move toward creating value in win-win discussions. In truly listening to and incorporating all points of view in an overall solution, you begin the process of thinking laterally in new ways.

In addition to this, you need clarity of the physical planning document in Goal #1. Finally, all-around commitment to the three goals must be expressed by all members of the planning team.

Strategic Planning Final Document

Keep it simple: 16 to 20 pages maximum; in overhead slide format

Sections/Documents	# of Pages
I. Introduction	2–4
1. Cover sheet with *Rallying Cry*	
2. Executive Summary; History	
3. Strategic Planning Model	
4. Acknowledgements	
5. Table of Contents	
6. Environmental Scanning and Strategic Issues	1–2
II. Ideal Future Vision and Strategies	
1. Vision/Back Up	1–2
2. Mission/Driving Force(s)	1
3. Values/Back Up	2–4
4. KSF Matrix/First Year Action Plan	2–3
5. SBUs/MPAs Clarified with Pro Formas	1–2
6. 3-Year Business/Department Planning Process	1
(Mini Strategic Plans for SBUs/MPAs, and Major Support Units)	

ORGANIZING TASK #13: TAILORING YOUR STRATEGIC PLAN

It's probably a safe bet that most of you have done some form of strategic planning before. If this is the case in your organization, it won't make sense for you to blindly adhere to each step of this Reinventing Strategic Management Model. Rather, you should *always* tailor it to fit your own needs by assessing what you already have, and coming to mutual consensus with your planning team on which steps will require greater time and effort. This is an essential task that is usually done at the very end of the Plan-to-Plan day in order to sum up the next process.

If, like most organizations today, you already have a sound vision/mission/values statement (provided it's clear, current, universally accepted, and understood within the organization), it will be more appropriate to concentrate on Key Success Measures/Goals and strategies, etc.

At this point, the planning team should carefully review the list below, prioritizing each line item in terms of its level of importance in your strategic planning process (based on a high/medium/low scale).

This tailoring of your strategic planning process to fit your particular organizational needs provides top management with another method for narrowing down, defining, and focusing on what's important — and culling out what isn't crucial at the same time. Once this is done, you can customize a strategic planning process to your exact needs.

Tip: Importance of Step #8

Preserving Step #8, Plan-to-Implement, as another separate, one-day session, is a must for bridging the gap from planning to implementation (Goal #1 to Goal #2). So we always ask our clients to give it an H (high) if they want us to help them. Without Step #8, the SPOTS syndrome will strike and we'll suffer a hit to our reputation. We'd rather pass up the money and preserve our reputation.

Reinvented Strategic Planning (Tailored to Your Needs)

Based on your current understanding of the Reinvented Strategic Planning and Change Management Models (and strategic management), please list the importance (H–M–L) of developing each potential deliverable for your organization.

Strategic Planning — Steps #2–5

1. _____ Environmental Scanning (SKEPTIC)
2. _____ Vision — Our Ideal Future, Aspirations, Guiding Star
3. _____ Mission — Who, What, Why We Exist
4. _____ Values — Our Guiding Principles, to Guide Organizational Behaviors
5. _____ Driving Force(s) — Positioning, Our Competitive Edge
5a. _____ Rallying Cry — Three to Six Key Motivational Words
6. _____ Key Success Measures — Quantifiable Measures of Success
7. _____ Current State Assessment
7a. _____ Scenario/Contingency Planning
8. _____ Core Strategies — Major Means, Approaches, Methods to Achieve Our Vision
8a. _____ Actions/Yearly Priorities Under Each Core Strategy

Business Units — Step #6

9. _____ SBU/MPAs Defined — Strategic Business Units/Market Segments, or Major Program Areas
9a. _____ Business/Key Support Plans — 3-Year Mini Strategic Plans for Units

Annual Plans — Step #7

10. _____ Annual Plans/Priorities (Department Plans)
11. _____ Resource Allocation/Strategic Budgeting (including guidelines)

Individuals/Teams

12. _____ Individual Performance Management System — Tied to Strategic Planning
12a. _____ Rewards and Recognition System — Tied to Strategic Planning

Bridge the Gap — Step #8

13. _____ Plan-to-Implement Day — Get Educated, Organized and Tailor Our Change Management Process/Structures

Focus on the Vital Few ("STAR" Results)

14. _____ Quality Products and Services
14a. _____ Customer Service

14b. _____ Speed/Responsiveness/Convenience for the Customer
14c. _____ Choice, Fashion, Control, Customized

Alignment of Delivery — Step #9

15. _____ Organization Structure/Redesign
15a. _____ Business Process Reengineering — To Lower Costs/Improve Response *(Customer Focused)*
15b. _____ Blow Out Bureaucracy (and Waste)
15c. _____ Information Technology — Technology Steering Group

Attunement of People/Support Systems — Step #9

16. _____ Professional Management and Leadership Competencies, Skills
16a. _____ Management Change Skills/Managing Strategic Change Skills
16b. _____ HR Programs/Processes — Employee Development Board
16c. _____ Values/Cultural Change Skills
16d._____ Employee Involvement/Participative Management Skills/ Empowerment
16e. _____ Strategic Communications: Knowledge and Skills

Yearly Update — Step #10

17. _____ Annual Strategic Review and Update

Teamwork

18. _____ Teamwork for Executive Team
18a. _____ Teamwork for Department Teams
18b. _____ Teamwork for Cross-Functional Relationships/Teams
18c. _____ Strategic Alliances

IN SUMMARY

The Plan-to-Plan step can make all the difference in how smoothly and effectively your planning and change process will go. The key is in assessing the organization, building your capacity (with leadership and support staff), and educating, organizing and tailoring the process to your specific needs. This is accomplished via the executive briefing and each of the 13 Plan-to-Plan organizing tasks. You'll then have already completed much of the hard work that engineers success of the plan up front, before you even begin.

Most organizations don't adopt this crucial Plan-to-Plan day. As for the Centre, we wouldn't even think of beginning actual planning until all of this was satisfactorily completed.

RECAP OF KEY CONTENT POINTS

- Before you begin the Plan-to-Plan step, make sure you are clear on what it is: i.e., schedule an executive briefing and an opportunity to organize your approach to the strategic planning process (i.e., assess, educate, organize, and tailor).

- Be specific and clear on the exact entity you're going to plan for (organization, geographic community sector, business unit, etc.).
- Identify the key issues that are critical to your organization's success up front, as a guide to keeping planning practical. (Use the critical issues list or an organizational assessment to accomplish this.)
- Make sure the top members of your collective leadership are personally ready and committed to leading your strategic planning and change management process. (In other words, conduct capacity building through team-building/visionary leadership priorities and skills training, right away.)
- Use Plan-to-Plan as an opportunity to problem-solve potential barriers to strategic planning that your organization may encounter — before you begin.
- Be sure to scan your organization's environment, both internal and external, to make certain you are not trying to create your plan in a vacuum.
- Don't blindly follow the ten steps of the planning model. Tailor your strategic plan in a way that best fits your particular organization.
- Make sure your strategic plan drives your budget (i.e., "strategic" budgeting) not vice versa.
- Your key stakeholders should include anyone who affects or is affected by the organization's strategic plan.
- Don't let your planning team grow beyond 14 or 15 individuals.
- Create a staff support cadre to support the planning team.
- Have an experienced external strategic planning facilitator who can play devil's advocate and facilitate strong egos, especially during the planning process.
- Incorporate a Parallel Process to integrate the planning team's progress with other key stakeholders, inside and outside the organization. Communicate, communicate, communicate.
- Set up clear, mutually agreed-upon ground rules that will be in effect for the entire planning and implementation process.
- Review and reaffirm all commitments to your organization's plan and the planning process, including the three main goals.
- Take 3 to 5 minutes at the end of each planning day to give yourselves feedback and to learn from your experiences. Ask the three key questions:

1. What can we continue to do?
2. What should we do more of?
3. What should we do less of?

"HOW-TO" ACTION CHECKLIST

1. "Look before you leap." Have at least a half-day executive briefing, in which all top management executives — including the CEO — understand and are in sync with the planning process. Consider including key stakeholders in this as well.
2. Hold a kick-off meeting to share with all key stakeholders the planning process and their role in it.
3. Select an external strategic planning facilitator to start the planning process, but also set up the staff support cadre right away, so you can eventually have the internal capacity to run this process yourself.
4. Complete all the Plan-to-Plan tasks either in a formal, half-day session following the executive briefing session, or informally with the CEO and top management team. Use the following list of 25 tasks as your checklist.

    1. Organization specifications sheet
    2. A high-performance organization mini survey
    3. Prework strategic planning briefing questionnaire
    4. Executive briefing on strategic management
    5. Personal readiness for strategic management
    6. Strategic planning problems/barriers
    7. Readiness actions and steps
    8. Organizational fact sheet for strategic planning
    9. Critical issues list
    10. Strategic planning staff support team/needed meetings
    11. Planning team membership
    12. Identification of key stakeholders
    13. Key stakeholder involvement
    14. Initial environmental scanning/current state assessment required (minimum of seven areas)
    15. Reinventing Strategic Management Model tailored to your needs
    16. Strategic planning link to budgets
    17. Organizational and individual leadership (self-change)
    18. Individual commitment
    19. Strategic implementation and change commitments
    20. Strategic planning updates communicated to others
    21. Energizers for meetings
    22. Strategic planning meeting process observer
    23. Action minutes format
    24. Meeting processing guide
    25. Closure/action planning

6 Environmental Scanning and the Parallel Process

Trust is a big part of successful change.
The way you build trust is by practicing the
politics of inclusion.

-David Osborne

AN ENVIRONMENTAL SCANNING SYSTEM

Environmental scanning is a topic that has been a staple in strategic planning for some time. However, we see two main changes in how it has traditionally been used.

First, the environment to be scanned is not that of the present, but is the time frame out to the end of the planning horizon and even beyond if possible. The idea is to become a futurist and try to understand and predict, as much as possible, what the future holds in store that could affect your organization.

Contrast this approach to the standard SWOT technique, which looks at the opportunities and threats in the environment as they exist today. It is important to conduct this type of scan each year as part of the planning and update processes. However, it is fundamentally different from the detailed, futurist environmental scan we are discussing. More and different details about the future come out when you look at all the many key factors in the environment using the SKEPTIC framework shown in Figure 6.1. To use this framework, the planning committee should answer the questions in Figure 6.1 individually and then discuss it as a group.

Secondly, environmental scanning should no longer be conducted once a year as part of the planning process. We recommend it be performed quarterly as part of the Leadership Steering Committee, guiding the implementation of the plan. As a minimum, conduct the scans no longer than 6 months apart. The world is changing too fast now. Don't get left behind.

HOW TO ACCOMPLISH ENVIRONMENTAL SCANNING

We recommend setting up a Strategic Environmental Scanning System (SESS), that includes the following six steps:

1. Identify the organization's environmental scan needs, especially for the next round of strategic planning (annual updates).
2. Generate a list of information sources that provide core inputs (i.e., trade shows, publications, technical meetings, customers, and Internet).
3. Identify those who will participate in the environmental scanning process. (They do not have to be members of the planning team.)

1-57444-278-3/00/$0.00+$.50
© 2000 by CRC Press LLC

93

What are the 5–10 environmental trends/projections/opportunities/threats facing us over the life of our Strategic Plan?

S Sociodemographics

K Competition

E Economics/Environment

P Political

T Technical

I Industry/Substitutes

C Customer

Note: Use this list as the content framework and "grounding" for the strategic planning process. Bring it out at the end of the planning process to ensure you've covered these trends adequately.

FIGURE 6.1   Environmental trends.

4. Assign scanning tasks to several members of the organization; form teams to do this.
5. Collect data on a regular basis.
6. Disseminate the information in a large group meeting on a yearly basis, and quarterly at the Strategic Change Leadership Steering Committee meeting.

Tip: It is best to have each scanning team assigned based on SKEPTIC. It also helps if you get a senior management sponsor for each team, using the natural roles that the different functional executives play, i.e., S (socio demographics) to the VP HR, E (economics) to the CFO, etc. In addition, ask for volunteers to assist them as part of their scanning team. Middle managers are crucial as a part of this, but they should volunteer based on their expertise and interests.

As an aid to this scanning, Figure 6.2 shows the Stakeholder Analysis with the world as a complex system. These environmental groups or "domains" can be part of the different teams' analysis. There are some specific feedback mechanisms and ways to look at these domains and they are listed here.

SPECIFIC FEEDBACK AND RENEWAL MECHANISMS: ENVIRONMENTAL DOMAINS

1. Customers
   - Customer data, surveys, perceptions, feedback, focus group
   - Non-customer data, surveys, perceptions focus groups
   - Advertising, marketing ROI
   - Customer profitability
   - Accounts receivable
   - Product quality
   - Segmentation data
   - Complaint handling, trends
   - Visits, meetings
   - Customer comment cards
2. Suppliers/Vendors
   - Visits, meetings
   - Sales potential
   - Annual reports
   - Accounts payable
3. Unions (Employee Involvement Programs)
   - Joint union–management committees
   - Safety, security data
   - Meetings with union leadership
4. Employees
   - Employee opinion surveys — morale, motivation, and communications — yearly, by units
   - Rewards — matching surveys, programs, diagnosis
   - Culture surveys, focus groups, action research
   - Deep sensing of employee perceptions
   - Task forces, think tanks, discussion groups
   - Unfiltered upward feedback meetings — employee/management meetings
   - MBWA (Management By Walking Around)
   - Job design, work simplifications
   - Organization effectiveness suggestion programs — not just productivity
5. Public Community/Society
   - Technology trends
   - Sociodemographic trends

- Issues management process
- Environmental impact
- Social responsibility program
- Advisory boards
- Community involvement

6. Government (Issues Management Process)
   - Lobbyist data
   - Legislative visits, reports (state/federal)
   - Legal reviews, compliance, spirit

7. Owners/Stockholders
   - Investor relations surveys
   - Annual meetings
   - Phone calls, trends

8. Competition
   - Competitor analysis
   - Industry financial comparisons
   - Niches
   - Trade shows
   - Strategic alliances
   - MBWA
   - Price analysis
   - Association meetings, seminars
   - Annual reports

9. Wall Street Financiers/Creditors
   - Visits, meetings
   - Analyst briefings
   - Annual reports
   - Diversify
   - Advisory board

10. Management
    - Administrative MIS reports
    - Financial reports (short-term/long-term)
    - Management data, opinions
    - Strategic planning process
    - Team building, diagnosis, executive retreats
    - Offsite meetings, overnights, Outward Bound team experience
    - Peer evaluations
    - Meeting evaluations
    - Performance evaluation, including company values

11. International
    - GNP, productivity, growth, and development
    - Economics, forecasts
    - Societal, cultural, country trends
    - International financial exchanges

Stakeholder = any group or individual who can affect or is affected by the achievement of the organization's objectives. The groups listed here are examples of categories of stakeholders.

FIGURE 6.2   Stakeholder analysis — the world as a complex system.

ARE YOU A FUTURIST AND STRATEGY EXPERT?

As we said, senior executives need to become futurists in order to keep looking into the future where they will live the rest of their lives. Obviously, the Internet, search engines, and industry publications should be part of your scanning process. In addition, I recommend that your scanning team regularly scan the following resources:

1. **Long-Term View**
   - *The Futurist* (monthly magazine)
   - World Future Society
   - *Science News* (16 pages, biweekly)
2. **Middle-Term View**
   - *Christian Science Monitor* (newspaper)

- *Trendletter*, John Naisbitt (8 pages, biweekly)
- *Kami Quarterly*, Michael Kami (Lighthouse Point, FL)
- Joseph Coates, DC/USA
- Charles Fetter, Canada

3. **Shorter-Term Trends**
   - *Globe and Mail* (Toronto)
   - *New York Times*
   - *Wall Street Journal*
   - Sound Books (executive summaries)
   - *The Economist* (weekly magazine)
   - Lots of weekly magazines (*Fortune, Business Week,* etc.)

4. **Systems Thinking**
   - Pegasus Communications – *Systems Thinker* (8 pages, monthly, Cambridge, MA)
   - Systems Thinking Press (Website)

5. **The Environment**
   - Jacques Costeau, *Calypso* (monthly magazine)
   - World Wildlife Foundation
   - Sierra Club, *Sierra* (monthly magazine)
   - Greenpeace

6. **The Internet**
   - Many Sources — Which do you use regularly?

In addition, there are a number of ways to combine being a futurist with becoming a strategy expert (another leadership skill for each individual/organization). This is the reason and purpose for being a futurist. Some ideas here include the following:

1. Become an expert on Systems Thinking.
2. Share/critique strategic plans/strategies/values of other organizations in magazines.
3. Conduct bite-size *strategy school* topic learnings each month/staff meeting.
4. Read books/listen to tapes about strategy — share with each other.
5. Invite speakers on strategic topics.
6. Conduct competitor analysis, focusing on their strategies.
7. Cover department/business unit issues in a 1, 2 sequence:
   - What are your strategies? Your values?
   - How does your issue/operational problem fit into your strategies/ values?
8. Benchmark *Best Practices* inside/outside your industry.
9. Become an expert on successful implementation as a "strategy-in-action."
10. Conduct positioning/driving force discussions and case studies of prominent organizations and use to clarify your own.

QUESTIONS TO PONDER

- What does SKEPTIC stand for?
- How do you set up an environmental scanning system?
- What is a stakeholder? Differentiate them from employees and customers.
- As a futurist, what are your favorite Internet sites? Why?

HOW DOES THE PARALLEL PROCESS WITH KEY STAKEHOLDERS OPERATE?

Another form of "scanning" is with your key stakeholders on your actual strategic planning decisions and documents. We recommend what we call our Parallel Process, based on our second premise that "people support what they help create."

This Parallel Process model provides the opportunity for optimum involvement throughout your planning and change process by all key stakeholders, be it your board, employees, middle managers, and stockholders as well as customers and any other external groups desired. We advocate "organized participation," unlike other models that often have either too much (public sector) or no (private sector) stakeholder involvement in the process.

Our experience with organizations focuses clearly on the dynamic tension between ownership of the strategies for change by the leadership team, and acceptance or buy-in to the plan by the key stakeholders, who are crucial to the successful implementation of the desired change. We have involved over 1000 people in Strategic Planning and Change Management processes this way and have met all objectives. This is because we conduct this Parallel Process in a very organized, planned, and participative way.

Briefly, we recommend a Parallel Process in which real-time meetings are held with key stakeholders after *each* phase/offsite meeting of the Strategic Planning and Change Management process.

The purpose is twofold: (1) to share information and provide feedback to the core leadership team in order to troubleshoot and improve the plans, and (2) to gain understanding, acceptance (i.e., buy-in), and commitment to the overall direction and implementation of the plan.

Typically, this is done in meetings held "in parallel" with the planning phases by first asking, "Is there anything fundamentally wrong with this draft document or direction?" Once this is clear, we ask for positive and negative comments in subgroup discussions using an interactive approach. Each subgroup has a facilitator (chosen from the core planning and change steering teams) trained to keep the process both positive and productive.

The tailoring of the details of key stakeholder involvement is determined by the core planning team prior to beginning the actual Strategic Planning and Change

Management process. This results in a much higher probability of successful implementation of your plan or major change.

PARALLEL PROCESS STEPS

1. *Analyze and select all of your stakeholders.* A stakeholder is any group or individual who is affected by the achievement of the organization's objectives. The groups listed in the Stakeholder Analysis in Figure 6.2 are examples of categories of stakeholders.
2. *Identify the "key" stakeholders.* Decide whose involvement in your Parallel Process meetings is key based on their importance to both the development and achievement of your Strategic Management (Planning and Change) process.
3. *Conduct your next planning or change leadership team meeting.* Decide in detail at the end of this meeting, exactly how to run your Parallel Process meetings by asking questions such as how do we involve our stakeholders? When and where should we meet, and who should attend? Which documents do we gather feedback on? etc.
4. *Conduct a short orientation and training preparation* with those planning team members involved in the Parallel Process to ensure that they are coordinated and comfortable with their efforts.
5. *Conduct the actual Parallel Process meetings as planned.* The purposes of these Parallel Process meetings include the following:
    1. To explain the Strategic Planning and Change effort and the stakeholder's role in it.
    2. To understand and explain the draft documents clearly.
    3. To give input and feedback to the core planning team, taking into consideration the following:
        - Guarantee — Feedback will be seriously considered.
        - Limitation — Input is gathered from many different people. Therefore, it is impossible for each person's input to be automatically placed in the final document exactly as desired.
    A thorough job of the Parallel Process results in fewer implementation problems and less resistance to change. When change happens cooperatively, people feel you're "doing it *with* them rather than *to* them."
6. *Collect feedback sheets and take them back to the full planning and change management team.* Include
    - Common themes and trends (vs. pet peeves),
    - A synthesis of the flip charts developed at this meeting,
    - Impressions brought back by the planning team representative.
7. *Have the full planning and change management team refine their plans based on the Parallel Process feedback.* There are two potential planning team problems here:
    - Completely rewriting documents unnecessarily (reinventing the wheel; ditching sound decisions already made).

- Replacing provocative words to make the document palatable (thus watering it down to meaningless or dual/mixed messages).

8. *Provide feedback on the changes made.* Once you have updated your plans, it is a good idea to share your input with those who were involved in your Parallel Process. One way is to provide a comparison of the old plan and the new plan, explaining your reasons for change. A second way is to highlight the changes on the new plans, much the same way a legal document is done.

Figure 6.3 provides an illustration of the entire process.

Parallel Process Meeting Options

There are a many things to consider when preparing for your Parallel Process meetings. Success in achieving your goals is determined by careful preplanning.

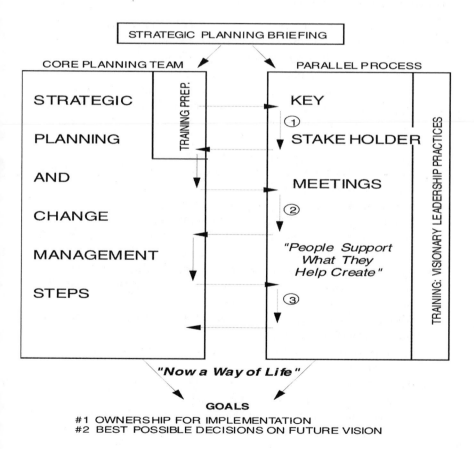

FIGURE 6.3 Set up the planning community.

Focus first on middle managers that are the strategic plan implementers and thus require special attention. They must take ownership of the plan and be committed to the change process.

For best results, get on the agenda of one of the regular meetings of your stakeholders — taking care to allow enough time to adequately present your material and gain their cooperation — or schedule special small group forums.

Take opportunities to present your plan at regular staff meetings and "all employee" meetings of core planning team members. If your organization is very large, use employee focus groups to break the job down into manageable sections.

You may also need a working session with the board of directors to get its approval and support of the entire plan and implementation process.

If holding public meetings, proper facility setup and management of large groups are tasks to be dealt with, as well as the fact that you have less control of who will attend your meetings (i.e., lack of key stakeholders in attendance).

PARALLEL PROCESS MEETING HINTS

1. Ensure that only members of the core strategic planning team hold these meetings, as they are the only ones with the knowledge to do so. Run the Parallel Process in teams of two to help each other.
2. Explain the strategic plan concept or model first.
3. Explain the documents next. You will be less defensive this way. Don't just read the documents; educate the participants. They must fully understand the concepts or intent and the specific meaning of key words and phrases.
4. Make sure "draft" is written on all documents.
5. Once the stakeholders start giving feedback, make sure you prove to them that you have heard them. The best way to do this is to:
   a. Repeat back the essence of their statements.
   b. Empathize with their feelings, not just the words.
   c. Write down their statements on a flip chart and check with them to ensure accuracy (or better yet, have a second facilitator do so).
6. Focus discussions on substance, on the spirit or intent of the documents.
7. If you must explain part of a document or letter, use phrases like, "The intent was ..." or "What was meant was ..."
8. Check their views regarding the documents that you've just reviewed. Are they in fundamental agreement?
9. At the conclusion, state actions you'll take, when you will meet with them next, and follow up.
10. Thank them.
11. Go to stakeholders if at all possible — take the first step.
12. Take documents to meetings in "bite-sized pieces" to make them digestible, rather than giving them the full plan all at once.

13. As a general rule, don't get feedback in a large group setting; break out into subgroups with facilitators for each one (use flip charts). Begin and end the meeting with the whole group only.
14. The best size for excellent feedback is 10 to 15 people (maximum).
15. It is often useful to script each meeting. If not, be sure to develop a common set of overheads for each meeting for consistency and clarity. Decide whether you want everyone to have handouts of all the documents and overheads.
16. Help stakeholders to be clear on means vs. ends and The Systems Thinking Approach that underlies good planning and implementation.
17. Allow enough meeting time for depth of questions and answers, or give participants time for ideas and reactions to be written down and turned in later to a central point.
18. Key Success Measures (KSMs) — also called corporate goal setting — are the most difficult documents to gain feedback on. Consider asking only about the areas of success to measure first, working on the actual measurements and targets later with *only* the parties responsible for their approval and accountability.
19. What do you do if you don't agree with feedback/comments? Collect data. Do not comment on it, unless it is a big item that is crucial to explain. This meeting is an information-sharing and feedback meeting; it is not a decision-making meeting. That is done at the next planning meeting.
20. Beware of gestalt vs. pieces — don't let them break materials down into isolated documents or paragraphs. They all go together and must be taken in context.
21. How do you redirect a vocal person? Use a flip chart to reword their comments, check it with them for accuracy, and then move on.

Parallel Process Meeting Sample Agenda and Materials

Agenda:
- Welcome, introductions, purpose, and agenda
- Strategic planning explained along with WIIFM (what's in it for me)
- Explain "draft" documents
- Gain feedback on the documents and record it on flip charts
- Closure/next steps

Overheads and materials needed (minimum):
- Strategic planning (A, B, C, D, E model) overview
- Agenda, purposes
- Parallel Process concept overheads
- Draft documents to be covered

	Strategic Management Process	Staff Support Team Role	Stakeholder Mtgs. (Face-to-Face)	SP Update (Internal Communications)
A	Step # #1 Plan-to-Plan	1a. Preparation for stakeholder mtgs/comms. 1b. Training of facilitators/planning team for stakeholder meetings →	(Combine mtgs. as appropriate) 1. Kick off mtg. of Strategic Planning Concept	After Each Strategic Management Session →
B	#2 Ideal Future Vision		2. Review Vision and Mission Review Values	
C	#3 Key Success Factors #4 Current State Assessment	3. Preparation for Current State Assessment (with Parallel Process Stakeholders) →	3. Review KSFs/ CSA Input →	
	#5 Strategy Development	5. Preparation for Parallel Process →	5. Review Strategies/ Yearly Action Priorities →	
	#6 Business Plans	6. Prep for 3-Year Business Unit Planning (Optional) →	6. Involved in Business Plans (by unit)	
	#7 Annual Plans	7. Preparation for Annual Department Planning and Large Group Annual Planning Review Mtg. →	7. Develop Dept. Annual Plans 7a. Attend large group review mtgs. →	
D	#8 Plan-to-Implement	8. • Final SP Document • Communications Rollout • Yearly Map of Implementation →	8. Attend yearly "kick off" implementation mtg. →	
	#9 Strategy Implementation and Change	9. Coordination of Strategic Change Leadership Steering Committee →	9. Involved in implementation (quarterly as appropriate)	
	#10 Annual Strategic Review (& Updates)	10. Preparation for Annual Strategic Review Sessions	10. Attend Parallel Process mtgs. all over again each year	

FIGURE 6.4 Parallel Process summary examples.

QUESTIONS TO PONDER

- Who are your key stakeholders?
- How do the participative management skills help or hinder the Parallel Process? Why?
- Describe a Parallel Process meeting.
- Why should you never let anyone outside the planning team lead a Parallel Process?

IN SUMMARY

Good luck in your Parallel Process. Remember that *"people support what they help create."* So either involve them in the Parallel Process during the planning and change process, or you will find that resistance will be far greater. In other words, "pay me now or pay me later."

RECAP OF KEY CONTENT POINTS

1. Senior management must be futurists as well.
2. Organizations need an environmental scanning system that provides senior management with data on a quarterly basis — yearly is now too long.
3. All "SKEPTIC" areas should be covered in a scan.
4. The Parallel Process is the way to involve many people in the planning process.
5. Be sure you have a "draft" to be reviewed in the Parallel Process meeting. Just get feedback on it: don't make decisions there, but later back in the Planning Team.
6. The Parallel Process has two purposes; increasing ownership and under-standing, as well as improving the quality of the product.
7. Be sure to cover the guarantee and limitations at all Parallel Process meetings.
8. There are many hints regarding Parallel Process best practices. Which five are most important to you?

"HOW-TO" ACTION CHECKLIST

1. Get volunteers to join each of the SKEPTIC Teams. Have each led by senior management.
2. Have all the environmental scanning teams report one after another so that the Planning Team has a full understanding of the entire environment.
3. The Parallel Process must be run only by core Planning Team members who have been privy to the full discussions.
4. Hold Parallel Process meetings on the workers' home territory to make the first step.
5. Middle managers/first line supervisors are the key players and should be first up in a Parallel Process round.
6. There are many meeting hints regarding this unique process — learn them well.
7. Hold Parallel Process meetings after each core Planning Team retreat — try it "bite sized."

7 Ideal Future Vision (Step #2)

The only limits, as always, are those of vision.

WHY IS THE IDEAL FUTURE VISION STEP IMPORTANT? WHERE SHOULD I START?

The Ideal Future Vision step (#2) is the first real action step in Reinventing Strategic Management. It is the step in which you formulate those dreams that are worth believing in and fighting for. Most importantly, this is where you set in motion the outcome of becoming a customer-focused, high-performance learning organization.

As in every facet of systems thinking, the Ideal Future Vision step must *begin with (and keep) the end in mind.* In this step, your collective leadership should begin the process of selecting those outcomes that you most want to achieve. Keep in mind that these outcomes directly influence the type of organization you will become. If the organization you see in your ideal future is high-performance and customer-focused, for instance, you need to select goals/measures (outcomes) that will help you achieve this. Typical outcomes for this type of organization would involve these six areas:

1. Customer satisfaction
2. Quality products/services
3. Profitability/retained earnings
4. Employee satisfaction
5. Contribution to society
6. Stockholder return

At this stage in beginning your strategic planning process, the cry of "It can't be done!" is irrelevant and unacceptable. This exercise isn't about limiting your organization's possibilities; it's about attempting to discover just what those possibilities can be.

Many organizations in the recent past have, at some point, hired a consultant to help them create their organizational mission and vision statements. Unfortunately, consultants often come in espousing the latest business trend or fad, essentially offering not much more than a piecemeal approach (shared vision only) to a systems problem. To illustrate, Louis V. Gerstner of IBM was quoted in the mid-1990s as saying,

The last thing IBM needs right now is a vision.

1-57444-278-3/00/$0.00+$.50
© 2000 by CRC Press LLC

As is apparent in the quote above, the last few years have seen vision and mission statements falling into what I call the "organizational development dumping ground" along with other business trends. As a result, these statements often end up being as superficial and meaningless as the paper they're printed on. I can't stress this strongly enough: your collective leadership must be completely committed to agreeing on the ends (vision) and working on the means (strategies) of achieving your Ideal Future Vision. Then it must work together in one team to make the changes necessary to achieve them. This is the only way in which your organization's vision statement can truly make a difference in how you run your business and serve your customer day to day.

Goal-setting is the #1 criteria for success in all the literature.

Example: The well-known study of 100 Harvard Business School graduates supports this very well. On following up with them 20 years later, researchers found that the 10 who had originally set clear goals with action plans owned 96% of the wealth.

After defining this Ideal Future Vision in a comprehensive way, it is then crucial that every member of your organization thoroughly comprehends your vision, and is totally committed to carrying it out. Your role is to develop in your employees an almost missionary zeal for the outcome of serving the customer — along with acquiring the skills and strategies for achieving it.

Example: I can't begin to stress the importance of having every organizational member understand and commit to your Ideal Future Vision. In fact, I've had two separate experiences in which, once the collective leadership of the organizations had come to mutual agreement on the organization's Ideal Future Vision, an executive on the senior management team decided to leave the organization because that vision wasn't the way he or she personally or professionally wanted to go. I actually considered this a healthy outcome, as I've never yet observed an organization successfully achieve its Ideal Future Vision when individual members of its collective leadership team aren't all pulling in the same direction. After all, if you can't all agree on your desired "ends," your "means" will never be in sync.

HOW TO BEGIN

Whatever you can do, or dream you can, begin it. Boldness
has genius, power, and magic in it.

-Goethe

The Ideal Future Vision step generates direction and order. Though it does not replace the common-sense fundamentals of running your business day to day, your organization cannot have an adequate sense of purpose without it. And, it is important that all organizational leaders participate in this key step.

In effect, the Ideal Future Vision step is where you focus on the outcomes and direction that will become the context for determining what you have to do to successfully implement your strategic plan. It's the point at which your collective leadership should step outside of all preconceived boundaries or limitations (and outside of your present business and habits) and begin to form a view of your organization's ideal future.

When your organization's collective leadership begins developing your Ideal Future Vision, don't be afraid to come from the position of not knowing all the answers. After all, you are seeking those answers that will define the best possible outcomes for your organization. Be willing to let go of what isn't working, and then develop and keep the detailed image of the future you desire in full view at all times.

> *Everything that can be invented has been invented.*
> *-Charles H. Duell, Director of U.S. Patent Office, 1899*

Being willing to go after what you really want is one thing. Defining what that is can be quite another. As the quote above so clearly illustrates, it can sometimes be extremely challenging just to step outside those boundaries of the world you've always known, and reshape the possibilities of that world by exercising your imagination. This failure to look beyond "what is today" — our familiar paradigms — to the possibilities of tomorrow, happens to all of us. Again, the following quote eloquently expresses this point:

> *Heavier-than-air flying machines are impossible.*
> *-Lord Kelvin, President, Royal Society, 1895*

CONFRONT YOUR PARADIGMS

Paradigms are a set of rules and regulations that: (1) establish boundaries, (2) set rules for success, and (3) show what is — and isn't — important. The world-famous futurist, Joel Barker, brought the paradigm concept dramatically to our attention in the 1990s. It was his observation that organizations (and people, too) establish a set of paradigms that eventually become so entrenched that they are never challenged.

Barker maintained that while these paradigms are useful in focusing attention, they tend to blind people from seeking effective strategies for future success. He argued that in order to become high-performance and customer-focused, organizations need to undergo a "paradigm shift," which poses the question: "What is impossible to do today ...but if it could be done ...would fundamentally change the way you do business?"

Many young people today look at the world of E-commerce and ask themselves this very question, hence all the new "Dot Com" start-up companies. Can you ask yourself this question?

Barker advised organizations that they should look outside their existing boundaries — in effect, learn to "shift" their paradigms. He believed that in order to be truly visionary, organizational leaders must become "paradigm pioneers;" i.e., they must be courageous and willing to take risks, even in the face of the unknown.

A typical example of past paradigm shifts would be humankind's progress in flight: from balloon to biplanes, to single-wing propeller planes, to jets, the Concorde, satellites and rockets, and finally (for now) to the space shuttle (what's next?).

Looking at the worlds of transportation and mass media electronics gives us wonderfully dramatic examples of paradigm shifts:

- In the field of transportation, humans first walked, then graduated to riding on animals, carts and wheels, then on to boats, trains, cars, and buses, and from there to mass transit and airplanes.
- Mass media electronics have shifted paradigms many times over in the span of a few mere decades. First came the tube, followed by the transistor, and in its present incarnation, chips.

And other, key paradigm shifts include the following:

- In California, the Poway Unified School District is focusing its energies on the outcome of *learning*, as opposed to the activity of *teaching*.
- Privatization of companies by the hundreds in Chile and Mexico, as well as city services in Philadelphia, Chicago, Dallas, etc.

Perhaps the most important idea to take away from this is that we can all choose our own paradigms, today *and* tomorrow. Completing the Ideal Future Vision step is a process that enables us to put aside reason *temporarily* and look beyond the present to the future as we would like it to be.

BECOME A SUPERIOR STRATEGIC THINKER

The well-known strategic planning expert, Gary Hamel, had this to say in a 1999 workshop brochure: "It's not enough to work harder, nor is it enough to just get better. Companies today have to learn how to get different — profoundly different."

Yesterday's business models are being supplanted by radically new ways of doing business. This isn't process reengineering; it's fundamental strategy innovation. Newcomers have created the lion's share of new wealth in many industries, and they have succeeded not by "executing better," but by changing the rules of the game.

In an increasingly nonlinear world, only nonlinear strategies will create new wealth. Yet few companies seem able to spawn imaginative, wealth-creating strategies. Strategy innovation, like quality, must be a deeply embedded, ubiquitous capability, and strategic thinking must be a daily habit, pervasive throughout the organization, rather than the province of a few individuals.

Thus, above all, see the future as an empty slate at first; approach it as a new beginning. You'll need to conduct an environmental scan of how the world is changing; then you'll be off and running in a proactive manner, thus creating your own Ideal Future Vision. In the words of Joel Barker, "You can and should shape your own future … and if you don't, somebody else surely will!"

THE IDEAL FUTURE VISION STEP — FOUR CHALLENGES

Completing the Ideal Future Vision step successfully requires taking your collective leadership through the following four main challenges.

Challenge #1: Shaping your organization's *vision statement,* or "guiding star."
Challenge #2: Developing a realistic future *mission statement* that states your organization's desired unique purpose.
Challenge #3: Developing your *core values* that collectively make up your organization's culture: "What we believe in."
Challenge #4: Identifying the desired *positioning* or future driving forces and the *rallying cry.*

These four challenges will be addressed in the following sections.

CHALLENGE #1: SHAPING YOUR ORGANIZATION'S VISION STATEMENT

- This should be idealistic, something you want your organization to aspire to — your vision of what the future looks like at time "X."
- Even if they're not fully attainable, your vision should include dreamlike qualities, future hopes.
- Develop an energizing, positive, and inspiring statement of where and what you want to be in the future.

Example: The Man on the Moon Vision: "I believe that this nation should commit itself to achieving the goal, before the decade is out, of landing a man on the moon and returning him safely to earth." — *President John F. Kennedy, May 25, 1961.*

The first challenge is developing your Ideal Future Vision (like Kennedy's) via a "visioning" process. This is probably one of the most complex components of the four. After all, you're asking your collective leadership to consciously step outside their familiar boundaries that exist in your day-to-day operations, and create new, previously unexplored scenarios just as President Kennedy did. It can be an intimidating process. Done correctly, however, it can become immensely rewarding.

Tip: Introducing the "Nine Dots Exercise" is an ideal, hands-on way to initiate group participation. You're probably already familiar with the problem of the Nine Dots, shown in Figure 7.1. It is an excellent example of the limits most of us place on our own abilities to imagine beyond that which we already know. Once you've been shown the answer — which is that there is no rule that says you can't go outside of the dots to complete the puzzle — it seems ridiculously obvious, yet all of us are usually so good at conforming to everyday rules and boundaries (i.e., paradigms), that we've almost forgotten how to "get outside the nine dots" to solve problems.

Instructions: Connect the nine dots in any way you can with the only instructions being – use four straight lines, connected beginning to end.

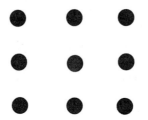

FIGURE 7.1   The Nine Dots exercise is an ideal method to use for initiating group participation.

To help you get "outside the Nine Dots," you will usually need to conduct an environmental scan to fully open up the unknown possibilities the future may present. By scanning the environment (Chapter 6) to see what is and will potentially be happening in your future, you'll avoid working in a vacuum. Most importantly, you'll have thought it through carefully enough to know whether you're actually creating an Ideal Future Vision, or merely hallucinating.

Once you conduct unfreezing activities such as the 9 dots and an environmental scanning process, then creating your Vision Statement (Challenge #1) involves these activities:

ACTIVITY #1: *LIST CURRENT BOUNDARIES OR PARADIGMS THAT EXIST IN YOUR ORGANIZATION*

It is important at this time to list current boundaries or paradigms. Doing this helps you identify the limitations that exist in your current thinking. Remember, perfectionism and boundaries can severely restrict your ability to create your Ideal Future Vision. When you brainstorm your ideal future (Challenge #1), you don't want to be limited creatively.

Some organizational boundaries to use as guidelines might include the following:

- Specifics at a future year, decade, etc.
- Your markets, customers
- Your values, culture
- Your core competencies and capabilities
- Your driving forces, distinctive characteristics
- Your geographic area
- Your history, environment, competitors, industry
- Your governance (public, private, shareholders, not-for-profit, etc.)
- The ideal you want

- Answering the "why" of your existence; doing what you do; societal needs (i.e., societal good/service to others)
- Your level of leadership, excellence, service, quality, etc.
- What you are known for, your reputation, image

Envision what your Ideal Future Vision would be like without these limiting boundaries. Also, focus on your key visionary desires and concepts, not on the exact wording just yet.

ACTIVITY #2: LIST IDEAS AND BRAINSTORM FOR YOUR IDEAL FUTURE VISION

Get all participants started in private brainstorming sessions. Encourage brainstorming participants to be creative, be innovative and limitless, and go for their ideals. Come back into a group session, with each participant putting up their lists for the group to address and compare.

At this point in the visioning process, you should begin developing consensus by getting a sense of the key areas in your visions. The partial list below is an example of an initial brainstorming document that Giant Industries, a medium-sized oil company, developed during its visioning process.

Giant Industries'
Vision Brainstorming List

Our Vision [Includes]:

1. Highest quality customer service
2. Using strategies to lead and guide our [organization]
3. [Creating] an integrated energy company that consistently leads our industry group relative to total stockholder return
4. Flexible and opportunistic in substantially increasing our supply and refinery capacity
5. Engage in related businesses
6. Good corporate citizen[ship]
7. Maintain a secure raw materials supply

ACTIVITY #3: CREATE A VISUAL PICTURE OF YOUR NEW PARADIGM AT YEAR X

Participants should now create symbols or illustrations for the new vision. Have them draw a visual picture of your new paradigm for Year X. This will aid greatly in establishing a crystal-clear image in each participant's mind of exactly what your new Ideal Future Vision looks like.

Lastly, when you've reached final consensus and checked for pitfalls, another subgroup of two to four people should then write a first-draft Final Vision Statement based on this consensus. After this draft has been formally reported to the total group and refined, use the Parallel Process to check it, then redo it one last time.

Example: After completing these activities, Eagle Creek, Inc. came up with the following:

Eagle Creek Vision

Our vision statement describes where and what we want to be in the year 2005. Theses are the future hopes and aspirations of Eagle Creek, Inc.

- Eagle Creek is the world leader in providing function-first, high quality, innovative travel gear with the spirit of adventure.
- We are driven by our total commitment to our core consumers and dealers within our globally responsible value system.
- We have a strategic management system directing aggressive marketing, sales, distribution, production and product development actions.
- We are continuously improving our dynamic learning and empowering work environment to increase growth, profitability, and employee ownership.

CHALLENGE #2: DEVELOPING A REALISTIC FUTURE MISSION STATEMENT

- The mission statement states what business you want to be in, vs. the activities you do today.
- It also states why your organization should continue to exist — its reason for being.
- Your mission statement concerns itself with the *content* of your business — what you produce, its benefits, and who you serve.

Sounds simple, right? But, in actual practice, mission statements often prove to be an elusive concept. Most organizations today have them, they just don't often have the "meat" of specifics to drive behaviors.

Most organizations need to define their philosophy more explicitly and clearly. The statements we see generally have no clear focus. Secondly, most statements are written in such vague language that they have little meaning.

Instead, you can begin developing a high-quality mission statement with the introduction of the Mission Development Triangle in Figure 7.2.

Have each person begin the exercise by answering — individually — the first three questions:

1. *Why* do we exist?
2. *Who* do we serve?
3. *What* do we produce as outcomes?

Once they've completed this on a individual basis, form the participants into three subgroups and have each subgroup develop a visual answer on a flip chart to the

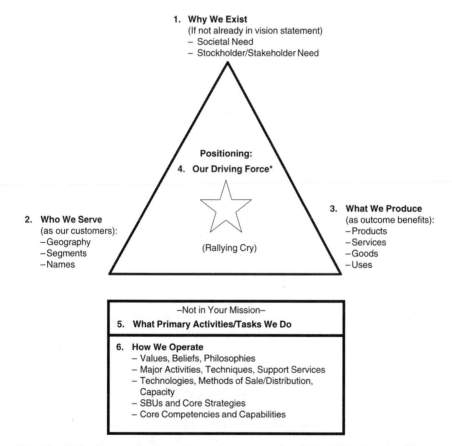

*Note: Your Driving Force can be either a who, a what, a why, or a how (1-2-3-5-6), but it must position you in the marketplace differently from your competitors.

FIGURE 7.2   Mission Development Triangle exercise. Adapted from P. Below, G. Morrisey, B. Acomb, *Executive Guide to Strategic Planning*, 1978; S. Haines, *Internal Sun Co., Inc. Working Paper*, 1979; and J.W. Pfeiffer, L.D. Goodstein, and T.M. Nolan, *Applied Strategic Planning: A How To Do It Guide*, Pfeiffer & Co., San Diego, CA, 1986.

same three questions. (Though at times the participants may feel these questions are repetitive, it's important that they go through the process of answering them — both individually and as a group — in order to come up with a true, synthesized list.)

Next, select one person from each subgroup to work with the facilitator in synthesizing the three charts into one. Take care not to eliminate any answer; filtering and closure will come later. Following this, the entire group should analyze each question from the synthesized list. Tests to ensure clarity and closure should include the following:

1. Does each *who* relate to a *what*, and vice versa?
2. Looking at the *why*, ask what will be better as a result of your existence as an organization? Does it tie to the vision statement?
3. Are the *whats* the outputs of your activities, as opposed to being the activities themselves?
4. What risk is being taken by this future mission; is anything changing?

Gain agreement on the exact words for each *who, what,* and *why.* Or, if you are following a Parallel Process, get general agreement on wording. Then assign a subgroup of three people to write a first-draft mission statement and bring it back to the group for final review, discussion, agreement, and closure. Considerations should include the following:

1. Is it brief, concise, and understandable?
2. Is it broad and continuing, but not so broad as to be meaningless?
3. Is it stated in results (output terms) vs. activities (inputs/throughputs)?
4. How does it fit with our old mission document?
5. Is it future-oriented?
6. Will it drive behavior in the organization?
7. What will be different in the future as a result of this mission?

Example: This mission statement, created by the highly successful Poway (California) Unified School District, reflects a forward-looking shift from the traditional educational paradigm of "teaching" to that of "learning":

We Believe All Students Can Learn

Our mission is to ensure that each student will master the knowledge and develop the skills and attitudes essential for success in school and society.

Another good example of a mission statement is that of BC Building Corp. in Victoria, British Columbia:

BC Buildings Corporation
Mission Statement

We are a Crown Corporation with a community presence throughout BC. Our mission is to support effective service delivery of government ministries, agencies of the Crown and other publicly funded organizations by:

- Efficiently planning, providing and managing accommodation and real estate solutions.
- Providing responsible stewardship of the assets and resources entrusted to us.
- Contributing to the sustainability of communities and our environment.

Our mission is achieved by our motivated, highly skilled, and dedicated team of employees.

When mission statements are fully developed, committed to, and implemented, organizations will truly see the "butterfly effect" take place, in which minuscule differences in the beginning abruptly become massive differences in the results. By shaping a succinct, clear mission statement, it will be much easier for your organization to stay on its self-directed track, constantly checking: *Is our mission teaching or learning? Railroads or transportation? Selling computers or information handling systems? Traveling in cyberspace?* You get the picture.

FIVE MISTAKES WITH MISSION STATEMENTS

Regardless of whether an organization is large or small, privately or publicly owned, or public or private sector, the mistakes I see over and over again fall into the following five areas.

Mistake #1: Mistaking the "How" As Being Part of the Mission

This is a big one; *most* people mistake the "how to" as belonging with the mission. Yes, *how* your business operates — its values, techniques, technologies, capabilities and strategies — is important enough to merit consideration in almost everything you do. In fact, you'll note it's included (#4), along with your organizational driving force/positioning (#5), in the earlier Mission Development Triangle.

It's important not to confuse means and ends, processes and outputs. A current example of this problem is the Malcolm Baldrige Award, which has been criticized for focusing exclusively on process, causing some award winners in the past to lose focus on their customers and their profits. Also, Deming's 14 Points — while significant — don't even mention the customer, resulting in further confusing management and TQM experts.

Mistake #2: Failing to Specifically Identify Your Customer

While most people mistake the "how to" as belonging in their mission statements, they also fail to dissect the who/what/why of their business — which is what the mission statement is all about. Only by dissecting the who/what/why of your organization will you end up with a true, workable mission statement that can serve you through transition and growth.

In particular, most mission statements fail to clearly define "who" the customer is. Instead, they merely refer, generically, to "the customer." Look closely at your mission statement; nine out of ten times, if it fails to clearly identify the customer, you are most definitely *not* customer-focused, no matter what you believe.

Mistake #3: The Control vs. Service Dilemma in Staff Departments

Staff departments usually find that they face serious issues when developing mission statements. The finance or human resources department of an organization, for example, can find the contrast between *control* and *service* issues confusing. The staff department's primary job may be controlling the organization's finances for the CEO, but they still need to fulfill the role of a service department to the rest of the organization as well.

Too often in these instances, the staff department will develop a mission statement based on organization-wide control issues only, while ignoring the service side of their role. We've all seen or been in organizations where the organization's policy manual is more comprehensive than any other document the organization creates; this is the result of basing the organizational mission primarily on control issues.

Keep in mind, also, that there is a difference between "serving" other departments in your organization and being subservient to them. *All* departments are important; each one just has different roles/missions. The single most important job of every organizational department is to identify and serve the customer — or to serve someone else who is serving the customer directly.

Mistake #4: Failing to Properly Define Your "Entity" in the Public Sector

Because its own defined entity and purpose is part of a larger continuum, the public sector often experiences difficulty in developing mission statements. It's often confusing to determine where their organizational entity ends and the rest of the industry or public responsibility begins. As indicated in Figure 7.3, this confusion can often result in poor direction and focus.

Thus, some of the public sector's most common mistakes in clarifying their mission include:

1. Confusing means and ends, or activities vs. results. This is very similar to the failure to eliminate the "how to" from the mission statement, and concentrate only on outcomes.

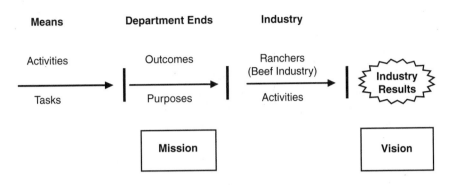

FIGURE 7.3   Public sector mission problems.

2. Trying to "do it all" themselves in a mission that is outside their roles and responsibilities (i.e., "do-gooders" vs. self-help missionaries). This assumes the public they serve is incapable of taking responsibility for itself, and instead are dependent on the government.
3. Failing to clarify, focus on, or even care about the customer they are supposed to serve. This often translates into a government organization seeing its real day-to-day mission as "serving upward" to politicians only.
4. Failing to distinguish between the business products and services that they provide and the staff support areas that will be necessary to support them. This is a result of not knowing "what business we're in" — or denial that you are even in a "business" at all.

Example: It is perfectly acceptable, for instance, for the San Diego Department of Health to create a rather broad vision statement, such as having "a high standard of health throughout San Diego County." In its mission statement, however, it needs to be much more specific, concerning itself with defining its particular role in achieving this countywide health standard vision.

Mistake #5: "Going through the Motions" Only

I'd like to insert a strong word of caution here. As in the strategic planning process itself, it's terribly easy to just "go through the motions," ending up with slick vision and mission statements that sound great, but say little and mean even less. Many people view these statements as the easy part of strategic planning, with the real work coming later, in strategy development. Therefore, they are tempted to just string nice-sounding words and phrases together for the sake of getting the task behind them. They see vision and mission statements as ends in and of themselves, not as the beginning of an ongoing strategic management (i.e., strategic planning and strategic change) process.

Also, vision and mission statements issued by top management all too frequently bear little relation to the day-to-day realities of an organization. As in Intel's CEO once said, "You look at corporate strategy statements, and a lot of them are such pap. You know how they go: 'We're going to be world-class this, and a leader in that, and we're going to keep all our customers smiling.'" Yet, nothing really changes.

As you develop your organization's vision and mission statements, beware of these traps. The truth is, your vision and mission statements are crucial components of your strategic planning process; in fact, they literally become the fundamental destination that guides you through every step of the planning and implementation process. For this reason, your vision and mission statements deserve your utmost attention and respect: after all, the more time and creative energy you invest at this stage, the easier your work will go down the line as you continue the rest of your strategic planning.

CUSTOMER-FOCUSED, HIGH-PERFORMANCE LEARNING ORGANIZATIONS

At the risk of being redundant, I think it's important to bring up the customer focus issue again here. Every organization should ask, and be able to answer, these three critical questions:

1. Who are our real customers?
2. What do they really want (including those things they don't even know about yet)?
3. How do we give them "value added" in whatever they want?

When analyzing who your real customers are, pay careful attention to the question of "internal" vs. "external" customers. There *is* a difference. When all is said and done, of course, your only real customer will always be the external customer who buys your product or service. However, you may exist to serve someone else internally in the organization, but external to your department. In the final analysis, it should always come down, again, to this: "My job is to serve the customer or to serve someone who does."

Don't lose this customer focus — it's altogether too easy to do so: Our purpose — customer satisfaction — the reason for being in business, often gets lost in the shuffle of corporate initiatives (i.e., Value-Chain Analysis, Enterprise Resource Planning, etc.).

From a synergistic point of view, your customers will increase if their needs are met; conversely, they will decrease when their needs are not met. Therefore, all of your organizational operations, processes, and procedures must be geared toward accommodating customer needs. And, as those needs change, you must continually anticipate the changes, and introduce and improve on new products, services, and systems.

Example: At Kalmbach Feeds, Inc., in Upper Sandusky, Ohio, they really care about their customer. Their mission details include the following:

Customer:

We are committed to doing whatever is necessary to assist our customers in achieving their goals by providing customized, innovative, and responsive products and services of the highest quality and value. We will go the extra mile and do whatever it takes to satisfy livestock and poultry producers.

In my experience, it is rare to find a high-performance organization in existence over the long term that doesn't make customer satisfaction its number one priority. Therefore, it's a pretty safe bet that if you want to be a high-performance organization, you will have to be clearly, emphatically, and totally customer-focused throughout every level and aspect of your business.

QUESTIONS TO PONDER

- Have you developed a vision statement that gets outside the "Nine Dots" and expresses your ideal future as an organization?
- Have you developed a mission statement that dissects the who/what/why of your organization?
- Do your future vision and mission statements only bear close relation to the day-to-day realities of your organization — or is it future-oriented to your ideal?
- As your collective leadership develops your vision and mission statements, has it continuously kept your customer clearly in focus?

CHALLENGE #3: DEVELOPING YOUR CORE VALUES

A leader's role is to manage the values of the organization; a leader's role is to harness the social forces in the organization, to shape, and to guide values.
-Chester Barnard, Past President, New Jersey Bell Telephone

- Core values are the principles that guide your daily organizational behavior.
- They specify *how* you should act while accomplishing your mission; your way — or *process* — of doing business.

- Your organization's core values must state not only how you will act at work, but also what you believe in.

In addition to customer focus, high-performance learning organizations invest heavily in defining and implementing their core values. The formation and observance of core organizational values has many productive outcomes. High-performance organizations use their core values as a stability factor for employees. When employees share organizational values, they feel more committed and loyal, identify more strongly with important organizational issues, and display a willingness to "get the job done."

Core values can contribute insight and direction when your organization is faced with unpleasant choices. In addition, they can serve as a rudder in tough times, helping your organization to pursue the high road of ethical conduct, respect, and dignity for the individual. Increased employee motivation, effort, and clarity of focus also serve to develop a competitive edge for your organization. Perhaps most significant, strong core values will be invaluable in guiding the 10,000 or more small decisions employees make daily.

As you develop your organization's core values, keep in mind that they must meet the following six criteria to be a core value:

1. Is it a collective belief organization-wide — simple and clear?
2. Does it determine the standards of acceptable work behaviors?
3. Will people know and care if this isn't followed?
4. Is it a value that will endure consistently over time?
5. Are there myths, rituals, or other well-known organizational stories to support its existence?
6. Is it crystallized and driven by the top management level?

Because their very nature requires them to be of key importance, core values are usually few in number. Some typical core values I consistently see in my work, as embraced by today's high-performance organizations, include:

- Quality/service/responsive/speed (customer-focused)
- Creativity/innovation/flexibility
- Wise, focused use of resources
- Energizing, motivating, and positive leadership
- Teamwork and collaboration
- Empowerment/accountability
- Mutual respect/recognition/honesty/dignity

Example: A great example of core values that benefit today's high-performance organization is the following list from Wal-Mart, put out under founder Sam Walton's mantra "A bias for action":

Wal-Mart Principles

- Managers are servants.
- The customer is the boss.
- Employees and suppliers are partners.
- Costs must be driven down to keep prices low.

In developing your own core values, your core planning team should individually complete the exercise in Figure 7.4. Once they have finished, they should then discuss, analyze, and evaluate each other's lists of values.

After this discussion, the team should develop a first draft of your core values statement, bulleting simple, clear phrases that have been arrived at by consensus. Keep in mind that you'll be troubleshooting it, so it needn't be perfect yet. Also at this time, your key stakeholders should be involved in a Parallel Process to give you feedback on whether anything is fundamentally wrong with the core values draft, whether anything should be added or deleted, and what the gaps are between your ideal core values and today's reality.

Option: Some organizations opt to conduct a personal values exercise first (Figure 7.5), since in reality organizational values are just the result of the values of management.

Once this has been done, the draft should be revised, and further analysis should be made. This analysis involves the following values audit, which enables the team to evaluate (1) which values are being followed most closely, (2) and least closely, (3) how to correct any imbalances, (4) if specific training is needed, (5) what (if any) policies need to change, and so on.

Tip: Why do an analysis of core values now? Employees at this point are often impatient to witness instant behavior changes in management; they want to see them "walk the talk." However, it usually takes 12 to 18 months to change behavior.

For this reason, once you have a completed values statement, there should be an assessment of the current status and uses of the values right away (Figure 7.6). While it should permeate all organizational activities, communicating the core values throughout the company — unless you're prepared to put them visibly into practice immediately — can be a sure way for senior executives to "shoot themselves in the foot."

With your core values firmly in place throughout your organization, there's one more element to consider: the implications of your organization's culture.

ORGANIZATIONAL CULTURE IMPLICATIONS

While core values are guides to organization-wide behavior, the collective behaviors in your organization make up its culture. Though "the way we do business around

Complete Column #1 (The Way It Should Be): Select 10 of the following values that have the most importance to your organization's future success.

Complete Column #2 (The Way It Is Now) at a later time (or as directed).

Column #1 The Way You Think it Should Be Ideally	Column #2 The Way It is Now (Can Also be Ideal)		
_____	_____	1.	Adaptation to Change
_____	_____	2.	Long-Term Strategic Perspective/Direction
_____	_____	3.	Energizing/Visionary Leadership
_____	_____	4.	Risk Taking
_____	_____	5.	Innovation/Creativity
_____	_____	6.	Marketplace Aggressiveness/Competitiveness
_____	_____	7.	Teamwork/Collaboration
_____	_____	8.	Individual/Team/Organization Learning
_____	_____	9.	Recognition of Achievements
_____	_____	10.	Waste Elimination/Wise Use of Resources
_____	_____	11.	Profitability/Cost Conscious
_____	_____	12.	Quality Products/Services
_____	_____	13.	Customer Service Excellence/Focus
_____	_____	14.	Speed/Responsiveness
_____	_____	15.	Continuous/Process Improvement
_____	_____	16.	Growth/Size of Organization/Revenue
_____	_____	17.	Contribution to Society/Community
_____	_____	18.	Safety
_____	_____	19.	Stability/Security
_____	_____	20.	Ethical and Legal Behavior
_____	_____	21.	High Staff Productivity/Performance
_____	_____	22.	Employee Development/Growth/Self-Mastery
_____	_____	23.	Dialogue/Openness and Trust
_____	_____	24.	Constructive Confrontation/Problem Solving
_____	_____	25.	Respect/Caring for Individuals/Relationships
_____	_____	26.	Quality of Work Life/Morale
_____	_____	27.	High Staff Satisfaction
_____	_____	28.	Employee Self-Initiative/Empowerment
_____	_____	29.	Participative Management/Decision Making
_____	_____	30.	Data-Based Decisions
_____	_____	31.	Diversity and Equality of Opportunity
_____	_____	32.	Partnerships/Alliances
_____	_____	33.	Excellence in All We Do

FIGURE 7.4 Organizational Values exercise — guides to behavior. Adapted from S. Haines, *Internal Sun Co., Inc. Working Paper,* 1979; J.W. Pfeiffer, L.D. Goodstein, and T.M. Nolan, *Applied Strategic Planning: A How To Do It Guide,* Pfeiffer & Co., San Diego, CA, 1986; and T. Rusk, *Ethical Persuasion Working Paper,* 1989.

here" seems a simplistic way to define culture, Figure 7.7 clearly shows how appropriate this definition really is.

This is an important element to pay attention to; a healthy organizational culture can go a long way toward supporting your organization's vision and mission statements. The old admonition, "do as I say, not as I do," however, no longer works in today's high-performance organization; the ill will generated by this approach can seriously impede the achievement of your vision and mission.

Because today's revolutionary change is causing organizations to change the way *they* do business themselves, organizational culture isn't something you can afford to ignore or treat lightly. Thus, one of your key strategies will be to create

Please rank order these from 1 to 15 with 1 being the most important to you personally
and 15 being the least important to you personally.

		Actual	**Desired**
1.	Having good relationships with colleagues	☐	☐
2.	Professional reputation/respect	☐	☐
3.	Achievement of organization/unit goals	☐	☐
4.	Teamwork and collaboration	☐	☐
5.	Leisure time for enjoyment/fun	☐	☐
6.	Wealth and prosperity	☐	☐
7.	Fitness and health	☐	☐
8.	Contribution/service to society/community	☐	☐
9.	Acknowledging/recognizing other's achievements	☐	☐
10.	Autonomy/freedom to act	☐	☐
11.	Personal growth	☐	☐
12.	Time with family/close friends	☐	☐
13.	Ethical behaviors	☐	☐
14.	Excitement and challenge	☐	☐
15.	Spiritual/religious time	☐	☐

FIGURE 7.5   Personal Values exercise. Adapted from S. Haines, *Internal Sun Co., Inc. Working Paper*, 1979; J.W. Pfeiffer, L.D. Goodstein, and T.M. Nolan, *Applied Strategic Planning: A How To Do It Guide*, Pfeiffer & Co., San Diego, CA, 1986; and T. Rusk, *Ethical Persuasion Working Paper*, 1989.

one desired culture throughout your entire organization. You will probably need a specific project resulting from your strategic plan in order to accomplish this. Your option will be to either begin it now or wait until you have completed strategic planning and then begin. Decide which makes the best sense for your organization, then develop the appropriate strategies and an action plan to implement it.

Tip: While it may be tempting to skirt around this issue, don't! While your organization's culture will definitely affect its core strategies, the reverse is equally true. In my observations, whenever strategy and culture collide, culture *always* wins out — *therefore, ignoring it will undo a lot of hard work.*

Whenever you decide to get started on your culture change strategies, you will need to begin by analyzing how many different subculture levels presently exist in your organization. Typically, organizations tend to have different subcultures at

Uses: Throughout the Entire Organization

The following are typical categories where Core Values should appear and be reinforced within an organization. Where else should they appear and be reinforced?

1. **Strategy**
   - Explicit corporate philosophy/values statement-visuals on walls; in rooms

2. **Operational Tasks**
   - Corporate and product advertising
   - New customers and suppliers vs. current customer and supplier treatment and focus
   - Operational tasks of quality and service

3. **Leadership**
   - Flow of orientation and assimilation
   - Job aids/descriptions
   - New executive start-up
   - To whom and how promotions occur (values consequence assessed); criteria
   - Executive leadership (walk the talk); ethical decisions; how we manage

4. **Resources/Technology/Communications**
   - Internal communication (vehicles/pubs)
   - Press releases, external pubs
   - Image nationwide (as seen by others)
   - Resource allocation decisions

5. **Structure**
   - Dealing with difficult times/issues (i.e., layoffs, reorganizations)
   - Organization and job design questions

6. **Processes**
   - Recruiting handbook; selection criteria
   - How applicants are treated (vs. values)
   - How rewards for performance operates, especially non-financial rewards
   - Role of training; training programs
   - Performance evaluation; appraisal forms (assess values adherence); team rewards
   - Policies and procedures (HR, finance, administrative, etc.); day-to-day decisions

7. **Teams**
   - Cross-dprtmnl. events, flows, task forces

8. **Macro**
   - Managing change (according to values)
   - Stakeholder relationships (vs. values)

9. **Feedback**
   - This analysis
   - Employee Survey
   - 360° Feedback

Quick Core Values Assessment and Why?

Best 2 - 3	1 - 2 Most in Need of Improvement
1.	1.
2.	
	2.
3.	

FIGURE 7.6   Core Values assessment and uses.

different levels throughout the organization, and they can frequently be at odds with each other. Common subculture levels could include (1) top executive, (2) upper management, (3) middle management, and (4) workers.

There are other kinds of subcultures that are often adversarial to one another, including field vs. headquarters departments, line vs. staff, or the manufacturing subculture and the marketing department subculture, and so on.

In addition, there are three key transformational change levers (Figure 7.8) to affect cultural change.

Organizational culture is a set of interrelated beliefs or norms shared by most of the employees of an organization about how one should behave at work and what activities are more important than others.

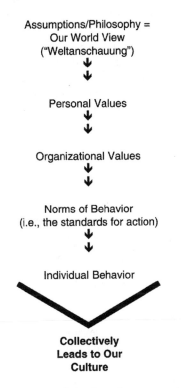

FIGURE 7.7   Organizational culture defined — the way we do business around here.

What Revolutionaries Take Over		What People in Organizations Want	
In addition to controlling the treasury They control:	– or –	**Financial rewards**	
1	Media	1	Communications Recognition Programs Stump Speeches
2	Schools (Education)	2	Learning and growth Training/Values Leadership Development
3	Police/Military (Controls)	3	Freedom to act/Accountability Rewards/punishment/pay Empowerment/policies (Strategic Management System)

FIGURE 7.8   Transformational change levers.

In Summary

Establishing or changing an organizational culture takes persistence and patience over the long haul. It's difficult, but it can be done. You'll need an organizational leader with an almost fanatical adherence to your core values, and one who never deviates during times of trouble.

Examples of entrepreneurs who have successfully created a strong culture that is resistant to change include Ray Kroc (McDonald's), J. W. Marriott, Sr., Bill McGowan (MCI), Izzy Cohen (Giant Food), and Walt Disney. They are all leaders who weren't afraid to change their own behavior first, thus lending credibility and believability to the importance of cultural change.

Remember, you can change your mission, you can change your strategies, and you can change your structure — but if you don't change your culture, it will only serve to defeat all the other changes you desire. Thus one example of a multiyear cultural change effort may be as follows.

Multiyear Cultural Change Effort — "Drip-Drip" Joint Developmental Experiences

Concept: Take the entire Senior Management Collective Leadership Team (up to 30 to 40 people max) through an intense 2 to 5-day training and development experience 1 to 2 times per year.

Goal: Use it to focus the attention, develop an action plan, and kick off to the entire organization your approach to one of a number of key topics of cultural change.

Suggested Sequence/Flow: (Put high, medium, and low on your priorities).

I. Initial Topics (in a tailored order)

II. Additional Key Topics in Cultural Change (in no order)

____1. Systems Thinking and Learning

____8. Creating the People Edge

____2. Reinventing Strategic Management

____9. Creating Customer Value

____3. Leading and Mastering Strategic Change

___10. Blowing Out Bureaucracy

____4. Strategic Leadership Development

___11. Organization and Process Redesign

____5. Conflict Management — Ethical Persuasion

___12. Learning and the Learning Organization

____6. Coaching for Commitment

___13. Effective Team Building (Teams Everywhere)

____7. Group Facilitation (and   ___14. Negotiating — Win–Win
Participative Decision Making)
for Leaders

                                      ___15. Train-the-Trainer for Managers

                                      ___16. Personal and Supervisory
Transition Management

                                    ___ 17. Excellence in Customer Service

---

CHALLENGE #4: IDENTIFYING THE DESIRED POSITIONING OR FUTURE DRIVING FORCES AND RALLYING CRY

The rallying cry states the essence of your organization's Ideal Future Vision step.

- This should be a crisp, motivational slogan — eight words or less (such as Ford Corp.'s *"Quality is Job One"* — that is easily remembered by all organizational members.
- Be sure it's a powerful, motivating force for your staff that is inspirational, believable, and repeatable on a daily basis across the organization.

To come up with a rallying cry, you'll need to first define your organization's positioning and/or driving force. This is the key single thrust within your mission statement around which your organization builds everything. It is also called Positioning, Driving Force, Grand Strategy, Competitive Edge/Advantage, Strategic Intent, Image, Reputation, etc. It is the way we differentiate ourselves from the competition in the eyes of the customer. It is sometimes called "the mother of all core strategies" as it defines "how we are driven" as an organization. The rallying cry is a concept

- to which all other functions, directions, decisions, and criteria are subordinated.
- that is usually comprised of the *whos, whats,* or *hows.*
- taken from your mission and values statements (*why* is a given).
- that is your organization's core or distinctive competency which makes it unique from your competition.
- that will sustain as your competitive edge over a period of years.
- that cannot be readily duplicated.
- that is either your current reality, or can become your reality within the period of time for which you are planning.

Your rallying cry that is derived from this positioning should not be treated as an advertising slogan. Instead, it should be used consistently throughout your day-to-day internal operations over the entire length of your strategic plan; you should not change it as you would, say, a slogan for your ad campaign. External use of your rallying cry is optional, and can promote an added-value concept.

Your rallying cry will act as a motivational force to continually remind internal staff of your vision statement. It is meant to be used over the long term, so it should be memorable, believable, and able to be repeated on a daily basis.

Example: Some of the particularly effective rallying cries of other high-performance organizations include the following:

- Disney: *We Create Happiness*
- Ford: *Quality is Job One*
- Canadian Standards Association: *Making Our Mark on the World*
- McDonald's: *Quality, Service, Cleanliness (QSC)*
- Poway Unified School District: *Excellence in Learning ... Our Only Business*

Tip: At first glance, many people view these rallying cries as hokey and unnecessary. I have most often observed this to be the case when the organization fails to clearly connect its rallying cry to its essence — in other words, to what the organization is all about. One effective way to approach this issue is to wait until the end of strategic planning to develop the rallying cry. Then, actively involve members of your organization through an organization-wide contest for the best rallying cry. To do so, you must make them aware of your strategic plan, make sure they understand its precepts, and then ask them to submit their own ideas (this helps not only in creating a sense of ownership organization-wide, but in the actual implementation, as well). Then, have top management publicly announce the winning phrase, and reward all those who submitted entries, as well.

However, first you must develop your "positioning" statement as the core part of your mission statement (or as a separate statement).

POSITIONING FOR YOUR COMPETITIVE ADVANTAGE

Positioning is an elusive concept, actually a Master's Degree level of strategic "thinking." Many organizations and their senior management can't even focus clearly on this concept as they try to be all things to all people.

In fact, positioning is quite the opposite — it involves trade-offs and choices of where to focus and make your reputation.

In researching this topic over a number of years, the Centre found that there are actually five key ways consumers/customers (each of us) look at what we buy. We look for "value," an overused word that is actually a ratio of what I "get" from you to what it "costs" me.

Photomation West of San Diego has its own definition that is quite similar, "the perfect balance of competitive pricing, outstanding service and unsurpassed quality."

We have synthesized research into a *World Class "Star" Results Model* with the five key points or ways to achieve your positioning. (Figure 7.9) As way to understand this further, try and develop what it means to you and your particular organization's positioning using the blank "Star" exercise in Figure 7.10.

$$\text{Perceived Customer Value} = \frac{\text{Outputs}}{\text{Inputs}} = \text{Multiple Outcomes}$$

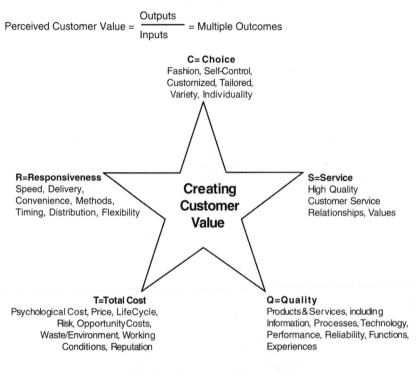

C= Choice
Fashion, Self-Control,
Customized, Tailored,
Variety, Individuality

R=Responsiveness
Speed, Delivery,
Convenience, Methods,
Timing, Distribution, Flexibility

Creating Customer Value

S=Service
High Quality
Customer Service
Relationships, Values

T=Total Cost
Psychological Cost, Price, LifeCycle,
Risk, OpportunityCosts,
Waste/Environment, Working
Conditions, Reputation

Q=Quality
Products & Services, including
Information, Processes, Technology,
Performance, Reliability, Functions,
Experiences

*Anticipating the Customers' Wants and Needs
For Products, Services, and the Intangibles*

FIGURE 7.9   World class "star" results — where's your competitive edge?

The key to positioning is to decide which one of the five points on the star you want to be your distinctive competency in the marketplace in the eyes of the customer vs. the competition. In regard to the other points on the star that the customer wants, you must be at least "competitive" with other choices the customer has. If not, that area of competency can become a competitive disadvantage (as was the case for Jack-in-the-Box after their food quality was in question in the mid-1990s when a few people died). However, trying to be all things to all people doesn't work — you must make trade-offs.

Examples:

- Nordstrom's and Marriott are known for service.
- Eagle Creek, Inc. is known for the *quality* and durability of its products (outdoor luggage, back packs, etc.).

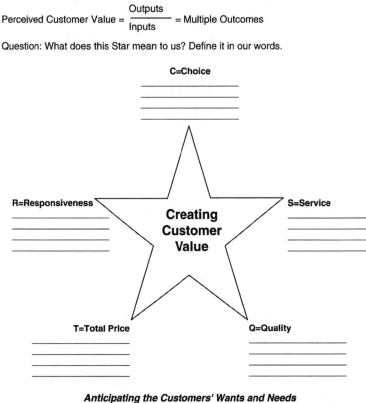

$$\text{Perceived Customer Value} = \frac{\text{Outputs}}{\text{Inputs}} = \text{Multiple Outcomes}$$

Question: What does this Star mean to us? Define it in our words.

C=Choice

R=Responsiveness

S=Service

Creating Customer Value

T=Total Price

Q=Quality

Anticipating the Customers' Wants and Needs
For Products, Services, and the Intangibles
Through The Systems Thinking Approach℠

FIGURE 7.10 Creating customer value — positioning.

- Gateway Computers is known for the *choices* the consumer has in terms of their needs for a computer.
- Wells Fargo Bank has increased its *responsiveness* uniquely in California by putting its branches and ATMs inside grocery stores — adding more convenience, making them safer, and providing longer hours of operation for their customers.

Total Cost Issue

The "cost" point of the star is what you must "give" to get the desired products/services above; hence "total cost" is the denominator in the "Customer Value Ratio." It's "total cost" that is at issue today because it is more than just what you pay for the products/services above. It also includes the negative psychological side to service, your reputation, the product's life cycle, waste, and working conditions, etc. Price is always an issue for us all. However it is not value. Value is the ratio described above.

Since we are discussing customer value, let's make it come alive for you by doing an assessment of your organization's customer value using the worksheet in Figure 7.11. You can use this to examine either (1) the competition or (2) your own customer segments vs. the five points on the Star Model.

Confusion on the Positioning Concept

Finally, some key points on the confusion inherent in this "$64 million dollar question," that is, the most important question each organization must answer and achieve. The confusion arises because executives often

1. Don't know the definitions of "positioning" or "value."
2. Find unclear the definition of the "customer" vs. stakeholders.
3. Find confusing what "exceeding" expectations (Customer Recovery Strategy) means.
4. Don't know what "high quality" stands for. Is it
   - Products/service?
   - Customer service?
   - Experiences?
5. Use the word "value" without understanding what it is. i.e.,

$$\text{Ratio of } \frac{x \ (\text{what we get})}{y \ (\text{what we give})}$$

6. Don't know the five options available to them on the Star Model (Figure 7.9) to achieve their positioning.
7. Find the terms confusing overall. Is there a difference between these terms below?
   - Core competencies
   - Identity
   - Reputation
   - Competitive edge/advantage
   - Strategy
   - Image
   - Perception
   - Positioning
   - Grand strategy
   - Driving force
8. Are unrealistic, wanting to be excellent in all five areas instead of choosing one in which to be distinctive as a trade-off/focus.
9. Don't understand that being competitive with the competition on the other four star points is OK.
10. Forget that lowest cost is not usually "value" in the eyes of the consumer.
11. Don't see "achieving" vs. "sustaining" your positioning as different.
12. Don't even know their own positioning and are highly unrealistic about how their organization compares to the competition.
13. Have no customer information on their positioning.
14. Believe that positioning is the same as "what we do well." Positioning must be what the organization does *better than* or *unique from* the competition in the eyes of the customer.

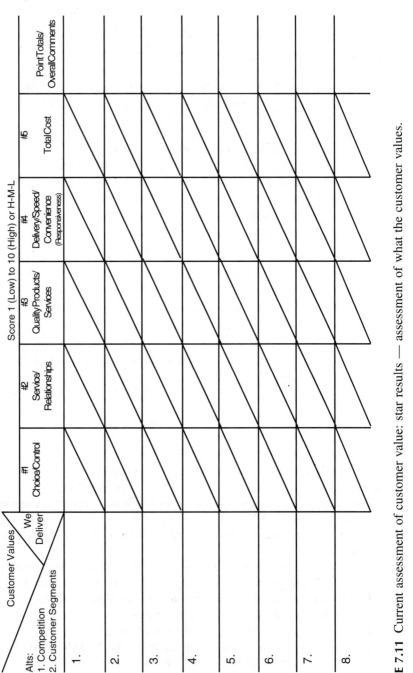

FIGURE 7.11 Current assessment of customer value: star results — assessment of what the customer values.

QUESTIONS TO PONDER

- Have you defined your organization's positioning or driving force, and developed an organization-wide, motivational rallying cry?
- Does your organization's rallying cry extract the essence of your vision, mission, and core values statements?
- Have you developed a set of core organizational values that you can adhere to, organization-wide, through the long-term?
- Have you defined your organization's subcultures, and the number of levels at which they exist?
- Do you have action plans for both creating one's desired culture and achieving your positioning throughout your organization?

IN SUMMARY

To effectively follow the systems thinking of the Reinventing Strategic Management Model, you must begin with a clearly defined Ideal Future Vision. Because its multiple components — vision, mission, core values, positioning, and rallying cry — are all important, shaping this vision will require patience and persistence.

The fact is that all of these components have value, but only as they exist together, as part of an overall, cohesive whole with your positioning as the core. If you do only some of them — or if you do them all, but take them no further — you'll in effect be shaping a temporary, piecemeal solution to a systems problem (and creating a SPOTS event).

RECAP OF KEY CONTENT POINTS

- The Ideal Future Vision step is the first real action step in strategic planning, and one of the recurring key elements for organizational success.
- The first challenge in the Ideal Future Vision step is to shape an organizational vision statement.
- The second challenge is a realistic mission statement that describes your organization's desired, unique purpose.
- The third challenge is the development of core values that make up your organization's culture: "What we believe in."
- The fourth is designing a rallying cry from your definition of your positioning or driving force, which states the essence of your organization.
- It is often better to wait until the end of strategic planning to develop a rallying cry, in order to really clarify the essence of your strategic plan.

- There are five major areas of confusion in developing a mission statement:
  1. Mistaking the "how" as being part of the mission.
  2. Failing to focus on the customer.
  3. Lack of clarity on "control" vs. "service" in departmental mission statements.
  4. Failing to properly define your "entity" in the public sector.
  5. "Going through the motions" only.
- In developing your vision and mission statements, it's critical that you clearly define your customer in specific terms.
- There are a number of major areas of confusion regarding positioning as well:
  1. Its definition.
  2. Its relationship to "value."
  3. Its importance and clarity/the need for trade-offs.
  4. Understanding lowest cost vs. value.
  5. The range of choices you have.
- Every component in the Ideal Future Vision step is important, as part of an overall, cohesive whole with positioning as the core.
- The Ideal Future Vision is necessary, but not sufficient for success. You must go further with the full strategic plan, annual plan, and implementation and change.

"HOW-TO" ACTION CHECKLIST

1. Develop a vision statement that "gets outside the Nine Dots" and expresses your ideal future as an organization.
2. Create a mission statement that clearly identifies the who/what/why of your organization.
3. Make sure your vision and mission statements relate closely to the day-to-day realities of your organization.
4. As you shape your vision and mission statements, be certain that you keep your customer clearly defined and in focus.
5. Develop a set of core organizational values that you can adhere to, organization-wide, through the long-term.
6. Define your current organizational culture and reduce the number of subculture levels throughout the organization.
7. Create an action plan that will enable you to shape a culture that is consistent throughout the organization.
8. Define your organization's positioning or driving force, along with an organization-wide, motivational rallying cry.
9. Make sure your organization's positioning and rallying cry contains the essence of your vision, mission, and values statements.

8 Key Success Measures (Step #3) or Goals

If you've never established quantifiable outcome measures of success for your vision, how will you know you've achieved it?

Reshaping Strategic Management requires a new approach to managing the entire entity or organization as a system. This can only be accomplished if you continually focus on your desired outcomes. By following some surprisingly pragmatic, common-sense steps, you can create the ultimate outcome of a high-performance, customer-focused learning organization.

As we saw in Chapter 7, Step #2 — creating your Ideal Future Vision — puts into words those ideals and beliefs that best represent your organization's desired future vision and values. Combining these ideals with your mission statement and positioning clarifies your Ideal Future Vision.

In order to steer your organization toward the tenets spelled out in your vision, mission, positioning, and values statements, you'll need to create methods for *measuring* them. After all, once you've defined your vision, the only way it can be meaningful, and the only way you'll know if you're reaching it, is through constant, steady measures. It's critical to remember here that any elements that are important — not just those that are easy or expedient — *can and should be measured*. It may take some creativity, but it can and must, be done. That's where Key Success Measures (or Goals) — Phase B of the Strategic Management model — come in.

Measuring is the first step that leads to control and eventually to improvement.
If you can't measure something, you can't understand it.
If you can't understand it, you can't control it.
If you can't control it, you can't improve it.

In the visionary stage of the Strategic Management model, it is necessary to temporarily suspend reality; to be able to look at what your ideal future would be if you had no restraints or restrictions of any kind. Now it's time for getting concrete with your vision through outcome measures of success — known as Key Success Measures/Goals.

The first step in developing your Key Success Measures/Goals is to identify the key phrases from your vision, mission, and values, and then determine methods by which they can be measured. As you begin the process of selecting those phrases that will ultimately serve as your organization's Key Success Measures, always keep

1-57444-278-3/00/$0.00+$.50
© 2000 by CRC Press LLC

in mind that they must represent the results or outcomes of actions the organization can commit to, live with, and be accountable for.

KEY SUCCESS MEASURES/GOALS ARE OUTCOME MEASURES OF SUCCESS

You need Key Success Measures (KSMs) to track your organization's continual improvement toward achieving its Ideal Future Vision. And, by establishing concrete guidelines for measuring organizational progress, they assist in developing a high-performance, customer-focused learning organization. The best KSMs are those that meet all the criteria of the following definition: *Key Success Measures (or Goals) are the quantifiable outcome measurements of an organization's vision, mission, and values on a year-by-year basis, ensuring continual improvement toward achieving your Ideal Future Vision.*

While we believe that "Key Success Measures" is the proper term for this, we have also used the term "Goals," against our better judgment. This is because too many organizations use this "Goals" term now, and we want this book and concept to be understandable to everyone.

Throughout the organizational literature, Key Success Measures go by many names. You'll hear them referred to as objectives, critical success indicators, corporate goals, etc. It doesn't matter what they're called, as long as everyone in your organization has the same clear idea of exactly what they are, i.e.: outcome measures of success.

However, the real value of establishing KSMs for your organization is that you can then use them to determine your successes, your vulnerabilities, and where necessary, appropriate corrective actions you can use to get the organization back on track. Otherwise, you run the very real risk of becoming an unguided missile, with no mechanisms for feedback. If you've chosen measures based on the definition above, you can use your KSMs to answer these questions throughout the implementation of your strategic plan:

1. How do you know if you're successful?
2. How do you know if you're heading for trouble?
3. If you *are* off course (in trouble), what corrective actions do you need to take to get back on track and achieve your Ideal Future Vision?

In order to balance long- and short-run considerations, every organization has a minimum of four key areas that must be measured and tracked in order to create an outcome-based measuring system:

1. Worker performance and attitude/learnings (employee satisfaction).
2. Key operational indicators that represent the leverage points in the organization.
3. Customer satisfaction.
4. Profitability and/or retained earnings (organization's financial viability).

Many of you have undoubtedly heard of "The Balance Scorecard" concept. Its areas of measurement roughly match our four above. Why is this so? It is because organizations are living systems with predictable outcomes: we both see the same thing. To understand how these four interrelate, see the Key Success Factors Circle (Figure 8.1).

In addition to these four factors, my experience and observations in both the public and private sectors have shown me an additional six areas of results that can have significant impact on the organization:

5. Innovative, quality products/services (TQM, etc.).
6. Productivity and efficiency (business reengineering of processes).
7. Physical and financial resources (resource allocation and management).
8. Manager performance and development/succession.
9. Social responsibility.
10. Environmental responsiveness.

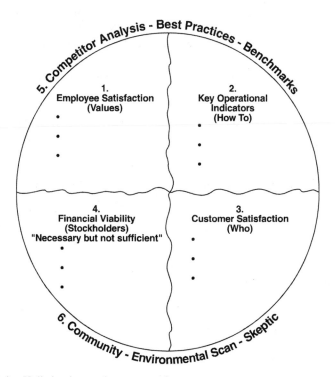

FIGURE 8.1   Holistic view — key success factors.

Some elements, such as organizational finances, are obvious and easy to measure. Though it is important and necessary to measure finances, it will not provide a complete, authentic organizational picture of success. Keep in mind that your vision has more outcomes in it than financial considerations alone. Other areas, such as employee satisfaction and customer service, can be complex and intangible, and require more creativity in devising ways to measure them accurately.

MEASURE WHAT'S IMPORTANT, NOT WHAT'S EASY

It is imperative at this point in strategic planning to take the time to develop these measures. If organizations opt for limiting their measurements to the most easily recognized and concrete areas, they narrow their focus on the organization's overall, desired outcomes. This ultimately limits their ability to "grow" and shape the organization.

We've all seen or experienced organizations that measure progress strictly by budgets and sales forecasts. It's easier to measure the financial side of things than the "people side" of an organization. What invariably happens, however, is that the financial departments then become the driving force of the company, with customers, products, and employees often being a forgotten measure in the organization's success equation.

Remember, it is only through customer satisfaction, innovative product strategies, and employee satisfaction — guided by professional management and leadership practices — that you sustain a competitive business advantage over time.

FINANCIAL VIABILITY IS NECESSARY BUT NOT SUFFICIENT FOR LONG-TERM SUCCESS

A good example of this point is illustrated by Giant Industries, Inc., a regional, integrated energy company located in Scottsdale, AZ. Soon after Giant merged with an exploration and production company and went public, it began to concentrate more and more on the financial end of its corporate activities. The upshot was that its high quality of customer service — which up to that point had been its original positioning and most important Key Success Measure/Goal — lost its focus.

Through strategic planning, Giant has a set of nine KSM areas:

1. Customer service quality
2. Shareholder value
3. Financial strength
4. Responsive/supportive leadership
5. Strategic/opportunistic growth
6. Stable supply of raw materials
7. Employee satisfaction/ethical behavior
8. Quality products
9. Safety   ·

Giant employs these KSMs to encourage continual focus on their overall customer service vision, rather than just on economics alone. The end result, even during the first year of implementation of their plan, has been a dramatic increase in stock price, along with a high level of favorable press.

> *Being financially viable prevents failure. Success is
> defined by how well we serve and keep customers.*

QUESTIONS TO PONDER

- What are your outcome measures of success?
- Do you limit your KSMs to financial measures alone?
- What else should be included?
- What is your terminology for this? Is it helpful or not?
- Is your organization one in which measurements and accountability come easily?

THE FAILURE TO FOCUS ON OUTCOMES

Another consideration to keep in mind as you select your Key Success Measures/Goals is the contrast of "activities and means," vs. "results and outcomes." It is often easy to quantify and measure your various activities and ongoing efforts, such as attendance, number of widgets produced, etc. However, your organizational activities only make sense if they're directly contributing to your desired outcome.

The outcomes are the reasons for your existence, rather than the activities. Too often the activities become ends in and of themselves in bureaucracies of all types, particularly in the public sector. This is why it's significantly more meaningful to stick to measuring results and outcomes.

Example: If you were to take the game of baseball and the San Diego Padres, in particular, 1999 was not a very good year for them as a baseball team. The player moves they made at the end of 1998 after playing in the World Series literally turned them into a bad baseball team.

In fact, what happened is that they failed to focus on their outcomes. For example, the outcomes that a baseball team would typically have would be: (1) to be financially viable, so as to avoid bankruptcy, (2) to win a pennant — or at least compete for it each year, as opposed to being in next to last place, (3) to build and sustain themselves toward this ongoing, desirable future, and (4) to provide entertainment and enjoyment for their fans. These would be typical outcome measures of success the Padres could pursue with a clearer vision of their future.

However, their failure to focus on outcomes has led them to primarily focus on one activity: cutting costs for the next 3 years until their new stadium is built. The predictable result of this focus on a solitary activity — not even on a strategy, such as financial viability — is that they will probably experience a reduction in attendance to around 2 million fans in 2000. In contrast, they drew about 3.5 million in 1998. By not focusing on outcomes, and focusing on only one *activity* (financial cost-cutting), ultimately they are almost guaranteed an outcome of major financial losses by the time their downtown ballpark is built. In the absence of clearly defined ends (i.e., outcomes or targets), we are forced to concentrate on activities and efforts, but we ultimately become enslaved by them.

SIMPLE KEY SUCCESS MEASURES

Though it's simple to explain this concept, it's difficult to do it well. The reason for the difficulty, as I mentioned earlier, is that some of your key vision areas aren't easily measurable. It is important therefore to get creative about translating these vision concepts into specific and quantifiable measures.

It might be helpful at this point to see some examples of strong KSMs, from both the private (see matrix, Figure 8.2) and public (Figure 8.3) sectors.

PRIVATE SECTOR KEY SUCCESS MEASURE (KSM) SAMPLES

1. **Customer satisfaction measures**. High-performance organizations dedicate a great deal of time and effort to determining customer satisfaction on a regular basis. "Regular" can mean quarterly or less, but this must be done a minimum of once a year. The most common first step is to utilize focus groups and conduct initial surveys to gather specific information on customer wants, needs, preferences, and expectations. The next step is to conduct external surveys of the customer base and compare results with data from the focus groups. Another key step would be to regularly benchmark the organization against its top competitors.

2. **Developing a "close to the customer" culture.** Organizations can take customer satisfaction a step further and build an organization-wide, "close to the customer" culture. This entails a series of internal and external survey assessments, continually comparing survey results against the progress within the organization's culture. (See our Key Commandments of a Customer-Focused Organization, in Chapter 2, for more detail.)

3. **Setting up a "Mystery Shopper" program.** Many organizations establish Mystery Shopper programs, as well as Mystery Diners and Mystery Fliers, thus setting up an anonymous program for gathering candid customer feedback.

4. **Employee satisfaction measures.** Most organizations today recognize their employees as a key resource. So many businesses are service-oriented these days, that organizations are beginning to feel that employee satisfaction is directly linked with customer satisfaction. At least once a year, organizations need to survey their employees' perceptions of how closely the organization is tracking its desired core values. Other measurements might include turnover rate, worker compensation costs, safety, etc.

5. **Financial viability measures.** Organizations need to closely track such measures as cash flow, return on investment, return on equity, net income after taxes, percent profitably, earnings per share, and revenue growth

KSM Overall Coordinator for is ___ Bob Brown, MIS Manager ___ (Name/Title)

KSM Areas (Headers) with Specific Factors for Each	Baseline Target 2000	Intermediate Targets 2001	2002	2003	Target 2004	Ultimate Target	Specific KSM Coordinator	KSM Achievement Accountability
1. Employee Satisfaction Factor: Conduct a yearly survey (vs. our Core Values) with a valid sample of our employees (use 10 point scale)	— Develop survey — Conduct it — Revise future targets	6.0/10	7.0/10	8.0/10	8.5/10	10/10	SH	
2. Customer Satisfaction Factors:								
A. Conduct a quarterly survey of a valid sample of our customers	— Determine their wants for quality products/services (Focus Group) — Develop/conduct survey — Revise future targets	7.5/10	8.0/10	9.0/10	9.5/10	10/10	CH	
B. Develop a "close to the customer culture"	— Benchmark vs. top 3 vs. 7 Tracks — Conduct assessment — Develop full program with milestones set	Full re-assessment/refine plan	Full re-assessment/refine plan	— To be determined during baseline (2000) —	Full re-assessment/refine plan	Culture achieved		
C. Set up a successful "Mystery Shopper Program"	— Use customer wants to set up program with evaluation scale; milestones	— To be determined once program set (2000) —				10/10	DM	
3. Financial Viability Factors:								
A. ROE	— Measures all factors	TBD						
B. % Profit (NIAT)		10%/year						
C. EPS	— Revise future targets	TBD						
D. Revenue Growth per Year		15%/year						

Note: These baseline targets must go on Priority Actions List for first year's Annual Planning.

FIGURE 8.2 KSM continuous improvement matrix (backwards thinking) — private sample.

KSM Overall Coordinator for is _____ Mary Smith, Controller _____ (Name/Title)

KSM Areas (Headers) with Specific Factors for Each	Baseline Target 2000	Intermediate Targets 2001	2002	2003	Target 2004	Ultimate Target	Specific KSM Coordinator	KSM Achievement Accountability
1. Teamwork/Partnerships **Factors:**								
A. # of partnerships in existence	0	5	8	10	13	All key areas	SH	
B. Yearly evaluation of their effectiveness vs. their charter (10 pt. scale)	Develop Eval. System & Charter Format	9/10				10/10		
2. Strategic Plan Effectively Implemented (i.e., Strategic Management System) **Factors:**							DM	
A. SCSC meets regularly	1 day/quarter							
B. Yearly comprehensive map developed and followed each year	yes — 100%							
C. All management evaluated in new appraisal form (using strategies and values as tools)—HR Audits	develop appraisal; train mgmt.	100% eval.						
D. Vital Few projects completed successfully	develop plan to phase in all 4 with targets leadership program completed	Organization Restructuring Completed	Quality/Service Completed	BPR Completed	New Game Plan Developed (all 4)	100% of all targets met		
E. Annual Strategic Review conducted —Action Plan developed —SP & Annual Plan updated	N/A	yes	yes	yes	yes			
3. Self-Funding **Factor:**							CH	
A. Percent of budget self-funding	Develop game plan Begin implementation with time tables	20%	40%	60%	90%	100%		
4. Decentralized Site Based Management Concept Functioning Effectively	Develop concept and terminology/evaluation tool Train mgmt. on it Benchmark it vs. top 3 competitors	Yearly independent assessment 33% effective	50% effective	75% effective	95% effective	100% effective	JM	

Note: These baseline targets must go on Priority Actions List for first year's Annual Planning.

FIGURE 8.3   KSM continuous improvement matrix (backwards thinking) — public sample.

each year. These are all the typical measures that Wall Street and the investment community look at to determine stock value.

6. **Customer reality check — the quality gap.** According to a survey conducted by the Quality Research Institute in the mid-1990s (published in *Training* magazine), customers remain disillusioned about so-called improvements in quality. Focusing on the retail, hospitality, and utility industries, the survey tried to discern degrees of success in corporate total-quality campaigns — both in the eye of the corporate executive and the customer.

- In retail, a majority of department store executives indicated a substantial rise in their service quality over the past 12 months — *only 20% of their customers agreed with this.*
- Also in retail, over 60% of discount store executives reported visible improvements in the quality of service — *only 30% of their customers believed the quality of service was improved.*
- Hospitality industry execs reported meeting customer expectations "almost all the time" — *only 40% of their guests agreed.* In all, the guests were much more happy with the quality of the physical facilities than with the service.
- More than 60% of executives in the utilities industry felt that their service quality showed marked improvement over the previous year — *only 9% of their customers could agree.*

These glaring discrepancies make the most compelling argument of all for clear, precise methods to measure outcomes. Only by using such methods as Key Success Measures/Goals can organizations determine how their internal assessments compare with their customers' perceptions. And only the customer's perceptions count — perceptions equal reality to them.

PUBLIC SECTOR KEY SUCCESS MEASURE (KSM) SAMPLES

1. **Self-funding measure.** In the public sector, staying within budget is often the ultimate goal. This is why it's so critical to track and assess what percentage of budget can be self-funded. There are alternative sources for funding available, such as using "in-kind" contributions, donations, and volunteer time and contributions, as well as formal fundraising.

2. **Alliance/partnership measures.** This measure often employs both quantity and quality measurements. Examples of this would be to survey the number of partnerships within or between organizations, and then conduct annual evaluations (most often using 10-point scales) of their effectiveness in light of their charter.

3. **Decentralized, site-based management and community service delivery concepts.** Empowering organizational members is a crucial strategy for success. It is imperative here to continually monitor the organization's balance between granting the rights of empowerment along with the

responsibility to support the organizational directives. Empowering people without clear understanding as to the direction doesn't create empowerment — it only creates chaos. Management training and the right tools/skills are essential here, as is a clear and shared future vision.

KSM Samples for All Organizations (Public or Private)

1. **Successful implementation of a strategic management system.** Every organization needs to develop a way to measure how successfully the strategic plan is being implemented. This can be accomplished through consistent meetings of the Strategic Change Leadership Steering Committee (SCLSC). Another measure would be to develop and track a yearly comprehensive map of implementation steps and outcomes. Also, a performance appraisal process can be developed (using strategies and values as tools) for regular evaluation of management and other employees. Organizations should also determine — on an ongoing basis — whether they are consistently implementing their leverage points for strategic change.

2. **Yearly strategic management systems update.** This is where you develop a follow-up step for your strategic management system. By committing to this critical annual review and update, you are in effect creating an automatic reminder process for regular evaluation of how the system is working. This is the point where you evaluate the success of your organization-wide implementation process. It is also an opportunity to make necessary revisions, both to the organization's strategies and its supporting budget.

It is important to focus on a small number of the most important success areas, so keep your organization's Key Success Measures/Goals at roughly 10 or less. Therefore, a good question to start with would be "is the KSM a key one throughout the organization?" One way to screen your KSMs for clarity and validity is to pose common-sense questions such as these:

- Does it overlap or duplicate any other KSMs?
- Is it a key indicator of your organization's success?
- Is it a tangible KSM that you can easily measure?
- Is it an actual report card, measuring results vs. activities?
- Are you willing to commit to and be accountable for these KSMs, year after year?

The most effective way to determine if your measures of success (KSMs) meet the test is if you are able to measure them by either (1) quality, (2) quantity, (3) time, or (4) cost. These four categories apply to potential KSM areas for any organization.

1. **Measuring quality.** The Navy Public Works Center in San Diego, California, views every other Navy base that it serves as its customer. Periodically, it conducts surveys of all of its customers, measuring the levels of customer satisfaction on a 10-point scale, then coming up with an average percentage of overall satisfaction. The Marriott Corp. requires managers to become "mystery diners" at all of its restaurants, thereby creating feedback on their services from the customer's perspective.

2. **Measuring quantity.** Quantity can be determined in a number of ways, such as internally monitoring the number of items produced with zero product defects. Other quantity KSMs could be the number of products produced within a certain time frame, or a ratio such as in tracking plant safety (number of industrial accidents per quarter, with a target of zero).

3. **Measuring time.** The element of time makes for a terrific KSM and organizational outcome. It forces you to examine and stay on top of the organizational processes involved in providing value to the customer. Federal Express uses its on-time delivery for overnight, 2-day, and 3-day deliveries as well as its 10:30 AM delivery guarantees as a way to be responsive to their customers and provide the value they want/need.

4. **Measuring cost.** Cost is another viable KSM; it is also an obvious one. Organizations can easily monitor budgets, the cost of product development, or staffing costs, to name just a few. It is easy and it can be a valid KSM; again, just remember that using cost as your *only* KSM is not enough.

I can't stress enough how critical KSMs/Goals are to every organization, public or private. It's very distressing to me to see that this skill of writing clear goals and committing to good outcomes is missing from many organizations.

In the private sector, the most common observation I've made is that of continually committing to financial goals alone. When one considers the unfortunate result of using only financial considerations as a measuring stick, it is easy to see why so many organizations experience confusion, ignore people and customer issues, and lack a clear sense of purpose.

The public sector, unfortunately, is even more vulnerable to missing the boat in developing measures of success. Because the public sector rarely focuses on the idea of its customer and other outcome measures of success, public organizations often become slaves to their activities. "Performance metrics" often means measuring "comprehensive activities," not Key Success/Outcome Measures. They often don't even attempt to measure outcomes.

Example: A large school system I worked with in the last few years did a great job in running a Parallel Process to develop ownership and commitment. However, it never reached consensus on a set of Key Success Measures/Goals to follow for its outcome measures of success. As a result of internal problems with the board of education, the superintendent resigned. His replacement lasted little more than a year. What the school system had was a common mission, vision, and values, but no set of clear, agreed-upon goals and measures with universal commitment.

Another example is the state of Oregon. In order to assess various state agencies for budgeting purposes, it has established its own Key Success Measures — their term for it is "Oregon Benchmarks." The state uses these to measure the state's quality of life and economic prosperity in a variety of areas. Unfortunately, it is analytical thinking run amuck, with over 800 total measures at last report!

Always keep in mind, the best KSMs are the ones that can be stated in simple, clear language. While there is no shortcut method for establishing these KSMs, once you've gotten the hang of it, it will save you enormous amounts of time and retraced steps later on in your implementation.

HOW TO DEVELOP KEY SUCCESS MEASURES GOALS

To begin developing the measures of success for your organization, there are two specific tasks that will help you determine the general areas from which you will extract your measurement areas:

1. It is critical at this point to pull out the key words and phrases from your vision, mission, and core values. To shape KSMs that will be recognizable throughout the organization, it's necessary to identify those key phrases that best define your organization's success.
2. It will also be important to agree on specific, key financial and operational success areas.

Once you've crystallized the key words and phrases that constitute success, the planning team must combine the answers for both of these tasks into a consolidated list. At this point, the team completes the development of the organizational KSMs by pruning them to no more than 10 areas to be measured (more than 10 areas makes it difficult to focus, and awkward to coordinate).

QUESTIONS TO PONDER

1. What are the key words and phrases from your vision, mission, core values?
2. What are other key financial/operational success areas?
3. You're aiming for no more than 10 KSMs. Can your planning team prune and combine their answers to the two questions above and come up with a consolidated list?

Now it's nuts-and-bolts time. Once you've established your 10 (or fewer) critical KSM/Goal area "headers" — such as alliances, employee work satisfaction, strategic management system effectiveness, financial success, customer satisfaction, and decentralized, site-based management — the next stage of development lies in defining the specific methods by which you will measure these headers. The alliance header, for example, could be measured by the number of partnerships in existence, and by a yearly evaluation of their effectiveness. The header of customer satisfaction can be measured by quarterly surveys, developing a "close to the customer" culture, or instituting a Mystery Shopper program.

Once you know how you're going to measure your KSM/Goal areas, you need to set definitive target dates for reaching them. If you are strategic planning for the year 2010, for instance, you'll have to establish specific targets for measuring individual KSMs each year up to the final target year of 2010. The most direct way to do this is to contrast your current-year baseline data (i.e., the present status of the individual goal/KSM) against where you want it to be when you hit your target year.

Tip: As I mentioned earlier, it's important that you define and narrow down your organizational KSMs. It will be crucial to conduct an ongoing Parallel Process to create buy-in from all key members of the organization. Once your list has been pruned down to 10 or fewer KSMs, make sure every individual that is affected has an opportunity to learn what each KSM is all about, and understands what is expected of them in achieving it. Always remember that people support what they help to create.

You'll probably have to do some initial research before you can determine the current baseline data on each of your KSMs. You will gain the best results by formally appointing an individual as an overall Key Success Measure/Goal Coordinator. In addition, each individual measure needs its own KSM/Goal Coordinator who will be accountable for the research, measurement, and reporting on it.

Also, it may be that you won't be able to assign a target yet, because the specific measurement (i.e., a customer satisfaction survey) is not yet in place. In this instance, you can create an action plan to develop the survey within the agreed-upon time frame. This will then serve as your initial baseline target year's measure of success.

LAYING IT ALL OUT: THE GOAL MATRIX

Now that we've discussed a range of KSMs that could be applied to both public and private organizations, it's time to review the formal, written framework: the KSM/Goal Continuous Improvement Matrix (see Public and Private Sample Matrices, Figures 8.2 and 8.3). This matrix is the final product in developing your outcome measures of success on a year-to-year basis; showing continuous improvement toward your Ideal Future Vision. It should be used as an organizational report card; it provides the organization with a concrete, visual method for tracking your results.

KSMs should be the primary tools for mapping your organization's progress and success through its strategic plan. By folding them together in this one matrix, the organization establishes an immediate, "at-a-glance" system for measuring overall success. (This matrix also serves as a terrific measuring system for any top management bonus program.)

The overall KSM/Goal Coordinator will keep your matrices up to date, and report progress every 2 to 3 months (at Strategic Change Leadership Steering Committee meetings) on actual vs. target results. Because KSM coordinators are an inherent part of the measuring and reporting process, they need to be individuals who are highly respected throughout the organization, with access to and support from senior management.

As you can see in the figures, the left column of the matrix lists the KSM areas, with their specific measures. The next several columns should list the regular yearly intervals at which your KSMs will be measured against actual performance.

Tip: Many organizations add a final column to the KSM Continuous Improvement Matrix for benchmarking. *Benchmarking* is a method by which the organization contrasts its own continuous improvement against its competition's best practices and measures of success. It is very valuable and informative to know your organization's results compared with your competitors, particularly in the private sector.

Benchmarking vs. the competition may or may not be part of your organization-wide KSMs. At the business unit level of the organization, however, they *are* Key Success Measures, and must be tracked as such. One last comment — be watchful in comparing competitive benchmarks, for it's rare that two firms in the same business sector function in exactly the same fashion.

In addition, it has become popular to set a "BHAG" (or Big Hairy Audacious Goal in the book *Built to Last*) for an organization. One of our clients, Sundt Companies, Inc., a $400 million a year construction firm based in Tucson, AZ, has a 10–100–1 BHAG. By the year 2010, they want $100 million in net worth, with $1 billion in yearly revenues.

KSM/Goal Priority Setting

Now it's time to set priorities. This is actually a two-phase process in which the planning team needs to: (1) place your KSMs in a forced ranking priority order, and (2) eliminate those KSMs that rank consistently at the bottom. Completing this process will help you focus on any remaining weak links, verify that you're measuring what's important (not just what's easy), and establish a natural order of priority.

It is also critical that the planning team specifically defines *how* it will measure success for those measures not already in existence. Be specific as to the length of time you estimate for each KSM. Without a concrete plan that includes dates and accountability, other priorities and crises will invariably demand the time and attention that you need to be spending on developing your organization's measures of success.

As you prepare to fill in the Key Success Measure Matrix that will be your primary tool in measuring the success of your organization's strategic plan, go through a quick mental checklist, answering the questions below.

QUESTIONS TO PONDER

1. Have we clearly identified key words and phrases from our vision/mission/values?
2. Have we developed clear, *quantifiable* measures of success?
3. Have we gotten feedback through a Parallel Process?
4. Have we identified specific measures?
5. Have we conducted troubleshooting on our measures of success?
6. Is there a coordinator for each KSM/Goal to be measured, as well as an overall KSM/Goal Coordinator?
7. Are we willing to use them as bonus measures after the first year for top and middle management?

Tip: For organizations that are not accustomed to measuring success (or making many measurements of anything), a simpler approach is to set specific goals for just the next year at first. Build the full matrix later. Be sure to set simple goals such as

1. Customer Satisfaction
   - First year, develop and implement survey; second year, 10% results improvement
   - No major (Top 10) customers lost
   - Two new major (Top 10) customers acquired
2. Employee Satisfaction
   - First year, develop and implement survey; second year, 10% results improvement
   - Turnover rate down 10%
   - Absenteeism rate down 10%
3. Financial Results
   - Revenues up 10%
   - Profits up 10%
   - Stay within budget
4. Product Development
   - Two new products developed and rolled out to customers
   - Second year, each product had $x in sales
5. Operational Results
   - Gross margin maintained (or up 10%)
   - One to two key leverage points in operations, i.e., zero defects, safety, etc.

IN SUMMARY

Establishing Key Success Measures/Goals is where your organization's vision starts to convert to reality. They are the culmination, on paper, of all your previous work on your organization's vision, mission, and values. As we reinvent Strategic Management for the 21st century, goals provide a unique tool for organizations to travel from high-level "soft" visions to defining outcome goals, then implementing and measuring them.

Using the KSM Continuous Improvement Matrix (Figures 8.2 and 8.3) as a tool, your organization will be able to chart the successful outcomes of its strategic plan. The matrix serves several purposes in your organization. For the executive team, it serves as an organization-wide report card at regular, specific intervals, keeping their attention focused on what's important. It also provides a quick, easy way to communicate updates on organizational progress for all employees. You can use a simple A, B, C, D, F scorecard grade just as schools do, in order to keep it simple (or confidential).

Visually tracking the progress of each KSM/Goal on the matrix acts as a motivator, reminding management and employees of how much they've accomplished. And because it measures outcomes in the key areas of the organization, it also makes an ideal progress report on which to base executive/management bonuses.

One note of importance, however, is to keep in mind that KSMs/Goals are often something new to the organization. It can normally take a year or more to get comfortable with them and understand how to get just the right measurements. Therefore, when new KSMs are established, consider them cast in sand initially, and expect to do some adjusting and tweaking along the way. Also, it would be imprudent at this stage to publicly broadcast them. Don't worry, though, they will begin to feel natural and will turn to concrete down the line.

It is critical to your progress that this matrix is kept up to date, and is continually communicated throughout the organization. As long as everyone is in touch with and comprehends the goals and measuring sticks represented by the organization's Key Success Measures/Goals, they will be better able to remain focused on the right outcomes.

At this point in strategic planning, you now know what your Ideal Future Vision is, and you have developed outcome measures of success — called Key Success Measures or Goals — to reach this vision. It is time to begin working your way back toward this future vision, beginning with today. The Current State Assessment outlined in the next chapter will probably feel like familiar territory. The Current State Assessment step is where that old endangered species — planners — have traditionally concentrated their time and energy: studying about today, versus building toward tomorrow.

RECAP OF KEY CONTENT POINTS

- Be sure to reflect the customer's point of view, both internally and externally.
- Measure all key elements of your Ideal Future Vision.

- Focus on outputs and results — except, possibly, for some crucial benchmarking on key processes/systems.
- Benchmarking vs. the competition may or may not constitute organization-wide KSMs/Goals. However, at the business unit level of the organization, they definitely *are* Key Success Measures/Goals, and should be tracked and evaluated as such.
- Be careful of competitive benchmarks, as rarely do two firms in the same business sector function in exactly the same fashion.
- Be sure to use the Parallel Process for the measures as well; ownership and buy-in are essential.
- Cost/benefits analysis applies to KSM/Goal development also. Use readily available data when at all possible.
- If your vision should change at any point, remember to change your KSMs/Goals accordingly.
- Outcome measures/goals are often something new to an organization; it may take a year or so to get used to working with them and to get just the right measurement. Consider them cast in sand at first; in concrete later. So don't publicly broadcast the exact targets too soon.
- Some measures — like performance improvement — are a long-term process; just tracking and measuring in the first year is a good result. Have patience.
- Tie your executive bonus/incentive pay and rewards to KSMs/Goals beginning in Year 2. This could be a separate project, but it is vitally important to success.
- Since KSMs are outcomes/results, they are often seen as goals or objectives, and the words can sometimes be used interchangeably. Be clear on your terms.

"HOW-TO" ACTION CHECKLIST

1. Determine your KSM areas, based on vision/values/mission and driving force(s). Do it first individually, then in subgroups, then the total group.
2. Set specific KSMs/Goals and measures (targets) for end-of-planning horizon (i.e., the year 2010), baseline year (current year), and even intermediate targets if possible.
3. If you don't have enough time or experience, just do the first year's measures — but do them! Set a deadline.
4. Assign accountability for each KSM/Goal measurement and also an overall Coordinator to collect/report the data.
5. Troubleshoot your measures to ensure they are outputs/results/core values, vs. means to an end. (Means should only be used when ends can't be

measured effectively or the means are absolutely essential/key leverage measures).

6. Define/agree on priorities for the measures (i.e., forced ranking of 10 or less).

7. Eliminate the lowest-priority measures if they are not critical or you have too many (10 is maximum).

8. If you do not currently have the specific measure in place, your target for the first year will be to set it up, and then in Year 2, establish it on an ongoing basis.

9. Set up the reporting format for KSMs/Goals and use it to track ongoing progress of target vs. actual.

10. Establish a measurement to find out whether the plan and the total strategic management system has become a practical reality — just like a yearly independent financial audit.

9 Current State Assessment (Step #4)

Tolerating dissent is an essential means by which societies cope with change.

-Peter C. Newman

ARE YOU WILLING TO TOLERATE HONEST ANSWERS?

Having established a set of quantifiable outcome measures — Key Success Measures/Goals — in the last chapter, you'll be able to successfully track the implementation of your strategic plan outcomes. Next, you must determine how much energy, time, and organizational resources you'll need to get from the input of where you are today to the output of where you want to be by Year X, or achieving your Ideal Future Vision. In order to do this, you'll need absolute, organization-wide clarity on where you are today, i.e., an assessment of your current state.

In earlier strategic planning eras — and even today — the Current State Assessment has been where planners spend most, if not all, of their time. The problem most executives and I have with this is that, once the assessment is complete and the findings written up in a sophisticated, glossy report, not much else happens. Other than telling us where we are today, this type of assessment fails to identify the gaps between today and tomorrow (i.e., our Ideal Future Vision). It also fails to develop specific action plans throughout the organization to close those gaps.

The first and most basic objective of our Current State Assessment (Step #4) is to honestly assess your current organizational performance against your Ideal Future Vision in many different ways.

Be aware when going into a Current State Assessment (CSA) that you must be prepared to accept *all* of its findings, not just the ones you feel good about. This is part of assessing your current state honestly. After all, you won't achieve your Ideal Future Vision unless you rigorously deal with everything that has the potential to block your path.

Once you've identified the gaps between "where we are" and "where we want to be," you need to problem-solve those gaps, and develop overall core strategies with specific actions or tactics for each one in order to close or bridge these gaps over the life of your strategic planning horizon.

Your CSA has two main components: an external assessment and an internal assessment. All of the areas necessary to completing both these assessments are outlined in this chapter. There may be areas unique to your organization, however, that should also be assessed. By following the approaches suggested here, you will

1-57444-278-3/00/$0.00+$.50
© 2000 by CRC Press LLC

be able to complete a Current State Assessment that reflects your particular organizational situation.

BEST PRACTICES RESEARCH

Throughout this chapter, both the internal and external assessments will have a number of minisurveys, designed to provoke thoughts and ideas and point you in the directions needed to conduct a full assessment. Though they're not meant to be all-inclusive, they are "thought-starters" for initiating further discussion and action planning.

These surveys have been systematically translated and interpreted from our research of the best practices of successful organizations and the main theorists and writers in each area. The implication is that today's successful organizations are not only surviving the revolutionary changes of the 1990s: they are also beginning to move into position for the new millennium.

GETTING STARTED

There are a few variables you'll need to decide prior to conducting a Current State Assessment, including:

1. How much time does the organization need to accomplish this?
2. How much expertise do we need or already have among the members of the planning team? The rest of the organization?
3. Has some Current State Assessment work already been done by other members of your organization or elsewhere that you can use?

Example: In working with the health care field in Arizona, I found they had access to a substantial number of published surveys that would pertain to their assessment, but that nobody had ever taken an organized and strategic set of actions on them. Rather than have them start from scratch on their SWOT (Strengths, Weaknesses, Opportunities, Threats), I advised them to incorporate the presentation of these studies, and the actions that had occurred, into this CSA Step #4.

For each area, they used outside experts to dissect and interpret the study, ultimately providing the planning team with an executive summary. They then consolidated the findings from these summaries into an overall, usable SWOT analysis that would lead them into developing strategies with action plans — Step #5.

CONDUCTING AN INTERNAL CURRENT STATE ASSESSMENT

*The systems view of organizations shows clearly that a
paradigm shift in one aspect (or element) of an
organization causes the need for paradigm shifts in
every aspect of that organization.*

Conducting an internal Current State Assessment in your organization will show you what gaps need mending to get from today to tomorrow. It will also enable you to clearly examine your "systems fit" and alignment throughout your organization in support of your Ideal Future Vision. Always remember, you'll need to incorporate a Parallel Process in your internal CSA, Step #4, as well as carefully checking with corresponding levels of your organization (and other stakeholders) for the influences and effects of each change that needs to take place. Another alternative is to have the SWOT completely done by the Parallel Process members.

There are also a number of categories that specifically target critical areas that are universal to any organization's internal CSA, including:

1. Organizational financial analysis
2. Core values analysis
3. Key Success Measures/Goals analysis
4. Strategic business design
5. Value-chain analysis
6. Management/leadership core competencies
7. Strategic human resource management area
8. Reward for total performance
9. Cross-functional teamwork
10. Core competencies
11. Technology assessment

These assessment categories are described in the following sections.

ORGANIZATIONAL FINANCIAL ANALYSIS

This is the most obvious place to begin, and you most likely will already have much of the data at hand. You'll need to look at your profit-and-loss statements and organization-wide budgets, and, to assess the capitalization within your organization, your balance sheets.

Example: As General Motors has clearly shown, getting your "financial house" in order is a vital necessity, but it isn't sufficient for long-term success. For GM, that success must now come through serving their customers with the products and services they need. They have been failing at serving their customers. They have been failing for over 10 years, as their market share has eroded every year from near 50% to around 27% as we write this.

CORE VALUES ANALYSIS

If your organization is one that approaches its core values as "nice, but not necessary," you're missing the boat. Core values, after all, are the main elements that make up your entire organizational culture, and without a unified and motivated culture, turning your organization into a customer-focused, high-performance entity won't happen. (See Chapter 7 for a detailed listing of typical areas where core values should appear and be reinforced within your organization.)

As you assess your core values, have your key stakeholders analyze each value according to your organization's adherence to it. Use your employees to do this. Don't just trust your own perceptions of this.

Example: In today's environment, the value of teamwork has advanced from "nice to have" to a Critical Success Measure. See the book *Built to Last* for a full look at the importance of values in many organizations.

KEY SUCCESS MEASURES/GOALS ANALYSIS

At this point, you should also look for any indications that you may have previously overlooked some immediate, critical items that should still be incorporated into your KSMs. Or, you may find that the ones you've already developed will suffice for measuring your organizational outcomes. However, make a final critique on each KSM vs. your baseline data of that measure.

STRATEGIC BUSINESS DESIGN

Empowered, educated people armed with technology
and information do not require the same organizational
framework that existed 100 years ago.
-James R. Houghton, CEO/Chairman, Corning, Inc.

A growing number of organizations today are analyzing one of the basic measures in their success: the system of jobs and the dynamics of operating relationships that constitutes the strategic business design of the organization. No matter what size your organization is, there are a number of dimensions that exist in all organizations that should support your positioning in the marketplace as detailed in Chapter 7. These include

- Administrative components
- Integration/differentiation
- Professionalization
- Span of control/structures
- Specialization
- People practices
- Delivery channels
- Technology/Internet

- Formalization
- Autonomy
- Centralization/decentralization
- Complexity
- Policies/procedures
- Delegation of authority
- Customer relationships

Traditional, hierarchical organizations are finding that the old motto of "That's just the way we do it around here" isn't working anymore. Today, hierarchical organizations are moving away from the executive/staff/line structure to a more integrative and horizontal (or cross-functional) fit. They're asking questions such as the following:

- How many layers of management should there be? (What is the minimum needed?)

- Where is the demarcation between needed staff and burdensome bureaucracy?
- How do we empower our employees to serve the customer better and to take more self-directed initiatives, rather than waiting to be told?
- How do we manage diverse organizations resulting from mergers, acquisitions, joint ventures, etc.?
- How do we organize geographically remote units, such as sales offices, factories or service centers?
- Can we design structures and processes to meet customers' needs, especially as they relate to speed, responsiveness, and flexibility/choices?
- How can we continually manage the improvement of structures and processes across boundaries?
- How is each job designed? Are we providing our employees with holistic (Plan-Do-Control) jobs?
- Following the concept of "strategic consistency and operational flexibility," what goes where under each function?

Finally, the organizational structure should usually be set up so that as many interdependent, cross-functional, horizontal tasks of the business or program area as possible are grouped together and placed close to the customer for maximum efficiency and effectiveness.

In any case, the old cliché "mission → strategy → structure" still holds true today. Any needed changes in your organizational structure depend on aligning it with your mission, strategies, and especially your positioning in the marketplace.

Example: Jack-in-the-Box has nicely recovered from its near demise as a result of poor quality food that caused the death of some customers. Now their "Jack Is Back" commercials reflect their favorable positioning with single adult males and their big juicy (i.e., high fat content) burgers.

Customer-Focused Structure

Customer-focused organizations organize by customer-focused units for all organizational products and services, using the "Lone Ranger" philosophy: "One customer equals one organizational representative." They organize by customer *markets,* customer *segments,* customer *geography.*

McDonalds, for instance, does it quite naturally by geography. In fact, their latest strategy is to be wherever their customers are — in schools, hotels, shopping malls, office buildings, Wal-Mart stores, airports, ships, etc. — even if the restaurants themselves are much smaller or less expensive than usual (i.e., McDonald's ExPress).

Strategic business design looks at the organization as a system, using our A, B, C, D, E Systems Thinking framework for a holistic view of the organization as it interacts in its environment. We now use it to examine the internal workings of the organization. Our extensively researched model is illustrated in Figure 9.1.

To view this model in greater detail, we have developed strategic business design assessment tools for high-performance organizations shown in Figures 9.2 and 9.3.

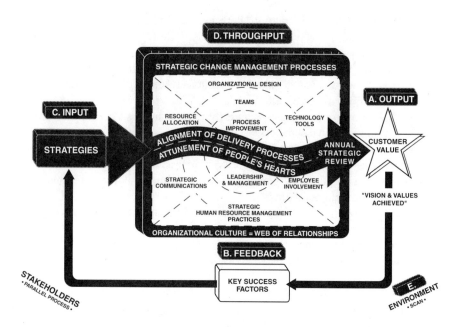

FIGURE 9.1   The organization as a system — creating alignment and attunement for your competitive edge. Courtesy of the Centre for Strategic Management, San Diego, CA, 1997 Revised. With permission.

VALUE-CHAIN ANALYSIS

Value-chain analysis consists of looking at your organizational systems and processes from the point of view of your customers and your vendors/suppliers as well. You go back to radically reengineer and simplify, thus removing all *non*-value-added elements. It's about collapsing cycle time (how long it takes to perform a specific function) down to the real task time. The main idea is to bring every level and operation of your suppliers and your organization closer to the customer, so that the customer gets your service or product more quickly, and with the highest possible quality.

   Example: Cardone, Inc., of Philadelphia, PA, the world's premiere remanufacturer of auto parts, has recently undergone a complete value-chain analysis. They are reducing their inventory cost by over $30 million.

   Tip: Survey your customers to find out the processes that are most important to them, where they have the most complaints, etc. Most top experts (i.e., Hammer, Conway, Deming, etc.) believe that, for a customer focus, each organization has only seven to ten processes that involve three or more functional departments — these should be your focus. Keep in mind, you don't reengineer *functions*, you reengineer *processes* (despite the proliferation of workshops today that try to tell you otherwise) that include your suppliers as well.

   Example: When done right, total quality, value-chain analysis, and business process reengineering type programs will make a huge difference in your organiza-

Directions: (1) Please circle the number that best describes your organization the way it is today. Then total up the scores at the bottom. (Refer to the "organization as a system" model in Figure 9.1 for details.)

(2) In addition, please run a line down the page connecting each circle as you go. The result is probably a zigzag showing where your organization's emphasis has been (high numbers) and not been (low numbers). The extent of your zigzag is the extent of your lack of congruence and fit of these parts of your organization towards its outputs.

		Reactive Organization A	Responsible Organization B	21st Century High Performance Organization C	Comments
A. 1.	Output Achievement of Results	1 2 3 4	5 6 7 8 9	10	
B. 2.	Feedback Feedback Loop	1 2 3 4	5 6 7 8 9	10	
A-C. 3.	Strategic Planning Strategic Planning	1 2 3 4	5 6 7 8 9	10	
D. 4A.	Alignment — Delivery Operational Tasks (Quality/ Service)	1 2 3 4	5 6 7 8 9	10	
4B.	Technology	1 2 3 4	5 6 7 8 9	10	
4C.	Resources	1 2 3 4	5 6 7 8 9	10	
4D.	Organizational Design	1 2 3 4	5 6 7 8 9	10	
4E.	Team Development	1 2 3 4	5 6 7 8 9	10	
4F.	Business Processes	1 2 3 4	5 6 7 8 9	10	
D. 5A.	Attunement — People Leadership and Management	1 2 3 4	5 6 7 8 9	10	
5B.	Employee Involvement	1 2 3 4	5 6 7 8 9	10	
5C.	Strategic Communications	1 2 3 4	5 6 7 8 9	10	
5D.	Human Resources	1 2 3 4	5 6 7 8 9	10	
5E. D.	Culture Change Strategic Change Mgmt. Process	1 2 3 4	5 6 7 8 9	10	
6.	Strategic Change Management	1 2 3 4	5 6 7 8 9	10	
7. E.	Annual Strategic Review Environment	1 2 3 4	5 6 7 8 9	10	
8.	Environmental Scanning (SKEPTIC)	1 2 3 4	5 6 7 8 9	10	

TOTAL SCORE = _____ (170 points possible)
A. High Performing Organization = 110 to 170 points
B. Responsible Organization = 60 to 110 points
C. Reactive Organization = 0 to 60 points

FIGURE 9.2 A high performance organization survey.

tion's success. General Electric has been highly successful in the past using something called "Workout," and now Six Sigma Quality Programs designed to work out the quality problems and bureaucracy existent in their business systems and processes.

Caution: Make no mistake, value-chain analysis can yield a huge strategic and cost efficiency result. It is absolutely necessary for success on an ongoing basis. Thus, you should plan for it probably once every few years.

MANAGEMENT/LEADERSHIP CORE COMPETENCIES

It is very easy for ignorant people to think that success
in war may be gained by the use of some wonderful
invention rather than by hard fighting and
superior leadership.

-General George S. Patton

◄────── *Paradigm Shift* ──────►

A diagnostic tool for understanding and managing accelerated change. / Organization as a System → Type Organization		**A.** Reactive Organization	**B.** *Industrial Age* Traditional Organization	**C.** *Systems Age* 21st Century High Performance Organization (Proactive)
A. Output	1. Achievement of Results	Survival Level & Conflict Only	Profitability OK or Within Budget	Customer Value/ Financial Results/ Clear Positioning
B. Feedback	2. Feedback/ Measures	Rarely Used (Closed System)	Financial/Operational Measures Only	KSFs-Key Measures of Success
A-C. Strategic Planning	3. Strategic Planning/Strategic Mgmt.	Survival Day-to-Day	3-Year Forecasts/ Operational Planning	Integrated Strategic Management System/Annual Strategic Review
D. Alignment (of Delivery Processes)	4A. Operational Tasks (Quality/Service) 4B. Technology 4C. Resources 4D. Organizational Structure 4E. Team Development 4F. Business Processes	A. Firefighting/Fix It (Low Quality) B. Out of Date C. Squeaky Wheel D. Fragmented E. Adversarial/ Individual Focus F. Personal Control	A. Maintain Only/ Obsolete Tasks B. Piecemeal Technology C. Incrementalism D. Hierarchy and Bureaucracy E. Functional Teams Only F. Department Controls	A. Reputation for High Quality/ Service B. Technology Fit/ Organization C. Resources Clearly Focused D. Networks/Flat Strategic Alliances E. Cross-Functional Self-Managed F. Customer-Focused (Value Chain)
D. Attunement (With People's Hearts and Minds)	5A. Leadership and Management 5B. Employee Involvement 5C. Strategic Communications 5D. Human Resources 5E. Culture Change	A. Enforcing Blame (Incompetence) B. Avoid Blame/Wait C. Minimal/Negative D. Poor People Mgmt. E. One Man Rule (Impose will)	A. Directing/ Controlling B. Obedient Doers C. Formal/Newsletter D. Low Risk Mind Set E. Command & Control	A. 6 Competencies (All System Levels) B. Empowered C. Strategic Positive/ Open Book D. Empwr. Employees to Serve Customer E. Partic. Leadership (Facilitate/Support)
D. Strategic Change Management Process	6. Strategic Change Management 7. Annual Strategic Review	No Follow-Through Not on Radar Scope	Isolated Change Projects Department Goals and Objectives	Transformational/ Integrated Change- Proactive Strategic Plan-Living/ Breathing Updated Document
E. Environment	8. Environmental Scanning	Rarely-Closed System	Today Only	Future/Full SKEPTIC

FIGURE 9.3   A high performance work organization: the organization as a system — summary of Best Practices research.

Of course, none of these innovations, changes, or restructurings can effectively take place over the long term without professional management and leadership practices. From our best practices research and my own observations, these practices are what I call the basic building blocks (or foundation) of business; without these, nothing happens.

People often talk about how "employees are our most important assets." I disagree. Employees are certainly your organization's greatest assets: but only if you — as their leader — *let them be!* Being in management and leadership, *you* are actually the most important asset, and the *only competitive edge difference* in any organization over the long term. Therefore, assessing yourself honestly and being open to continuing leadership development is the best competitive advantage any organization can possess over time. All this talk about the core competencies of an organization misses the most obvious point: that the most important core competency any organization must have is strategic management and leadership.

To reach consensus in this area, have each member of your core planning team, as well as other key stakeholders, fill out the survey in Figure 9.4 according to how they view your organization's leadership management.

Tip: As a profession, managers generally don't devote the time and energy to skills that are essential for effective management and communication. Do they even know what those skills are? Do they even know why it's considered a profession?

Example: Kalmbach Feed, Inc., has made a strategy in this area one of their top priorities. In their first year of implementation, they have conducted a needs assessment and developed a leadership model with workshops, along with attendance from the CEO on down. Managers were trained by this author and the Centre for Strategic Management to become instructors as a key part of all this as well. They used the six natural levels that appear in Figure 9.4 parts 1 and 2 — Leadership development competencies.

STRATEGIC HUMAN RESOURCE MANAGEMENT AREA

By now you know that if you want your organization to survive and grow, you're facing both short- and long-term substantial change. And it's not only change in your technologies, customer contact, or organizational design, either; its change in your people management practices as well.

As this era continues, your organization's strategic human resource management practices will be more important than ever. For this reason, it's imperative that you carefully assess your human resource management best practices using the seven levels of Living Systems we saw earlier to strengthen leadership competencies. These Best Practices are detailed in Figure 9.5.

Creating the People Edge: "Best Practices"

I. **The Throughputs Processes: People Edge Best Practice Areas**
    A. Area 1: Acquiring the Desired Workforce (Individually)
        1. Identifying *core organizational competencies* and individual capability requirements.
        2. Developing diverse, flexible, safe, and *alternative workforce arrangements.*
        3. Conducting workforce, succession and retention planning.
        4. Installing *career development,* and employee assistance practices that assist employees in managing their own careers and lives.
        5. Implementing recruitment, selection and promotion methods to hire, orient, and assimilate the desired employees.

I. Optional Instructions: #1 ☐ How skilled are you in these corporate leadership skills yourself?
                            #2 ☐ How well does this occur now for the person you are rating?
                            #3 ☐ For your organization and its management?

II. Instructions: Please circle the # or N/A that applies.   _____ (name)

Topic	Current State Assessment					Score and Comments
Self or Others: Management of Organization:	(1) No Skills -Reactive Orgn. -Survival Only	(5) Some Skills -Responsible Orgn. -Traditional Control	-1990s High Perf Orgn. -Proactive Orgn. Emprmnt.	(10) High Skills	N/A Not Applicable	
Level #1-Enhancing Self-Mastery (Personal)						
1. Personal & Life Goal Setting	(1) 2 3 4	(5) 6 7	8 9	(10)	N/A	**Level 1:**
2. Balancing Life (Body-Mind-Spirit)	(1) 2 3 4	(5) 6 7	8 9	(10)	N/A	Total Score: _____ /5 =
3. Acting With Conscious Intent	(1) 2 3 4	(5) 6 7	8 9	(10)	N/A	_____ (average)
4. Ethics and Integrity Displayed	(1) 2 3 4	(5) 6 7	8 9	(10)	N/A	
5. Accurate Self-Awareness	(1) 2 3 4	(5) 6 7	8 9	(10)	N/A	
Level #2-Building Interpersonal Relationships						
6. Caring About Others	(1) 2 3 4	(5) 6 7	8 9	(10)	N/A	**Level 2:**
7. Effectively Communicating With Others	(1) 2 3 4	(5) 6 7	8 9	(10)	N/A	Total Score: _____ /5 =
8. Mentoring and Coaching Others	(1) 2 3 4	(5) 6 7	8 9	(10)	N/A	_____ (average)
9. Managing Conflict Effectively	(1) 2 3 4	(5) 6 7	8 9	(10)	N/A	
10. Supporting Innovation and Creativity	(1) 2 3 4	(5) 6 7	8 9	(10)	N/A	
Level #3-Facilitating Empowered Teams						
11. Practicing Participative Management	(1) 2 3 4	(5) 6 7	8 9	(10)	N/A	**Level 3:**
12. Facilitating Groups Effectively	(1) 2 3 4	(5) 6 7	8 9	(10)	N/A	Total Score: _____ /5 =
13. Delegating and Empowering Others	(1) 2 3 4	(5) 6 7	8 9	(10)	N/A	_____ (average)
14. Training and Developing Others	(1) 2 3 4	(5) 6 7	8 9	(10)	N/A	
15. Building an Effective Team Around Them	(1) 2 3 4	(5) 6 7	8 9	(10)	N/A	

FIGURE 9.4   Leadership development competencies.

	(1)	2	3	4	(5)	6	7	8	9	(10)	N/A	
Level #4-Collaborating Across Functions/ Departments												
16. Installing Cross-Functional Teamwork	(1)	2	3	4	(5)	6	7	8	9	(10)	N/A	
17. Integrating Business Processes	(1)	2	3	4	(5)	6	7	8	9	(10)	N/A	
18. Valuing the Differences of Other Depts.	(1)	2	3	4	(5)	6	7	8	9	(10)	N/A	**Level 4:**
19. Serving Others in the Organization	(1)	2	3	4	(5)	6	7	8	9	(10)	N/A	Total Score: ___/5 =
20. Managing People/HR Mgmt. Processes	(1)	2	3	4	(5)	6	7	8	9	(10)	N/A	___ (average)
Level #5-Integrating Organizational Outcomes												
21. Reinventing Strategic Planning	(1)	2	3	4	(5)	6	7	8	9	(10)	N/A	
22. Strategically Communicating Organization-Wide	(1)	2	3	4	(5)	6	7	8	9	(10)	N/A	
23. Positioning the Organization vs. the Marketplace	(1)	2	3	4	(5)	6	7	8	9	(10)	N/A	**Level 5:**
24. Leading Cultural Change	(1)	2	3	4	(5)	6	7	8	9	(10)	N/A	Total Score: ___/5 =
25. Designing and Organizing Effective Change Structures	(1)	2	3	4	(5)	6	7	8	9	(10)	N/A	___ (average)
Level #6-Creating Strategic Positioning												
26. Scanning the Global Environment	(1)	2	3	4	(5)	6	7	8	9	(10)	N/A	
27. Practicing Interest-Based (Win-Win) Negotiations	(1)	2	3	4	(5)	6	7	8	9	(10)	N/A	
28. Managing External Alliances	(1)	2	3	4	(5)	6	7	8	9	(10)	N/A	**Level 6:**
29. Networking Externally	(1)	2	3	4	(5)	6	7	8	9	(10)	N/A	Total Score: ___/5 =
30. International Sophistication/Effectiveness	(1)	2	3	4	(5)	6	7	8	9	(10)	N/A	___ (average)
Energizing Forces												
31. Level 1-Perception of Self-Awareness	(1)	2	3	4	(5)	6	7	8	9	(10)	N/A	
32. Level 2-Reputation for Integrity	(1)	2	3	4	(5)	6	7	8	9	(10)	N/A	
33. Level 3-Recognition of the Interdependence With Others	(1)	2	3	4	(5)	6	7	8	9	(10)	N/A	
34. Level 4-Values providing service to others	(1)	2	3	4	(5)	6	7	8	9	(10)	N/A	**Level 7:**
35. Level 5-Understands/agrees with the organization's Vision and Values	(1)	2	3	4	(5)	6	7	8	9	(10)	N/A	Total Score: ___/6 =
36. Level 6-Believes in mutual influence and synergistic efforts	(1)	2	3	4	(5)	6	7	8	9	(10)	N/A	___ (average)

Grand Total: _____ (360 possible) /36 = _____ (average)

FIGURE 9.4 Continued.

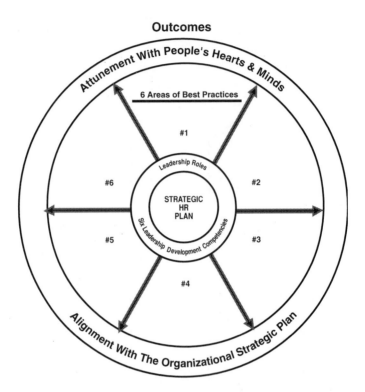

FIGURE 9.5   Focus areas of the six rings–six people edge Best Practice areas.

   B. Area 2: Engaging the Workforce (One on One)
       6. Installing Performance Management Systems that attune individ-
           ual and team behavior with strategic direction and core values
           (i.e., goal setting, coaching, appraisal, and development).
       7. Linking remuneration and compensation systems to capability
           and performance.
       8. Creating recognition systems that reinforce strategic direction and
           core values.
       9. Providing flexible benefit programs to meet changing employee
           and employer needs.
      10. Dealing effectively with poor or inadequate performance/disci-
           pline problems and grievances.
   C. Area 3: Organizing High Performance Teams (Team)
      11. Understanding, designing and developing teams, task forces, and
           team skills.
      12. Developing small unit team leaders/supervisors.
      13. Developing empowered, self-directed employees, work teams and
           accountability.

14. Establishing participative management skills for management to lead teams in conducting business.
15. Developing programs that reward and reinforce teamwork.

D. Area 4: Creating a Learning Organization (Department to Department)

16. Developing and spreading learning and intellectual capital quickly across the organization by all employees to include life-long learning practices.
17. Institutionalizing Systems Thinking as a new approach to better thinking, understanding, and acting. Keep it simple: "simplicity on the far side of complexity."
18. Developing human resource measurements and information to help the sharing of learning, including cataloging corporate knowledge.
19. Promoting the value of debriefing and learning from our experiences, mistakes, and successes.
20. Creating ways to encourage creative thinking and innovation.

E. Area 5: Facilitating Cultural Change (Organization-Wide)

21. Engaging in a continuous process of communications dialogue, discovery, and assessment to deepen everyone's shared understanding of the organization's vision and desired organization culture vs. its current status.
22. Shaping and developing the collective management skills in support of the desired culture.
23. Aligning and streamlining all human resource processes, programs and systems with the core values and strategic direction.
24. Designing and organizing structures and people management roles needed to facilitate change to the desired culture.
25. Developing strategic change experts, agents, and capabilities of all employees to support and implement the desired organizational changes.

F. Area 6: Collaborating with Stakeholders (Organization to Environment)

26. Developing the environmental knowledge, awareness, and skills of employees to operate in a global environment.
27. Understanding, developing and maintaining strategic alliances and networks, including outsourcing.
28. Maintaining the positive people environment and competitive advantage in the marketplace.
29. Creating an intense customer focus and commitment by all employees.
30. Collaborating and balancing value contribution to employees, customers, shareholders, community, cultures, and countries.

II. **More Inputs: Leadership Roles and Six Leadership Development Competencies**

31. Defining roles in creating The People Edge by management, staff, and human resources.

32. Installing a Strategic Leadership Development System and an Executive Development Board.
33. Developing leadership competencies. (See list of six competencies in the Centre's Leadership Development System).
34. Partnering on staff, management, customer, and human resource functions and roles.
35. Adding human resource value through a strategic approach and structures.
36. Articulating the strategic direction and core values over and over again (stump speeches).

III. The Fundamental Core Input: Strategic Human Resource Planning

37. Developing a Strategic Human Resource Plan to position the organization's human resource practices and processes to consistently add value to employees, customers, shareholders, and the community.

IV. The Outer Circle: Outcomes and Results

38. *Alignment with the Corporate Strategic Plan* — need for the overall organization to have people-related values and vision, and to develop strategies that deal with people-related business issues resulting in added value to the customers.
39. *Attunement of People's Hearts and Minds* — the "edge" in the marketplace created by people when their hearts and minds are fully invested in their work.
40. *#1 Core Competency* — how close are we to creating the People Edge by increasing the range and depth of our strategic leadership competency (and associated) through each of our middle and senior management members.

REWARDS FOR TOTAL PERFORMANCE

As the traditional hierarchical structure continues to diminish in favor of a more horizontal, cross-functional design, the traditional methods for rewarding exceptional performance also fall by the wayside. That doesn't mean that organizations no longer need to reward performance, however.

The first step toward choosing the reward method that's right for you is to examine a broader perspective of (1) financial, and (2) nonfinancial rewards.

Financial Rewards

Rewarding performance on a financial basis can take a number of varying forms:

1. Base salary	2. Merit increase
3. Promotional increase	4. Adjustment increase
5. Incentive awards	6. Benefits
7. Pay for knowledge	8. Employee stock ownership

Many medium to large-sized organizations use some or all of these financial rewards for performance. However well they worked for the hierarchical organization, they are not the right ones *alone* for today.

Example: Everyone — and I mean everyone — with any background in the psychology of organizations agrees that the seductively simple "pay for performance" doesn't work, yet it is continually perpetuated by senior management. In recent years, average merit raises under pay-for-performance nets the average employee the princely take-home pay of $10 more a week. After 12 months of work and results, this is hardly enough to motivate anyone to do anything.

Nonfinancial Rewards

Monetary incentives aren't the only acceptable way to reward performance — far from it. With today's changing marketplace, in fact, most organizations simply are unable to tie performance to money in a meaningful way, say 10% to 15% of salary. The public sector never has.

More and more, today's high performance organizations are turning to nonfinancial performance compensation with great success. In best practices research on employee needs in France, Canada, and the U.S., and my own surveys I've conducted hundreds of times, the top three answers to employee needs are

1. Recognition for a job well done
2. Growth and development (learning and training)
3. Responsibility (opportunity for freedom of thought and action, i.e., empowerment)

On the average in each survey, money's importance almost always comes in at fourth place. Once again — it's necessary, but not sufficient for most of us.

Example: Organizations most commonly reward individuals, but the truth is, jobs usually get done through teamwork. The missing link here is that we're rewarding exclusively on one aspect of the job; the individual part. Though this is necessary, it's not sufficient.

Gauging Performance

Now let's look at ways to gauge actual performance. Performance is about (1) results vs. your core strategies, and (2) behavior vs. your core values at three levels:

* Individual work accomplishments
* Teamwork achievements
* Organizational results

To determine if your reward system is effective, complete the chart in Figure 9.6. Look at what types of performances your organization assesses and rewards and, if changes are needed, specify who should be responsible to lead this change.

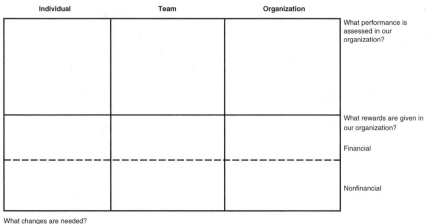

FIGURE 9.6 Internal assessment: performance and rewards — rewards for total performance assessment.

Example: Remember, rewards must reinforce your new Ideal Future Vision, not the past. Almost all organizations I have worked with do *not* have a reward system that supports their future vision/mission/values. Managers that do not have a reinforcing reward system are, in effect, shooting themselves in the foot. The organization is blindly pursuing its future vision in spite of the lack of a good analysis, change, and fit of their reward system to the vision.

CROSS-FUNCTIONAL TEAMWORK

More and more organizations are turning toward a horizontal structure — organizing around processes, rather than individual, hierarchical functions (Figure 9.7). Cross-functional teamwork is becoming an essential ingredient for success. And without teamwork, a total focus on the customer in today's changing marketplace won't happen.

Example: A good example of the horizontal effect is in Motorola's Government Electronics group. Making customer satisfaction its driving force, this group reshaped its own supply management organization. Rather than being a separate entity, it is now a successful *process* — with its external customer as the end product.

If your organization is like most, you've probably initiated some team activities, but are searching for ways to incorporate more cross-functional teamwork effectively. To determine where and how teams would work best in your organization, use the matrix in Figure 9.8.

Example: It is becoming self-evident that maximum use of self-directed work teams yields reduced costs, shorter cycle times, and greater customer responsiveness. General Electric's lighting business successfully did away with its traditional organization design, in favor of a structure where a senior team (made up of between 9

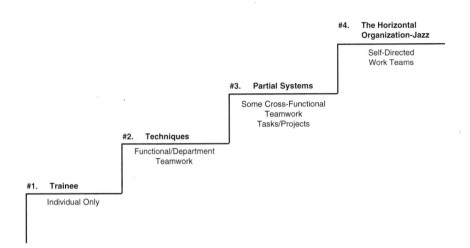

FIGURE 9.7 Level of teamwork in any organization — cross-functional teamwork and horizontal organizations.

and 12 individuals) supervise close to 100 processes worldwide. (This includes anything from maximizing production machinery to designing new products.) A multidisciplinary team oversees and is responsible for meeting each goal of each process.

Caution: Make sure the skills training and motivation are available to all workers. However, don't forget to train the supervisors and senior managers first, so they really *can* walk the talk. Remember, leaders are your most important asset!

CORE COMPETENCIES

The last element of your internal assessment should be a study of your organization's core competencies. This is about gaining a realistic sense of what your organization is particularly good at, in order to continually build on its strengths, as well as eliminating your weaknesses.

Exercise: There are three primary steps or questions you need to follow when identifying core competencies:

1. First, define how these core competencies compare to your desired future ideal for your driving forces. What core competencies do we need across the organization to achieve our future vision?
2. Next, ask "What are our existing core competencies? Are they the same across the organization — or not?"
3. Finally, look at possible alternatives for your organization if it couldn't fulfill its existing core competencies.

Tip: When looking at the primary core competency of your organization and its senior management, and the leadership skills of your collective management

Cross-Functional Teamwork Emphasis	#1 Individual Focus	#2 Functional/Dept. Teamwork	#3 Some Cross-Functional Teamwork	#4 Self-Directed Work Teams
1. Shared Vision/Strategies	Senior Management's Job Only	Dept. Mission & Plans Only	Sharing of Dept. Plans/ Regular Follow-up Mtgs.	Every Dept./Level Uses Strategies as Organizing Focus
2. Organization-Wide Strategies (or goals)	Specific KRAs for my Job	Dept. Goals Only	Project Teams for Certain Strategies	All Have Strategy Sponsorship Teams
3. Leadership/Management Skills	Traditional Boss – Subordinate Skills	Participative Mgmt. Skills	Trainer–Coach Facilitation Skills for Managers (T-C-F)	T-C-F Skills at all Levels—"Every Employee a Mngr."
4. Core Business Processes	Individual Job Focus	Dept. Processes	Some TQM/BPR	Organize Company Around These
5. Supplier/Customer Contact	Only If In Your Job Description	Certain Depts. Only as Interface	On Special Occasions or Cross-Functional Projects	Normal Part of Everyone's Job in Cross-Func. Teams
6. Organization Design — Hierarchy	Standard Vertical Bureaucracy/ Job Descriptions	Emphasis on Dept. Teamwork & Team Building	Cross-Functional Projects/Tasks Often Set Up	Cross-Func. Teams With Shared Leadership/Mgmt. (Team Advisors)
7. Physical Set-up/Location	Offices/Cubicles for Individuals	Each Dept. Separate	Project Meetings and War Rooms	Cross-Func. Team Members in Same Open Location
8. Resources, Communications, and Techology	Based on Your Job & Need to Know	Openness & Participation in Dept. Resources	Access to Cross-Functional Projects Resources, Communication & Technology	Open Book Mgmt. Across Orgn.—Info Available to All
9. Rewards System	Adversarial/Individual Focus	Dept. Teams Only Rewarded	For Cross-Functional Projects	Standard Cross-Func. Team Rewards
10. Percentage of Organization Managed by Cross-Functional Teams	0%	10%	20–40%	50%+

Type of Teamwork

FIGURE 9.8 Cross-functional teamwork — the horizontal organization.

team, use our six natural levels of leadership competencies mentioned earlier in this chapter and in Chapter 2.

TECHNOLOGY ASSESSMENT

Today's rapidly changing world is driven, in many ways, by the dramatic changes in information technology and telecommunications technology and their infinite number of combinations. Thus, a new imperative is to see where you stand on the use of technology as a competitive business advantage.

   Example: Arthur Andersen's website (**www.arthurandersen.com/6p-awards**) lists eight key questions (Figure 9.9).

1.	Are employees able to access computer and telephone networks from remote locations?	☐ Yes	☐ No	☐ Not Sure
2.	Do all employees share a common software platform?	☐ Yes	☐ No	☐ Not Sure
3.	Can your customers place orders with you electronically?	☐ Yes	☐ No	☐ Not Sure
4.	Is the primary form of internal communications electronic (e-mail, bulletin boards, voice mail)?	☐ Yes	☐ No	☐ Not Sure
5.	Do most of your workstations have processors the equivalent of a Pentium® or better?	☐ Yes	☐ No	☐ Not Sure
6.	Does your company use "distance learning" to educate its employees?	☐ Yes	☐ No	☐ Not Sure
7.	Does your company have a technology manager who is part of its top management team?	☐ Yes	☐ No	☐ Not Sure
8.	Can your employees run software applications when the network is down?	☐ Yes	☐ No	☐ Not Sure

FIGURE 9.9   Is your company taking full advantage of today's technology?

SUMMARY

Now that you've thoroughly assessed the current state of your organization internally, you should have a pretty fair idea of what is working. You should also have a clear grasp of what needs to be changed in order to get from where you are today to where you want to be tomorrow. Now it's time to turn to your organization's external environment.

QUESTIONS TO PONDER

- Are you honestly willing to accept *all* of your Current State Assessment findings — not just the ones you feel good about?
- Do you already have previous assessment work that could be used now?
- Have you conducted thorough financial and core values analyses?
- Have you made certain your organization has the right Key Success Measures in place? Where do you stand with them?
- Is your rewards/appraisal system reinforcing your strategies and values?
- Have you assessed your leadership and teamwork (two key areas)?
- Have you carefully examined all your organizational processes from a customer perspective, and made action plans for any necessary reengineering?
- Do you have strong people practices in the six natural levels of strategic human resource management?
- Have you clearly identified your organization's core competencies?

CONDUCTING AN EXTERNAL CURRENT STATE ASSESSMENT

It's simple — those with the latest and most comprehensive market information have a clear advantage over those who don't.

-American Demographics

There is no shortage of potential areas you may wish to focus on during your external Current State Assessment. Here is a partial list of external assessments frequently used; you may want to add some of your own as well.

1. Organizational life cycle
2. Competitor analysis
3. Customer focus
4. Market orientation and segmentation
5. Value mapping products and services (positioning)
6. Market share and growth rate
7. Product/market certainty mix

These areas of external assessment are described in the following sections.

ORGANIZATIONAL LIFE CYCLE

Obviously, all organizations go through similar life cycles: (1) the research and development phase, (2) start-up end growth, (3) the mature business phase, (4) decline, and, hopefully, (5) a renewal phase.

It's important to differentiate the mature phase from the declining phase. If you fail to recognize the difference, it could prove too late for possible renewal.

Example: Years ago, AT&T and IBM were both in antitrust lawsuits with the government. While IBM won their suit and had it dropped, AT&T did not, and was forced to break up into the seven "Baby Bells."

There was an interesting outcome of this. While AT&T and the Baby Bells were forced to change, the Baby Bells ultimately underwent a successful renewal and various recombinations to create new competitive market forces. IBM, however, continued on from its mature phase into a decline phase, and is only now renewing its old marketplace dominance through re-creating itself as a service organization. It's a great case for proving that winning in the short-term doesn't mean long-term success and vice versa.

As the matrix in Figure 9.10 indicates, there are a number of measures that go into studying your organization's life cycle: industry maturity, competitive position, market share objective, and sales volume. There are five questions you need to consider when evaluating your organization's life cycle:

1. Where are we on the life cycle matrix today?
2. Where do we want to be in the future?
3. Where are we likely to be in the future (given no proactive changes)?
4. What are the implications for today (i.e., competitors, customers, growth-rate, market share, profitability, liquidity, substitutes, technology)?
5. What are the implications for the future?

COMPETITOR ANALYSIS

Your external assessment won't be complete without a thorough, in-depth analysis of your competition. You need to look not only at how they sell their product or service, but also what has and hasn't worked for them, market share, and future projections and strategies.

Conducting an in-depth competitive analysis is of great value to your own planning; it gives you a clear picture of how crowded your market is and initiates ideas on how to capture more of it.

Use the list below as a framework to conduct an analysis of your top three competitors.

- Vision, mission values, and driving force(s)
- Core strategies, outcome measures or goals
- Current state assessment (SWOT)
- Market share and customer reputation/positioning
- Pricing strategy
- Background of key executives
- Technology perspective
- Core competencies and capabilities

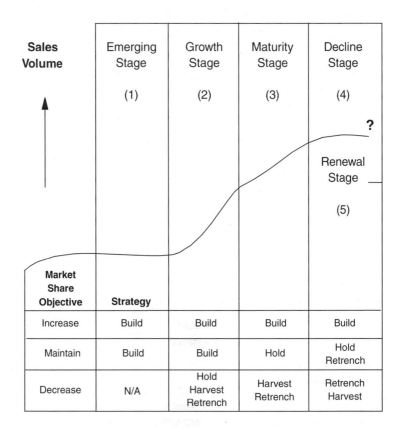

Sales Volume	Emerging Stage (1)	Growth Stage (2)	Maturity Stage (3)	Decline Stage (4)

Renewal
Stage

(5)

Market Share Objective	Strategy			
Increase	Build	Build	Build	Build
Maintain	Build	Build	Hold	Hold Retrench
Decrease	N/A	Hold Harvest Retrench	Harvest Retrench	Retrench Harvest

Time ⟶

Where are we?
a. Dominant
b. Leading
c. Important
d. Tenable
e. Weak
What are its implications?

FIGURE 9.10 Organizational life cycle matrix.

Conducting this type of competitive benchmark will help you accomplish two things: (1) you will gain a greater understanding of exactly what you're up against, and (2) you will get a better overall sense of your industry.

CUSTOMER FOCUS

I've seen it over and over again: organizations that do not have a clear focus on who their customers are (and what they want) have fewer customers — and considerably less profit. Just saying you're already customer-focused — or want to be — won't cut it; the customer *always* knows the difference.

To determine if your organization really is customer-focused, use the survey in Figure 9.11 to get to the heart of the matter. Honestly assess your organization's adherence to these Key Commandments of a Customer-Focused Organization discussed in Chapter 2.

If you're already following these commandments in your organization, congratulations; you truly are a visionary. If not, this is a perfect time to examine your weaknesses as well as your strengths, and create a series of actions toward improvement.

Being truly customer-focused also means incorporating ongoing customer recovery strategies (CRS). When you do make a mistake with a current customer, it is important to use effective customer recovery strategies (listed below).

"Customer Recovery Strategy" Design Characteristics for Unsurpassed Customer Service

At the "Moment of Truth":

1. Focus on the 5–10 year ROI of the customer.
2. Focus on your long-term image and reputation. (Remember, unhappy people tell 11 others; happy customers tell 4 others).
3. Empower the person at the "moment of truth" to be creative and innovative to surpass the customer's expectations as to solving the problem.
4. Provide expenditure authority to do the above.
5. Ensure accountability (= responsibility) at the "moment of truth."
6. Focus recovery on future business (i.e., 50% next time; free next time, etc.).
7. Speed up the recovery — at the "moment of truth."
8. Develop a "Customer Guarantee" and live up to it/surpass it.
9. Ensure your CRS deals with fast responsiveness, being knowledgeable, having empathy and sensitivity, as well as both the tangibles and intangibles.
10. What else?

Five Levels of Recovery Strategy Mastery: Which do we do?

_____1. Deny it's our problem. (I just work here.)
_____2. Fight their concern but eventually give in to them. (They won.)

Mastery Skill Level →	A. Trainee		B. Techniques					C. Systems Orientation		D. Jazz Player	Comments
The Key Commandments	Going Out of Business		Dogged Pursuit of Mediocrity					Customer-Focused		Art Form	
1. Close to the Customer	1	2	3	4	5	6	7	8	9	10	1.
2. Executives out in the marketplace	1	2	3	4	5	6	7	8	9	10	2.
3. Know and anticipate customers' needs	1	2	3	4	5	6	7	8	9	10	3.
4. Surpassing customer needs is driving force	1	2	3	4	5	6	7	8	9	10	4.
5. Survey the customers' satisfaction	1	2	3	4	5	6	7	8	9	10	5.
6. Have clear positioning in the marketplace	1	2	3	4	5	6	7	8	9	10	6.
7. Focus on Creating Customer Value	1	2	3	4	5	6	7	8	9	10	7.
8. Quality Customer Service Standards	1	2	3	4	5	6	7	8	9	10	8.
9. Customer input and focus groups	1	2	3	4	5	6	7	8	9	10	9.
10. Moments of Truth–all staff/1 day/year	1	2	3	4	5	6	7	8	9	10	10.
11. Business processes reengineered	1	2	3	4	5	6	7	8	9	10	11.
12. Structure based on marketplace	1	2	3	4	5	6	7	8	9	10	12.
13. Reward customer-focused behaviors	1	2	3	4	5	6	7	8	9	10	13.
14. Have a clear policy, recovery strategies	1	2	3	4	5	6	7	8	9	10	14.
15. Customer-friendly-people	1	2	3	4	5	6	7	8	9	10	15.

Total Score = _____ (150 possible)

FIGURE 9.11 Survey — are you a customer-focused organization?

_____3. Meet their expectations. (Customer is always right.)

_____4. Meet their expectations and then do something else beyond it that they don't expect (including an apology).

_____5. Do #4 and fix the underlying system or process problem of which it might be a symptom.

Getting customers is hard and expensive; *keeping* them — by meeting their expectations and then doing something more that they don't expect — will pay off over and over again in the long term.

MARKET ORIENTATION AND SEGMENTATION

This is where you evaluate how market-oriented your organization really is. You need to assess a number of organizational characteristics, such as the following:

- Are we easy to do business with?
- Do we keep our promises?
- Do we meet the standards we set?
- Are we responsive?
- Do we work together inside the organization to provide coordinated and quality service?

In my experience, though many organizations protest that they already know and are close to their customer, few really are. It's unfortunate, but it's a fact. In conducting this portion of your external assessment, it is imperative that you carefully scrutinize your customer base. After gathering this data, bring it back to the group of planning team members for discussion, feedback, and action.

To get a better sense of whether your organization is concentrating its energies on the most profitable customer base, you should also look at the cost/value ratio of your customer. Ask planning team members and key participants to fill out the chart in Figure 9.12.

Identifying your customers according to who they are, how they do business with you, and how much it costs your organization to retain them will quickly help you to pinpoint where the most profitable customers are.

By focusing on your customer, you will gain a clear, sharp image of just exactly who your present and future customers should be. The more you concentrate on this criteria, the more quickly you will truly become a high-performance, customer-focused organization. To restate the obvious, without customers, you won't even *have* an organization — much less a profitable one.

VALUE MAPPING YOUR PRODUCTS AND SERVICES (POSITIONING)

You'll need to create an actual "map" of your products and services, assessing where the value of each — their position — stands in the marketplace. This is an attempt

Instructions: Define A through G below for either ☐ Today or ☐ Desired in the next three years for our:

A. Main Market Segments	B. Key Customers	C. Main Products and Services	D. Value of Market Segment (H-M-L)	E. Market Share	F. Main Industry Competitors	G. Industry's Life Cycle

FIGURE 9.12 Marketplace worksheet.

to determine how you stack up against your competitor's lines, and how your product or service's quality is perceived.

Organizations often make the mistake of thinking that getting the product out there in the marketplace is enough, but that's just not so. The fact is, product mapping and positioning has a great deal to do with your customer's perception of your product and the organization behind it.

As the graphic in Figure 9.13 illustrates, a Value Map poses these questions of each of your products or services: (1) Where do we stand in price, quality, and perceived value? and (2) What actions do we need to take if we want to increase or change this line in the future?

Perhaps most importantly, creating a map from your customer's perspective will give you a total, overall perspective of which areas — such as cost, quality, features, delivery, and customer responsiveness — your products and services are the most (or least) competitive in.

Example: Many organizations compete only on a commodity (or price) basis, such as today's airlines (Ring #1 in Figure 9.13). It's usually better to compete on brand — such as Proctor & Gamble's retail products, Tide, etc. (Ring #2). The best way to go, however, is to focus on Rings #3 and #4, the overall product *and* service package, i.e., Marriott, Nordstrom's, and Disney.

MARKET SHARE AND GROWTH RATE

Once you've sized up the competition, it's time to take a serious look at how much of the market you already have, and how much of it you want to have. As the familiar General Electric and Boston Consulting Group matrix shown in Figure 9.14 indicates, you'll need to look at analyzing (1) your market share, and (2) your market growth rate. Then you can decide what actions you should take for consistent growth and profitability over the next few years. You'll need to analyze which of your products or services are strong, and which ones you might consider letting go to free up your resources.

Once you've carefully evaluated your market share strengths and weaknesses, use the matrix in Figure 9.14 to develop the strategies to succeed in your market. That way, you'll end up with a complete portfolio management set of strategies for all your SBUs and products.

Use this data to consider and shape different strategies that can position your organization in its marketplace and be sure to match the results you'll expect with each strategy.

PRODUCT/MARKET CERTAINTY MATRIX

Now that you've studied your products and business units, it's time to break your evaluation down further still, by looking at your specific product (or services) lines. Use the same criteria for each end product that you used to judge your business units, asking

1. Are we changing this product or service?
2. What are the implications — or risk — of this change?
3. What actions should we take, and at what point?

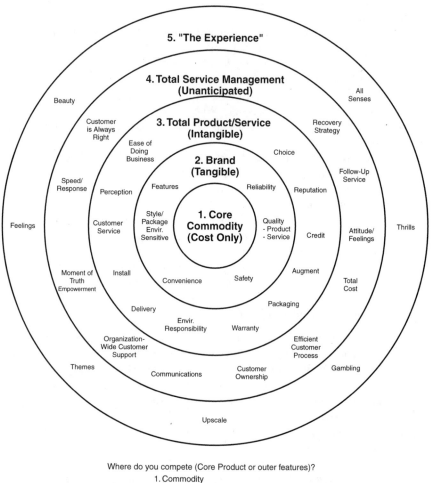

Where do you compete (Core Product or outer features)?
1. Commodity
2. Brand
3. Total Product/Intangibles
4. Total Product and Services Package/Unanticipated
5. The Experience

FIGURE 9.13 Value map: total "package" perspective — to create customer value (both products and services combined).

Develop a growth share matrix, showing each product's profitability on gross margin. In addition, judge each one by its market and customer segment, developing a matrix that identifies projected success rate, similar to that shown in Figure 9.15.

Whether you're taking an existing product to a new market or evolving it into a new but related product that will sell to a different market, always, *always* analyze it carefully against the backdrop of a matrix like the one in Figure 9.15. Otherwise, you're entering an uncharted course on not much more than a whim or a guess —

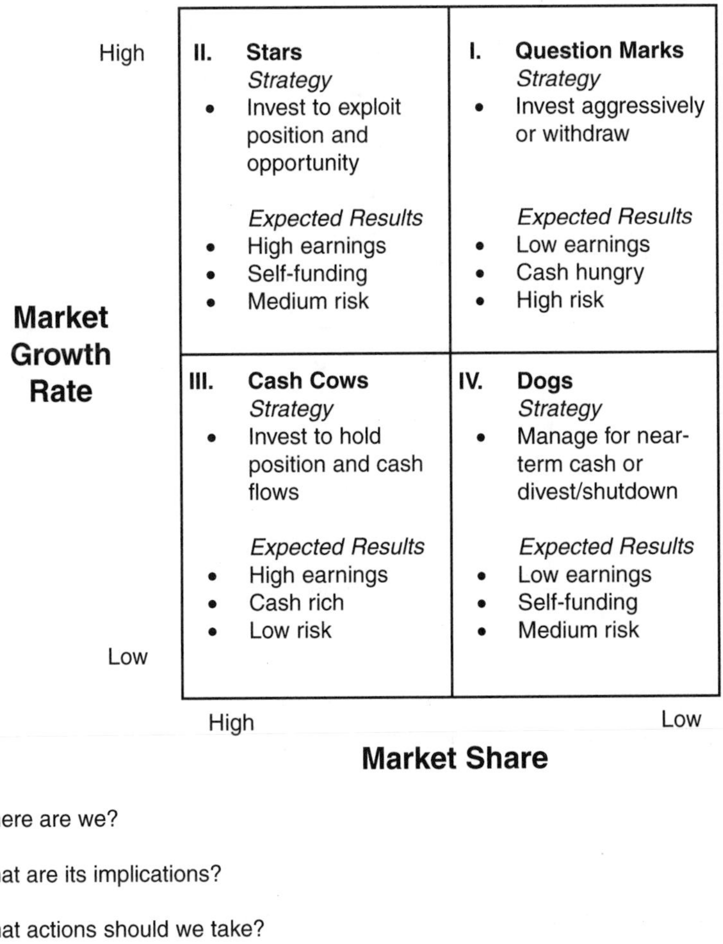

	High	**II. Stars**
		Strategy
		• Invest to exploit
		  position and
		  opportunity
		
		Expected Results
		• High earnings
		• Self-funding
		• Medium risk
			I. Question Marks
			Strategy
			• Invest aggressively
			  or withdraw
			
			Expected Results
			• Low earnings
			• Cash hungry
			• High risk

Market Growth Rate		**III. Cash Cows**
		Strategy
		• Invest to hold
		  position and cash
		  flows
		
		Expected Results
		• High earnings
		• Cash rich
		• Low risk
			IV. Dogs
			Strategy
			• Manage for near-
			  term cash or
			  divest/shutdown
			
			Expected Results
			• Low earnings
			• Self-funding
			• Medium risk

	Low	High	Low

Market Share

1.   Where are we?

2.   What are its implications?

3.   What actions should we take?

FIGURE 9.14 Growth share matrix. Adapted from B.C.G. and G.E. Portfolio Matrix.

and we all know the story of where that got IBM when they wanted to sell PC Junior's (a new but related product) to a consumer market (a new, unrelated market). On the matrix, they had only a 20% probability of success; the PC Junior has long since had its demise.

Example: A good example of this kind of foreplanning in the auto industry would be the success Toyota experienced when it wanted to bring a new product (the Lexus) to a new, but related, upscale market.

Another not so great example was when Sears wanted to introduce financial services (a new, unrelated product/service) to what it gambled on being a new, but related customer (their in-store customers). In fact, however, it was trying to reach a new customer (financial service buyers in general), and failed to achieve the success it wanted. Sears is presently reversing this strategy.

Products (or Product Lines)

Markets (Customer Segments)		Existing	New, but Related	New and Unrelated
	Existing	90% *Very High Certainty*	60%	30%
	New, but Related	60%	40%	20%
	New and Unrelated	30%	20%	10% *Very Low Certainty*

1. New products/same customers = 60% success rate.
2. New products/new customers = serious problems with any success.

FIGURE 9.15 Product/market certainty matrix (Z model). Adapted from Hayden and A.T. Kearney (1987 FIMA tape).

The benefit of going through this exercise is that it forces you to concentrate on the probability of each product's success, and identifies up front those that could be problematic.

QUESTIONS TO PONDER

- Have you analyzed your external key stakeholders and defined how you will respond to their needs so that you'll stay focused on your Ideal Future Vision?
- Do you know what phases your organizational and industry life cycles are in right now?
- Have you made a thorough, in-depth analysis of your competition?
- Is your organization structured around customer-focused units?
- Are you clear on your market orientation, and on whether you're concentrating on the most profitable customer base?
- Have you developed a Value Map of your products and services, as well as their market position?
- Do you know how much of your market you already have, and how much you want to have in the future?

CONDUCTING A STRENGTHS, WEAKNESSES, OPPORTUNITIES, THREATS (SWOT) ANALYSIS

Once you've completed your assessments — both internal and external — the final step necessary is creating a Strengths, Weaknesses, Opportunities, Threats (SWOT) analysis.

The basic concept is this:
Internally: Build on your <u>S</u>trengths
Eliminate or cope with your <u>W</u>eaknesses
Externally: Exploit your <u>O</u>pportunities
Ease and lower your <u>T</u>hreats

A SWOT analysis allows your planning team and key stakeholders to tie up any loose ends uncovered in your Current State Assessment, and answers any previously unresolved organizational issues. It's one of the most critical steps of your entire assessment, as it incorporates both your external and internal assessments into one summary that is usable and practical.

When identifying your SWOT, your planning team and key stakeholders should be looking for any element or characteristic that will either help or hinder your organization in its attempt to achieve its Ideal Future Vision. There will more than likely be many entries on both sides of the coin; you should therefore be sure to include all of the internal and external assessments outlined in this chapter.

Once you've drawn up a draft of internal weaknesses and strengths, ask planning team members to list corresponding "action implications" next to each entry. See the Summary Analysis in Figure 9.16 as an example of the format to use to ensure your SWOT is action-oriented. Many are not.

Tip: It is possible to apply the SWOT framework at the divisional, departmental, or SBU/support group level. If you decide to utilize it this way, you'll have one internal SWOT, but two externals: one that is external to your department, and one that is external to your organization (i.e., a SWOT–OT analysis).

Once you have completed the SWOT analysis, you will have a realistic, comprehensive list of potential actions that can be used to jump-start your brainstorming for the next step of planning; creating core strategies.

RECAP OF KEY CONTENT POINTS

- When conducting your internal and external assessments, be willing to honestly accept all findings, not just the positive ones.
- In your internal Current State Assessment, be sure to include thorough evaluation of these ten points:

Instructions: Use one page like this for each letter in the SWOT assessment.
Based on the assessment tasks, which are the most important factors to consider in the strategic planning?

Which Factors Are Most Important? List Answers	Action Implication Over the Planning Horizon
1.	
2.	
3.	
4.	
5.	
6.	
7.	
8.	
9.	
10.	
11.	
12.	
13.	
14.	
15.	
16.	
17.	
18.	
19.	
20.	

FIGURE 9.16   Summary analysis — assessment.

1. Organization financial analysis
2. Core values analysis
3. Key Success Measure analysis
4. Strategic business design/high performance
5. Business process reengineering/value-chain management
6. Management/leadership competencies
7. Key human resource practices
8. Reward for total performance
9. Teamwork
10. Core competencies
11. Technology assessment

- In your external Current State Assessment, be sure to include evaluation of these ten areas:

  1. Organizational life cycle
  2. Competitor analysis
  3. Strategic Business Unit (SBU) information
  4. Customer focus/customer recovery
  5. Market orientation and segmentation
  6. Value map of products and services (positioning)
  7. Market share and growth rate
  8. Product/market certainty

- Be sure to conduct a SWOT analysis (with action implications) as a summary, to digest all your analysis into a usable form.

"HOW-TO" ACTION CHECKLIST

1. Analyze your organizational finances and core values. Evaluate them on their capacity to support your Ideal Future Vision.
2. Assess your organization's strategic business design to determine if it will "get you where you want to go." Then redesign it as necessary.
3. Evaluate your organizational processes from your customer's point of view.
4. Make sure you have the management and leadership skills you'll need.
5. Look at organizational reward systems, both financial and nonfinancial.
6. In conducting your Current State Assessment (CSA), it is best to do so utilizing cross-functional teams of middle/first-line management (or other key stakeholders) in order to get a full picture of your organization's current performance. Prior to starting the assessment, decide which CSA tasks you want to conduct, then set up cross-functional teams to do the actual work.
7. Scrutinize organizational core competencies and their fit with your desired future.
8. Analyze what phases your organizational life cycle is currently in.
9. Make an in-depth analysis of your competition.
10. Defend why each of your SBUs should continue to exist.
11. In your market orientation analysis, make sure you're concentrating on your most profitable customer base.
12. Develop a Value Map of your products or services, and define their market position.

13. Do an in-depth analysis of your current market share and define how much your future market share should be.
14. Look closely at each product line; determine the implications or risks inherent in any changes you may make.
15. Complete your internal and external Current State Assessments with a summary of the data in usable form such as Strengths, Weaknesses, Opportunities, Threats (SWOT) analysis.

10 Strategy Development (Step #5)

*If you always do what you've always done, you won't
always get what you've always gotten because the
world has changed.*

-Stephen G. Haines

SHARED STRATEGIES

Step #5 — strategy development — works on creating the core strategies and action items that will help you bridge the gaps between your Ideal Future Vision, and the Current State Assessment you've just completed.

The result of this step will be three to seven core strategies to be implemented organization-wide. When put into practice, these shared strategies become the primary means to your desired end — your Ideal Future Vision. In essence, these core strategies will become the "glue" that keeps your organization focused in a consistent, customer-focused fashion year after year. A shared vision is what everyone talks about. *Shared strategies* are what most workers more readily relate to.

NEW MANAGEMENT STRATEGIES FOR NEW TIMES

The 1990s saw a proliferation of new strategies as organizations tried to cope with the revolutionary changes of the decade. Even now, organizations are facing multiple levels of change, with more certainly to come. Thus, *don't reform — transform* your company.

Because we're living in a time of virtual revolution, it will take more than simple "tuck-and-cut" solutions. Organizations need new visions, new strategies, new programs, and most importantly, new actions. In short, being "micro smart" (incremental thinking), yet "macro dumb" (lack of systems level thinking) won't work anymore.

STRATEGIES FOR THE 21st CENTURY — REVISITED

What can and will work for organizations facing the unknowns of a new century is to greet these changes with enthusiasm, looking at them as new challenges and strategic opportunities. As mentioned in earlier chapters, there was good news in the proliferation of new strategies that arose in response to the tremendous change of the 1990s, particularly these 15:

1. **Enterprise resource planning (ERP).** Corporations have begun to develop integrated, automated computer and telecommunication systems

1-57444-278-3/00/$0.00+$.50
© 2000 by CRC Press LLC

(Intranets) across the entire organization at all their remote locations. One input, one time, with electronic databases available to all. This has become big business: IBM and others have gotten into this market, as well as becoming "service bureaus," processing other's data and transactions.

2. **Electronic commerce.** Dot com companies are starting up daily as entrepreneurs all over the world are using the Internet as the new delivery channel of the 21st century. We've still only just begun, as Lucent Technologies has the ability to increase the digital volume through the pipe (fiberoptic cable) over 80 times through the use of color. Almost every organization today is, or should be, restructuring its business model and economics through the use of the Internet.

3. **Flexibility.** The revolutionary changes occurring now in the global marketplace are not diminishing. Indeed, looking ahead, it is likely that they will multiply. Customer-focused organizations that envision success in their future must be able to develop strategies with built-in flexibility and agility. For instance, in formulating their core strategies, Giant Industries, a major Phoenix, AZ oil company, and Poway Unified School District in southern California are both determined to be opportunistic and flexible in how they run their businesses.

4. **Speed.** Both Toyota and Daimler-Chrysler have incorporated speed as a core strategy. If done well, shorter cycle times can lower cost, improve product quality, and produce better customer response time. Neither General Motors nor most European automakers have successfully implemented this core strategy as yet.

5. **Horizontally integrated products (related products/by-products).** Ethanol plants are catching on in a big way; in Canada, communities are now being developed around them. Ethanol is an alcohol-based additive to gasoline, creating less need in the U.S. and Canada for importing oil. As the centerpiece for horizontal, community-wide integration, it also creates (1) steam for generators and electricity, (2) a mash that is used to feed cattle, and on the front end, (3) a need for grain as the primary ingredient. Thus an ethanol plant links ethanol production to farming, cattle ranching, electricity, and the distribution business (pipelines or trucks).

6. **Networks and alliances.** This is an innovative strategy that's rapidly becoming a favorite one. Organizations all over the world are finding they can't do it alone. Who would have thought that Microsoft and Apple would have joined forces? In Canada, MCI formed productive alliances with Bell Canada and Stentor. The Japanese have been successfully forging alliances like these for some time now, with their Kieretsu interlocking companies. *Caution:* Whether this strategy really works is a complex matter. Too many organizations seem to be rushing pell-mell into this strategy. It requires careful crafting, constant communications, and more.

7. **Value-added.** "More value for the same money" is becoming a hot strategy in manufacturing and retail industries of all kinds. Organizations

are looking at products and services from a "total package perspective," trying to determine where they are most competitive. Is it in their core product or in its more intangible features? An example is the Maxima, which Nissan is promoting as a luxury sedan, stressing that the buyer gets better quality and more value at the same price. Retail brand products, too, need to look at value add-ons, as more and more generic products beat them in size and cost.

8. **Environmentally improved/based products.** Environmental protection and its "3 Rs" — reduce, reuse, recycle — is good business for everyone these days. No longer are we hearing as much about the "business vs. the environment" debate. Now we find that most things that are good for the environment are good for many businesses as well. Also, the strategy of marketing products as "environment-friendly" is dramatically on the rise (i.e., products that can be recycled).

9. **Mass customization (or marketing one to one).** Toyota is aggressively taking advantage of improved manufacturing capabilities that link with the latest in telecommunications, allowing customers to select a base model with individual specifications and receive delivery in Japan a very short time later.

10. **Commonization/simplification.** Honda does a value analysis on every one of its products and its components, researching those elements of the product the customer really doesn't need or care about. By trimming these elements out of the product — or reducing their costs — their production costs go down, and they can offer their customers the same value for a lower price.

11. **Value-chain management.** In a management-supported, organization-wide rethinking of employee roles, General Electric created a culture without boundaries through something called "WorkOut" and now "Six Sigma" that works the entire value-chain from supplier to the customer. "You have to have … input from people who know the work best," says GE's CEO Jack Welch. "The more involved the workforce is in your decisions, the more they own them, and they make far better decisions."

12. **Organizational learning.** Numerous business writers (Senge, Peters, etc.) are reintroducing a common-sense notion to business as it moves into the 21st century. It emphasizes that with change being a given, we're going to need to learn how to cope with change on an individual and organiza- tion- wide basis. To do this, we must begin to create "learning organiza- tions," in which learning is an ongoing, normal part of the organizational structure. This is starting to happen even in big companies such as GE, Microsoft, and Lucent Technologies (former Bell Labs). The "learning organization" concept also implies that effective leadership must be the foundation for change and implementation of your vision of a customer-focused, high-performance organization (i.e., Right Answer #3).

13. **Automated Employee morale/benefits — focus on work.** Corporations have begun to recognize that, in addition to salary, employees are con-

cerned with providing for their "families," in all the current diversity of that term. Therefore, many corporations today are introducing increased family support programs as a part of their employee benefits package. This can include anything from family leave, child care resource centers, community and volunteer time, and wellness centers, to the more conventional elements such as employee stock-purchase plans, life insurance, tuition assistance, retirement, and capital accumulation plans (401K plans). For example, Stride Rite Corp. offers its employees all of these benefits, as well as offering an employee volunteer program, and child/elder care services. The good news is that companies now automate their internal personnel services so they can become "self-service" for the employee; better responsiveness and accuracy at a lower cost.

14. **Management and leadership practices.** Keep in mind, in all the research on the Vital Few Leverage Points for Change, management and leadership practices have been singled out as the foundation for everything else an organization does. In actual fact, the phrase "employees are our best asset" can only be true when the organization's leadership and management creates an environment conducive to motivated employees. Thus, when all is said and done, high management skills and leadership practices are really your greatest asset. Giants in management and leadership practices include Exxon, GE, and Shell.

15. **Simplicity.** Simplicity is defined by Bill Jensen in *Strategy & Leadership*, March/April 1997, as
    - "A common focus
    - Clear and concise goals
    - Tools to achieve the objectives
    - Information readily available to all employees
    - Sufficient training and direction to do the job
    - All activities linked to serving customer needs
    - A tangible and measurable outcome
    - Meeting the company's mission/vision"
    and further by Stephen G. Haines as a lack of "politics," a focus on logic and common sense, the Rule of Three, etc. As of yet, few companies are using this strategy even though the highly successful Southwest Airlines does this with only one kind of aircraft for its entire fleet (Boeing 737s).

KISS — KEEP IT SIMPLE, STUPID[1]

Listen to the leading lights of marketing these days and you come away with two distinct and seemingly contradictory messages.

The first could be encapsulated in the well-worn phrase, *keep it simple, stupid.* Customers have ever-shorter attention spans and zero tolerance for mixed signals.

---

[1] Source: *Harvard Management Update,* January 1999.

They don't want confusion, complexity, or clutter. Companies should do one thing well — and tell people about it all the time.

The other message relies on a second familiar phrase: *constant change*. Today's customers roam the world (virtually, if not literally) with ever-expanding and ever-changing needs. They have no loyalty to any supplier. Companies focus on one thing at their peril; the real challenge is to be constantly adapting to what customers want today.

Keeping it simple. Think Wal-Mart Stores. Think Southwest Airlines. "In a world where everyone is after your business," writes marketing consultant Jack Trout in his latest book, "you must supply your customer with a reason to buy you instead of your competitor. If your company has such a reason, you must then 'package' it into a simple word or set of words that is positioned in the ultimate background, the minds of your customers and prospects."

This is what Trout calls positioning, and it is an essential ingredient of keeping your message simple and stable. It's much the same set of ideas championed by Michael Treacy and Fred Wiersema in the 1996 book, *The Discipline of Market Leaders.*

Keeping it simple in this way seems like a no-brainer until you realize how many companies don't project a clear, unique identity. Just check out the ad campaigns, as Trout does in his book. IBM's "Solutions for a Small Planet" theme fails to point out the company's unique ability to "put all the pieces together" through integrated computing.

If the image doesn't carry the core message of what makes each company different from its competitors, Trout implies, the company doesn't know what it's doing.

Some keys to simplicity (for overall organizations) compiled by Steve Haines and the Centre include the following:

1. "Rule of Three" and "Three Times Rule"
2. 80/20 Rule
3. The Systems Thinking Approach
4. KISS mindset
5. Single page documents
6. Simplicity Rule — *P. Crosby*: "Let's make a rule that we can't use anything I can't explain in five minutes"
7. Flexibility — "Strategic Consistency and Operational Flexibility"
8. Fundamentals — *P. Crosby*: "We could learn a lot from military training"
9. Thank you cards
10. *Alan Landers*: Simple, Yet Powerful Rewards:
    - Celebrate the moment
    - Recognize the effort
    - Time with the boss
11. What else?

SIMPLICITY AND COMPLEXITY

Below are quotes from three notable thinkers on the subject of simplicity and complexity.

> *I wouldn't give a fig for the simplicity this side of*
> *complexity but I'd give my life for the simplicity on*
> *the far side of complexity.*
> *-Justice Oliver Wendell Holmes*

> *Any idiot can simplify by ignoring the complications. But, it*
> *takes real genius to simplify by including the complications.*
> *-John E. Johnson, TEC Chair (The Executive Committee)*

> *For every complex problem there is a simple*
> *answer and...it is always wrong.*
> *-H. L. Menkin*

FOUNDER OF SIMPLICITY

Ludwig Von Bertalanffy, the founder of General Systems Theory, is the "genius" and major leader and pioneer of the 21st century systems thinking orientation and its resultant simplicity ... through our holistic, synergistic, and integrated thinking called The Systems Thinking Approach.

Nobody's saying that dealing with ongoing, revolutionary change will be easy, but as the examples above indicate, there exists a wealth of potential growth and success through new strategies that incorporate more teamwork, greater empowerment, and faster, smarter new leadership.

PUBLIC SECTOR STRATEGIES OF THE 21ST CENTURY

In the public and not-for-profit sectors, widespread disappointment in the general quality or lack of services plus high taxes are creating the same need for new strategies that the private sector is experiencing. Many public sector organizations are now aggressively seeking and implementing strategies that are more like those used by the private sector, including those 15 that I articulated earlier in this chapter.

In addition, their strategies include

1. Steer, not row (facilitate vs. do-it-yourself).
2. Empower communities and customers to solve their own problems rather than simply deliver services.
3. Encourage competition rather than monopolies.
4. Be driven by missions, not rules.
5. Be results-oriented by funding outcomes rather than inputs.
6. Meet the needs of the customer, not the bureaucracy.
7. Concentrate on earning and making money rather than spending it.

8. Stop subsidizing everyone. "User pay" through charging user fees.
9. Invest in preventing problems rather than curing crises.
10. Decentralize authority.
11. Solve problems by market influences rather than public programs.
12. Reduce regulations; cut out bureaucracy and low risk taking.
13. Privatization (except for essentials not provided elsewhere).

These 13 strategies (some adapted from Osborne and Gaebler's book, *Re-inventing Government*) are being employed in the restructuring of the public and not-for-profit sectors.

Example: These strategies are actually quite similar to those of the private sector, and have been used extensively in New Zealand over many years. Also, beginning in 1993, Premier Ralph Klein of Alberta, Canada, has been called "a dog with a bone" by strenuously adhering to these strategies. Vice President Al Gore's *Reinventing Government Initiative* is another example of such strategy, as are those of many U.S. States — Oregon, Wisconsin, Minnesota (Gov. Jesse Ventura), etc.

Regardless of what strategies you and your organization choose, however, there are two types (of strategies) that every organization needs. These are explained in the following section.

BOTH CUTTING AND BUILDING STRATEGIES ARE NEEDED

Are you "planning not to lose"
or "playing to win?"

In developing your core strategies, one thing to avoid is the fallacy of thinking in terms of financial strategies, such as cost cutting, alone. By their very nature, many financial strategies are really cost-cutting strategies; they cannot stand on their own and produce long-range solutions. Strategies such as retrenchment, turnarounds, cost reductions, divestitures, reorganizing, value-chain management, business process reengineering, and lay offs may all be necessary to reduce overhead costs and sustain financial viability. Keep in mind, however, that they are mostly "cutting" strategies that keep you from failing (i.e., "playing not to lose").

You'll need other core strategies that are "building" you toward your ideal future (i.e., "playing to win"), such as TQM, Service Quality, Capacity Building (Leadership), product innovations, etc. In order for any strategy that involves "cutting" to be successful, it must be consciously coupled with a strategy of "building" toward your customer-focused vision. One without the other won't work long term. *Caution:* In addition to striking this balance between cutting and building, keep in mind that you'll need a good supply of patience — results aren't usually instantaneous. It's important to recognize that you'll need to "hang in" there during the transition from cutting strategies to building strategies.

Example: In other words, if your organization chooses to defray expenses by cutting down on employee training or production costs, it also needs to consider the future-building strategy of customer satisfaction. In this way, you can be sure you aren't mistakenly reducing your employees' skills in implementing any customer recovery strategy, or eliminating a feature of the product that has perceived value to your customer.

Example: In making technology decisions, you need to ask yourself three key questions:

1. Will it improve our ability to serve our customers?
2. Will it improve productivity?
3. Will it empower my people to get the information they need more quickly and accurately?

Too often CEOs are uncomfortable with technology and allow the "techies" to make these large and expensive decisions instead.

QUESTIONS TO PONDER

- Have you developed three to seven core strategies for bridging the gaps between your Ideal Future Vision and your Current State Assessment?
- In developing your strategies, have you taken into consideration the 15 new strategies for the 21st century?
- In the public or not-for-profit sector, have you used some of the 13 entrepreneurial principles of government to address your public's disappointment in the quality and lack of services available to them?
- Are you integrating building strategies as well as cutting (i.e., financial only) strategies?
- Finally, do you have a small number of focused core strategies (remember, the smaller the better)?

DEVELOPING CORE STRATEGIES; PUBLIC AND PRIVATE

Corporations are successful not because of the hundred and one good little actions they take to save money on paper clips and telephone calls, but because of one or two major strategies that are brilliant.

-Dr. Michael J. Kami

You may not realize it, but if you've been doing a good job of building your vision, mission, values, and Key Success Factors, you've been talking strategy all the way along. Whenever you talk about ends or desired outcomes, you've already talked about strategy. Now you need to draw from all those conversations, the elements you'll use to develop core strategies.

When developing your organization's core strategies, keep in mind that they should serve you in the following ways:

1. Core strategies should define your competitive business advantages, leading to long-term sustainable organizational viability.
2. They should help you select how you define, organize, and grow the elements or SBU parts of your business.
3. They should help you determine your overall organization design and structure, along with individual job design/employee initiative characteristics, and philosophy.
4. Core strategies must lead to a list of action items for each core strategy, over the life of the planning horizon. These action items are long-term, unifying directions for the lower levels of the organization.
5. Core strategies will become the "glue" (or yearly goals and objectives or shared strategies) around which to organize your annual planning process.

In addition, extensive best practices research by Ernst & Young and the American Quality Foundation (previously mentioned), as well as our own Centre for Strategic Management research on the Vital Few Leverage Points for strategic change led us to the same conclusions: There are only *three universally beneficial practices* with a significant impact on performance, regardless of an organization's starting position.

1. Strategic planning/deployment (implementation)
2. Customer-focused business process improvement methods
3. Continuous broadening of your range of management practices to make additional gains in performance

The rest is a "fit" (or systems thinking approach) question of organization, environment, performance.

Such conclusions have led us at the Centre to focus on the following three core intervention technologies with all our clients. *The research all verifies that the way to organizational success is through choosing the "Right Answers" that are the main premises of this book:*

Right Answer #1: Institutionalize a strategic management system (Strategic Planning and Strategic Change Management).

Right Answer #2: Create professional management and leadership practices and skills as the only long-term competitive advantage.

Right Answer #3: Use our Systems Thinking Approach; focus on outcomes, serving the customer being primary.

You'll need to develop a maximum of three to seven core strategies to successfully achieve your outcome of focusing on the customer. If your organization is like most, you'll probably end up selecting too many strategies, as there are a wealth of opportunities in today's global and Internet changes. However, if you want to be successful, you'll need to collectively commit to cutting to no more than three or four. It is important to keep core strategies to a small number. Implementing and coordinating more than three or four usually becomes unmanageable, as you're trying to be all things to all people, as we have noticed in our discussion of positioning.

In my doctoral research on U.S. savings and loans (prior to their demise), I discovered that among the most profitable savings and loans, the average number of core strategies was three. Among the top 200 U.S. savings and loans, the worst performers had five or more core strategies.

This 60% increase in the number of strategies the worst savings and loans chose consistently weakened their concentration and attention to their real issues. The overall conclusion of this and much more research was that carefully selected, core strategies were essential to achieving a customer-focused, high-performance organization.

Example: In the late 1980s, Imperial Corp. of America — a $13 billion, nationwide savings and loan holding company based in San Diego — decided on diversification as the best avenue for growth. The CEO and CFO developed a matrix of 231 business niches that they could conceivably enter. Of these 231 areas, they settled on 114 different products and delivery niches. They saw these as the best areas, as they had the highest profit margins.

The problem with this rationale is that high profit margins usually indicate high risk. In addition, Imperial experienced great difficulty in managing such a large number of disparate businesses, each requiring different strategies and professional management. The Resolution Trust Corp. ended up taking Imperial over and liquidating it, costing taxpayers over $1.3 billion in the 1990s.

In any case, every organization should tailor its core strategies to its own unique situation and risk level. My consulting projects have involved me in developing and implementing many of the strategies outlined here; from defining "what business we're in," and profiling (and strengthening) marketplace position, to Total Quality Management and Leadership (TQM/TQL), to value-chain management, to linking budgets to strategies, and to restructuring. However, the driving force of any organization as a system should always be based on the outcome of being a customer-focused, high-performance organization.

FACING CHANGE AND DEALING WITH IT

In order to survive the changes that have already taken place, as well as those yet to come, organizations today must examine the way they respond to change. Change is not going away anytime soon; if anything, it will be knocking at our door more and more frequently. Change is inevitable, but how it affects us is often determined by how we react to it. If we look at change as an expected visitor, rather than an unwanted guest, we can condition ourselves to accept it as a natural part of organizational life.

This attitude entails looking for the right answers and reinventing our strategic planning and implementation process so that it can be flexible enough to accommodate change. Though this sounds simple enough, implementing strategic planning and setting a strategic management system structure in place creates change, which I refer to as the Rollercoaster of Change (see Figure 10.1, adapted from numerous disciplines, including *Death & Dying*).

Though this sometimes comes as a surprise to people, it makes sense for two reasons: (1) the *reason* you are planning is because you need things to change, and (2) the *outcome* of setting all that planning in motion is The Rollercoaster of Change that can ultimately result in the desired organization-wide outcomes, but that also requires enormous skill and leadership to successfully manage through the rough times of change.

I named this the Rollercoaster of Change and began incorporating it into my work in the late 1970s, when it became apparent to me that this was often where the strategic change and implementation process got bogged down. Too often, organizations would do all their planning, conduct a Parallel Process, then go into the implementation stage full of high hopes. If change was not felt quickly, however, or was met with resistance, organizations would have a tendency to scrap the whole process, thus negating all the good, hard work they had done originally.

The reality, however, is that most major change — whether an organization is conducting strategic planning, a turnaround, or a competitive business renewal — happens over a long term of 3 to 5 years. Organizations must learn to bridge the gap between planning and its implementation with disciplined persistence. By showing

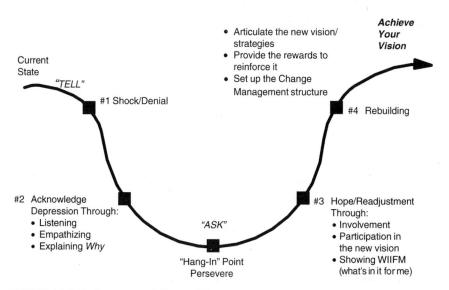

FIGURE 10.1 Rollercoaster of Change.^{SM}

organizations how to get through the Rollercoaster of Change, and to expect resistance as a natural part of the process, I have experienced vastly higher rates of successful implementation.

Cost cutting as a strategy is a good example of what takes place in the Rollercoaster of Change. As I previously indicated, it is almost always the first, inevitable step in any change effort. Because cost cutting is such an obvious and pervasive step, it's important for you to understand that initiating this process causes a natural reaction of shock, anger, and depression. As organizational leaders, you must prepare yourselves and your employees for this, and find ways to manage and weather it successfully.

WHAT IS GOING TO CHANGE?

Another way to make change less intimidating is to clearly demonstrate, organization-wide, what specific paradigm shifts and changes to expect from the core strategies. For instance, let's say one of your organization's core strategies is to "make TQM happen." Spell out, in simple terms, that you're going to need to go *from* TQM being just another buzzword, *to* having it as an integral part of your culture. The strategic business plan below from the Navy Public Works Center (PWC) in San Diego, California, gives other good examples of some typical paradigm shifts to expect from strategies.

NAVY PUBLIC WORKS CENTER
SAN DIEGO, CALIFORNIA

STRATEGIC BUSINESS PLAN

Core Strategy #1: World-class delivery machine (Innovation)
   Core Strategy Statement: Improve our processes, align our organizational structure and leverage technology to create a World Class Products and Services Delivery Machine.
   Paradigm Shift: *From* Improved Products and Services Delivery
                    To World Class Products and Services Delivery

Core Strategy #2: Sharpen Client Focus
   Core Strategy Statement: Delight our Warfighters through integrated client focus and teamwork throughout the region.
   Paradigm Shift: *From* Improved Customer Relations
                    To Proactive Customer Relations

Core Strategy #3: Business Evaluation and Planning (Operations)
   Core Strategy Statement: Establish our world-class position by aggressive business evaluation, planning, and product line management.

Paradigm Shift: *From* Competitive
               To Dominant

Core Strategy #4: Personal Leadership by Everyone (People)
  Core Strategy Statement: Fully realize personal leadership and team-
work to enable all of us to deliver great performance.
  Paradigm Shift: *From* Inconsistent Personal Leadership
                To Principled-Centered Leadership

You *can* survive change by articulating and using the "from–to" changes as you
not only make the required *cuts* but also *build* your core strategies for the future in
a participative manner. These will generate involvement, hope, readjustment, and
renewed commitment, enabling the organization to start building (or rebuilding) its
competitive advantage and customer-focused vision. Figure 10.2 shows how all this
fits into the Rollercoaster of Change.

One final word about handling change; remember the strategy of simplicity. It's
a truth of human nature that we don't experience fear or apprehension in situations
that are easy to get our thoughts around. Keep this thought in mind all throughout
the shaping, choosing, and implementing of your core strategies.

CREATING STRATEGIC ACTION ITEMS

For each core strategy, every organization needs a set of strategic action items (SAIs)
to achieve that strategy over the planning horizon. Thus, there are four steps to
consider when creating really excellent core strategies:

1. Ensure that you have a crystal clear strategy statement for each core
   strategy to guide the action items.
2. Be clear also on any paradigm shifts (i.e., "from–to") that are indicated.
3. Limit yourself to 5 to 15 (maximum) major items for each strategy to
   focus the changes.
4. For every strategy you want to accomplish, set/list three top action priorities for the next year.

SETTING ACTION PRIORITIES OVER 12 MONTHS

Once you've reached consensus on your strategic action items, you'll need to set
the top three to five action priorities for each strategy over the next 12 months. These
will provide direction for everyone in setting their annual, departmental, and individual goals. In effect, if you have six core strategies and three top priorities for
each one, you have eighteen top priority actions to accomplish as an organization
over the next year.

Example: Best Western International, Inc., developed 7 strategies and 20 action
priorities. For the first year of implementation, an *average of three actions* per
strategy is recommended.

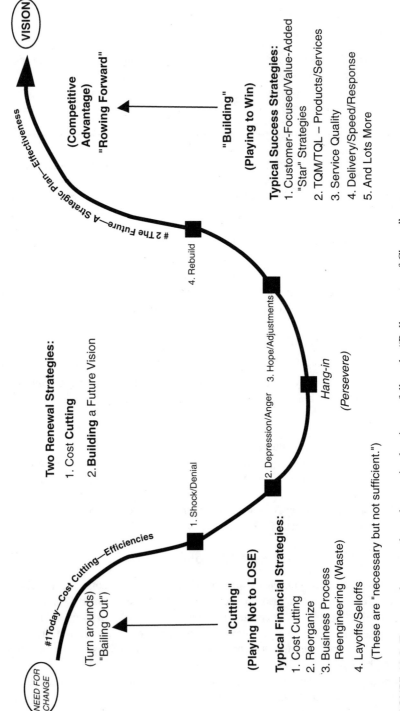

FIGURE 10.2 Turnarounds, renewals, and strategic planning — follow the "Rollercoaster of Change" sequence.

DEVELOP STRATEGY SPONSORSHIP TEAMS

> *Never tell people how to do things. Tell them*
> *what you want them to achieve and they will*
> *surprise you with their ingenuity.*
>
> *-General George S. Patton*

The next step in strategy development is to form cross-functional teams of senior management change agents. Forming cross-functional teams is about creating organization-wide, enthusiastic commitment to your core strategies.

Asking the hierarchical organization to change is insane: it was built to maintain the status quo that exists today. In order to change, you need a "critical mass" of change agents, and the best way to accomplish this is through volunteer senior management strategy sponsorship team (SST) members (and others) choosing what they're particularly passionate about. This is especially true for organizations of more than 200 employees.

For each core strategy, ask for volunteers from the senior members of the core planning team to act as "champions." Be careful to seek out these individuals wherever they have a passion to see the particular change occur. In this way, they will likely be proactive in fulfilling their champion roles, which are:

1. To be kept informed of the status of the core strategy's actual implementation — to keep the strategy alive.
2. To actively support and perform a leadership role in advocating the core strategy across the organization.
3. To cajole, agitate, and otherwise push and influence the people organizationally responsible to implement this core strategy to keep it moving forward (i.e., reverse the entropy that usually occurs with achieving change within a day-to-day context).
4. To advise and recommend actions needed to achieve this strategy.
5. To actively track and monitor the core strategy's success and report on it at quarterly SCLSC meetings.

> *In any business, the toughest things to succeed at,*
> *with the highest failure rates, are the newer things,*
> *the less certain thing. It should be a very high*
> *priority to put the best darn senior relevant person*
> *you have full-time on a new product in order*
> *to make that acorn become an oak tree.*
>
> *-Josh Weston, Chairman and CEO*
> *Automatic Data Processing, Inc.*

Once you've gotten the first champion to volunteer for their "passion," have all other planning team members volunteer to champion one or two of the core strategies: this will comprise the core of your strategy sponsorship teams. Use the chart in Figure 10.3 to list all team members, and remember to be clear on the roles of SSTs in contrast to the line organization.

STRATEGY SPONSORSHIP TEAMS (SSTs)

Roles of these SST champions — to keep the strategy alive

1. To be kept informed of the status of the core strategy's actual implementation.
2. To actively support and perform a leadership role in advocating this core strategy across the organization.
3. To cajole/agitate and otherwise push and influence the people organizationally responsible to implement this core strategy to keep it moving forward (i.e., Reverse the entropy that usually occurs with achieving change within a day-to-day context).
4. To advise and recommend actions needed to achieve this core strategy.
5. To actively track and monitor the core strategy's success and report on it at quarterly SCLSC meetings.

Champions for Strategic Plan Implementation

SST For Each Core Strategy (Sponsors, Leaders, Champions)	Line Manager (Still Accountable for all Core Strategies)
1. Accountable to be Devil's Advocate; to cajole, push, lead, agitate for these to change/succeed. 2. Report quarterly to the SCLSC on the status of the Core Strategy. Use the KISS method—mostly verbal reports/dialogue is desired. 3. Receive all department plans for this Core Strategy. Review/critique them. 4. Support and work with line managers on coordination and achievement of this Core Strategy. Do it in a way to ensure line manager has no surprises at the quarterly SCLSC meeting. 5. Can increase in size beyond the Strategic Planning Committee membership if needed.	1. Continue to be accountable/responsible for actions/results. 2. Develop annual department plans for your area of responsibility around each Core Strategy in order to support, contribute to, and help achieve each one. 3. Track, monitor, correct, and reward achievement of the actions. 4. Work with and keep SST informed of actions/priorities of the annual plan company-wide. 5. Can be a member of SST as well. 6. Participates in the quarterly SCLSC meeting discussions/future actions.

Possible Secondary Role for SST	*SST Non Role (Absolutely)*
6. Can grow beyond SST concept into becoming a proactive coordinator or task force (half way to becoming accountable).	7. Do not take over the line managers' direct accountability and allow them to assume a passive role.

FIGURE 10.3   Accountability and responsibility of each core strategy.

When developing your teams, be sure to spread out the planning team members so that each strategy team has roughly the same number of participants. Each person should choose a Strategy Sponsorship Team based on their passion and energy in seeing that the core strategy is actually achieved. Your end goal is to have a balanced mix of cross-functional team members, not necessarily just people with the direct line responsibility to implement the core strategy.

Tip: SSTs can also be supplemented by key stakeholders. However, keep each team at six to eight people (maximum) for ease of group dynamics/actions. Also, keep SSTs verbal, fluid, and dynamic. Whatever you do, don't bog them down in reports and paperwork.

QUESTIONS TO PONDER

- Do your core strategies focus on your positioning to create competitive business advantages?
- Is the change (from–to) affected by these strategies clear throughout the organization?
- In developing your external marketplace strategies, have you focused on all the customers' needs on our Star Model (Chapter 7).
- What is your strategy on E-commerce and alternative delivery systems?
- Have you made accommodation for the Rollercoaster of Change?
- Do you have both cutting and building strategies?
- Are you playing "not to lose" or playing to win?
- Do each of your core strategies have corresponding action items that are prioritized over the next 12 months?
- Have you created Strategy Sponsorship Teams (SSTs) that will "champion" each core strategy in its implementation?

STRATEGY PAGE STANDARD FORMAT

As a way to clarify and simplify your strategic plan, Figure 10.4 provides one way to show all the key strategic planning documents on a single page for each strategy. It is an excellent way to create simplicity on the far side of complexity.

IN SUMMARY

Again and again, on this very front, organizations in the U.S. are still struggling to learn the same three lessons:

First, we have used up all our strategic reserves, or slack. The only slack still remaining is the boundless energy, creativity, and self-confidence of the American people, if only we could harness those resources to our advantage once again in this information and Internet era.

Second, the age of unrefined mass production and mass consumption is over. This is the age of highly refined, specialized niche markets, all the way to one to one marketing.

Third, every strategy that created success in times of stability and plenty now produces failure in these times of worldwide competition and dynamic changes (the "failure" of success — "things will be good because they always have been"). As Jack Welch said, "If you're doing things the same way as you did them five years ago, you are probably doing something wrong."

Key Success Factors Related to This Strategy							
Factor	Measure	Target '99	2000	2001	2002	2003	2004
1.							
2.							
3.							

1. **Strategy Title** (3 words max): _____

2. **Strategy Statement:** "To_____

    _____ "

    (Action-oriented **sentence** of what the strategy is.)

3. **From:**   **To:**

    (How is the strategy changing – alternative is "continue to _____.")
    (Keep it short, focused phrase of 2–8 words)

4.	**Strategic Action Items** (over the next 3 years):	Lead	By When
	*1.		
	*2. (Simple declarative statements of actions;		
	3. start with action verbs.)		
	4.		
	*5.		
	6.		
	7.		
	8.		
	9.		
	10+. (Be all inclusive – more is better)		
	11+. (the more specific, the better)		

5. * = Top priority **must do** actions for the next 12 months (average 3 per strategy).

FIGURE 10.4 Strategy page standard format.

By implementing solid, future-based, growth-oriented core strategies — and carrying them out consistently and persistently over the life of the planning horizon — organizations will not only find that they have learned these lessons, they will also find themselves thriving into the third millennium.

I will end with what I think is the best strategy of all; "having fun."

Four Principles of Having Fun in an Organization

1. We Play (We Don't Work)
2. ("Go ahead") Make Their Day (Involve Customers)

3. Be There (Be Present)
4. Choose Your Attitude

Pike's Market Fish Company
Seattle, Washington

RECAP OF KEY CONTENT POINTS

- Your organization will need to develop a small number (3 to 7) of core strategies for bridging the gaps between your Ideal Future Vision and your Current State Assessment.
- When developing your strategies, consider these newer strategies for the 21st century:
  1. Enterprise resource planning
  2. Electronic commerce
  3. Flexibility
  4. Speed
  5. Horizontally integrated products
  6. Networks and alliances
  7. Value-added
  8. Environmentally improved products
  9. Mass customization
  10. Commonization/simplification
  11. Value-chain management
  12. Organizational learning
  13. Automated employee morale/benefits
  14. Management and leadership practices
  15. Simplicity
- In order to successfully reinvent your strategic planning and implementation process, you must make accommodation for The Rollercoaster of Change.
- Also, be sure you integrate "building" as well as "cutting" (i.e., financial only) strategies. Remember, you've got to play to win.
- Have corresponding strategic action items (SAIs), prioritized over the next 12 months, for each of your core strategies.
- Create strategy sponsorship teams that will "champion" each core strategy.

"HOW-TO" ACTION CHECKLIST

1. Ascertain that your vision/mission/core values and Current State Assessment (including SWOT) are final, and then develop your new core strategies.
2. Develop a small number (3–7) of core strategies for implementing your organization's strategic plan. Make sure they serve you in the following ways:
   1. They should focus your competitive business advantages, leading to long-term, sustainable organizational viability.
   2. Core strategies should help you determine your overall organization design and structure, along with individual job design, employee initiative characteristics, and philosophy.
   3. Core strategies should act as the "glue" (or "shared strategies") around which you'll organize your annual planning process.
3. Develop core strategies that accommodate change, including both cutting and building strategies. Don't be afraid to be very specific, indicating exactly what you're changing to, and exactly what you're changing from.
4. Ensure your organization has clarity of any "from–to" paradigm shifts that will result from your new core strategies.
5. Develop cross-functional teams of change agents — called strategy sponsorship teams — led by senior management. Also, assign a volunteer senior member of the core planning team as a "champion" for each core strategy.
6. Each strategy should have its own strategic action items (SAIs), carried out over the life of the planning horizon. Once SAIs have been agreed upon, set the three to five top action priorities for each strategy over the next 12 months. If you have 6 core strategies with 3 top priorities each, you'll have a total of 18 top priority actions.
7. As soon as you've finished your list of top priority actions, make a list from this of actions to be taken in the next week, month, or quarter. Do NOT sacrifice the implementation of your new strategic plan to hesitation, confusion, or inaction.
8. Finally, remember to take each stage of your strategy development through a Parallel Process, giving all levels of your organization's workforce the opportunity to buy into their strategic plan.

11 Business Unit Planning (Step #6)

> *A multi-division company without an overall strategy is not even as good as the sum of its parts. It is merely a portfolio of non-liquid, not-tradable investments which has added overhead and constraints. Such closed-end investments properly sell at a discount from the sum of its parts.*
>
> *-Bruce Henderson, Founder, Boston Consulting Group*

STRATEGIC BUSINESS UNITS: THE BUSINESSES YOU ARE IN

To make optimum use of the core strategies that will take your organization to its Ideal Future Vision, you'll need to carefully define what businesses you are in. You do this by identifying your Strategic Business Units (SBUs). (See Figure 11.1.)

Strategic Business Units are the business or line elements (or parts of the organization) that make up your total corporate or organizational entity. Generally speaking, SBUs can be identified if they meet these criteria:

- They produce and market a well-defined set of related products and/or services.
- They serve a clearly defined set of customers, in a reasonably self-contained geographic area.
- They compete with a well-defined set of competitors.

In many of today's organizations — particularly those that are of a multibusiness structure — it's not always a simple matter to clearly identify and define Strategic Business Units. More detailed SBU criteria would include the following:

- Existing as separate and distinct units, generally more self-contained, with their own mission and strategic plans (under the organization-wide plan and strategies).
- Usually, SBUs are about "what we do," not "how we do it."
- They can be the business transactions you perform for a customer (but not the values or support functions).
- Usually, they are based on your driving force(s) or core strategies.

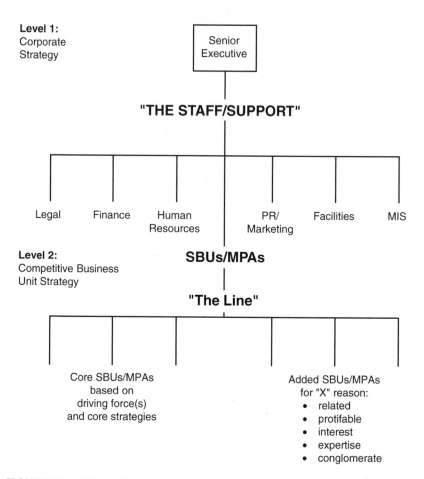

FIGURE 11.1 SBUs, MPAs, Divisions, Units, etc.

- They are often representative of specific skills and expertise (i.e., core competencies).
- They could be specific areas focused on specific, desired results or outcomes (but not just activities).
- SBUs should exist where the preponderance of your business is with outside customers (as opposed to sister departments or divisions).
- They should be units that have the authority to implement and adjust plans once approval is granted.

To determine exactly (1) what businesses you want to be in the future, and (2) what it will take to get there, clarifying your Strategic Business Units is extremely important. It forces you to evaluate your overall portfolio of businesses to be sure you know why you're in each of these businesses, and to properly allocate your resources accordingly.

Example: General Motors has, in effect, three main business units (SBUs): (1) Hughes Aircraft (defense industry), (2) GMAC (finance), and (3) vehicle (cars and trucks) production.

SBUs need to fit within an overall corporate strategy of relatedness (such as GMAC) to an organization's driving forces or core strategies, or to its core expertise or competency. Any other reason should be honestly and clearly articulated (even if it isn't a good reason). This underlying honesty should incorporate reasons such as profitability, a champion's interest, or the building of a powerful conglomerate (such as GE).

In the public sector, unfortunately, there is no such equivalent to a clearly identifiable Strategic Business Unit. As you might guess, this makes for a lot of the confusion you may encounter when running, or dealing with, public or not-for-profit organizations.

In my work with the public sector, this has been a recurring problem. For the sake of clarity, I've coined the term "Major Program Areas" when referring to Strategic Business Units in public and not-for-profit organizations.

Example: In British Columbia's Ministry of the Environment, there are (1) the Fish and Wildlife program, (2) the Water Management program, (3) the Lands and Parks program, and (4) the Environmental Protection program (includes water, air, and some lands). Additionally, there are six geographical regions with responsibility for all these programs across the province.

This is a confusing structure, as there's no clear, identifiable construct by category — such as natural resources, inhabitants, or activities — upon which to define their businesses. For instance, how do you organize your thinking about their business units? Is it (1) a construct around inhabitants, such as fish and wildlife? If it is, then what happens to birds? Or is it a construct around (2) the natural resources of the earth, such as water and land? If so, then why is air not included? Even more confusing, there's a further construct (3) of responsibility for all of these programs by the six different regions mentioned above.

This is a perfect example of why each organization needs to clearly define its business units — using either the Strategic Business Units (SBUs) or Major Program Areas (MPAs) terminology — in order to determine if what it presently has will take it toward its desired future outcomes. With three different constructs all in use concurrently, it's no wonder this Ministry of the Environment has a difficult time trying to run its separate programs and regions: not only are they all separate from one another, none of their units are interlocking in any way. It's an obvious example of why it's important to pick one construct and follow it.

MATCHING YOUR STRATEGIC BUSINESS UNITS TO YOUR MISSION STATEMENT

Everyone talks about sticking to the knitting, but a lot
of companies don't know what their knitting is.
-Benjamin Tregoe, Chairman, Kepner-Tregoe

Your organization's mission statement is all about "who, what, and why you're in business." Strategic Business Units and Major Program Areas represent the various "whats" within the mission statement, and therefore must be grounded in it. As the earlier example of General Motors illustrated, it's imperative that your SBUs support that statement. If they do not, you've either got to change the statement or change the SBUs, or settle for running a confusing operation.

Once you've clearly defined your SBUs, you're ready to determine (1) *which* SBUs need enhancement, growth, or change, (2) whether you'll need to *add* any SBUs, and (3) exactly *how* (including how *much*) they need to change and grow over the life of your strategic plan. This must be accomplished because your Strategic Business Units usually represent the smallest subdivision for which you can develop a distinct, separate business strategy. They also represent the level at which you actually compete with other organizations in your industry, especially within conglomerates.

In order to get the fullest possible implementation of your organization's overall strategic plan, it is essential that these subdivisions create business plans of their own. Failure to do so will leave your organization with an overall blueprint — the strategic plan — but no specific, concrete actions for implementing the plan through your separate business units or program areas.

The goal here is not to invest in isolated projects that produce separate or incremental benefits, but to develop well-positioned business clusters whose synergy creates advantages that beat the cost of capital, increase return on investment, and build lasting shareholder value. To achieve this goal, an organization's management needs to develop overall core strategies that generally hold true for related business clusters, not just for one business at a time.

There are four basic mechanisms through which ongoing SBU synergies create value:

1. **Shared resources/activities.** SBUs or MPAs can share common activities — such as research and development, engineering, procurement, production or operations, pooled sales forces, marketing programs, distribution channels — thus achieving scale economies (such as at Proctor and Gamble).
2. **Spillover benefits of marketing and R&D.** Even when marketing and R&D activities aren't shared, businesses in a cluster often capture some of the indirect benefits of marketing and R&D expenditures that are made by sister businesses. For example, General Electric's research in turbine engines helped its aircraft engine business.
3. **"Similar" businesses (with the same core competencies).** Core competencies of knowledge and skills (both technical *and* managerial) can be shared across businesses in similar domains; i.e., similar technology industries or situations where retail marketing skills are key, such as Sony's miniaturization or Wal-Mart/Sam's Club.

4. **Shared image.** Individual business units in an organization gain in value by being strongly identified as members of the highly regarded corporate whole, like Disney's movies, theme parks, stores, and products, but *not* like Saturn disavowing its GM connections.

Other reasons for organizations to possibly add new SBUs might include

- **Evaluation.** Adding an SBU can make you better able to evaluate their inner workings, see if their products or services can be easier to create, bring you closer to your market, or improve their productivity.
- **Financing.** New SBUs are often considered because of the potential synergy they would offer the existing organization, again reducing such costs as training, development, production, cost of capital, cash cow potential, etc.

These are some of the reasons for adding new SBUs in order to better fulfill your overall organizational mission. To avoid vague, unclear, or irrational logic in this, however, there are six specific questions you'll need to be able to answer:

1. What is the *driving thrust or focus* for future SBU development that will help maintain or grow your desired core competencies?
2. What is the *scope of products* and *customers/market segments* that will (or will not) be considered?
3. What is the future *emphasis* or *priority* and mix for products and customers/market segments that fall within that scope?
4. What *key capabilities* or *competencies* are required to make this SBU's vision happen?
5. What does this SBU vision or direction imply for *growth and return* expectations?
6. What management expertise do we have that will help us in this SBU/MPA? How is it (will it be) better than others already in it?

Use the task in Figure 11.2 to help evaluate the pros and cons of new SBUs/MPAs. By following the 80/20 rule — keep 80% of your businesses in core competencies, 20% maximum outside your core competencies for additional resource allocation — you'll almost always stay on the right path when defining or changing your SBUs.

PRIORITIZING YOUR SBUs/MPAs

Once you've identified the existing, new, or altered SBUs, you'll need to fulfill your overall mission and start prioritizing them. As the matrix in Figure 11.3 shows, you do this by defining the size and percentage of each SBU/MPA as it will appear at the end of your planning horizon (i.e., Year X), then contrast it with today's status regarding its desired growth rate.

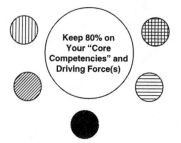

Instructions:
1. Allocate a maximum 20% outside your knitting to the bees—but do it with a "laser beam" vs. a "shotgun."
2. List new SBUs/MPAs here to see what % of your business you are expanding out of your core.

20% MAXIMUM RESOURCE ALLOCATION

Bees/Laser Beam Areas	% Money	% People	% Time	Materials
1.				
2.				
3.				
4.				
5.				
6.				
7.				
8.				
9.				
10.				
11.				
12.				
Maximum Total =	**20%**	**20%**	**20%**	**20%**

FIGURE 11.2 Stick to your knitting vs. bumble bees.

As you develop this future-oriented pro forma matrix for your organization's SBUs, consider these possible uses and implications of the matrix:

1. Plan the business/product/services direction at a concrete level for the next 2 to 3 years.
2. Analyze expected profit performance in specific ways.
3. Define which SBU/MPA businesses, products, or services your organization should, or should not take part in.
4. Decide on the amount of focus you desire within your overall vision/mission.
5. Prioritize and allocate resources, energy, and time.
6. Enhance image/marketing and employee efforts.
7. Conduct an environmental scanning and competitor analysis.
8. Ensure functional plans for all departments to support the business units as well as the organization as a whole.
9. Determine the degree of risk you are willing to take and are taking.

YEAR _____

Instructions: List the SBUs/MPAs you want the organization to have at the end of the planning process. Only after getting agreement on these should the rest of the matrix below be filled in/agreed to.

SBUs/MPAs	$ Amount of Business	% of Total	% Energy	Mission/Values Strategies Criteria	Why Will It Exist? (*RPIEC)
1.					
2.					
3.					
4.					
5.					
6.					
7.					
8.					
9.					
10.					

*Code: **R** = Related; **P** = Profitable; **I** = Interest of Champion; **E** = Expertise of a few people; **C** = Conglomerate
Note: *MPA = Major Program Area (a Public Sector Term)

FIGURE 11.3 Target goal.

10. Determine if you are going outside your core competencies and competitive edge.

It is crucial to closely analyze the factors of risk, driving force(s), organizational focus, and competitive approach. Without this careful analysis, you may be seduced further away from your mission/vision, rather than closer. The "X" test in Figure 11.4 can help you determine the risk and the validity of a new SBU or MPA.

Developing this careful evaluation of each SBU will help you in discovering and prioritizing viable business units that will take your organization to its chosen mission. In addition to analyzing risk and all the other corresponding factors, keep these common sense-basics in mind:

- Grow where the business is; don't try to make a market where none exists.
- Keep close to the customer's needs.
- Don't assume a good manager can run anything.
- Don't load down the producing people with nonproductive chores such as administrative reports.
- Debt is *not* your friend.

If the SBU/MPA you're looking at (1) doesn't predict a solid client relationship with a corresponding revenue, (2) doesn't foresee a hefty, long-term profitability, (3) doesn't have reasonable marketing and production requirements, or (4) won't give your organization a chance to earn top market positions, chances are it's a high-risk, relatively low potential SBU.

"X" TEST

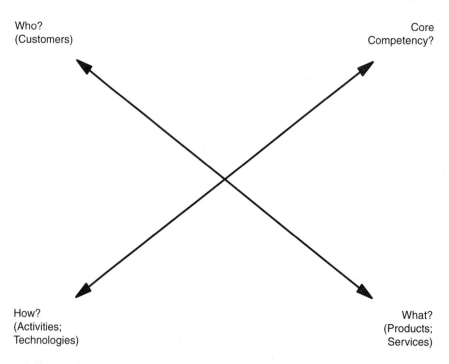

Who?
(Customers)

Core
Competency?

How?
(Activities;
Technologies)

What?
(Products;
Services)

* If a new SBU, product/service, or customer produces a change in more than one
   axis, the probability of failure is very high.

** If the change is in the driving force(s)/positioning, it is especially risky.

FIGURE 11.4 "X" — test for risk in changing positioning. Adapted from S. Haines, 1979.

Once you've assessed which SBUs/MPAs are right for your organization, set
your projections in motion by drawing up a formal scope paper and set of recommendations (see the model below) as to why you want to expand your SBUs. This
will help you further cement your thinking on the specifics involved in each
business unit.

NEW SBU/MPA

1. Scope Paper
   • What is the purpose of the SBU/MPA?
   • How does it relate to the organization's overall vision/strategies?
2. Business Case
   • What is the value added?

     a. Business plans, objectives, and timetables
     b. Overall organization value-added
     c. Good management practices/expertise of leaders to be used (from research — this is a key success factor)
3. Plus
   • Do a complete ROI analysis (return on investment).

MICROSMART VS. MACRODUMB: THE PORTFOLIO QUESTION

If you don't stand for something, you'll fall for anything.

Failing to focus on and prioritize your SBUs/MPAs can drastically reduce their results down the line. You run the risk of thinking at the *micro level* (analyzing projects, products, services, and programs at the business level — making decisions on the merits of the individual case), rather than the more holistic, *macro level* (analyzing a complete portfolio of business areas, lines, projects, programs, and elements — with decisions made as a totality).

I call this being *microsmart, yet macrodumb*. Strategic decisions need to consider your entire portfolio of business units (and potential ones, as well).

Example: One of our clients is in the high-tech field. The underlying question is, does he stay with his current technology, go to new technology, expand geographically across the U.S., go into peripheral business areas, or something else? This is a true portfolio question, because each possibility makes some sense in and of itself. However, if he tries to do all of them at once, he will end up failing.

And, while all this close SBU analysis may seem a bit much, the fact is that unless you evaluate SBUs/MPAs against your vision/mission and then prioritize any changes and actions they will require, it's a sure bet they won't be long-term, viable business units in today's world of dynamic change.

QUESTIONS TO PONDER

• Are any of your SBUs outside of (or do they expand beyond) your positioning/driving force(s) and core strategies and competencies?
• Have you assessed which SBUs/MPAs will need to be changed — or which new ones added — in order to fulfill your overall mission statement?
• Have you judged the level of risk involved, and can you ensure the risk is prudent?
• Do you have specific plans to deal with the risk?
• Can your SBUs/MPAs compete for the #1 or #2 spot in the marketplace, as they do at GE? If it's not #1 or #2, they sell it off.

- Are you "sticking to your knitting" by focusing on your core competencies, or are you in danger of trying to become "all things to all people?"
- Do the SBUs/MPAs outside your core related businesses reflect clear thinking and a rationale for their (continued) existence?
- Have you limited any new SBU searches to no more than 15% to 20% of your total effort and resources?
- Have you prioritized how you will allocate your future resources (money, people, time, materials) among all your SBUs/MPAs?

OVERVIEW: DEVELOPING THREE-YEAR BUSINESS PLANS FOR SBUS/MPAS

Now that you've clearly defined and prioritized your business units, the next step is to create a *three-year business plan* for each one. Each SBU or MPA must do this in order to compete successfully. Of course, it is important that each of these business plans derive from your organization's overall strategic plan, to exploit any synergistic possibilities.

Caution: Unfortunately, business planning is an area that is commonly missed by organizations. Passing it by can be a serious misstep. Without bringing the overall strategic planning down to the business unit level (in a "waterfall effect" fashion, as shown in Figure 11.5) organizations waste most of the hard work that has gone into their overall strategic plan for change.

In addition, you'll need to develop three-year business plans for all major support units, such as finance, MIS, human resources, legal, etc. Because these departments serve internal customers, however, they are, by their very nature, ideally required to wait until each SBU/MPA has completed its own business plan. It will be difficult for them to properly plan prior to that, because they won't know what each business unit (their customer) is going to need from them in the way of support.

Once organizations have built their strategic plan, however, they are often close to or getting close to beginning their yearly budget cycle, which makes it difficult to focus and devote the time necessary for three-year business planning. To offset this potential dilemma, you will have to skip business planning — for now — and go directly to building your annual plan and strategic budget (see Chapter 12 for more detail on this). Once that's done, you can come back later and build your three-year business unit and major support plans. While this isn't the ideal sequence, it is almost always the reality of the planning and budgeting cycle in my experience.

USING SYSTEMS THINKING IN YOUR THREE-YEAR PLANNING

Building three-year business plans for SBUs/MPAs follows exactly the same systems thinking process (A, B, C, D, E phases) that you used for overall strategic planning. However, it is actually much faster and easier, as you already have the organization-wide strategic plan to use as a guide and context within which to build your business plan.

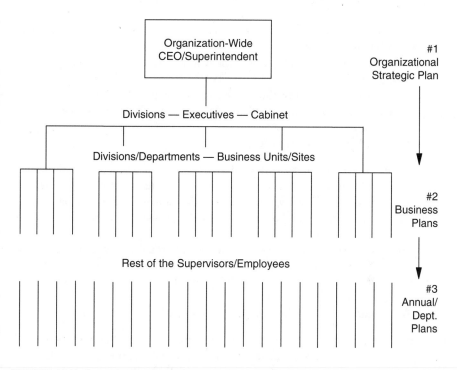

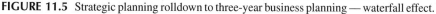

FIGURE 11.5 Strategic planning rolldown to three-year business planning — waterfall effect.

The first step in three-year business planning is Plan-to-Plan again, then begin developing a three-year business plan and document. Begin with Phase E — Environmental Scanning — then reacquaint your SBU/MPA with Phase A (Output: vision/mission/values) of the organizational strategic plan, and get a feel for how your particular unit fits within it.

Plan-to-Plan

Just as in your organization-wide strategic planning, there are specific guidelines for these business and program planning processes you need to focus on during the Plan-to-Plan day.

1. Conduct this entire process as a participative and open experience.
2. Have a core planning team of 15 or fewer people.
3. Involve key stakeholders with a Parallel Process:
   • Unit employees
   • Key organizational executives
   • Focus groups
   • Data exchange/other interface groups
4. Balance your time efficiency with preparation work vs. the need to develop ownership through "struggling" with the issues.

5. Review the organization's strategic planning document first in any planning offsite.
6. Conduct a values discussion (personal/organizational) to uncover issues and build teamwork.
7. Conduct a final plan review once the plan is done (daylong meeting with 30 to 60 people).
8. The standard amount of time for business planning is 5 days: 2 days on Phases A and B, 2 days on Phase C, and 1 day on Plan-to-Implement.

Phase A — Outcomes: Ideal Future

First, use the same vision as that of the overall organization — only one per organization, remember — then develop a mission statement for the business or major support unit, specifically defining how the unit will fulfill its part of the organization-wide mission. It should show why the business unit should exist in its own unique fashion.

For the final part of Phase A, review the overall organizational core values and determine if the unit will support those values. (Generally, it should and there's usually no need for additional values development.)

Phase B — Feedback: Key Success Measures/Goals

For Phase B (feedback, creating outcome measures of success), study the overall organization's Key Success Measures/Goals, then develop corresponding measures for your own unit, showing specifically how each SBU/MPA will link in helping to achieve the overall organizational Key Success Measures/Goals. Depending on the particular measure, the business unit could have the same one, or something that complements it. You may also add a few others that are unique to your unit.

For instance, if an organizational KSM/Goal states the goal of having at least a 9 on a 10-point scale in customer satisfaction, every unit must have the same goal. However, if one of the organization's KSMs states a specific, desired revenue and profit, each SBU would have a piece of this measure within its individual business unit. Together, all the SBUs should collectively accomplish the overall revenue and profit targets of the total organization.

Caution: The question of how to hold the SBU/MPA accountable for its "profit" can get a little tricky. There are different options on how to do this. (Figure 11.6.)

The proper answer as to where to hold them accountable is #4 in Figure 11.6, gross margin. However, organizations frequently hold the SBU/MPA accountable for its profit level *before* taxes (#6), but *after* allocation of overhead expenses (#5). Since the allocation of overhead expenses is something usually done by the finance department, though, it is not something the SBU has much control over.

The result of this #6 "accountability" level is often destructive infighting among SBUs and overhead support functions over allocated expenses. Since it's a win–lose situation, the worst part is that this allocation squabble adds nothing to the bottom line — or to customer satisfaction.

1. Where to hold the SBU/MPA accountable (at levels #4, #6, or #8)?

Standard Income Statement (P/L):

1.	Sales Revenue		_____
2.	C.O.G.S. (direct cost)	−	_____
3.	SBU operating costs (G/A)	−	_____
4.	Gross Profit/Margin	=	_____
5.	Organization-Wide Headquarters Operating Expenses (G/A) (Indirect Expenses/Overhead Allocated to the SBU)	−	_____
6.	SBU Profit Before Taxes	=	_____
7.	Taxes	−	_____
8.	NIAT	=	_____

> **The game is won or lost**
> **at the gross profit/margin line**
> *–John Zaepfel*

2. Discuss/agree on this as a key to accountability/responsibility.

3. If #5 is not the responsibility of the SBU/MPA, who is accountable/how do you get accountability/responsibility there?

FIGURE 11.6 KSMs for SBUs — accountability levels.

Example 1: A good example of this dysfunctionality was the method Sunoco adopted while the author worked there earlier in his career. A vertically integrated oil company, Sunoco broke itself into many different business units, and told each unit to compete and sell on the outside. Instead of developing into strong, externally oriented companies, the business units ended up vying for profits by trying to manipulate the allocated corporate overhead expenses and transfer pricing. Needless to say, this decentralization was a huge mistake and made serious inroads into Sunoco's overall long-term financial viability. It resulted in an ongoing, relentless demise that continues even today.

Example 2: On the other hand, for many years the Marriott Corp. has held their SBUs and properties accountable for gross profit/margin only. They have seen good results with SBUs matching their responsibility with their accountability.

A Marriott hotel, for instance, may have 40% gross margin accountability, but no accountability for corporate overhead expenses. This has created an environment in which each SBU and property exercises active daily control over its own gross margin to ensure success. If 40% is the target, then it follows that 41% is better, but 39% is not so good. This matches accountability with responsibility, and makes for a much more black-and-white, manageable scenario. Whatever formula your organization comes up with, its own best interest lies in finding ways, other than through turf battles, to control corporate overhead.

Phase C — Inputs: Core Strategies

In Phase C (Input) there are two key steps. In Step #4, Current State Assessment, each unit will need to know its own strengths and weaknesses internally, as well as its external opportunities and threats. Each business unit's planning team must look at all of the tools available to conduct its Current State Assessment, and then employ the ones that are most appropriate for them.

For Step #5, Developing Strategies, each unit needs to look at the organization's overall strategies and determine if it can apply some or all of those strategies to the unit, or if it will need to develop additional strategies specific to the unit in order to achieve its mission.

To do this successfully, you may want to make an analogy to the game of chess, posing such "down-board," longer-term questions as the following:

- Who is the competition?
- Where does the unit stand in terms of "market share" and the competition?
- In what way does the unit want to win vs. the competition; i.e., what is its overall strategy? (Remember, there *are* different strategies: win, lose, stay the same.)
- What "pawns," "knights," or "rooks" must the unit lose in order to win?
- Can the unit suffer these losses and still maintain integrity and consistency with its mission and values?
- What is the best opening move for the unit?
- What responses can the unit expect from its competitors, as well as from its employees?

Prior to finalizing its core strategies (Step #6), the unit should identify exactly what change is expected as a result of implementing each strategy: what it's changing from, and what it's changing to. And, it is imperative for the SBU to develop 5 to 15 Strategic Action Items for both the immediate priority and future implementation of its strategies over the three-year planning horizon.

Once you've agreed on your Strategic Action Items for each strategy and have created a clear "from–to" statement, it's time to finalize annual plans and budgets. (This will be covered in greater detail in Chapter 12.)

Phase D — Throughput/Actions: Implementation

Lastly, in Phase D, each unit will be dealing with throughput, strategy implementation, and change. Chapter 14 will cover this phase in depth.

In total, the processes involved in business/support unit planning generally require about 5 days to complete, and can be accomplished competently by following the steps shown in the business planning flowchart in Figure 11.7.

PLANNING AT THE SBU'S PRODUCT LINE/SERVICE LEVEL

To develop the most viable business plan for your SBUs/MPAs, you may need to create a product development committee (PDC) for new product development. The PDC is made up of key executives and specialists to plan, develop, track, and budget all future or enhanced products and services within each existing SBU/MPA.

The PDC is often a committee in charge of a variety of projects, and as such can utilize project management techniques and skills. Key points to address in product development include the following:

1. Is it a priority (i.e., 10% to 20% of time/energy going toward new products or businesses)?
2. Are there adequate resources devoted to it? Capital needs?
3. Does the SBU/MPA communicate well with the rest of the organization so all units know when to anticipate new products, services, or directions?
4. Is there strong senior management commitment to product development?
5. Is there a consistent strategy and direction for product development?
6. Are the right people involved in product development?
7. Is there a clear set of product development steps, accountability, authority, milestones, and reporting procedures? Are they clearly understood and utilized?
8. Are the product development timetables realistic and adhered to?
9. Is there a cross-functional team effort and shared goals across the organization for product development?
10. Are people open and honest about the issues and results during product development?
11. Is there department/senior management accountability and rewards for product development efforts and support?

Product development, particularly new product development, usually requires multiple levels of organizational approval. Because product development also has direct impact on the SBU/MPA business plan, it's crucial to include these product development steps in your planning.

As you can see here, product development steps have a marked similarity to those involved in creating a business unit plan:

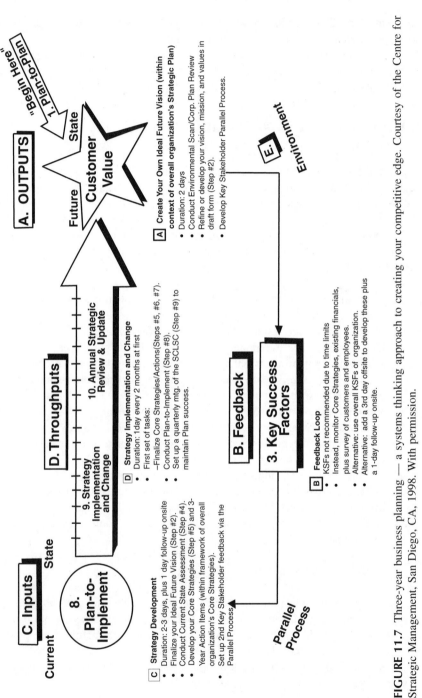

FIGURE 11.7 Three-year business planning — a systems thinking approach to creating your competitive edge. Courtesy of the Centre for Strategic Management, San Diego, CA, 1998. With permission.

1. Explore markets and competition for needs and wants.
2. Brainstorm ideas.
3. Initial development of all high potential concepts.
4. Screen down the number of concepts with customers, clients, users, etc.
5. Conduct a competitive product analysis.
6. Develop a 3-year pro forma.
7. Develop the product prototype.
8. Pilot test the prototype for performance.
9. Market test the product/packaging.
10. Modify the product/packaging as necessary.
11. Prepare for full-scale commercialization.
12. Launch the product.
13. Conduct a post-launch debriefing.
14. Monitor/correct product success.

When working on product development in conjunction with business unit planning, it's particularly important to identify what your market segmentation will be, and then develop support strategies around the four *P*s of marketing:

*P*roducts/services
*P*lace/geography
*P*romotion/sales/marketing
*P*rice

In many markets, price is a particularly critical and complex issue. If your organization is faced with competing against market price, you'll need to consider such questions as

1. Where can you find important purchasing criteria of which either buyers or competitors are not yet aware?
2. Are there ways in which you can shift the purchasing decision-makers within a buying organization to make your organization's uniqueness more valuable?
3. Are there barriers you can erect to protect that uniqueness and prevent competitors from imitating?
4. Can you find multiple sources of differentiation?
5. Can you reduce cost in activities that do not affect buyer value?
6. Can you command and sustain a price premium in selling to well-informed, upscale buyers?
7. Can you isolate and lower the costs of the activities you perform to differentiate your organization from its competitors?

When looking at pricing, you'll need to define your organization's objectives around the issue of price. As you can see in Figure 11.8, once your organization has agreed on its core orientation — be it profit, sales, volume, or status quo — there are many possible pricing objectives. Whatever pricing objectives you decide on —

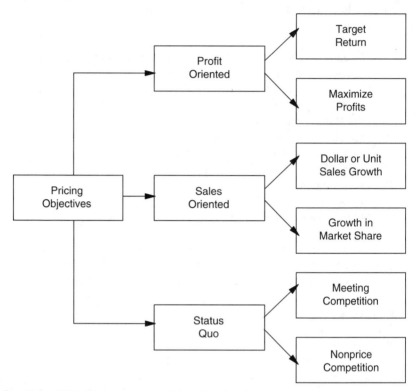

Question: which of these are your pricing objectives?

Do you agree/disagree as a planning team?

FIGURE 11.8 Possible pricing objectives/strategies.

from maximized profits, dollar or unit sales growth, market share growth, etc. — they will be the foundation for at least one, and maybe more of your SBU strategies. So choose carefully, and make sure the objectives are ones you can believe in.

SUPPORT NEEDS FOR BUSINESS UNIT PLANNING

It is important to keep in mind that this type of planning is comprehensive enough to create its own support needs. For instance, if your organization develops business plans for its five SBUs/MPAs, and three-year plans for its four major support units (all in addition to the overall organization-wide strategic plan), you could be looking at nine different business plans.

Because of this, be sure your organization has the internal support resources it needs to facilitate the development of these plans and their corresponding change management processes. If it already does, that's wonderful. If you feel there's a need for more support that's not already in place, you may need to assign and train appropriate individuals.

Example: At SaskEnergy, there was a shortfall of internal support personnel needed to carry their strategic planning through to the business unit level. Following a short, intensive training session, they ultimately created a cadre of nine skilled individuals to facilitate the process, as well as nine others who act as SBU support personnel.

QUESTIONS TO PONDER

- Have you brought your overall strategic planning down to the business unit level, with three-year business plans for your SBUs/MPAs/major support units?
- Do these plans follow exactly the same systems thinking, A, B, C, D, E phase process as in your overall strategic planning?
- Have you created a product development committee (PDC) for new product planning?
- Have you identified your market segmentation, and developed corresponding supportive strategies that incorporate the four P's of marketing?
- Have the support needs of your SBUs/MPAs been met?

IN SUMMARY

As you evaluate and build business units that will pay off on your bottom line, always keep in mind that they all must reflect your organization's core strategies. If there aren't clearly defined ties to the strategies that will help you achieve your Ideal Future Vision, poorly planned business units can quickly drain your organizational resources, knocking you off your desired path before you even realize it.

On the other hand, well-thought-out business units with clearly designated, prioritized plans and strategies, can be your organization's greatest asset. No matter what needs arise in assessing your SBUs or MPAs, make sure they're taken care of. Once you have a crystal-clear understanding of what each business unit is all about, and have made certain that the resources they need will be provided, these organizational "pieces" will reward your organization with a healthy, profitable, business "whole."

In sum, you need to take strategic planning down to the Strategic Business Unit/Major Support Department level of your organization as a system. Whether you do it in sequence or after Step #7 (Annual Planning/Strategic Budgeting), or choose not to tie it to your annual budget cycle, just make sure you do it. Failure to do so is a major mistake — it's impossible to create a critical mass for change without it. Consider the math:

6 Strategic Business Unit plans x 15 people on each planning team

= a total of 90 new change agents.

RECAP OF KEY CONTENT POINTS

- Evaluate your SBUs/MPAs to determine if any are outside your position-ing/driving force(s) and core strategies/competencies.
- Ascertain which SBUs/MPAs will need to change or be added in order to fulfill your organizational mission statement.
- Make sure you know the risk involved, and have specific plans to deal with it.
- Bring every step of your SBU/MPA planning back to your organization-wide core strategies.
- Limit your new SBU searches to no more than 15% to 20% of your total effort and resources.
- In your three-year business unit planning, be sure to follow the same systems thinking, A, B, C, D, E phase process as in your overall strategic planning.
- Incorporate new product development in your business unit planning.
- Identify the market segmentation of each business unit product or service, and develop support strategies that include the four Ps of marketing.
- Be sure to accommodate the support needs of each SBU/MPA business plan.

"HOW-TO" ACTION CHECKLIST

1. Define the SBUs/MPAs that currently exist in your organization.
2. Define the present revenue/profitability expectations of each SBU/MPA.
3. Delineate the desired future of each SBU/MPA, along with their future revenue/profits at the end of your planning horizon (Year X).
4. Develop criteria for SBU or MPA selection/exclusion/dropping — espe-cially the customer/market research.
5. Analyze each SBU/MPA based on that criteria; incorporate some tradi-tional analysis tools as well (i.e., risk, focus, etc.).

6. Force-rank a set of priorities of the remaining SBUs/MPAs.
7. Analyze these decisions from a holistic perspective. Make sure you haven't lost any core competencies by selective individual decisions.
8. For those SBUs/MPAs dropped or excluded, make a choice to either say "no" to the customer, or to develop strategic alliances/partnerships with others to provide for them.
9. Establish goals/targets for overall organization growth rates of volume and profitability.
10. Develop a three-year business plan for each SBU/MPA.
11. Establish an ongoing system to manage the changes resulting from your prioritization.
12. Develop product/market plans, organization structure, teams, and budgets to achieve your SBU/MPA targets, then adjust or reiterate this cycle where necessary to match resources with targets.

12 Annual Plans and Strategic Budgeting (Step #7)

Making the tough choices includes choosing where to leverage the organization.

SHARED CORE STRATEGIES: THE ORGANIZING PRINCIPLES OF ANNUAL PLANS

The art and skill of sharing and prioritizing. I've referred to them frequently in the last two chapters, but this is where you must make them real and turn the strategies into a viable, ever-present planning tool. In Chapter 10, we put in all the hard work of developing core strategies and setting priority actions to accompany each strategy. In Chapter 11 we defined and planned for your Strategic Business Units. It would be difficult, even demoralizing, to see all that work go down the drain at this point, but without setting annual plans under each core strategy, that's exactly what can happen. In case you don't believe this, see the following wake-up call and "reality check."

STRATEGIC MANAGEMENT REALITY CHECK

Talk is cheap. This is apparent from the results of a survey of more than 500 small and midsize companies that was conducted by the Oechsli Institute. Many of the employees say management's actions don't support the mission statement and that their company's workers don't understand what's expected of them. Worse, 8 out of 10 managers, salespeople, and operations employees say they are not held accountable for their own daily performance.[1]

Instead, we will use the Systems Thinking Approach of looking at the Seven Levels of Living Systems again. It is obvious that you need to cascade your planning down through all the organization's levels, from organization-wide to strategic business units to tactical department annual plans to individual performance appraisals (Figure 12.1).

The key to the Cascade of Planning is "Strategic Consistency and Operational Flexibility":

---

[1] *Source:* Performance Survey, the Oechsli Institute, Greensboro, NC, *Inc. Magazine*, July 1992.

1-57444-278-3/00/$0.00+$.50
© 2000 by CRC Press LLC

You don't implement a Strategic Plan
— *but* —
You do implement an Annual Plan
Based on the Strategic Plan

5 Year Strategic Plan
↓
3 Year Business Plan
↓
Annual Plan Priorities and Budgets
↓
Department Work Plans
↓
Individual Performance Plans

(The Glue: Shared Strategies and Common Values)

To help yourself focus on this point, always remember that the strategic plan is your blueprint — the overall design of your "house" — but it is not, and never will be the "house" itself (i.e., implementable in and of itself). Developing annual departmental plans and budgets based on your core strategies and annual priorities gives you the details that are necessary to make that "house" livable.

The sad truth is that this is where many organizations fall under the weight of their carefully designed strategic plan. Simply circulating a copy of their strategies with no corresponding, visible actions or expectations sends organization members a clear message: "Okay, we've [the planning team] done our part — now you're on your own to do yours. Oh, and do whatever you want, as there aren't any priorities or focus."

This is what leads to the infamous SPOTS (Strategic Plan On the Top Shelf ... gathering dust) syndrome. It's also abdication by senior management at its very worst. At it's very best, it's naive. In either case, it's unacceptable behavior for senior management.

The fact is, senior managers must persevere at this point, and give guidance on how they expect employees and their corresponding Strategic Business Units to "do their part." In order to avoid the very real possibility of your plan getting lost in the "I don't know what they expect *me* to do!" shuffle, you now must have each manager develop realistic annual plans (with the clear priorities of your organization's core strategies) and detailed expectations (remember the Strategic Action Items in Chapter 10). Then back it up with the necessary resources for implementing your core strategies.

This annual planning and budgeting (Step #7) is what I call the beginning of real strategic consistency and operational flexibility, and it is crucial. Remember, empowerment without direction is chaos.

Example: The fast food company, Jack in the Box, reexamined its strategic plan in light of some economic difficulties they encountered. In doing so, it quickly

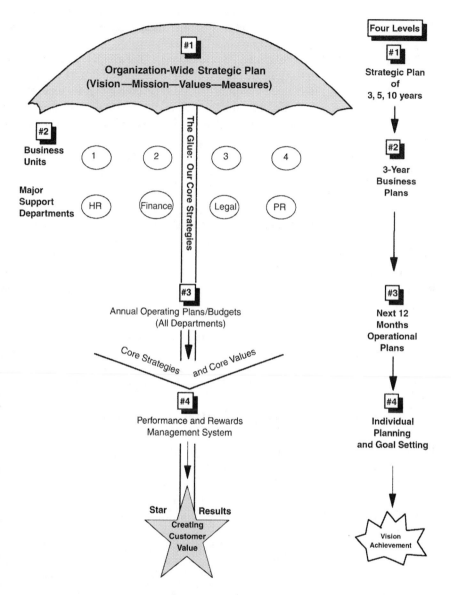

Key: Use the Core Strategies as the "Organization Principles" at all levels.

FIGURE 12.1 Cascade of Planning: shared strategies — strategic consistency yet operational flexibility.

became clear that they needed to rethink their economic structure and reprioritize their way of doing business.

Using their strategic plan as a focal point, they made major changes, including the layoff of more than 50 people. Before they got started, however, they determined that the main priority was avoiding any change that would derail or diminish any of their competitive strategies, and that this priority needed to be present in every change decision that was made.

Example: Another good example of prioritizing is the city of Saskatoon, in Saskatchewan, Canada. In its strategic plan, it chose seven core strategies as themes. Planners then came up with three priorities per strategy, giving them a total of 21 specific, clear priorities for change within the calendar year. These were then used as guides to each department's annual plan, as well as to the city's budgeting decisions.

CRAFTING EFFECTIVE ANNUAL DEPARTMENT "WORK PLANS"

Once you've chosen your core strategies and annual action priorities, you'll need to make up blank annual planning forms for each core strategy, with only the strategy shown at the top of each page. Use the format in Figure 12.2 as a guide for all departments in developing their annual plans. By having everyone use the same format and the same organizing frameworks (i.e., core strategies), you accomplish two things:

1. Establish the same key ways to communicate and work together around core strategies.
2. Focus everyone on organization-wide core strategies, and *not* on separate department goals or turf issues. There really should be no such thing as a departmental goal or objective; there should only be the department's contribution to the organization's overall core strategies.

If you must have departmental goals or strategies, then slot them under the organization-wide core strategies for consistency, e.g., under Core Strategy #3, list Goal 3.1, Goal 3.2, etc.

In any case, when completing the planning form, each department head should consider the following:

- What should our department actions be for supporting this strategy?
- How do our actions under each core strategy support the top-priority Strategic Action Items (SAIs) identified by management for this year?
- What resources or special support will we need?
- Who (specifically) will be responsible for seeing this through?
- What is a realistic target date for accomplishing this?
- How will we measure our progress?

Lastly, the "Who Else to Involve" column on the annual work plan (Figure 12.2) is critical to fill out, especially in a functional organization where horizontal or cross-functional teamwork is key to success, and not department or turf battles.

Department: _____

Date: _____
Fiscal Year _____

_____ : Strategy/Goals: _____

Yearly Pri #	Action Items (Actions/Objectives/How?)	Support/Resources Needed	Who is Responsible?	Who Else to Involve?	When Done?	How to Measure? (Optional)	Status

FIGURE 12.2 Annual work plan format (for functional/division work plans also).

Your department annual plans, then, should present your organizational core strategies as the organizing principles, with each one having a list of actions that must be completed in the coming year to support each strategy.

LARGE GROUP ANNUAL PLAN REVIEW AND APPROVAL

Even with the most thorough plans, it isn't enough to simply have each department develop its own annual plan. In order to accomplish true systems thinking, the entire organization needs to be aware of each department's annual plans. Remember that organizations are composed of interrelated parts, not silos.

To fully commit to achieving your Ideal Future Vision, which serves as the focus for your strategic plan, your entire collective leadership (i.e., your top 30 to 60 people) must actively participate in a large group annual plan review and problem-solving meeting. Understanding and ownership by everyone is the key to implementation success. Figure 12.3 illustrates how we do this.

This step is rarely done in organizations once departmental annual plans are created. The message seems to be "I'll do my job, you do yours," with neither side looking at or discussing the other's plans. (Isn't this analytical thinking at its worst?)

The specific details of holding this one-day large-group off-site meeting include the following sequence:

Integration of Plans Required in Three Ways
   1. Vertically
   2. Horizontally
   3. With key stakeholders (i.e., the web of functions/relationships)
First Round: Demonstrate this process. Use a fishbowl and an "easy" department plan.
Second Round: Break into three to four presentations and subgroups for more "air time" (maximum 10 to 20 people per subgroup).
Steps for Each Subgroup Presentation
   1. Distribute the department plan.
   2. Have each subgroup member read it individually while the presenter sets up a flip chart and assigns a note taker to capture all comments.
   3. Present the department plan first for clarification only (participants take notes for later discussion) using the form in Figure 12.2.
      a. Overview plus vision/mission review and fit.
      b. Details of annual department work plan.
   4. Get reactions from participants:
      a. What to add/delete/modify?
      b. Is the "who else to involve" column correct?
   5. Presenter and recorder pull together/share with the group a summary of the comments on the flip chart at the end of the day's meeting:
      • Key learning
      • Changes to plan

Tasks:

1. *Small group* presentations by all major department heads (# = _____)
    on their Department Annual Work Plans.
2. To the collective leadership/management of the entire organization (# = _____).

Large Ballroom:

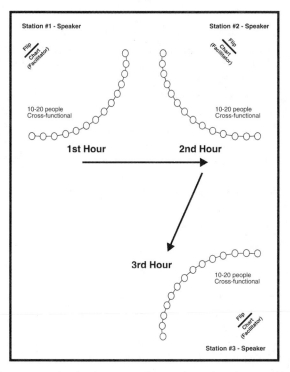

Philosophy: Small group, cross-functional teams meeting together and moving around in hourly activities create greater interaction, more energy, commitment, understanding, buy-in, and teamwork to implement the Strategic Plan.

Large group "dog and pony" presentations are boring at best!

FIGURE 12.3 Large group annual department reviews (and large group — whole system — team building).

- Implications for budgets/resources
- Implications for implementation
- SBUs/MPAs
- Changes needed to mission, values, KSFs

Third: Repeat Steps 1 through 5 above with a second and third subgroup (i.e., rotate subgroups each time; keep presenters at the same location).

Fourth: At the end of the day, review each presentation summary in Step 5 above in the total group (to ensure further/total integration).

Fifth: Have the CEO and/or key executive team members present how they are going to lead the change process.

After the Off-Site:

1. Revise your department plan as necessary.

2. Gain supervisor approval.
3. Tie it to budgeting process.
4. Implement it.
5. Achieve results/track and monitor.

At this point, you may be thinking, "Just what I hate — large group "dog and pony" shows — boring, boring, boring!" However, nothing could be further from the truth. What I'm advocating — and have seen work, time after time — is lots of small group interactive reviews going on at once.

Following the off-site large group review, have departments make any necessary revisions to their plans. Then assign a planning coordinator to collect all the plans together in one place. Then have that person split the department plans out by core strategies, and send them to the appropriate strategy sponsorship teams (SSTs) for future use. These SSTs can use them in annually monitoring, tracking, following-up, and reporting on the core strategies' status across all departments to the Strategic Change Leadership Steering Committee that will be set up.

ACCOUNTABILITY AND RESPONSIBILITY

Peter Drucker, writing in *Training & Development Magazine* (October 1998), has the following to say on the subject of accountability and responsibility.

> I have written, I would say, as much about leadership as most of today's prominent experts on the subject, but I have always stressed that leadership is responsibility. Leadership is accountability.
>
> As for separating management from leadership, that is nonsense — as much nonsense as separating management from entrepreneurship.

INDIVIDUAL LEVEL OF PERFORMANCE

Once annual plans are complete for departments, there is one more level of systems in the Cascade of Planning that needs close attention.

Failure to accomplish human resource management's seven "must do" projects below will set you up for negative reinforcement for all employees in regard to your future vision. Remember, your organization is usually set up to maintain today's status quo; that's why revamping your human resource management processes to support the future vision is essential.

Complete the following seven HR projects *first* — even before strategic change and implementation. Be sure to budget for them as well.

1. Redo your performance appraisal form/procedures to reward your core strategies and values.
2. Redo your executive "performance management system" to ensure the strategic plan gets down to executive accountability, and to reinforce and model your core values and strategies.
3. Modify your entire formal and informal rewards system (pay and nonpay) to ensure they reinforce and support your future direction.

4. Redo your recruiting, hiring, succession planning, and promotional criteria and processes to promote your strategic plan and direction.
5. Redo your orientation and assimilation processes (i.e., "smart start") to start people off with the values, shared strategies, and culture of your strategic plans.
6. Redo your training and development systems to build and reinforce your values, shared strategies culture, and future vision — especially leadership and management skills (not just knowledge and awareness).
7. Develop a strategic human resource management three-year business plan for the organization to support its organization-wide strategic plan, and specifically the "people" strategy every organization invariably has as a part of its strategic plan.

STRATEGIC BUDGETING: THE DIFFERENCE BETWEEN ADEQUACY AND EXCELLENCE

At this point, we assume that future revenue projections have been set through your Key Success Measures/Goals, business planning, and core strategies. Your task now is to show profit and return on investment to your board of directors (or show a zero profit in the public sector).

The annual budgeting and resource allocation process done at the completion of strategic planning is what I refer to as "strategic budgeting." This is because the emphasis here has everything to do with strategy, focus, and priorities — but very little to do with money alone. For most organizations, intelligent budgeting and careful resource allocation can mean the difference in successful implementation.

In strategic budgeting, the allocation of funds is determined by the annual priorities that are crucial to the achievement of your organizational vision, rather than by department or division power struggles. To be truly strategic, budgeting and resource allocation must meet the following five criteria:

1. It should reinforce and focus on your Ideal Future Vision and Key Success Measures/Goals.
2. It must support your strategic plan's top annual action priorities under each core strategy.
3. The criteria for your budgeting decisions must be the top priorities from your strategic plan.
4. Your budget priorities must match up closely to the core strategies.
5. It must result in your being able to fund and run your day-to-day business and be able to fund needed future changes as well.

We all know how tough these changing times are on budgets; the challenge is to find new and innovative ways not only to reduce costs, but also for increasing revenues and income. The idea is to find (or create) options with which to face tough budget choices, such as the following:

- Delete old budget items that are no longer valid, then add new items, based on your strategic plan.
- Look at your organization-wide core strategies, evaluating what to add and what to delete. Set priorities among strategies or set priority actions *within* each strategy (i.e., top two to four actions in each strategy for the coming year).
- Assign macroallocation to each department, leaving the decisions on how they achieve it up to each department.

Remember, the key is not to cut or increase budgets evenly across the board, but to make *simultaneous budget cuts and additions* that are based on your strategic plan criteria. Rather than a fixed budget driving your strategic plan, *your plan should always drive your budget.* Not looking at it this way will almost always prevent the successful implementation of your plan. Luckily, it's a negative result that can be avoided.

The strategic budget must be integrated with and linked to your strategic plan and your annual plans. This can take up to 2 years to do properly, with around 40% to 70% incremental implementation in the first year, then coming to full implementation in the second.

QUESTIONS TO PONDER

- Have you prioritized your organization's core strategies?
- Are you creating annual plans that support the organization-wide implementation of these core strategies?
- Are you committed to a large group review: a 1- to 2-day team-building meeting off-site in which your collective leadership (i.e., your top 30 to 60 people) reviews and problem-solves your annual plans?
- Have you kept this review meeting to a maximum of your 12 most important annual plans?
- Does your organization's budgeting and resource allocation:
  1. support the implementation of your strategic plan?
  2. reinforce and focus on your vision, Key Success Measures/Goals, and core strategies?
  3. enable you to fund and run your day-to-day business, as well as funding any necessary future changes?
- Are you looking for ways not only to cut costs, but also to increase revenues and income?

TEN WAYS TO ESTABLISH YOUR BUDGET AND RESOURCE ALLOCATION APPROACH

If money was what it took to be a success, then how
did Japan and Germany rise from the ashes?

Looking at today's global economy, the traditional biases as to the roots of economic success are changing. According to Anthony Carnevale in his book, *America and the Economy*, as well as many others, economic success is no longer based on natural resources, financial investments, saving rates, scarcity, free markets, or a military presence, but on the ability to intelligently prioritize a loosely connected set of economic and social processes with technology. How else do you explain the Japanese and German successes since World War II?

Because of a rapidly changing environment, it's more important than ever to reexamine our methods for focusing and allocating resources that will support our strategic planning and direction. I have yet to run across an organization that has all the funds it needs to explore every single revenue-generating possibility.

With today's drastic budgetary shortfalls and the need to invest in technology, the real trick is staying away from the rather simplistic cutting methods of the 1990s (i.e., across-the-board cuts on departmental budgets or employee compensation). It has been proven over and over that they simply don't work.

Also, these tight budget restrictions require more drastic budget cuts in order for the organization to become globally competitive in today's "Internet society." The result is that the economic structure of many industries is being altered (lowered) today, through the use of electronics, telecommunications, and E-commerce.

When weighing the priorities based on your strategic plan, use the ten ideas below or a combination of these for cutting and/or reallocating your organization's funds in a more focused (i.e., strategic) way:

Assign

1. Macro allocations only (and let managers allocate to their departments).
2. Carry out activity-level budgeting (zero-based budgeting).
3. Require 5–10–15% budget cut projections and plans, and cut each differently, based on their plans.
4. Budget "hold-backs" for Request for Proposals (RFPs).
5. Require new initiative programs (NIPS) for all new funding.
6. "WorkOut" the bureaucracy (eliminate waste) and then rebudget.
7. Reengineer your business' economic structure (radical reengineering) — now called "value-chain management," as it includes suppliers and customers.
8. Promote learning as a critical resource.
9. Initiate a recognition and awards program to lower costs and improve service.
10. Promote fund-raising and alliances/volunteerism (public sector).

These ten approaches to budgeting and reallocation are described in the following sections.

ASSIGN MACRO ALLOCATIONS ONLY (AND LET MANAGERS ALLOCATE TO THEIR DEPARTMENTS)

Consider macro allocation by top management for each SBU/MPA/major support department (i.e., a pie chart). Require reallocation within existing department resources to respond to new priorities (but be sure to allow more flexibility to switch funding and priorities).

Another variation would be to have all departments create bottom-up budgets once top management has decided on the needs/cuts.

CARRY OUT ACTIVITY LEVEL BUDGETING (ZERO-BASED BUDGETING)

Reexamine your organizational priorities at the activity level, focusing all the way through the organization. Have everyone force-rank their activities/projects, along with budget and people cost implications.

Once this is done, reorganize the list from the highest priority ranking to the lowest priority. Then, fill in whatever resources you'll need to support each activity. Draw a line where your resources are "used up." Finally, reach consensus through discussion and ranking as to what activities will now be included in your budget, and what to delete that is below the "used up" line just mentioned.

In carrying it through in this manner, you'll more clearly tie your budget to specific actions. Also, it will be easy to spot and troubleshoot any activities that do *not* have enough resources to support them.

Example: Marriott Corp. does this every few years as a corporate priority since they know that "waste" creeps into every budget, year after year. This is how they combat it.

REQUIRE 5-10-15% BUDGET CUT PROJECTIONS AND PLANS

Make more drastic budget cuts; for instance, identify $Z\%$ (i.e., 2 to 3%) of nonsalary "people-associated" costs that could be cut (things such as travel, office, equipment, etc.).

Another possibility would be to have everyone recommend cuts of $Y\%$ (i.e., 10%) in their area, even if your goal is $X\%$, say, 5% overall. This gives you flexibility to cut more or less in other areas. Then, reallocate some or all of the savings back to departments based on their initiatives toward the core strategies.

Yet another possibility is to ask for projected cuts of 5%, of 10%, and of 15% from each department, along with what plans or projects would be affected. Then, cut departments individually and in different amounts, based on your strategic priorities.

Example: The government of Alberta, Canada, did this as a part of its radical, successful restructuring in the 1990s. The Centre was fortunate to be the province's strategic planning trainer during that time.

BUDGET "HOLD-BACKS" FOR REQUEST FOR PROPOSALS

Set aside $X\%$ (i.e., 2% to 5%) of your budget for a Request for Proposal (RFP) process to further new pilot programs/experiments to take you toward your vision of the future.

Example: When I was an executive with Imperial Corp. of America, this was an ongoing part of our successful budgeting process.

ENCOURAGE NEW INITIATIVE PROGRAM FOR ALL NEW FUNDING

Have your employees recommend new initiative programs/projects (NIPS) that tie directly to the criteria in your strategic plan. Make sure budget and people costs and rationale are associated with each one.

If your organization is testing specific NIPS in an attempt to increase profits, and you find that it can't be done with existing staff, you'll need to make a business case for each project. When seeking NIPS staffing approval, you should be able to show improved or maintained productivity ratios, increased profits, and/or reduced costs.

To make the best possible case for your NIPS, be sure to incorporate the return on investment (ROI) principles below

1. Expenditures are an investment of capital resources at the present time for a return in the future that is *more valuable* than the present expense.
2. Management, however, always has a variety of options for investing capital. Your proposal must compete with the return from a variety of potential projects that would be funded.
3. *Hurdle rates* are key. Treasury notes might be 7% ROI with no risk. A return of 12% might be the minimum acceptable return for any project with some risk. Net present value (NPV) is also a consideration.
4. You must show that your project compares favorably with all other projects; clear superiority is key.
5. Underlying assumptions and past documentation should be clear; existing case stories must be conservative to be creditable.
6. The period of return of the project's investment is key; the earlier the better, and at most within 3 years.
7. The opportunity costs lost elsewhere to fund your project are key — management only has so much capital.

Example: The Environmental Protection Agency in British Columbia goes after new initiative programs on a yearly basis; in fact, it's the way it allocates resources to run day-to-day operations.

Note: The next five approaches are too late to begin at strategic budgeting time. You need to start them earlier in the year, so that their results in cost savings will be evident at budgeting time.

"WorkOut" the Bureaucracy (Eliminate Waste)

Set up a broader, reengineering "WorkOut" process (such as that at GE) to

- Eliminate bureaucracy
- Empower and delegate to staff
- Streamline workflow inefficiencies

If your organization is unable to experiment with revenue-increasing possibilities at this time, but you still need to cut your budget, then address it now: delays only end up costing more in money and motivation down the road.

One of the quickest, most obvious ways for cutting costs is to get rid of all the old ways (i.e., waste) that are no longer producing results. This is known as *continuous improvement*, and it's amazing how many of us give it lip service, but how few of us really do it. Instead, we just go along, continuing to do what we've always done — whether it still works or not.

To eliminate waste, you need to first define it. Waste is anything other than the minimum amount of equipment, people, materials, parts, space, overhead, and work time essential to add value to your product or service.

Reengineer Your Business' Economic Structure (Radical Reengineering)

Make major structural changes to change the way you do business at a lower cost (i.e., "aides" vs. full-fledged professionals). Doing more with less is what the 21st century is all about, but there are ways to approach this with the foresight necessary for carrying you into the future. Don't look at this only in the "now" — project into the future and consider possibilities from all sides:

- Flatten your organization by continuously empowering the employees.
- Lower manufacturing costs on nonvalue-added items (i.e., lean manufacturing).
- Radically reengineer your customer-focused business processes to be more streamlined, quicker, and lower in cost (i.e., value-chain engineering).
- Use your human resources well; fully utilize and challenge people.
- Eliminate all deadwood.
- Know your customers' priorities.

- Imagine: if you weren't doing it this way, how would you do it?
- Check your span of control — control it.
- Keep statistics: they'll flag patterns and give a historical perspective.
- Look at how much profit a profit center must make to keep an overhead/staff department working.
- Find the time to understand people; educate them both within and outside of your unit.
- Are you doing the wrong things right?
- Ask for an evaluation.
- Think of your department as "Staff, Inc." — be entrepreneurial, not bureaucratic.

Example: Hershey Foods in 1999 underwent a value-chain analysis in conjunction with installing an automated Enterprise Resource Planning (ERP) system costing about $125 million. As a result, over Halloween they lost $100 million in sales, because the ERP didn't work properly. Watch it!

Promote Learning as a Critical Resource

Invest some time and energy in your most critical resource; learning. Are there other existing resources that you could use to achieve your vision such as focus, motivation, commitment, new knowledge, technology, innovation and creativity, best practices emulation, leverage, or continuous improvement projects. If so, get to work on incorporating them now. Look at it as an investment in your organization's future.

In reality, most organizations still treat people as a fixed asset with a fixed cost, rather than as a variable-output human being.

It is well known that many companies tolerate employees who produce as low as 20% of their abilities, when most could produce 80% of their potential output on a sustained basis without stress overload. When properly trained, empowered, motivated, focused, and freed from bureaucratic systems, we are powerful learners who can produce more results faster and better than ever before.

Initiate a Recognition and Rewards Program

Set up a recognition program, rewarding actual, documented cost savings rather than suggestions. Suggestions are a dime a dozen; it's actual cost savings you really want.

Example: Though suggestion programs aren't generally well received in the U.S., I've set up such cost-saving types as above, including one that successfully documented up to $3 million in cost savings in the first year alone.

Because financial rewards can be prohibitively expensive, find ways to reward people in nonfinancial ways, too. Set up ceremonies, gifts, outings, time off, and other forms of recognition such as our Olympic recognition program (see below).

AN OLYMPIC RECOGNITION PROGRAM THAT WORKS
(reward at three levels; bronze, silver, gold)

1. Select one or two key outcomes you want, based on your strategic plan, such as lower costs, improved customer service, etc. Reward results and achievement, not ideas or suggestions.
2. Key program nomination characteristics;
   • Anyone can nominate anyone else or any team, including themselves.
   • Nominations are for anyone or any team who has actually achieved a desired outcome.
3. Ideas and proposals are not rewarded; achieving actual results is rewarded (i.e. saving $11.00, receiving a customer service thank you, etc.).
4. Publicize this program widely. Set up a simple one-page form on colored paper to fill out. Make the form widely distributed and available.
5. Hold large group meetings on a regular basis (quarterly?) with everyone eligible in attendance. If the organization is spread out, hold regional meetings and possibly one big annual meeting. It is best to make this meeting a quarterly business meeting with the *recognition* of winners as the main attraction. Some other business topics might include the following:
   • Discussion of Key Success Measures or outcome business results.
   • A guest speaker on a key topic, such as one of your key strategies or core values.
   • Discussion of one or two key core strategies and their importance and priorities.
   • Celebration of successes — social time such as a buffet lunch, end of day nonalcoholic happy hour, etc.
6. Set up a Peer Review Committee to review the submissions for documented outcomes. The goal is to get as many "winners" as possible; not to create winners and losers (i.e., multiple winners — compete against yourself only). Keep the results hidden until the meeting itself.
7. The basic concept here is the "Olympic Games": bronze, silver, and gold winners. Bronze goes to anyone who wins at any quarterly meeting. Silver goes to all the big winners. And Gold is reserved for the top three to five biggest winners. Do not single out one big final winner.

FUND-RAISING AND ALLIANCES/VOLUNTEERS (PUBLIC SECTOR)

Start fund-raising as one of your more important organizational functions. Acquire endowments/annuities for long-term funding. Recommend new ways to increase revenue, such as fund drives, alternative sources for funds, or in-kind donations and grants.

Example: Not-for-profit organizations need to become experts at this type of activity. As an example, some of my clients in public school systems now even have full-time fund-raisers and a complete "Fund-Raising Pyramid" (Figure 12.4).

In addition, attract volunteers and/or strategic alliances to better enable your organization to leverage the resources you have.

A Word about Public Sector Budgets

Budgeting in the public sector can be especially frustrating. More and more, however, organizations in this sector are refusing to wait, choosing instead to find ways to be more proactive, raise money themselves, and/or make their own budget reallocations, using many of the ten approaches listed above.

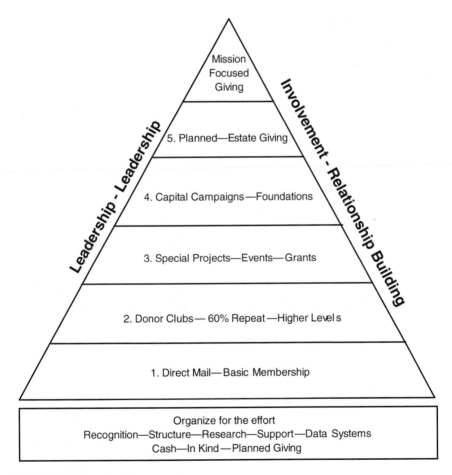

FIGURE 12.4 Fund-raising pyramid.

Through fund-raising, grant research, user/polluter pay, volunteer help, in kind contributions and other methods, not-for-profit organizations are making substantial inroads into bringing in financial resources that aren't based on taxes or state and federal allocations.

Tip: The need for strategic budgeting in the public sector is best articulated in this excerpt from the September 1991 issue of *Shipmate,* the alumni magazine of the U.S. Naval Academy:

> Many would argue, and convincingly, that it is the responsibility of the Congress to provide all the resources needed by the Superintendent [to run the Naval Academy]. The simple truth, however, is that the Congress does not, never has, and probably never will do so. The government provides what might be termed the absolute necessities; it is others who bridge the gap between adequacy and excellence.

INDIVIDUAL PERFORMANCE MANAGEMENT SYSTEMS

People do what you inspect ... not what you expect.

-USNA, circa 1964

Once your annual plan and accompanying strategic budgets are in place, two other crucial management systems must be installed:

1. A performance management system.
2. A rewards and recognition system.

Both the performance management system and the rewards/recognition system should be formulated and viewed as two separate but closely related change projects. The key to it all is the infamous performance appraisal that must be tied to your strategic plan. Figure 12.5 illustrates one very simple way to do this.

RESPONSIBILITY–ACCOUNTABILITY AND EMPOWERMENT

I have never used the word empowerment and never will.
I consider it a despicable word. I have always talked of
responsibility and only of responsibility. Only if there is
responsibility can there be authority — that too is the first
lesson of political science.[1]

-Peter Drucker

---

[1] *Source: Training & Development Magazine,* October 1998.

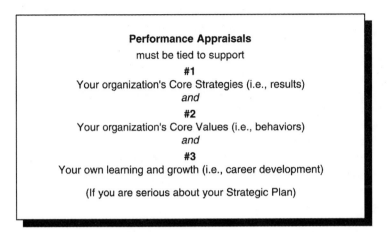

Performance Appraisals
must be tied to support

#1
Your organization's Core Strategies (i.e., results)
and

#2
Your organization's Core Values (i.e., behaviors)
and

#3
Your own learning and growth (i.e., career development)

(If you are serious about your Strategic Plan)

—— **Result: A Four Page Performance Management/Appraisal Form** ——

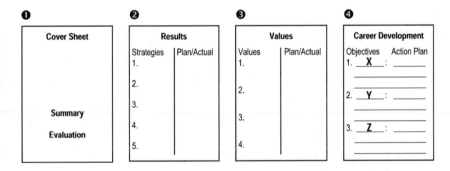

FIGURE 12.5 Performance appraisals … KISS — tied to strategic planning.

FINALIZING THE STRATEGIC PLAN AND RALLYING CRY

Once you've completed your annual plans and budgets, it's time to put the finishing touches on your strategic plan. From here, your next step will be the actual implementation of your plan.

One of the best ways to begin bridging the gap from planning to implementation is to hold an organization-wide "rallying cry" contest. Include every member of your organization in this contest. Also, rather than having winners and losers, emphasize multiple winners; everyone who participates is a winner — be sure to recognize them when they do participate. Then, select finalists, reward them all, and gain consensus among top management on one rallying cry that best represents the essence of your strategic plan.

QUESTIONS TO PONDER

- Has your organization reexamined its strategies for budgeting and allocating resources that will support your strategic plan?
- Are you staying away from simplistic 1990s across-the-board cuts on departmental budgets and employee compensation?
- Have you studied and incorporated several of the ten approaches to budget and resource allocation?
- If your organization is in the public, not-for-profit sector, are you exploring proactive ways to bring in supplemental income that isn't based on state or federal funds — such as fund-raising, grant research, volunteers, alliances, user pay?
- When your annual plan and budget are in place, will you be installing both a performance management system and a rewards and recognition system — and, if so, is it one that recognizes teamwork in addition to individual achievement?

IN SUMMARY: STRATEGIC CONSISTENCY AND OPERATIONAL FLEXIBILITY

No matter what you've done in the past, if you don't start developing your annual plans and budgets around your core strategies you won't be competitive in today's marketplace. It's not simply a case of top-down or bottom-up strategic planning; that's an outdated, either/or concept. It is now a matter of *strategic consistency* — at the strategic planning level — with *operational flexibility* at the annual and individual planning levels.

There are many more creative and proactive ways to approach planning, budgeting, and resource allocation these days than ever before. I've attempted to provide you with ten of the most results-oriented strategic budgeting approaches my clients have originated. Hopefully, these will be useful to you and will also inspire you to create many of your own.

RECAP OF KEY CONTENT POINTS

- To develop an effective annual plan, you need to make sure everyone focuses on organization-wide core strategies, *not* on separate department or turf issues.
- Make sure each department's actions for each core strategy support the top priority strategic action items (SAIs) identified by senior management.

- In the large group review, your collective leadership should compare all annual plans against your vision, mission, values, strategies, and Key Success Measures/Goals.
- In strategic budgeting, allocation of funds is determined by priorities that are crucial to the achievement of your organizational vision, rather than by department or division power struggles.
- It is important to study many different, proactive approaches to cutting/reallocating your organization's budgets in a more focused way.
- To cut costs in order to eliminate waste, you need to first define waste. *Waste* is anything other than the minimum amount of equipment, people, materials, parts, space, overhead, and work time essential for added value in your products or services.
- When seeking structural changes to do business at a lower cost, don't look only in the "now" — project into the future and consider possibilities from all angles.
- More and more, organizations in the public sector are finding ways to be more proactive and raise money themselves, rather than waiting for funding. They also use volunteers and strategic alliances.
- To ensure employee motivation and commitment to your plan, be sure you have both a performance management system and a rewards and recognition system in place, including a new performance appraisal tied to your strategic plan.
- In moving from planning to implementation, create a sense of ownership among employees through a "rallying cry" contest.

"HOW-TO" ACTION CHECKLIST

1. Prioritize strategic action items (SAIs) under each strategy; use your core strategies as the organizing principles of your annual plans.
2. Develop departmental annual plans, including all senior department heads.
3. Have your collective leadership (your top 30 to 60 people) actively participate in a large group annual plan review and problem-solving meeting.
4. Your top executives (i.e., CEO, President, COO, Superintendent, Executive Director, etc.) should present their personal leadership plans of what tasks they will personally do to help guide the plan's implementation.
5. At the close of your large group review, be sure that each participant prepares and presents one or two quick, easy actions they will take under each strategy over the next two weeks.

6. Review and adopt some of the ten ways to establish your approach to budgeting and resource allocation.
7. Design a performance management system and supporting appraisal form that enables individuals to set goals based on the strategic plan, as well as to take accountability and responsibility for their part in the overall plan.
8. Create a rewards and recognition system that reinforces employee commitment and rewards contribution, while encouraging individual success with specific, tangible rewards and/or recognition.
9. Bridge the gap from planning to implementation by holding an organization-wide "rallying cry" contest.

Part 3

Mastering Strategic Change: "Where the Rubber Meets the Road"

13 Plan-to-Implement (Step #8)

*Overvaluing "strategy" [by which many companies mean
big ideas and big decisions] and undervaluing execution
leads not only to implementation shortfalls...but also to
misinterpreting the reasons for success or failure.*

-Rosabeth Moss Kanter

PLAN-TO-IMPLEMENT DAY

The implementation of your strategic plan really is "where the rubber meets the road." You've put a backbreaking amount of energy, time, and care into defining the *content* of your strategic plan and its Ideal Future Vision. Now it's time to put these thoughts and visions into action through the *processes* and *structures* of change, in ways that will carry you successfully into the future.

The *processes* of change are the series of actions you set in motion to implement your plan, i.e. how change will occur, for both individuals and teams, and throughout the organization. The *structures* are the design and mechanisms you use to manage that change. Most important, you must be careful to create change mechanisms that will affect the change you want, but won't compromise those day-to-day activities that are crucial to your organization's success. Setting this up is the purpose of Step #8.

Changing behaviors always requires deep feelings.

To help organizations answer questions that are raised at this point, you'll usually need at least a 1-day, off-site meeting we call "Plan-to-Implement." It is similar to the Plan-to-Plan concept (Step #1), and consists of three similar parts: an executive briefing and educating on change session in the morning, and both organizing and tailoring tasks for change sessions in the afternoon.

The key to the Plan-to-Implement day is that it must always follow the completion of your strategic and annual planning. Keeping it separate from any and all planning activities is the only way I've found to maintain the integrity and the focus necessary for successful implementation. Remember that Goal #1, developing the strategic planning document, is completed. Now is the time to bridge the gap from Goal #1 to Goal #2 — ensuring successful implementation and change.

The fact is, most of us don't think about managing change much at all, and if we do, it's in fairly simplistic terms. Even with all the current talk on the importance of managing change, there still exist a number of myths surrounding strategic change and implementation, such as these:

1-57444-278-3/00/$0.00+$.50
© 2000 by CRC Press LLC

"Change is easy; we just need to follow our instincts."

"The *organization* needs to change, not me personally!"

"Senior management just needs to get the *others* to change."

"If only *senior management* would change!"

"Once we get past these tight times, we'll be fine."

"Without the resources, we can't implement the strategic plan."

"Once we know what to do and change, it will get done by the normal organization just by doing our day-to-day jobs." This is my personal favorite.

In the past, these myths may have provided us with some level of success in dealing with isolated change. However, in order to grow and survive in today's world of rapid change, we need to approach change both pragmatically and strategically.

MORNING SESSION: EXECUTIVE BRIEFING AND EDUCATING ON CHANGE

The purpose of the first (morning) segment of the Plan-to-Implement day is to debrief, demystify, and educate executives on the change issues facing your organization as a result of your new strategic plan. This segment concentrates on four primary categories:

1. The skill levels necessary to leading and mastering strategic change.
2. The Rollercoaster of Change as the key process for managing change.
3. A menu of infrastructures that may be necessary for leading and managing the change
4. Understanding organizations as systems, in order to change them.

LEADING AND MASTERING STRATEGIC CHANGE

Defining your *processes* of change and creating the *structures* for change are what I refer to as "mastering strategic change." It is the point at which everything you now do will affect everything you want to achieve later on. Before reaching that point of mastery, however, managers and executives must be clear on some basic elements of change.

To start, it's a good idea to take an inventory of what change skills you may (or may not) already possess. Most of us, at one time or another, make the mistake of thinking that we already have high-level, change-related survival skills: after all, we've all lived through change and survived it, right? Chances are, whatever skills you're thinking you have aren't really successful change skills at all, but rather learned, "knee-jerk," compensating techniques used in isolated past changes or crises.

Simply put, there is a world of difference between *surviving* change and *leading and mastering* change. *Surviving* change is reactive. It places you in the role of a victim of change. Survival is just that — survival. You don't come away with skills that can assist you in implementing future change. On the other hand, *leading and mastering* strategic change is about developing viable change mechanisms that you control over the long term.

I'd probably be safe in assuming that readers of this book have reached the "mastery" level in some area of their professional lives such as operations, accounting, legal, finance, engineering, human resources, etc. Change is no different from any of these areas, in that it is a profession with scientific data on what does (and doesn't) work, and it can be mastered. Remember our Seemingly Simple Element #1: Planning and Change is a primary part of leadership and management.

The *first cardinal rule* of change that managers should know is that *organizations* don't change — *people* change. Instead of approaching change in terms of changing the way the organization does business, you must first change and model your own behavior. Only then can you hope to assist in the behavior changes of the people who make up your organization. Though people resist change, I frequently find that the real stumbling block for leaders is that they don't know their behavior patterns are at odds with their goals in the first place. As a leader yourself, getting regular, honest feedback so you can change your own behavior is vital. This is Level #1 of our Six Natural Levels of Leadership Competencies: self-mastery.

The *second cardinal rule* of change is that existing organizational structures cannot be the same as the ones you'll use for large-scale change. Contrast the characteristics of change activities with the day-to-day activities of running your organization. You'll quickly see that people and their current structures have too much of an investment in the status quo and current habits to be able to readily change their ways, despite their good intentions (thus bringing to mind the old adage, "the road to hell is paved with good intentions"). Asking the current organization to change itself is just plain unrealistic. It is designed to perpetuate the status quo.

The *third cardinal rule* of change is that change, by its very nature, almost always loses out to the day-to-day operational demands. Because of this, it's imperative that you create change mechanisms (processes and structures) that are separate and distinct from your day-to-day activities. You have managers, tasks, processes, and structures involved in day-to-day activities. You also need managers, tasks, processes and structures set up to manage the change.

> *If any of your new paradigms, ideas, or changes were*
> *rationally, politically, or culturally easy, you would have*
> *done them already ... so don't underestimate the*
> *difficulty you're going to have in successfully*
> *implementing your strategic plan.*
>
> *-Stephen G. Haines*

In initiating your change effort, it's also important to expect that the desired changes resulting from your new strategic plan will be fragile. You should assume that they will need to be nurtured, protected, encouraged, and rewarded. Doing this in an ongoing, consistent manner can result in permanent and healthy strategic change.

No matter how beautifully you've constructed your organization's change effort, if your top management does not set aside the time to manage and lead the process personally, it won't go far. The only way to make change efforts work over the long term is to continually focus on the organizational vision and mission — an inherent part of top management's role. If your senior management delegates its accountability in these areas, it sends a message throughout the organization that your change effort is not an organizational priority. This is such a simple concept, yet executives miss this point over and over again.

THE ICEBERG THEORY OF CHANGE: CONTENT, PROCESS, AND STRUCTURES

To understand our Iceberg Theory of Change, we must begin with the understanding of the three realities of life that we encounter continuously: the *content* of our thoughts and discussions, the *process* we are undergoing at the moment, and the *structures* or context around which the content and process take place.

Designing, building, and sustaining a customer-focused, high-performance learning organization requires a balance in how organizations spend their time and energy between (see figure below):

1. The *content* (tasks, goals) and focus of the business.
2. The processes — how we work on the tasks (behaviors).
3. The infrastructures within which the content and process operate.

Content   Processes

Infrastructures

It requires persistence, disciplined persistence to do this.

> ***Content Myopia*** *is our failure to focus on processes*
> *and structures, yet successful change is dependent*
> *on processes and structures.*

The best way to describe how your organization can create and improve customer value while undergoing major changes (positioning goal) is through our Iceberg Theory.

In an iceberg, it is the 87% of the iceberg that is below the waterline that is dangerous. In organizations, it is the lack of focus on the underlying processes and infrastructures needed for effective change that sinks the change. These take time to install and work effectively, even after you understand the need for their installation in the change effort.

MANAGING THE ROLLERCOASTER OF CHANGE – THE KEY PROCESS

Major change takes two to five years...even with
concentrated, continuous, and effective actions.
                                                                                        -Stephen G. Haines

In managing large-scale organizational change, looking at how people naturally react to change is crucial. Every field that addresses itself to change has its own theory on how people experience change. The interesting thing is that, whatever theory you look at, a similar pattern emerges. As I've mentioned in previous chapters, years ago I came to call this series of behaviors The Rollercoaster of Change. As we saw repeatedly, it consists of four primary stages:

1. Shock and denial
2. Depression and anger
3. Hope and readjustment
4. Rebuilding

The Rollercoaster (Figure 13.1) exists as a reality of life. It describes and explains the key concept and framework of how change occurs, no matter what the type of change. Whether you are dealing with change at the individual, interpersonal, team, family, organization, community or societal level, this is all you need to know.

This Rollercoaster is a simple way of understanding the dynamics of how to effect positive changes of all types. Cycles of "stability–change–instability–new stability–and change all over again" are normal and natural. Don't fight them; use them to your advantage!

You must manage and lead yourself first, and then help others through the four stages of the Rollercoaster (illustrated in Figure 13.1). Keep in mind, though, that everyone goes through these stages at different rates, depths, and times.

STAGE #1: SHOCK AND DENIAL

As a leader of change, you must be extremely well prepared to give advance notice and clear expectations regarding your desired changes. Then, in the first week after announcing the change, you must be available and accessible to others to repeat the desired change and its rationale over and over.

Example: The question is not *if* each employee will go through the Rollercoaster, but *when,* how deeply, how long it will take, and whether he will successfully reach the other side. This last question of reaching the other side successfully is quite an issue for most organizations. Executives are trained in the skill of telling others what

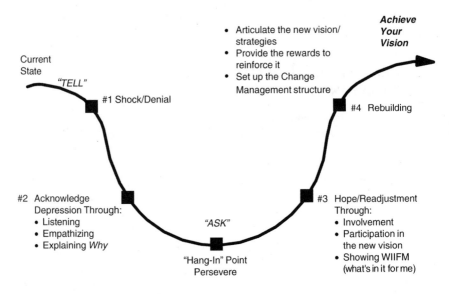

FIGURE 13.1 Rollercoaster of Change.

to do. In The Rollercoaster of Change, telling is only the "skill" of inducing shock, denial, and depression in your employees.

It is a given that each of us will go through the losses associated with stages #1 and #2 of the Rollercoaster (shock and depression). However, going through stages #3 and #4 (hope and rebuilding) is optional, and depends on someone leading the change process effectively. Self-mastery is the ideal, of course.

STAGE #2: DEPRESSION AND ANGER

The other problem with the Rollercoaster is the fact that once you start through it, you cannot go back and erase what you started. Instead, attempting to reverse changes already begun just kicks off another Rollercoaster, only this time from the spot at which you tried to reverse the process. Since this is usually at stage #2 (depression), it generally means that the new Rollercoaster will take employees deeper down into depression. Rarely will it get you out of the hole you are digging for yourself, your firm, or your employees.

People can be helped through stage #2 (depression) by this sequence: (1) listening, (2) asking questions, (3) empathizing, and (4) constantly explaining the vision and why it is significant. Letting people experience first-hand the executive's presence and rationale for the change is also crucial.

In other words, depression is normal and to be expected, as is resistance to change. The worst thing an executive can do is to push someone or tell him he should not feel the way he does. The more resistance you express to an employee, the more he will resist you as well (action–reaction).

STAGE #3: HOPE AND ADJUSTMENT

You must clarify each person's new role and required new norms of behavior, then gain maximum involvement and understanding of how to achieve the new vision and values on their part by emphasizing WIIFM (What's In It For Me).

The only way through stage #3 and up the right (and optional) side of the Rollercoaster is through leadership. In other words, you must be Drucker's "mono-maniac with a mission" having "persistence, persistence, persistence" in implementing, correcting, and improving the changes as you go. Involving people in the change is essential for the adjustment and hope of stage #3 to occur. The key is involvement in the "how to," not the decision on "what." The "what" should already have been decided in a participative fashion, such as using our Parallel Process (people support what they help create).

STAGE #4: REBUILDING

In this stage, you empower the fully committed individuals and teams to promote your vision and values.

In summary, the Rollercoaster and stage #4 highlight the issue of how difficult it is to create a critical mass in support of your desired changes. The importance of getting people to "buy in" but also "stay in" throughout the Rollercoaster (and its bottoming-out) process is critical.

This Rollercoaster is the basis of change, as it is natural and normal and all you need to know about change. Its uses are many (see below).

The Rollercoaster of Change
The Natural Cycles of Life and Change

Major Questions	Major Uses
1. Not if, but when to go through shock?	1. Personal transitions
2. How deep is the trough?	2. Employee self-management
3. How long will it take?	3. Stages of learning — all types
4. Will we get up the right side and rebuild?	4. Interpersonal relationships
5. At what level will we rebuild?	5. Coaching sequence
6. How many different rollercoasters will we experience?	6. Dialogue and discovery
7. Are there other changes occurring?	7. Conflict management

8. Will we hang in and persevere?

9. How do we deal with normal resistance?

10. How do we create a critical mass for change?

8. Situational leadership tasks

9. Teams, groups, meetings

10. Strategic planning

11. Core strategies (cutting/building)

12. Overall change management

THE CHALLENGE: 5 CHOICES

Stages #3 and #4 present a challenge to excellence in self-mastery and in leadership. There are five directions in which these stages can go (Figure 13.2). Remember the left side (the "loss" side) of the Rollercoaster is a given and the right side is optional. So which will it be?

1. **Incompetence** — Going Out of Business
2. **Technical** — Dogged Pursuit of Mediocrity
3. **Management** — Present and Accounted for Only
4. **Leadership** — Making a Serious Effort
5. **Visionary Leadership** — Developing an Art Form

Though the four stages of the Rollercoaster present a rather simple version of change, there's nothing simple about analyzing and redirecting people's behavior patterns. This is a complex undertaking that must address itself to the serious questions above. This is why we call it The Rollercoaster of Change. If you look at a real rollercoaster from afar, you'll see how complex it looks, with all its turns and loops. Change is equally complex. Thus, it is natural and normal that both management and employees will experience anger, depression, and frustration (i.e., step #2) during a change effort. All of us tend to view change, at least initially, as a loss of some kind. Once we've experienced these emotions and bottomed out, however, and we can actually see the changes take hold, we often feel the return of hope.

NATURAL CYCLES OF CHANGE

All the experts on various Seven Levels of Living Systems use this same change framework. They just use different terms as Figure 13.3 shows.

Why are the 20 uses of The Rollercoaster of Change shown in Figure 13.3 all basically the same? It is because this curve is how the natural way life on earth occurs and has occurred forever. Take a look at the following cycles and see what else you can add.

HISTORICAL AND NATURAL — CYCLES OF CHANGE AND LEARNING

The Environment (Earth)
- Santa Ana winds
- El Ninos, tides, ocean
- Volcanoes
- Earthquakes, plate movement
- Seasons
- Moon
- Day/night
- Whale/bird migration

Economics
- Bull/bear markets
- K-wave
  (long wave — Nikolai Kondratieff, 1926)
- Recessions, depressions
- Profit taking
- Inflation

Civilizations
- Inca/Aztec/Mayan empires
- British empire

- French empire
- Spanish empire
- Japanese dynasties
- Chinese dynasties
- African empire
- Roman empire
- Greek empire
- Persian empire
- USSR
- Current Western civilization

Ages
- Hunting, gathering, migratory
- Agriculture
- Industrial
- Information
- Systems (biogenetics– 2000)

Industries
- Start-up
- High growth
- Maturity
- Decline
- Renewal

Travel
- Walk
- Animals
- Row boats, canoes
- Carts, wheels
- Automobile

- Bus, ships
- Mass Transit
- Airplanes, flight

Flight
- Balloon
- Wright Brothers — biplanes
- Single wing propeller
- Jet planes
- Concorde (plane)
- Satellites, rockets
- Space shuttles

Life
- Birth/death
- Food cycle
- Food chain
- War/peace
- Growth/decline

In today's world, experts talk about chaos and complexity theory. These two theories are really just part of systems thinking in the view of this author (Figure 13.4).

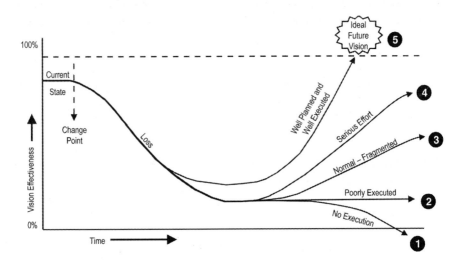

FIGURE 13.2 The five choices of change and levels of excellence.

Out of the complexity and interdependence of today's technology and society, combined with the chaos of fundamental and turbulent change, will ultimately come discovery of the natural and spontaneous new orders, structures, and visions. But what new orders, structures, and visions?

This "order" is that of the natural systems all around us, whether it is our bodies, our teams and families, our organizations, society and the many aspects of our natural world and environment. Thus, chaos and complexity are a natural and normal part of the process of discovering new orders from the natural systems and cycles of life. Yet, only our Systems Thinking Approach can provide the needed framework and the elegant simplicity to fully understand it. Hence, there is another way to look at the Rollercoaster in Figure 13.4.

Because major complex and chaotic change takes 2 to 5 years, being persistent in guiding and riding this Rollercoaster and its 20 uses successfully through the span of your planning horizon is a must. Senior management needs to plan ahead for this Rollercoaster, investing as much time and energy as it takes for everyone to get through it. Management should continually articulate your Ideal Future Vision, so employees are clear on why they're going through change. In addition, you'll need to set up a change management structure to build their confidence in your ability to actually lead and manage the change.

> *A basic truth of management — if not of life — is that*
> *nearly everything looks like a failure in the middle …*
> *persistent, consistent execution is unglamorous,*
> *time-consuming, and sometimes boring.*
>
> *-Rosabeth Moss Kanter*

Cycles of Change — Uses	Today #1 Shock	#2 Depression	"Hang-in"	#3 Hope	Future Vision #4 Reconstruction
I. Systems Thinking Concept					
1. Systems Thinking	Boiled Frog (Analytical Thinking)	Chaos and Complexity	Persevere, Yet Curious	Switch Paradigms (spontaneous self-org. in nature)	Systems Solutions
2. "Entropy" (Natural and Normal)	Loss of Energy	Run Down	Renewal	New Energy	Constant Energy
3. Change (Lewin/Beckhart)	Unfreeze	Crisis	Persist	Beginning Hope Norming	Refreeze Continuous Improvement on New Vision
		Change/Transition Management (SCLSC)			
II. Self-Change					
4. Understanding People/ Change (Death and Dying)	Shock/Denial	Depression/ Anger/Blame	Maximum Immobilization	Hope/ Acknowledge/ Readjust (Acceptance)	Rebuilding/ Constructive Work
5. Employee Actions	Don't Overreact	Ask Questions/ Express Feelings/ Be Skeptical	Don't Give Up	Get Involved/ Answer WIIFM/ Be Hopeful	Understand Vision/ Be Committed/ Take Action/ Fit Into System
III. Interpersonal Changes					
6. Relationships (Wil Shutz)	Inclusion Desire	Control Issues	Growth Desire	Openness	High Performance
7. Proper Structure of Management Interactions with Employees	Highly Directive/ Low Supportive	Highly Directive/ Highly Supportive	Transition/ Persistance	High Supportive/ Low Directive	Low Supportive/ Low directive
8. Situation Leadership (New Leadership Skills)	**Tell**/Direct (Train)	**Sell**/Ask (Coach)	Persevere	**Participate** Involvement (Facilitate)	**Delegate** Within System (Empower)
9. Management's Specific Tasks	Change Self First/ Appreciate/ Everyone changes at different rates and depths	Skeptics are my best friends/Empathize/ Listen/Explain Why/ Face-to-Face Mtgs.	Be Consistent/ Model the Way	Seek Involvement/ Show WIIFM/ Challenge the Process/Celebrate the Heart	Shared Vision/ Articulate Again & Again/Enable Others/Systems Fit, Alignment & Integrity

FIGURE 13.3 The Rollercoaster of Change: change in energy levels and their many uses (a primary concept of Systems Thinking are these natural cycles of change).

In some ways, management is called on to play the role of guidance counselor; listening, understanding, seeking involvement, and coaching people forward. Motivation, hope, and involvement can grow and take hold if managers help employees see What's In It For Me? (WIIFM). Concurrently, employees need to be apprised

	Today #1 Shock	PHASES		#3 Hope	Future Vision #4 Reconstruction
Cycles of Change **Uses**		#2 Depression	"Hang-in"		
III. Interpersonal Changes (Continued) 10. Coaching	Contact/Purpose	Chaos or Compatibility	Continuous Relationship	Contract/Norms	Collaboration/Work
IV. Team Change 11. Group Dynamics Stages	Forming	Storming	Hang-in Point	Norming	Performing
12. Dialogue and Discovery	Denial	Defend	Discussion	Dialogue (2-way = learning)	Discovery (of applications)
V. Intergroup Change 13. Learning Stages (People–Teams-Organizations)	Activity/Experience	"What" Process the Activity/ Feelings/Trends	Transition to Learning/Action	"So What" What have we learned? (learnings)	"Now What" Apply the Learnings (application)
14. Conflict	Conflict	Raw Debate/ Polite Talk	Desire for Resolution	Disciplined Dialogue (skills)	Skillful Discovery (seek truth)
15. Change in Diversity	Tell Policy	Deep Resistance	Persevere	Slow Acceptance	Higher Performance
VI. Organizational Change 16. Strategic Management System (Include Strategic Change	Where are we today? (our Current State Assessment)	What actions do we need to take? (content, processes, and structures) "Holding On" "Letting Go" Align/Fit of Parts			Where do we want to be? (our vision, values, and measures)
17. Two Different Strategies (Alignment)	I. "Cutting" Staff Cuts/Reorganize/Cost-Focused		Fit of System/ Persevere; Don't Back Off	II. "Building" Future Vision/Strategies/Quality/ Service/"Customer-Focused"	
18. Organizational Life Cycle	Maturity	Decline	Death or Renewal	Growth	New Maturity
19. Cultural/Values Change (Attunement)	Shock/Unfreeze Status Quo	ControL/Education, Communications, Rewards/Sanctions	Rebuild Morale/ Motivation	Create Critical Mass	Reward/Empower New Culture
VII. Orgn.-Environment 20. Partnerships/Alliances	Scouting/Entry/ Contract	Buyers Remorse	Openness and Conflict Mgmt.	Clarify Goals, Values, Norms & Trust	High Performing Alliance

FIGURE 13.3 Continued.

of the role they must play. They should be discouraged from overreacting, and encouraged to ask questions, get involved, and be committed.

If all of this sounds like a lot of hard work, you're right — it is. However, there is only one thing that's even more difficult, and that's trying to evade or ignore this

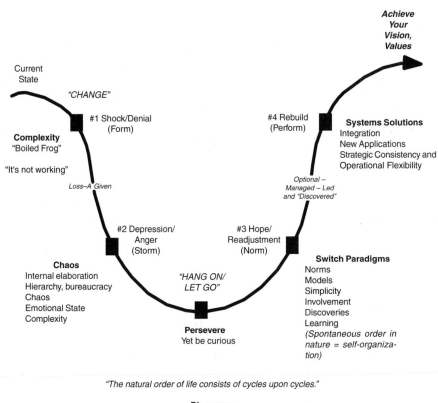

"The natural order of life consists of cycles upon cycles."

Discovery
"Discovery consists in seeing what everyone else has seen
and thinking what no one else has thought."
—Albert Szent-Gyorgi

Chaos and Complexity
Chaos and complexity are a normal and natural part of the process of change
—of discovering new ways of being and achieving new visions.

FIGURE 13.4 The Rollercoaster of Change and Systems Thinking.

Rollercoaster. The left side of the Rollercoaster's curve is a given, but the right side is optional. It depends on management's abilities to lead and manage it effectively.

That's why change, especially major change, does not come cheap. One of its costs is this psychological and emotional rollercoaster that people experience when reacting to change. But if you hang in there and persist, the payoff will be a high-performance, customer-focused organization that will continue to grow into the new millennium.

WORKSHOPS ON LEADING AND MASTERING STRATEGIC CHANGE

I think it's important to note here, that while the Plan-to-Implement morning session gives you a good overview for understanding the afternoon organizing and tailoring tasks segment, this half-day executive briefing won't provide enough detail or skills to help you achieve your own mastery (or systems) level of change.

In working with organizations at this point, we recommend all management levels attend a 2 to 3 day, in-depth, experiential and emotionally stimulating training simulation on leading and mastering strategic change. In this, management truly begins to have a deeper awareness and understanding of many of the previously discussed concepts and how to make implementation happen.

Knowledge of change such as I've just described is difficult enough — *skills* and *attitude* are critical and make the difference. In addition, workshops and a system for developing leadership skills are also essential. Learning the practical skills of trainer/coach/facilitator and conflict resolver are the leadership skills of the 21st century, in our view.

This is critical to every organization's change effort; after all, before your managers can effectively change behavior, including their own, they must first understand existing behaviors and develop new skills. Mastering these skills is also critical because of the span of time involved: remember, major change usually takes 2 to 5 years to achieve lasting results.

QUESTIONS TO PONDER

- Have you held an executive briefing and educating segment in your Plan-to-Implement day to debrief and educate your executives on the change issues facing your organization as a result of your strategic plan?
- Does your collective management team understand our Iceberg Theory of Change and the three key realities of content–process–structure?
- In following the first cardinal rule of mastering change, are you trying to change people and their behaviors (including yours)?
- Are you developing change structures that are different from day-to-day structures?
- Is your top management setting aside time to lead the change process personally?
- Has management made a commitment to guiding and leading employees through The Rollercoaster of Change and its 20 uses?
- Have you committed to enhancing your management's understanding of change with separate, multiday workshops on change and leadership practices?

AFTERNOON: ORGANIZING AND TAILORING CHANGE TASKS — PRIMARY CHANGE STRUCTURES

In the second, or afternoon segment of the Plan-to-Implement day, all of the structures that are necessary to organize your change effort should be decided.

Over the years, we have watched and participated in change efforts that have failed and some that have succeeded. The key to much of this, in our opinion and that of other followers of the discipline of systems thinking, is structure. It is the framework or context within which we play out our work, our lives, and our change efforts. Thus, we have compiled a list of change structures that have helped organizations of all types succeed in major change.

1. **Visionary Leadership** — CEO/Senior Executives with Personal Leadership Plans (PLPs, Figure 13.5)
   - For repetitive stump speeches and reinforcement
   - To ensure fit/integration of all parts and people towards the same vision/values
2. *°**Internal Support Cadre** (informal/kitchen cabinet)
   - For day-to-day coordination of implementation process
   - To ensure the change structures and processes don't lose out to day-to-day activities
3. **Executive Committee**
   - For weekly meetings and attention
   - To ensure follow-up on the top 15 to 25 priority yearly actions from the strategic plan
4. **Strategic Change Leadership Steering Committee** (formal) — replaces or is the Strategic Planning Team
   - For bimonthly/quarterly follow-up meetings to track, adjust, and refine everything (including the Vision)
   - To ensure follow-through via a yearly comprehensive map of implementation
5. °**Strategy Sponsorship Teams**
   - For each core strategy and/or major change effort
   - To ensure achievement of each strategic/change effort, including leadership of what needs to change
6. °**Employee Development Board** (Attunement of People's Hearts)
   - For succession, careers, development, core competencies (all levels), performance management/appraisals
   - To ensure fit with our desired values/culture and develop employees as a competitive edge
7. °**Technology Steering Committee/Group**
   - For computer, telecommunications, software fit and integration
   - To ensure systemwide fit/coordination around information management
8. °**Strategic Communications System (and Structures)**
   - For clear, two-way dialogue and understanding of the plan/implementation
   - To ensure everyone is heading in the same direction with the same strategies/values
9. °**Measurement and Benchmarking Team**

- For collecting and reporting of Key Success Factors, especially customers, employees, competitors
- To ensure an outcome/customer-focus at all times

10. *Accountability and Responsibility System** — all levels
   - For clear and focused three-year business plans and annual department plans that are critiqued, shared and reviewed, as well as individual performance appraisals
   - To ensure a fit, coordination, and commitment to the core strategies and annual top priorities

11. *Whole System Participation Team** (can combine with #8)
   - For input and involvement of all key stakeholders before a decision affecting them is made. Includes Parallel Processes, Search Conferences, Annual Management Conferences, etc.
   - To ensure a critical mass in support of the vision and desired changes

12. *Rewards and Recognition Programs** (can combine with #6)
   - For recognizing and paying people for strategic management accomplishments
   - To ensure reinforcement of the Accountability and Responsibilities System

13. *Organization Redesign Team**
   - For studying and recommending what redesign of the organization is needed
   - To ensure synergy of the strategies, structures, processes, policies, values, and culture

14. **Possible External Change Structures**
   - Advisory board of directors
   - Strategic alliances/partnerships
   - Customer/vendor focus groups
   - Union-management committee
   - Community special interest group (SIG) sessions
   - Community forums
   - User groups
   - Industry/member conferences
   - Value-chain council

The following sections describe some of the change structures from the list above in greater detail.

VISIONARY LEADERSHIP — PERSONAL LEADERSHIP PLANS FOR CEOS AND SENIOR EXECUTIVES

The primary task is to have senior management develop individual personal leadership plans (PLPs) that define the personal tasks they will do as their value-added

---

* Subcommittees of the Strategic Change Leadership Steering Committee

contribution to the change effort. You see, most senior executives don't present annual plans.

So the question becomes, what *are* they "bringing to the table" as it concerns your core values, the change effort, and core strategies?

PLPs are vital to building senior leadership's commitment to your change effort. Unless your top managers are willing, as leaders, to personally change, your organization won't change either. Employees look at their management and think, "Why should I change — they're not going to change!" Leaders must "walk the talk" as well as model openness in their own behaviors through presenting their PLPs.

In this task (to be accomplished and presented at the large group annual review meeting or the first Strategic Change Leadership Steering Committee meeting) each executive develops his or her own personal leadership plan, stating clearly what he or she will do to further the change effort, including actions and commitments:

1. Have each senior management member determine his or her personal leadership commitments regarding the implementation of your strategic plan.
2. Have a written and verbal personal commitment made to the Core Planning Team/SCLSC.
3. Leaders should answer this question: What am I personally going to do to lead and ensure our strategic plan is successfully implemented (i.e., my personal commitment/guarantee)?

Format for Personal Leadership Plans

- Use the same "Annual Planning Form" everyone uses to respond to the following statement (see Figure 13.5):
  I commit and guarantee that my personal tasks regarding strategic plan implementation in the next year will be the following.
- At the end of this form, the following is suggested.
  My "Allocation of Attention" to this in the next 12 months will be _____ % of my organizational work time.

Sample Actions

1. Articulate the vision with employees in all meetings/discussions (over and over).
2. Create a sense of urgency to achieve the Core Strategies/changes. Dip down into the organization on the issues to show personal interest.
3. Model the Core Values, especially those ranked "most in need of improvement."
4. Personally reward, recognize, and reinforce the new behaviors, results, and progress toward the vision.

To ensure the success of our Strategic Plan, I will need to develop my own personal leadership competencies as well as take specific action to demonstrate my own efforts to anchor my leadership within the organization.

A. Personal Leadership Development

Competency/Skill	What's to Be Undertaken	Time Frame
1.		
2.		
3.		

B. Demonstrating Personal Leadership in the next year, I will:

Action	Target Area	By When
1.		
2.		
3.		

Signed: _____   Date: _____

Print Name: _____   Title: _____

FIGURE 13.5 Personal leadership plan.

5. Communicate (and communicate and communicate) and dialogue without defensiveness. Listen, listen, listen.
6. Be open to personal learning, feedback, and skills development toward the vision. Set up your own personal development skill building program

Senior management should focus on the following leadership skills for managing change:

- Energizing the organization towards the vision with personal time spent on following up core strategies. (Senior management time is recognizably the scarcest resource.)
- Enabling employee achievement by reducing barriers to empowerment.
- Being a champion of a specific change through a strategy sponsorship team (SST).

- Trying out new behaviors; not needing to "know it all" and being willing to learn.
- Visiting operations, field offices, and key customers on a regular basis, sharing the vision through "stump speeches" and looking for feedback on customers.
- Reorganizing weekly and monthly executive committee meetings to reflect desired changes, in particular reviewing the top-priority actions.
- Setting up specific ways for all senior management to focus on the Vital Few (i.e., direction, quality of service, desired culture, and leadership skills).
- Being the first ones to go through any needed Visionary Leadership Practices skill building or Mastering Strategic Change workshops.
- Leading the Strategic Change Leadership Steering Committee.

Again, if you truly want to strategically change your organization so that it achieves your vision, then your top managers must be willing to personally model, mentor, and coach others as a regular part of their job descriptions.

INTERNAL SUPPORT CADRE —
THE REPLACEMENT FOR PLANNERS OF THE PAST

Though your top management needs to be actively leading and conducting follow-up status checks regularly and with the steering committee, your organization will also usually require a support staff to manage your change effort between meetings. Figure 13.6 illustrates the individuals or functions usually included in the makeup of this cadre/work. These are general guidelines for structuring your internal support cadre; the size and requirements of your particular organization will determine the number of individuals that's best for you. Keep in mind though, that these are probably permanent tasks in your organization (since change is so constant) and build them into your regular structure.

Even for small companies, as a minimum you will need one person who has 51% of his/her time focused on these responsibilities: sometimes this is the CEO's executive assistant.

Resources will be needed to effectively manage any transition. Identify those resources necessary for each change action and specify who will be responsible to supply them.

EXECUTIVE COMMITTEE — CHANGE LEADERSHIP

It is crucial that the first group to buy in to the "people support what they help create" theme is the executive group themselves. Consultants often forget this. The executive committee meetings, whether conducted weekly or less frequently, should break the agenda into two parts, in the following order:

1. Address the change issues, and ensure that the top-priority change issues are properly implemented in a timely manner.
2. Address the day-day-operational issues as time permits.

List Staff Support Team Names:

Position	Typical Tasks	Name
1. Planning	Strategic/Annual Planning Business Planning Current State Assessment	
2. Finance	• Key Success Factor Coordinator • Budgeting • Current State Assessment	
3. Human Resources	• Performance/Rewards Mgmt. • Training and Development	
4. Communications	Updates after Each Meeting Print Final Plan/Plaques Rollout Plan	
5. Administrative Assistant	Logistics/Follow-up Laptop Mintues/Document Revisions Drafts Strategic Plan	
6. Internal Coordinator **coordinates** or does 1–7 himself/herself	**Minimum List** Parallel Process Internal Facilitator Coordinates Entire Process Facilitates/Supports the Change Steering Committee Teach Org. about This	
7. External Consultant	Facilitates Planning/Change Teams Develops Internal Coordinator Devil's Advocate/Tough Choices Advisor on all Planning/ Change	

FIGURE 13.6 Staff support team.

STRATEGIC CHANGE LEADERSHIP STEERING COMMITTEE — THE #1 ABSOLUTE FOR SUCCESS

You must set up a Strategic Change Leadership Steering Committee (SCLSC), led by top management, to guide and control the overall implementation of any large-scale, organization-wide strategic planning and change efforts. Failure to do so is a guarantee of failure in implementation. This is our number one absolute.

The normal "cascade" strategy for implementing change
is usually ineffective, because memories remain embedded
in the way the organization works after the change. This
applies particularly if the change relates to the culture
rather than to work practices or systems.

-Dick Beckhard

Changing the Essence

This is a new way to run your business, giving equal weight to managing desired changes, in addition to the ongoing daily management of the organization.

The purpose of the SCLSC is twofold:

1. To guide and control the implementation of any large-scale, organization-wide strategic planning/change efforts undertaken through the Reinventing Strategic Planning Model or The High Performance Organization as a System Model.
2. To coordinate any other major performance improvement projects going on in the organization at the same time; to ensure fit with the time and energy demands of ongoing daily business activities (i.e., systems fit, alignment, and integrity).

Criteria for Steering Committee Membership

1. Senior management leadership teams for today and the future.
2. Informal or formal leaders from parts of the organization that are key to implementation.
3. Core Steering Group Implementation Staff Support Team, including overall change management coordinator, KSM and ESS coordinators, and internal facilitators.
4. Credible staff who are knowledgeable of the strategic plan that was developed.
5. Key stakeholders who share your ideal future vision and are willing to actively support it.

Committee Meeting Frequency

1. Phase I: Monthly or bimonthly as the process begins.
2. Phase II: Quarterly, only after the process is functioning smoothly (and if rapid change is not needed).

Example: At Sundt Corp, in Tucson, Arizona, there is an established, ongoing leadership team with 15 of its top executives that meets regularly to review the plans.

Needless to say, there is an unusually strong sense of ownership and involvement with their strategic plan's implementation.

Without a Steering Committee, there is no check-and-balance system making sure that the change effort doesn't lose out to the demands of your organization's day-to-day business activities.

STRATEGY SPONSORSHIP TEAMS

Ask for senior and middle management volunteers to be Strategy Sponsorship Team leaders. Leaders should have particular passions for each of your organization's core strategies and serve as the strategy team's ongoing champions. Have other members of your core planning team (and others from the large group meetings) sponsor one or two of the core strategies that are their particular passion as well, with six to eight members (maximum) for good group dynamics and informal meetings. These individuals will form your Strategy Sponsorship Teams.

EMPLOYEE DEVELOPMENT BOARD — LEADING THE PEOPLE EDGE STRATEGIES

This concept will be covered in more detail in the next chapter, however, it is key to transforming your people into your competitive edge, starting with your collective management team. HR is the support to this board of senior executive team members, not the leaders in their own right. Our board concept is a Proven Best Practice, yet it is fundamentally different from the way most organizations operate.

TECHNOLOGY STEERING COMMITTEE/GROUP

With Enterprise Resource Planning fast becoming the norm (especially in medium and large firms), the need for this specific change committee is more important than ever. Leaving the technology changes to the technologists is a mistake of the highest order by senior management, especially since the cost of these systems can literally bankrupt an organization if you are not careful.

COMMUNICATION SYSTEM AND STRUCTURE — COMMUNICATE, COMMUNICATE, COMMUNICATE

Once your strategic planning document is finalized, you'll need a communications rollout. Josh Weston, Chairman and CEO of ADP, Inc., explains it best:

> Most people think they've communicated when they've sent out a memo that describes something, or in today's age you might send out an audiocassette or a videocassette, that says what you want to say. That's not communication; that's a one-way street. Nothing is communicated unless it's been read or heard, also understood, then believed, and furthermore, remembered. I have found in our business, among other things, you must be multi-media. We take advantage of audiocassettes, of videocassettes, the written word, and lots of informal meetings in order to say and say yet again that which has been said, in order to reinforce important communication.

In order to be certain your strategic plan is, indeed, being understood, you'll need to decide how you will handle a communications rollout, both organization-wide and with key stakeholders, to create a critical mass of understanding.

In addition, you will need ongoing communications throughout the change effort. You can never communicate too much.

KEY SUCCESS MEASURES CADRE — MEASUREMENTS AND BENCHMARKING TEAM

One of the most obvious organizing tasks is to ensure you have a clear and account-able (even if it's small) cadre of people to carefully and continually track your Key Success Measures/Goals (KSMs). Remember that KSMs must measure your strate-gic plan's outcomes as embodied by your vision, mission, and values.

Regular tracking of your KSMs not only gives your organization more control and clarity over its own progress, it also reinforces the concept of continuous improvement, since your measures or targets should increase each year.

COMPREHENSIVE YEARLY MAP OF THE CHANGE PROCESS — ACCOUNTABILITY AND RESPONSIBILITY SYSTEM

The Yearly Comprehensive Map, shown below, is the focal point around which the success or failure of your strategic plan's process of implementation revolves. Its purpose is to create a specific, "by the numbers," monthly implementation process and plan that are visible and easy to track and follow. Completing this task by tailoring it to your organization is actually the primary task of the afternoon session.

By putting down, in black and white, those specific actions that will take place in the 12 months immediately following your planning, organizational members go beyond compliance and begin to build active commitment to your vision. Then, turn the management of this "map" over to your overall change coordinator. It is a great way to tie all your accountability for the plan into one follow-up system.

Example: One of the primary reasons Hal Kluis, CEO of Evans Communications in Turlock, California, is currently enjoying terrific profits and growth is due to the company's persistence and patience with its follow-up process.

CREATE A CRITICAL MASS FOR CHANGE — WHOLE SYSTEM PARTICIPATION

For true, lasting change to occur, you must build a "critical mass for change." That means building an organization-wide mass of commitment to achieving the imple-mentation of your strategic plan. To gain this ongoing commitment to your plan, you'll need to rely heavily on the second Seemingly Simple Element #2: people support what they help create.

It can take 1 to 2 years to fully build your critical mass. Following is a summary of many of the ways to do this discussed earlier in this book.

Yearly Comprehensive Map

(TAKES 2 YEARS TO INSTITUTIONALIZE)

Date

June–Year #1	1.	Begin Strategic Planning (Plan-to-Plan: 1 day)
July– Oct	2.	Do Strategic Planning (5– 8 days overall)
November	3.	**Develop Annual Work Plans/Budgets***
Jan–Year #2	4.	**Conduct Large Group Department Plan Review (1 day)***
Jan	5.	**Conduct Plan-to-Implement (1 day)***
April	6.	Quarterly Steering Committee Review Session – or bimonthly–
July	7.	Quarterly Steering Committee Review Session
April– July	8.	**Develop 3-Year Business Plans*** **(for Business Units/Major Support Departments)**
September	9.	Evaluate Plans' Year #1 Success—Reward based on results
Oct–Dec	10.	**Conduct Annual Strategic Review (and Update: 2– 4 days overall)***
Jan–Year #3	11.	Develop Updated Annual Department Work Plans/Budgets
Jan	12.	Conduct Large Group Department Plan Review (1 day)
April	13.	Quarterly Steering Committee Review Session –or bimonthly–
July	14.	Quarterly Steering Committee Review Session
Oct–Dec	15.	Institutionalized—StrategicReview/Update Again— *The plan as a way of life*

*These are the steps often missed, resulting in failure to implement your Strategic Plan.

Critical Mass for Change Strategies

- Hold Parallel Process and large group employee meetings whenever possible.
- Modify strategic plan drafts using the Parallel Process, listen and review.
- Develop and share annual plans each year for all departments/divisions.
- Implement simple changes and actions quickly — right after annual plans.
- Develop three-year business plans involving both key stakeholders and staff.
- Create trust in your leadership by being open, via the Strategic Change Leadership Steering Committee and on a daily basis. Involve skeptics and listen to them.

- Use Strategy Sponsorship Teams as change agents for tracking and reporting.
- Continue to hold Parallel Process meetings with key stakeholders throughout.
- Put out updates after each Strategic Change Leadership Steering Committee.
- Answer "What's In It For Me" (WIIFM) for employees on a regular basis.

Though building a critical mass takes time, it's worth it. Every step, no matter how small, takes you closer to your future vision and further cements employee commitment and it virtually guarantees the successful implementation of your plan.

The "Lily Pond" Example: A good way to look at this is to imagine a lily pond. The premise is that it takes 30 days to fully populate the pond with lily pads, and that each lily pad creates a second one (i.e., doubles the number) each day. How many days does it take to fill half the pond with lily pads? One quarter of the pond? Answer: 29 days for half, 28 days for one quarter.

REWARDS AND RECOGNITION PROGRAMS

Obviously, the most direct way to build individual commitment to your strategic plan is through rewarding performance. As an organizing task, assign accountability and timelines to look at your present reward system. The first thing to do is to make sure your formal performance appraisals are based on each individual performing in ways that further your core values and strategies. More than likely, your current appraisals are still based on old strategies. If so, it's time to make some changes. The same holds true for your performance management and incentive program, as well as the Olympic recognition program mentioned in Chapter 12.

ORGANIZATION REDESIGN TEAM — FOR WATERTIGHT INTEGRITY

Once your strategic plan and your desired positioning is clear, then designing your organization to fully support that direction is essential. A Strategic Business Assessment and Redesign project is a standard methodology for organizations such as our Centre for Strategic Management. See Chapter 14 for details.

Again, most organizations lack watertight integrity in how they operate. This is why reengineering experts see the average firm as having 30% to 40% waste or fat.

SUMMARY

Each of these processes and structures, from your strategic plan rollout, through developing personal leadership plans, to creating a critical mass for change, is covered in the afternoon session: the organizing and tailoring tasks segment of a Plan-to-Implement day. It may not be necessary to give each one equal emphasis: perhaps your organization has just recreated, in-depth, its performance and rewards system, for instance, and doesn't need to do more than highlight the topic. However, each Organizing and Tailoring Task must be present and accounted for in your Plan-to-Implement day. After all, these are the "10,000 little things" that make the difference between ongoing successful implementation of your plan and the good old SPOTS syndrome.

QUESTIONS TO PONDER

- What are the four phases of the Rollercoaster of Change? Which one are you least skilled at, and why?
- Name the four core change structures that you feel all organizations should adopt if undergoing large-scale change. Why?
- What other structures from our list of 14 does your organization currently need? Do any of them exist right now?
- How is your plan implementation going right now? Would it benefit from a Plan-to-Implement day even now? Why or why not?
- How skilled are you in leading and mastering strategic change? What skills do you need to improve?

RECAP OF KEY CONTENT POINTS

- At the completion of your strategic planning, conduct a Plan-to-Implement day with three segments: executive briefing and educating, and both the organizing and tailoring change tasks.
- The cardinal rule of change is that you must design and develop structures for managing change that are separate from existing, day-to-day organizational structures.
- You must prepare for and be ready to manage the four phases in the Rollercoaster of Change on a constant basis, as people change at different rates and speeds:
  1. shock and denial
  2. depression and anger
  3. hope and adjustment
  4. rebuilding

"HOW-TO" ACTION CHECKLIST

1. Develop an initial rollout and communications plan.
2. Establish an organization-wide annual plan reflecting the strategic planning priorities for the first year.
3. Align the budget to reflect the strategic planning priorities.
4. Build all department/division/unit annual plans around the organization-wide annual priorities or goals.
5. Establish a yearly map, or master work plan, for 12-month implementation and follow-up. It should include three-year business plans for any SBUs/major support departments that don't yet have them.
6. Establish a Key Success Measure/Goal monitoring, tracking, and reporting system.
7. Revise your performance and reward system to support your new vision, core strategies, and values.
8. Build an internal support cadre with the expertise and skills to coordinate the strategic plan's implementation and change management.
9. Ensure key Strategy Sponsorship Teams are set up to build a critical mass for change.
10. Make sure all members of management in your organization become experts in the 20 uses of the Rollercoaster of Change.
11. Choose from the list of change structures needed and select those that will help you be successful in creating customer value.

14 Strategy Implementation and Change (Step #9)

Changing people's habits and ways of thinking is like writing your instructions in the snow during a snowstorm. Every 20 minutes you must rewrite your instructions. Only with constant repetition will you create change.

-Donald Dewar

Many times, managers read long-range plans, nod in agreement, and then wait for something to happen. A good example is when organizations begin a quality improvement process, which usually includes a strategy of changing the culture.

If nothing really visible starts happening right away, management tends to panic. Somehow they expect the process itself to magically do all the work — that having educated their employees, formed teams, and told them to start holding improvement meetings will automatically start some sort of mystic plasma flowing. They don't realize immediately that management has to lead, and in some cases, drag people along. Failure to do so shows a lack of integrity on management's part.

If you always do what you've always done,
you won't always get what you've always done,
because the world has changed!

-Stephen G. Haines, 1991

This is why it's a good idea at this time to check your system's overall alignment, attunement, and watertight integrity. This deals with each part of the organization and its relationships to others. Each part of your organization's system must be aligned with every other part in support of the vision. *This is the real task of strategic change by senior management.*

To accomplish true system fit, alignment, attunement, and integrity, you must develop *commitment*, not merely compliance, to your new vision. You'll need constant repetition, follow-up tactics, and techniques for ensuring success, dealing with resistance, maximizing commitment, and minimizing disruptions. Because the level of change you're dealing with tends to generate disruptive fallout in the organization, it's important to create situations as needed in which there can be quick, visible successes — with all the attendant ceremony and hoopla.

Example: The Navy Public Works Center in San Diego (a virtual city government of 3000 workers) has an excellent weekly executive board meeting and strategy review, created specifically to engineer successful implementation of its strategic plan.

1-57444-278-3/00/$0.00+$.50
© 2000 by CRC Press LLC

As you begin the implementation of your strategic plan, always pay attention to the cultural changes that will need to take place. The attention can't be limited to top or bottom levels only. It's also important to be aware of the various levels of possible difficulties in any organization. In particular, pay attention to middle management. It's called this because these managers are caught "in the middle" and are frequently the ones who block change. They've often worked hard to get where they are, only to have the new "empowerment" culture undermine the authority they took so long to acquire. Remember, employees are your greatest asset, but only if management allows them to be. So focus here on the middle management and first-line supervisors, not just on the workers.

Tip: Of course, the reality is that there will be some backsliding from time to time, but by anticipating it, it is possible to combat it and overcome it. To look realistically at how difficult it will be to install your strategic change effort, consider such factors as the following:

1. Executive willingness and time commitment
2. Size of your organization; it's geographic locations, number of levels, and Strategic Business Units
3. Amount of change
4. Fundamental/radical cultural shifts caused by the change
5. Cross-functional teamwork issues
6. Changes needed in knowledge, attitudes, and skills (competencies)

In the end, management action, or lack of it causes most problems in change efforts. Systems alignment, attunement, and integrity are difficult to develop, much less maintain, and require tough actions on senior management's part at all levels, not just with its direct reports (remember, it's organization-wide change you want).

However, the bigger conflict and failure ultimately is not to face up to these issues. Every time I hear the word "vision," I think of a big, complicated, political-sounding document that everyone nods to, but no one takes seriously. When that happens, systems alignment and attunement go begging and the organization maintains no watertight integrity.

INSANITY:
Doing the same things in the same way,
yet expecting different results.

-Stephen G. Haines, 1991

Senior management needs the courage of its convictions. Wanting to be liked instead of respected is a blueprint for failure — and one I see all too often today. It's no longer fashionable to be a strong leader. Nonsense!

THE STRATEGIC CHANGE LEADERSHIP STEERING COMMITTEE (SCLSC) IN OPERATION

*"The transition from the current state to the future state
has traditionally been underestimated, understaffed,
and inadequately addressed."*
-Bill Veltrop, Exxon Corp. Executive

As we said, the #1 essential step in making sure the implementation of your strategic plan is underway is to establish your Strategic Change Leadership Steering Committee (SCLSC) with regular meetings. The mission of this committee is to regularly check, adjust, and report on the progress of overall implementation. It needs to meet at least quarterly, and in each meeting it should address the three purposes below:

1. Reviewing and scanning the environment for any changes that effect the organization.
2. Reviewing the status of Key Success Measures/Goals vs. targets by the KSM Benchmarking team.
3. Reviewing the core strategies, strategic action items, and department plans that support them by the strategy sponsorship teams (SSTs).

The Strategic Change Leadership Steering Committee is the organization's primary instrument in advancing implementation, and as such, it should use its meetings as much more than a casual check or status report. The SCLSC should act as a motivator, communicator, coordinator, problem solver, and when necessary, mediator.

A typical daylong SCLSC meeting should not only ask in-depth questions about Key Success Measures/Goals, core strategies, and annual plans. It should also problem-solve performance issues, evaluate and make suggestions on priority changes based on environmental changes, coordinate major performance improvement projects, and communicate progress on all of the above to key stakeholders throughout your organization. See below for a typical agenda.

Change Steering Committee (Standard Meeting Agenda)

Note: This interactive strategic planning implementation follow-up day should include learning, change management, and team building.

1. **Welcome:** Agenda, Logistics, Norms, current to-do list reviewed.
   • Interactive "change" icebreaker.
   • Where in the yearly planning cycle/map are we?
2. **Review Status** of Key Success Measures/Goals vs. targets (KSM Coordinator).

3. **Learning Activity:** Conduct communications and interpersonal skills, coaching, presenting, facilitating, team building, or other change management skills needed to have the committee work effectively, and for the change to succeed.

4. **Review Core Strategies,** strategic change projects, and top-priority annual action items (strategic sponsorship teams/presenters — be interactive, questions and answers, etc.).
   - List top three successes to celebrate.
   - List top three issues/concerns and problem-solve them.

   Note: Rollercoaster of Change — Each topic needs to answer three questions:
   - Where are we as a team on this Rollercoaster?
   - Where is the rest of the organization? Differences: location, department, level.
   - What actions are needed to bring us all through these desired changes?

5. **Review of Annual Plan Status** (or business/functional plans).
   - For each department, follow-up results obtained.
   - Maintain the organization's "systems fit, alignment, and integrity" with any other major changes.

6. **Changing Priorities? Environmental Changes?** (SKEPTIC): What are they? What should we do about them?

7. **Deepen Change Management Understanding and Assessment:** Each meeting covers one new change management tool and applies it to an issue/strategy:
   - Best practices list
   - Customer-focused
   - Empowerment criteria
   - Cross-functional teams
   - HR management practices
   - High performance survey
   - "Change implications" list
   - Menu on alignment/attunement
   - Leadership development competencies
   - Positioning/customer star results

8. **Communications to Key Stakeholders** (continue the Parallel Process).
   - In writing and face-to-face.
   - Stump speeches.
   - Unit/department meetings also (cascade communications).

9. **Next Steps.**
   - To-do list reviewed — assign accountability/timing.
   - Next Change Steering meeting — prepare agenda.
   - Next year's timetable for annual strategic review/planning and budgeting cycle.

10. **Process — How did it go?** (both the day and the Strategic Change Management process overall).

Last, and most important, there should be an all-management meeting and all-employee meeting following each SCLSC meeting whenever possible. This will serve to cascade the SCLSC direction, results, and discussions in face-to-face settings throughout the organization.

In all of this, it should be obvious that solid and timely communications are crucial to the success of any major change effort. Senior leaders need "stump speeches" composed of the key parts of the strategic plan. Your communications goals might include the following:

- Gain greater commitment to the organization's strategic plan.
- Develop more trust and honesty: be blunt — speak the unspeakable.
- Build the credibility needed for effective leadership — be human, admit mistakes.
- Focus your organization's efforts on critical issues and top annual priorities.
- Communicate more directly and effectively with a broader constituency — to all stakeholders.
- Identify the organization's key messages over and over again (stump speeches).
- Use your own personality, passion, and voice to increase leverage as a leader: be yourself — be unique.

Communications and Emotions

Teddy Roosevelt was right about the bully pulpit:
"Some look at the evidence and believe that if their conclusions are logical, others should accept them automatically. That's not good enough. You have to communicate — constantly, emotionally, and directly."

There is a proliferation of communications discussions about the need for improvement in most organizations (is it a symptom or the root cause?). Regardless, a failure to understand some of the basics of good communications is startling. It includes the proven notion that one has to tell someone about changes that effect them *four times* before they really hear and understand it. Some other key basic communications points are given in Figure 14.1.

Executives need to be experts on all of this during Step #9, strategy implementation and change. Unfortunately, many are not.

ORGANIZATIONS AS SYSTEMS

Every organization is perfectly designed to get the results it is getting. Thus, if results are less than desired, the design should be changed. That includes adjusting structure, work processes, linkages, and information flows to meet new needs.

-Keeping Current, Quetico Centre, 1994

One-to-One Conversation

Communication Methods	
Words=	7%
Tone=	38%
Body Language=	55%
Total=	100%

Small Group Discussion

Large Group Discussion

Video Conference

What you do speaks louder than what you say!

Telephone Conversation

Conference Call   "2 way"

— —

Voice Mail   "1 way"

Pager

Handwritten Letter

E-Mail

Fax

Typewritten Letter

Mass-Produced Letter

We Remember Approximately:
10% of what we *read*
20% of what we *hear*
30% of what we *see*
50% of what we *see* and *hear*
70% of what we *say* and *do*
90% of what we *explain as we do*

Newsletter

Brochure

News Item

Advertisement

Handout

Repetition Increases Understanding
1st time=10% retention
2nd time=25% retention
3rd time=40–50% retention
4th time=75% retention

FIGURE 14.1 Ladder of communications effectiveness (repetition–repetition–repetition).

A second area in which executives need to be experts during Step #9 (strategy implementation and change) includes understanding that their organizations are living and complex systems. It is much more than organization structure alone, although even that has become more complex these days as Figure 14.2 shows. There are now three areas that make up a firm's human resources, (1) staff, (2) contingent workers, and (3) external strategic alliances, all of which are crucial to having the resources needed to effectively implement your strategic plan.

In our earlier discussion of the morning session of the "Plan-to-Implement" day, the last part of the Executive Briefing segment looked at all of the pieces of an organization: its structure, budget, people, processes, technology, teams, boundaries, vision, customers, suppliers, leaders, jobs, services, quality, and more.

We then proceeded to evaluate how to find a framework or model that can make sense out all of these pieces. Executives need to put them together in some organized and structured *"mental map."* If they can, it will assist them in better understanding

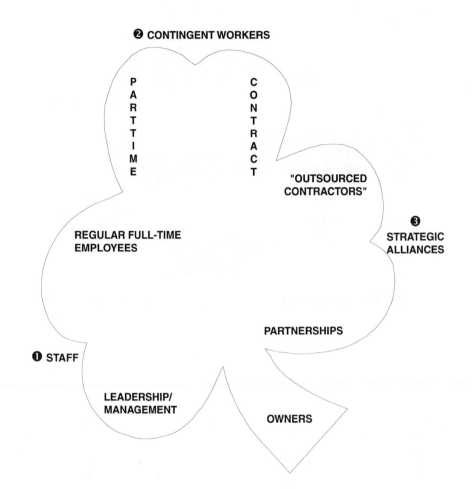

FIGURE 14.2 The shamrock organization. Adapted from Drake International, 1985 and Doug MacNamara, the Banff Management Centre, 1998.

how to change all the parts to fit better into an integrated system that can support their desired outcomes (i.e., your vision and/or achievement of improving customer value).

The Organization as a systems model, shown in Figure 14.3, has the same A, B, C, D, E phases as our Reinventing Strategic Management Model, as they are both based on the Systems Thinking Approach. Again, the model's most fundamental characteristic is that it is a way to look at and assess each organization as a system. The key is, if you change one piece of the system/organization, you'll need to adjust all the other pieces to a greater or lesser extent, in order to make the organization continue to run effectively as a whole.

In other words, changing the organizational parts to a good fit with each other leads to synergy (i.e., 2 + 2 = 5). Conversely, when the organizational parts are in conflict, having turf battles, or simply not working (or fitting) together, suboptimizing

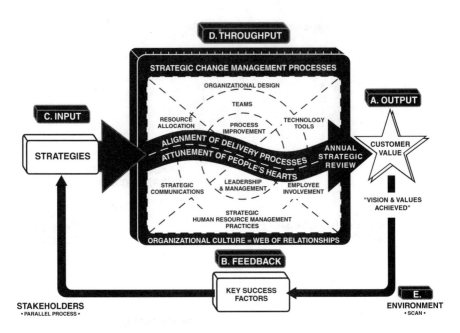

FIGURE 14.3 The organization as a system — creating alignment and attunement for your competitive edge. Courtesy of the Centre for Strategic Management, San Diego, CA, 1997 Revised. With permission.

will be the inevitable, organization-wide result (i.e., 2 + 2 = 3). Remember the analogy about trying to make the world's greatest car, using different makes and models for each piece and ending up with a car that wouldn't fit together and would never be able to run?

In our initial research on strategic change and organizational systems models, we were primarily seeking the best way for managing radical, long-term change. We found, in comparing 13 different, popular organizational change models, that none of them treated the organization as a system.

It was also surprising to note that, of these 13 models, only two included values or technology issues, only four even mentioned the customer (unbelievable!), and only one incorporated a strategic change management system for guiding the necessary change that became the norm of the 1990s and will continue into the foreseeable future.

Thus, we developed the "organization as a system" model (Figure 14.3) to describe any organization as a system, large or small. It focuses on our Systems Thinking Approach, as opposed to the traditional (and still most common) analytical organizational models, which are static, hierarchical, and incomplete. These analytical models largely ignore the organization's customer, technology, environment, feedback, and the dynamic nature of today's world. Instead, they focus on the more superficial, hierarchical structure with its separate workings of the internal pieces/departments. The systems approach, on the other hand, provides an expanded, *structural design of organizations as living systems* that more accurately reflects reality. It was expressed in *Inc. Magazine* (November 1993), as follows:

> Peter Senge of MIT writes about asking executives who they think is the leader of a ship crossing the ocean. The usual answer is the captain or the navigator, but he answers that it's the designer of the ship, because everyone on the ship is influenced by its design.

The high-performance organization that's flexible enough to grow through change in the 21st century will need each part of its overall system to be healthy and work synergistically. If a working systems model and common mental map exist within your organization, you'll be able to more easily pinpoint specific problem areas during Step #9, strategy implementation and change. It will also become easier to evaluate how all the parts of your system work together, leading to more effectiveness.

Along with this model, we researched the best practices at high-performance organizations. The result is the High-Performance Survey that was included in the Current State Assessment, Chapter 9. It is based on our Organization as a System model here. Go back and see how its ten parts seem to fit, complement, and even overlap with one another. Look it over carefully, intuitively. The High-Performance column is a list of the proven best practices we know today. It will prove to be of high importance when initiating a Strategic Business Design during the first year of implementation. It is critical to accomplish in order to redesign the alignment and attunement of the organization in support of your new and changed future vision and positioning with watertight integrity.

STRATEGIC BUSINESS DESIGN — OF AN ORGANIZATION AS A LIVING SYSTEM

Using a common and shared organizational systems model has tremendous advantages. Not only is it practical as a fundamental template or model, it also provides a superb diagnostic tool for analyzing your organization and all its subunits, as well as checking the fit, alignment, attunement, and watertight integrity with your overall vision and positioning. It is also extremely useful as a common, interactive structure for communicating and working together to change parts and relationships within your organization to be better able to achieve your vision.

Strategic business design is no longer centralized vs. decentralized, but strategic consistency and operational flexibility.

Question: How do you design your business, leadership, organization, processes, and people practices to support your Ideal Future Positioning and Vision?

Answer: With an integrated and holistic strategic business design for your entire organization to maximize its synergy toward your vision (i.e., watertight integrity of design).

The following are some topics of a strategic business design:

1. Shared visions/values and shared strategies
2. Shared values and strong culture
3. Strategies and tactics
4. Formal structure and formal design
5. Strategic consistency and operational flexibility
6. Centralization and decentralization
7. Job descriptions and roles/responsibilities
8. Policies and procedures and accountability
9. Functions and business processes
10. Compensation and rewards/recognition
11. Full-time employees and part-time/contract employees
12. Positioning/core competencies and outsourcing/strategic alliances
13. Product-based and customer-focused

In Sum: Mission   Strategy   Structure (i.e., strategic business design).

Strategic business design is composed of two parts: (1) assessment and (2) design. Sample forms to use for this needed effort sometime during the first year of strategic plan implementation are given in Figures 14.4 and 14.5. While we have included them here to begin educating the reader about this key first-year project, it needs a much more extensive treatment than we have room for in this book. We plan to make it the topic of a future book.

Based on the past, which 1–3 items of all the components of the Organization as a System Model is your organization likely to fail to implement successfully? (i.e., "The best predictor of future performance is past performance.")

#	Components most likely to fail to be implemented	Result of the failure	Actions to take to counter this

FIGURE 14.4 #1 Use: organization assessment summary.

ROLLERCOASTER OF CHANGE:
PRINCIPLES AND TECHNIQUES OF CHANGE

When making the major changes in any organization based on a strategic business redesign project, the potential negative impact on employees is huge. In order for executives to navigate the Rollercoaster of Change effectively, some *key principles of change* must be well understood. See below for a best practices list; these principles of change are research-based, not matters of personal opinion.

1. Any change in any one part of the organization affects other parts of the organization — the "ripple effect." (An organization is a system and a "web of relationships.") Leaders need to pay constant attention to an integrated fit/alignment and attunement. If not, entropy will take over and a run-down organization will slowly deteriorate.
2. People are funny: change they initiate is viewed as good, needed, and valuable. Change that is forced on them is met by some form of resistance, no matter what the nature of the change.
3. People need predictability — physical, psychological, and social. It's an offshoot of the basic need for security.
4. People will feel awkward, ill at ease, and self-conscious; they need information and reassurance over and over again.
5. People will think first about what they will have to give up — their losses; let people cry, mourn, and grieve the loss.
6. People will feel alone even though others are going through the same change. Structure interactions and involvement for people to feel a sense of community.
7. People also need variety, new experiences, growth, breaks in routine, and creative outlets.
8. The communications power in explicit vision and values is enormous. People want to believe.
9. Only one to three themes (maximum) should be chosen in order to give people focus.
10. People change at different rates, depths, and speeds; they have different levels of readiness for change.
11. Excellence is doing 10,000 little things right — that is strategic management in execution.
12. "Structures" exist; their design influences everything else.
13. "Processes" exist; the only issue is their focus and effectiveness.
14. There is a need for a continual change management process — the hierarchical organization has a difficult time changing itself.
15. The stress of change on people is enormous, but can and must be managed for successful change to occur. People can only handle so much change; don't overload — it causes paralysis.
16. Being open to feedback doesn't have to be avoided, but it can be painful; yet it is growth-inducing, as you have more information with which to improve.

17. Employees can be a bottom-line competitive business advantage, but only if management first becomes the advantage.
18. People will be concerned that they don't have enough resources; help them get "outside the Nine Dots."
19. If you remove pressure for change, people will revert back to old behaviors; relapses are natural and will occur.
20. We rarely use what works despite the fact that proven research is available on change management.

— Adapted from John Laurie, Ken Blanchard,
Bill Pfeiffer, and Stephen G. Haines

What components of your organization will/should be impacted by the major change/strategy you propose? Which change/strategy?: _____

Which Components are Impacted and How?	Action Needed/Implications
Phase A	
1. _____ Vision	
2. _____ Mission	
3. _____ Organizational Values	
4. _____ Organizational Culture	
5. _____ Organizational Identity/Image and Positioning	
6. _____ Strategic Plan	
7. _____ Quality Services	
8. _____ Customer Service	
9. _____ Quality Products	
10. _____ Customer Choices	
11. _____ Lower Cost Products/Services	
12. _____ Speed/Responsiveness	
Phase B	
13. _____ Key Success Factors — Outcome Measures (List) _____	
_____	
_____	
Phase C	
14. _____ Other Core Strategies (List): _____	
_____	
_____	
15. _____ Dept. Annual Plans	
Phase D	
16. _____ Operating Tasks	
17. _____ Leadership Development System/ Skills	

FIGURE 14.5 #2 Use: organization design for action planning: strategic change impact exercise — creating a high-performance organization using the A, B, C, D, E phases and the "organization as a system" model.

Which Components are Impacted and How?	Action Needed/Implications?
18. _____ Empowerment	
19. _____ Key Internal Stakeholders (List): _____ _____ _____	
20. _____ Staffing Levels (Recruitment/ Downsizing/Selection)	
21. _____ Facilities/Equipment — Physical Resources	
22. _____ Communication Processes	
23. _____ Resources (Financial/All)	
24. _____ Technology	
25. _____ Organizational Structure/Design	
26. _____ Job Design/Definition	
27. _____ Strategic Business Units (SBU)	
28. _____ Succession Planning	
29. _____ Rewards System (Pay/Non-Pay)	
30. _____ Performance Appraisal	
31. _____ Training and Development	
32. _____ Business Processes	
33. _____ Policies and Procedures	
34. _____ Team Development	
35. _____ Annual Strategic Review (& Update)	
36. _____ Change Management Structures	
E Environment	
37. _____ Environmental Scanning System	
38. _____ Key Environmental Stakeholders (List): _____ _____ _____	

FIGURE 14.5 Continued.

— A Challenge —
Be deadly serious over the long term…
or don't even attempt change…
You'll screw it up.

"In life, what you resist, persists."
Constant reinforcement is needed.

To carry out these principles in a practical way requires people sensitivity and street smarts coupled with proper reflection and planning time. Below are some techniques to help executives understand the Rollercoaster and assist them through the "ups and downs" when implementing major change.

Ways to Unfreeze an Organization
(Induce Phase I: Shock/Denial and Phase II: Anger/Depression)

1. Share what competitors are doing.
2. Explain your organization's finances and profit/loss statement.
3. Share your organization's vision and future ideal.
4. Clarify the impact on the organization and employees of a particular situation or issue.
5. Conduct an organizational survey. Feed it back to "X."
6. Collect interview data and feed it back to "X."
7. Re-explain job expectations and standards of performance.
8. Change the reward system (individual, team, organization-wide).
9. Discuss changes in the environment that impact the organization.
10. Discuss why there is a need to change.
11. Explain the organization's strategic plans and direction and why they are chosen.
12. Set goals with employees.
13. Examine employee data, such as turnover, etc.
14. Conduct an unfiltered upward feedback meeting.
15. Change the roles of key informal leaders.
16. Feed back customer perceptions and data.
17. Conduct focus groups of employees or customers.
18. Change the location of management offices to be closer to the workers.
19. Set up task forces to analyze issues and recommend solutions.
20. Explicitly evaluate employees (including senior management) on your espoused values.

Factors Needed to Successfully Go through the Stages of Change
(Phase II: Anger/Depression and Phase III: Hope/Adjustment)

1. This is a time of high uncertainty and anxiety.
   a. Communicate frequently downward about the change and change process.
   a. Develop feedback mechanisms to hear the employees' questions and concerns and then find a way to conduct two-way dialogues.
2. Don't react emotionally to employee concerns and resistance. Empathize and understand it. Let people talk it out. Then try to deal with the underlying issues (i.e., read between the lines).

3. Let people have a clear understanding of why the change is necessary.
4. Let people have an opportunity to critically cross-examine the leader(s) and verify for themselves the necessity for change.
5. Give people occasions to talk through their feelings of loss and detachment from the old ways.
6. Have methods by which people affected by the change can participate in some aspect of change to control their destiny.
7. Have management develop and organize new support systems to establish the new state.
8. Develop a positive climate about the change by evoking a clear and positive "common vision" of what the end state of the change will look like.
9. Show people how the change can personally help them and their needs.
10. Relate the change to employee values.
11. Develop teams (not just groups or departments) and a value and a reward for teamwork.
12. Work closely with the informal leaders of the organization.
13. Provide employees with an opportunity to increase their learning and competence about their jobs and about the change.
14. Develop and communicate about your well-planned transition management process to give employees a sense of security and knowledge that you are in control and in charge of the changes.

QUESTIONS TO PONDER

- How often should the Strategic Change Leadership Steering Committee meet throughout the year? Why?
- Who should be on the Steering Committee? Why?
- How would you go about conducting a strategic business design in the first year of implementation?
- How many committees (from the Change Structures list of the previous chapter) do you think an organization of 1000 employees should have? Why?
- What are some things that senior management should do to assist employees through the Rollercoaster of Change in a major reorganization?

ATTUNEMENT WITH PEOPLE'S HEARTS AND MINDS — THE PEOPLE EDGE

As stated in the previous chapter, one of the key list structures for accomplishing change is an Employee Development Board. It is the place where the senior executive team can focus on developing employees as a competitive edge over the competition. Every strategic plan we have ever assisted on has included one or more people strategies. However, what should be included in this strategy is a mystery to many executives.

Organizations and senior management need to understand that you don't "align people," as the saying goes. You must focus on the *attunement with people's hearts and minds* as human beings and living systems, not mechanical assembly line robots.

EXECUTIVE/EMPLOYEE DEVELOPMENT BOARD CONCEPT: "INVEST IN YOUR PEOPLE FIRST"

The people management practices of any organization should be viewed as a system of people flow from hiring, through their careers, and through retirement and/or termination. Making this all happen is the responsibility of senior management; usually best done through an EDB (Executive/Employee Development Board) focused solely on this framework and creating people as a competitive business advantage.

This board reinforces senior management's responsibility to carry out "stewardship" responsibilities toward themselves and the rest of the employees. The best way to carry this out is to conduct a Strategic "People Edge" Plan to fully define and implement your corporate strategic plan's people strategy.

In essence, this board is responsible for the human resource management flow and continuity, linking staffing to business strategy via

- Hiring
- Selection (up/lateral)
- Succession planning/core competencies
- Developmental jobs/experiences
- Leadership development system
- Training: classroom (internal, external)·

- Organization design/structure
- Sociodemographic trends
- Rewards/performance
- Workforce planning
- Employee surveys of satisfac tion/360° feedback

A mechanism/structure of how to achieve management continuity is needed (i.e., a linking pin of boards) (see Figures 14.6 and 14.7).

Executive/Employee Development Boards (EDB)

1. **Purpose:** To proactively manage and create the organization's People Edge
2. **Number of EDBs:** Using the linking pin concept (see Figure 14.7)

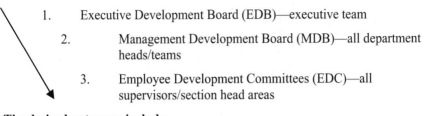

1.   Executive Development Board (EDB)—executive team

2.   Management Development Board (MDB)—all department heads/teams

3.   Employee Development Committees (EDC)—all supervisors/section head areas

The desired outcomes include:

Right person — Right job — Right time — Right organization — Right skills

FIGURE 14.6 The structure necessary to form a linking pin of boards.

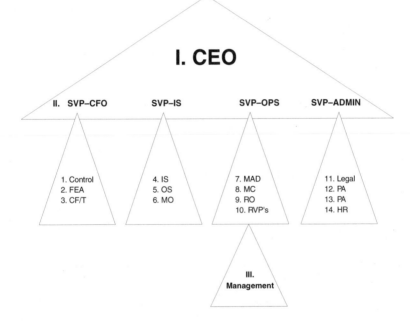

FIGURE 14.7 The linking pin concept.

   I.   First level — Executive EDB
   II. Second level — Four SVP EDBs
   III. Third level — 14 Management EDBs

3. **Management of Each EDB**

   A. **Chair**
- Senior officer responsible for stewardship of area
- Manage the EDB
- Links to higher-level EDB
- Responsible for EDB decisions/actions/follow-up

    B. Members
- Direct reports of each chairperson
- Responsible for succession presentations
- Must wear a corporate hat in the meetings for them to be successful
- Represent their employees as well

    C. Secretary/HR Rep
- Provides content input
- Ensures employee fair treatment
- Handles minutes and logistics
- Ensures process occurs properly
- Is the linkage person laterally to EDBs
- Provides follow-up continually on EDB desired actions

4. **Meetings:** As necessary, but initially quarterly or monthly depending on rollout of tasks (see below).

5. **Rollout:** Recommend initially that only Executive EDBs be established so that officers can gain experience with the process prior to involving directors in 14 officer areas.

Sample Monthly Executive Meetings

Week 1	Operational/Business Issues
Week 2	Strategic Planning and Change Process/Status
Week 3	Strategic Change Issues
Week 4	Customer Satisfaction
Week 5	Executive/Employee Development Board (EDB)
Quarterly	Staff, promotion, succession, development

    This Employee Development Board should focus on the Six People Edge Best Practice Areas shown in Figure 14.8, which are based on the extensive research of the Centre. We examined eight key, well-known authors in the human resources field and found none of them had all of our six levels of best practices. As you will see they are same six natural levels of the leadership competencies mentioned earlier in this book. Both best practice lists are based on the *Seven Levels of Living Systems,* as clarified by systems thinking researchers years ago. Only two of these eight key authors had even the beginning elements of a systems approach.

    The questionnaire shown in Figure 14.8 details the *Six Levels of People Edge Best Practices* (and their 30 associated people programs and 9 other key inputs and outcomes). It is provided for the reader's detailed understanding and use as an assessment tool.

I. Optional Instructions: #1 ☐ How skilled are you in these best practices yourself?
                     #2 ☐ How well does this occur now for the person you are rating? _____ (name)
                     #3 ☐ For your organization and its management?

II. Instructions: Please circle the # or N/A that applies.

Topic	(1) No Best Practices –Reactive Orgn. –Survival Only				(5) Some Best Practices –Responsible Orgn. –Traditional Control					(10) High Level Best Practices –1990s High Perf. Orgn. –Proactive Orgn. Emprmnt	N/A Not Applicable	Score and Comments
Self or Others: Management of Organization:					Current State Assessment							
Level #1–Acquiring the Desired Workforce												
1. Identifying organizational competencies	(1)	2	3	4	(5)	6	7	8	9	(10)	N/A	
2. Developing alt. workforce arrangements	(1)	2	3	4	(5)	6	7	8	9	(10)	N/A	
3. Conducting workforce/succession plng.	(1)	2	3	4	(5)	6	7	8	9	(10)	N/A	
4. Installing a career development program	(1)	2	3	4	(5)	6	7	8	9	(10)	N/A	**Level 1:** Total Score: _____ /5 = _____ (average)
5. Hiring desired employees	(1)	2	3	4	(5)	6	7	8	9	(10)	N/A	
Level #2–Engaging the Workforce												
6. Installing a Performance Mgmt. System	(1)	2	3	4	(5)	6	7	8	9	(10)	N/A	
7. Linking compensation to performance	(1)	2	3	4	(5)	6	7	8	9	(10)	N/A	
8. Creating recognition systems	(1)	2	3	4	(5)	6	7	8	9	(10)	N/A	**Level 2:** Total Score: _____ /5 = _____ (average)
9. Providing flexible benefits	(1)	2	3	4	(5)	6	7	8	9	(10)	N/A	
10. Dealing with poor performance	(1)	2	3	4	(5)	6	7	8	9	(10)	N/A	
Level #3–Organizing High Perf. Teams												
11. Developing team skills	(1)	2	3	4	(5)	6	7	8	9	(10)	N/A	
12. Developing small unit leaders	(1)	2	3	4	(5)	6	7	8	9	(10)	N/A	
13. Developing empowered teams	(1)	2	3	4	(5)	6	7	8	9	(10)	N/A	**Level 3:** Total Score: _____ /5 = _____ (average)
14. Establishing participative management	(1)	2	3	4	(5)	6	7	8	9	(10)	N/A	
15. Developing team rewards	(1)	2	3	4	(5)	6	7	8	9	(10)	N/A	

FIGURE 14.8 Best Practices — creating the people edge.

Topic Self or Others: Management of Organization:	Current State Assessment											Score and Comments
	(1) No Best Practices −Reactive Orgn. −Survival Only			(5) Some Best Practices −Responsible Orgn. −Traditional Control				(10) High Level Best Practices −1990s High Perf. Orgn. −Proactive Orgn. Emprmnt.			N/A Not Applicable	
Level #4—Creating a Learning Organization												**Level 4:**
16. Spreading learning quickly	(1)	2	3	4	(5)	6	7	8	9	(10)	N/A	
17. Institutionalizing systems thinking	(1)	2	3	4	(5)	6	7	8	9	(10)	N/A	Total Score: ____/5 =
18. Developing HR measures	(1)	2	3	4	(5)	6	7	8	9	(10)	N/A	
19. Learning from our experiences/mistakes	(1)	2	3	4	(5)	6	7	8	9	(10)	N/A	____ (average)
20. Encouraging creative thinking	(1)	2	3	4	(5)	6	7	8	9	(10)	N/A	
Level #5—Facilitating Cultural Change												**Level 5:**
21. Understanding the desired culture	(1)	2	3	4	(5)	6	7	8	9	(10)	N/A	
22. Developing collective mgmt. skills	(1)	2	3	4	(5)	6	7	8	9	(10)	N/A	Total Score: ____/5 =
23. Integrating HR with strategic direction	(1)	2	3	4	(5)	6	7	8	9	(10)	N/A	
24. Designing organizational structures	(1)	2	3	4	(5)	6	7	8	9	(10)	N/A	____ (average)
25. Developing change experts/capabilities	(1)	2	3	4	(5)	6	7	8	9	(10)	N/A	
Level #6—Collaborating with Stakeholders												**Level 6:**
26. Developing global skills	(1)	2	3	4	(5)	6	7	8	9	(10)	N/A	
27. Understanding strategic alliances	(1)	2	3	4	(5)	6	7	8	9	(10)	N/A	Total Score: ____/5 =
28. Maintaining a positive environment	(1)	2	3	4	(5)	6	7	8	9	(10)	N/A	
29. Creating customer focus	(1)	2	3	4	(5)	6	7	8	9	(10)	N/A	____ (average)
30. Collaborating with all stakeholders	(1)	2	3	4	(5)	6	7	8	9	(10)	N/A	

Grand Total: _____ (300 possible) /30 = _____ (average)

FIGURE 14.8 Continued.

Again, how to create the People Edge should be the topic of an entire book on its own. However, suffice it to say that each organization needs to develop a "strategic" People Edge plan for its human side of the organization. This is not the responsibility of the Human Resources Department, but of senior management. Human Resources needs to be involved, but it is not invested with fiduciary responsibility for the employees.

IN SUMMARY — EFFECTIVE IMPLEMENTATION AND CHANGE

Step #9 is a multifaceted step. In fact, it really isn't a step at all. Rather, it is the difficult 80% of the effort in vision achievement, composing most of the 12 months of the strategic management yearly cycle. Strategic planning is important, but it is only 20% of the effort. Carrying out the regular meetings of the Strategic Change Leadership Steering Committee (SCLSC) is the most important element for success throughout the year. We have never seen a really successful change without it.

RECAP OF KEY CONTENT POINTS

- The regular meetings of the Strategic Change Leadership Steering Committee are the most important element for success in any change effort.
- Know the difference between simply surviving change and mastering it, i.e., developing viable change mechanisms that you can use to try and control change over the long term.
- The first cardinal rule of change is that *organizations* don't change ... *people* do.
- If your top management doesn't set aside the time to manage and lead your change effort, it won't go far. Employees watch what management does — *and* what it doesn't do — for clues to its real priorities.
- In order for your change effort to succeed, understand that your organization is a living, breathing system and use the *Organization as a Systems Model* to ensure the system's fit, alignment, and watertight integrity.
- This entails the need for a *Strategic Business Design* project in the first year of implementation.
- A second project in the first year of implementation is the need for an *Employee Development Board,* comprised of senior management. They must "flesh out" their people-related core strategy through a Strategic People Edge Planning process.
- It is a critical senior management task to check your change management system for its fit, alignment, and integrity with respect to your vision on a constant basis.

"HOW-TO" ACTION CHECKLIST

1. Set up an ongoing Strategic Change Leadership Steering Committee to manage the change process.
2. Make sure top management practices ongoing, active leadership in your change process.
3. Put an environmental scanning system in place — both yearly and in quarterly Strategic Change Leadership Steering Committee meetings.
4. Create an ongoing Key Success Measures/Goals tracking team that reports to the Steering Committee on a regular basis.
5. Set up Strategy Sponsorship Teams to report regularly to the Steering Committee on the achievement of the core strategies and strategic action items.
6. Set up a communications committee to ensure successful regular communications throughout the change effort to all employees.
7. Set up an environmental scanning system and team to track environmental changes and report regularly to the Steering Committee.
8. Set up an Employee Development Board to conduct and implement a Strategic People Edge Plan for the organization. It should be tied to your corporate strategic plan's Core Strategy regarding people (and there always is one).

15 Annual Strategic Review and Update (Step #10)

Thinking is easy. Acting is difficult. To put one's thoughts into action is the most difficult thing in the world.

-Goethe

To persist in keeping your implementation up and running successfully year after year as a strategic management system — even after the newness has worn off — you'll need to conduct a yearly follow-up to diagnose the overall success of your implementation. Also, be sure to recycle and update your strategic plan and its annual priorities, continuing to improve toward your Ideal Vision as you go. In a way it's like a "Continuous Improvement Helix," as shown in Figure 15.1.

Each year, every organization has a yearly independent financial audit. However, a yearly independent strategic management audit is rarely found in the management literature, in practice, or even on management's or the board of directors' radar screens.

Instead, Step #10, the Annual Strategic Review and Update should include a review, assessment, and a feedback report, with recommendations from an external, unbiased perspective on the status of your organization's strategy implementation. This assessment process concerns itself with two overall purposes/goals:

1. To assess management's attention to the strategic management system and implementation process itself.
2. To assess management's attention to actual results and achievement accomplished under the strategic plan.

Paying attention to only one of these two goals in not very effective, as Figure 15.2 reflects. The result of this update should be the following four outcomes:

1. Updating your strategic plan.
2. Clarifying your annual planning and strategic budgeting priorities for next year.
3. Problem-solving any issues raised in the assessment of either goal above.
4. Setting in place next year's comprehensive map of implementation, annual plan, and strategic change management process (SCLSC, etc.).

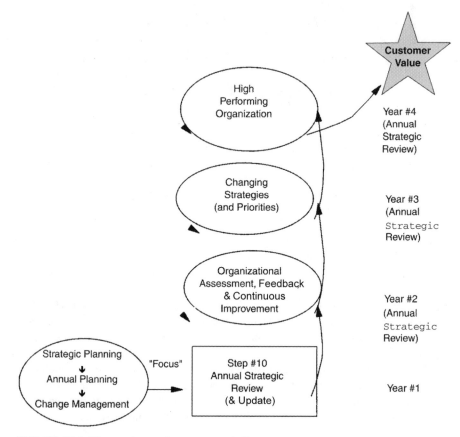

FIGURE 15.1 The continuous improvement helix.

YEARLY ASSESSMENT — THE FIRST STEP

There are many ways to collect the data for the Current State Assessment portion of the Annual Review:

- Interviews with senior management.
- Interviews with the internal support cadre.
- Documents, records, agendas of all change and planning processes and meetings.
- Focus group meetings, possibly with the SSTs, middle management, first-line supervisors, and cross-functional teams of employees.
- Focus groups of customers.
- Interviews with external stakeholders, board members, suppliers, and customers.

Specific feedback and renewal mechanisms include the following:

Instructions: Based on the framework and goals below (#1 and #2), every organization needs to conduct an independent yearly follow-up and diagnosis on how they are performing. This is key to "learning to be a customer-focused high performance organization."

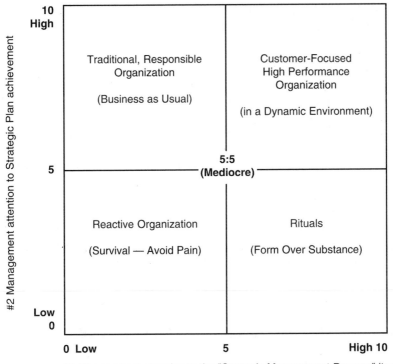

Question: Where do you see yourself on this framework?

FIGURE 15.2 Annual strategic review.

1. Issues management process (government, community, stockholders, stakeholders)
2. Environmental scanning system
3. Competitor analysis
4. Financial reports (short-term/long-term)
5. Industry financial comparisons
6. Customer data, surveys, perceptions, feedback, focus groups
7. Noncustomer data, surveys, perceptions, focus groups
8. Technology trends
9. Sociodemographic trends

10. Employee opinion surveys (morale, motivation, communications) — yearly, by units
11. Rewards: matching surveys, programs, diagnosis
12. Culture surveys, focus groups
13. Administrative MIS reports
14. Deep sensing of employee perceptions
15. Advertising, marketing ROI, and research
16. Management data, opinions, meetings
17. Task forces, think tanks, discussion groups
18. Strategic planning process
19. Unfiltered upward feedback meetings
20. Team building diagnosis, executive retreats, and checkups
21. Action research
22. Structured experiences, feedback and learning
23. Job design, work simplifications
24. Organization effectiveness suggestion programs (not just productivity)
25. Employee involvement programs, meetings
26. Peer evaluations
27. End of meeting evaluations
28. Employee/management meetings
29. Off-site meetings, overnights, outward bound team experience
30. Performance evaluation, including company values
31. MBWA (Management By Walking Around)
32. Strategic Change Leadership Steering Committee

ANNUAL REVIEW MEETINGS — THE SECOND STEP

Once your assessment is completed, a yearly strategic update of your plan needs to be made. You don't need to spend time on a brand-new strategic plan each year, but you do need a refresher or annual update of the plan. This is much quicker than the original planning process, but it is a must. Your yearly update should consist of completing the full A, B, C, D, E Reinventing Strategic Management Model, only in a much briefer fashion.

1. Complete a brief Plan-to-Plan as necessary.
2. Start with a 2-day off-site meeting that includes these tasks:
   - Recheck your strategic plan — its vision, mission, values, and Key Success Measures — quickly and briefly, as an overview to see if they are still relevant.
   - Conduct the Strengths, Weaknesses, Opportunities, Threats (SWOT) analysis, preceded by a feedback of your independent strategic management system audit and assessment.
   - Refine your core strategies. (Year to year, core strategies pretty much stay the same, but in any given year, one or two may have changed or fallen off, and one or two others may have been added.)

- Reset your annual strategic action items/priorities and accountability. This task will represent the bulk of this off-site meeting's work. Most of last year's priorities will be completed, and you'll need to create new ones, as well as rollover the next phases of some current projects.
3. Conduct a Parallel Process for feedback from all key stakeholders.
4. Hold another 1- to 2-day review meeting to finalize your updated strategic plan (and especially the annual action priorities for next year).
5. Then, require all your key department managers to again develop their annual plans within the context of your core strategies as the organizing principles.
6. Following this, you should hold a 1- to 2-day large-group annual plan review meeting as before, to ensure all department plans are correct and in sync with each other.
7. Develop strategic budgets.
8. Reenergize the Strategic Change Leadership Steering Committee, Strategy Sponsorship Teams, etc.

Constantly I am asked how often organizations should *completely redo* their strategic plans in addition to these annual updates. Realistically, in today's changing world, I believe that a plan can last only 2 to 3 years before it needs to be completely redone. On the other hand, you should expect to do a new plan, or revise your existing one, whenever your organization experiences major change in its direction (new or changed goals), its environment (marketplace), or its leadership (if the CEO leaves, for instance).

Tip: The Annual Strategic Review and Update (Step #10) is key to being a high-performance learning organization. Without a strict adherence to this part of the process, you won't need to worry about how long your change effort is taking — you simply won't have one. This yearly renewal process is based on the systems thinking concept of "entropy," in that as soon as the strategic plan is developed and implemented, its consequences and environmental changes indicate a need for a redesign soon after. Hence, the key concept of the strategic plan as a "living, breathing document" is crucial. Rigidly holding to the plan is as bad as no plan at all.

Thus, the ideal Strategic Management System is an inexact, adaptive, learning, ideal-seeking system. Flexibility and agility are paramount.

QUESTIONS TO PONDER

- Have you had an *independent audit* of both your organization's strategic management system and the results of your plan?
- Are you communicating organization-wide, with each planning update session?

- Does your organization have a Strategic Change Leadership Steering Committee, led by top management, to guide and control the annual review and update of your strategic plan?
- Do you have an internal support staff to manage your update?
- Have you created a yearly map for the next year, showing a specific implementation plan, and have you allocated the proper resources for it?
- Are there Strategic Sponsorship Teams in place for championing your core strategies again for the second year?
- Are you continually tracking progress on your Key Success Measures/Goals?
- Has your organization's senior management led this review and also developed individual Personal Leadership Plans for themselves?
- Are you building individual and team commitment to your plan with an effective performance and rewards system?
- Is your organization firmly committed to an Annual Strategic Review and Update (similar to its yearly independent financial audit)?
- Is your strategic plan recycled yearly?

TIME COMMITMENT

The time commitment to complete this Annual Strategic Review depends on a number of circumstances, such as

1. Self-awareness and existing teamwork skills of the leader and senior management.
2. Conflict-management and problem-solving skills of the team.
3. Degree to which the key stakeholders have a harmonious view of the organization's future.
4. Availability of data required for the review.
5. Planning team composition, group size, and strategic orientation.
6. Priority of the update process itself — comprehensive, quick, or low priority.
7. Amount of key stakeholder involvement and parallel process meetings.

IN SUMMARY: ACHIEVING GOAL #3 — BUILD AND SUSTAIN A HIGH-PERFORMANCE ORGANIZATION

This chapter lists the ongoing key tasks for an effective Annual Strategic Review and Update (Step #10). These tasks are crucial to keeping your plan fresh, up-to-date, relevant, and focused toward your desired future. That is why we have identified it as Goal #3 in Strategic Management: "Build and Sustain High Performance."

Setting these last three Strategic Management chapters and steps (#8, #9 and #10) into motion as ongoing, organization-wide change management processes enables you to come full circle each year, all the way through the A, B, C, D, E yearly cycle. They will provide your organization with the necessary content, process, and structure for successfully implementing and updating your strategic plan and making solid progress toward achieving your vision, year after year. After all, how did we put a man on the moon during the decade of the 1960s? Step by step, task by task, and year by year — just like any good strategic plan.

RECAP OF KEY CONTENT POINTS

- Conduct a yearly follow-up and independent diagnosis of your performance regarding your plan's successful implementation, as well as the establishment of your Strategic Management system.
- Conduct a yearly recycling and updating of your strategic plan and all its components, the full (A, B, C, D, E) model.
- Take the time you need to do this right. However, it is usually only about a third to half of the time it took to build the plan in the first place.
- Only three to five themes (maximum) as continual priorities for the organization.
- Give constant attention to an integrated fit and corporate view. Don't put up with poor teamwork and performance.
- Renewal, feedback, and issues identification don't have to be sacred cows. Welcome problems, not complacency.
- Excellence is doing 10,000 little things right. A Strategic Management system is a continual improvement in execution: a constant agitation and dissatisfaction with the status quo and a desire to find new and better ways to do everything.

"HOW-TO" ACTION CHECKLIST

1. Use an independent auditor for your update to ensure it is an unbiased assessment.
2. Involve your people throughout this review, using the standard Parallel Process, especially middle management.
3. Have middle management help with the SWOT assessment to get more input.
4. Be sure to carefully repeat all the tasks in Step #7, Annual Planning and Strategic Budgets (Chapter 12) and Step #8, Plan-to-Implement (Chapter 13).

5. Republish your plan, produce tri-fold and other plaques and cards to reinforce your plan again.
6. The stress of change on people is enormous, but it can be prioritized and managed, or it will manage you.
7. "Processes" exist; the only issue is their focus and effectiveness. Manage the *process* of change/updates.
8. The communications power in explicit vision and values — use it face-to-face.
9. Use what works — the proven research is in.

Part 4

Getting Started: Different Options and Customized Applications

16 Strategic Management Applications

Nothing splendid has ever been achieved except by those
who dared to believe that something inside them was
superior to circumstances.

INTRODUCTION

Though it is easy to feel powerless and battle-weary amid the rapid-fire change of today's environment, it is a constant that we must learn to deal with and overcome. Avoiding it, and the tough choices that come with it, will only leave the future health and performance of your department or organization to be determined by circumstances beyond your control.

By using the Systems Thinking Approach, however, and thinking backwards to the ideal future you envision, it is possible to implement innovations that are custom-fit to your organization/department — innovations that raise you above those circumstances you can't control, and give you an overall approach that you *can* control.

THE ABCs OF STRATEGIC MANAGEMENT REVISITED

A systems thinking approach to strategic management cannot be successful unless you remember to incorporate the A, B, C, D, E phases of the system:

1. Creating your ideal future — your *output*
2. Measurements of success — the *feedback* loop
3. Converting strategies to operations — the *input* to action
4. Successful implementation — your *throughputs*/actions
5. Accomplished within our rapidly changing global environment

In recapping the underlying concept of the Reinventing Strategic Management Model, we've seen that the systems thinking approach to strategic management boils all planning issues down to five main questions within the five phases of the systems model:

Phase A (Future Outcomes): Where do we want to be?
Phase B (Feedback): How will we know when we get there?
Phase C (Today's Input): Where are we now; what strategies should guide us?
Phase D (Throughput Actions): How do we get there?
Phase E (Environment): What is/will be changing in the environment? (Ask on an ongoing basis.)

The beauty of approaching your planning and implementation this way is that no matter where you are in your planning or actions, you can maintain a focused, systems perspective, make adjustments in response to change or, if necessary, even change direction by simply stepping back, reviewing these questions, then having the courage to move forward on the answers, always focusing on the outcome.

Though you do not need to religiously adhere to the ten steps this book outlines for strategic management via the systems approach, you do need to incorporate each of the five phases in order to successfully implement your strategic management system. The five A, B, C, D, E phases are the framework for each and every step in the Reinventing Strategic Management Model; they are also unique to this systems model (no other planning/change processes in existence today includes all five phases).

As this systems model comes from the scientific discipline of the General Systems Theory, its characteristics were set up to be generically applied to all open/living systems. It is these characteristics that make this approach timeless and universal. Using the five-phase systems approach to strategic planning and change means you can apply it to anything — and I mean anything. Whether you're planning for an organization, a department, a project, or even yourself or your own family, this systems thinking approach works for any and every kind of system.

MANY USES OF THE FIVE PHASES OF SYSTEMS THINKING

This section illustrates how to use this generic, five-phase, systems thinking approach in these specific applications:

1. Comprehensive strategic planning
2. Strategic Planning Quick (SPQ)
3. Microstrategic planning
4. Three-year business unit planning/major support department planning
5. Strategic change projects
6. Strategic life planning (personal and family)
7. Team effectiveness
8. Problem solving
9. Project management

The differences between these various uses are substantial, and illustrate how widely this approach has been successfully applied. Who knows … after learning the five-phase systems approach, you will probably end up finding a completely new application for your particular environment. For the purposes of this chapter, however, I've chosen the applications that I have used the most in my work with organizations and individuals.

COMPREHENSIVE STRATEGIC PLANNING

Comprehensive strategic planning, of course, is what this book is all about: developing in-depth strategic plans and implementing change efforts that enable any organization to successfully install a new strategic management system that will help you achieve your Ideal Future Vision. This complete, 10-step model is most applicable to larger organizations that need to galvanize (in one direction) an entire organization made up of thousands of people.

Even with the full ten steps, though, the key is to tailor it each time you conduct strategic planning, rather than following the same rigid application. It needs to fit your organization's unique requirements at that particular time. In general, this comprehensive strategic planning will require approximately 12 to 16 days over a period of 7 to 10 months (but obviously less, if tailored differently), as shown in Figure 16.1.

While 7 to 10 months may seem like a lot of time, it is really setting up the annual cycle for managing the organization as a system in a strategic fashion. If you

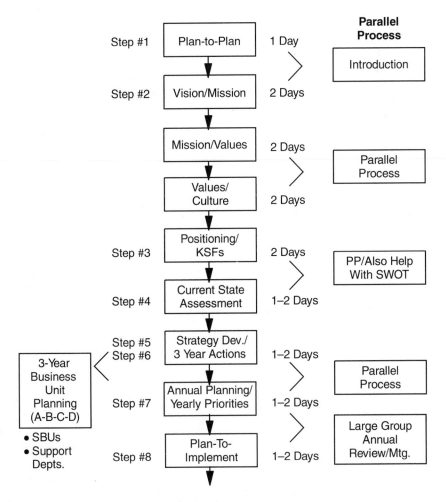

FIGURE 16.1 Comprehensive strategic planning.

can keep this more outcome-oriented perspective in mind, it will probably make more sense to you over the long haul.

The suggested timeline generally consists of two, 2-day off-site planning sessions each month for the number of months required, based on your tailoring. Plan on about a month's time between each meeting in order to hold a series of Parallel Process meetings in which you'll conduct a review of the strategic plan developed so far with your key stakeholders.

Example: You will find many examples of successful comprehensive strategic planning processes we have conducted such as Sundt Corp., Giant Industries, BC Buildings Corp., SaskEnergy, Poway Unified School District, and the Alberta Department of Agriculture (city of St. Albert, Alberta), Navy Public Works Centers (both in San Diego, California, and Norfolk, Virginia), etc. throughout the pages of this book.

STRATEGIC PLANNING QUICK

The reality in this fast-paced modern world is that we sometimes just don't have the time available to go as in-depth as the comprehensive strategic planning suggests. Time and speed, especially, are key competitive advantages today. Also, there may be any number of other reasons you would not be in a position to enter into comprehensive strategic planning at this time, such as the following:

- Crisis — have to act quickly
- Need to rapidly refocus, in a new direction
- Limited time available
- Smaller-size organization
- Limited resources
- New to strategic planning — need to "test the waters"
- Awaiting new senior management/major board changes, but want to get started

Typical businesses that have successfully used the Strategic Planning Quick (SPQ) model are small-to-mid-size organizations. The Reinventing Strategic Management Model can be tailored to conduct viable strategic planning from start to finish in only 5 days of off-site meetings, over a period of 2 to 3 months. As you can see in Figure 16.2, the steps and step numbers designated in the comprehensive strategic planning model are the same for this SPQ model — they're just condensed.

Though Strategic Planning Quick can be done off-site, in 5 days, you should plan on conducting an informal Plan-to-Plan session beforehand, as prework. In all, there will be two, 2-day off-sites, with time in between for two Parallel Processes, finishing with a 1-day off-site meeting. If you're considering this framework, keep in mind that it also should be tailored to fit your specific needs. For instance, instead of 5 days, either 4, 6, or 7 may be best for you.

Example: Such entrepreneurial organizations as Community Care Network, KVP Systems, Evans Telephone, Royal Electric, Eagle Creek Inc., Santel Federal Credit Union, Laser Machining Inc., Rockwell Federal Credit Union, California

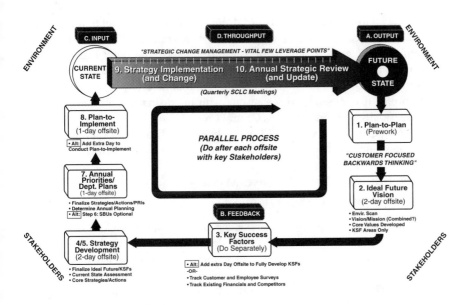

FIGURE 16.2 Strategic planning quick (SPQ): 5+ days — a Customer-Focused systems solution to creating high performance. Courtesy of the Centre for Strategic Management, San Diego, CA, 1995 Revised. With permission.

Coast Credit Union, Pulse Engineering, and British Columbia's Mineral Titles branch have used Strategic Planning Quick with excellent results.

MICROSTRATEGIC PLANNING

Microstrategic planning often represents an organization's first foray into authentic *strategic* planning. It is also sometimes used by very small (50 or fewer employees) organizations or by small departments within an organization. It is modeled on Strategic Planning Quick, but instead of two 2-day off-site meetings, it is condensed down to only two 1-day off-sites (Phases A, B, C). Following these 2 days of off-sites, you'll immediately need to set up and begin the quarterly Strategic Change Leadership Steering Committee meetings (Phase D) and Environmental Scanning (Phase E).

Because the tightness of microstrategic planning lends itself to a certain rigidity, and because most work must be done "off-line," you must make sure that the entity you're planning for has a strong feedback loop. Also, since you won't have time to concentrate on Key Success Measures/Goals, you should instead focus on and monitor core strategies and existing financials, along with surveys of both customers and employees. As you complete this Key Success Measures/Goal off-line, gain approval later.

Caution: One last word of caution. Microstrategic planning requires quicker decisions, with time for only one Parallel Process. Be sure you do all preliminary work off-line as prework, saving the meeting time for any key consensus discussions that are needed to address crucial issues. Unless you firmly commit to incorporating this Parallel Process, you run a strong risk of lower creativity and futuristic thinking and even a lower level of support by key stakeholders who don't feel involved in the plan's creation. Above all, remember, that people support what they help create. Successful implementation (Goal #2) is the real goal here.

Example: It *is* possible to see results with microstrategic planning. It's been done successfully with firms such as Central Credit Union, Wheeler Frost Associates (a small financial services firm), AEA Credit Union, Leachman Cattle Co., and a strong community foundation, the Health Care Alliance, among others.

THREE-YEAR BUSINESS UNIT PLANNING/MAJOR SUPPORT DEPARTMENT PLANNING

If you look at a large corporation's strategic planning as an example, you'd typically see planning done for five or more years in length. Below the corporate wide level, though, there are many different line departments or business units. In addition, there are major support functions such as public relations, human relations, finance, legal, etc. Each of these line and support units needs its own strategic plan, usually called 3-year business plans. To review business unit planning, see Chapter 11.

Example: Some excellent examples of where this has been done in organizations conducting the larger, comprehensive strategic planning process include Giant Industries, Sundt Corp., SaskEnergy, Poway Unified School District, and British Columbia Ministry of the Environment, Lands, and Parks.

STRATEGIC CHANGE PROJECTS

Most change efforts falter because they pursue only a partial systems solution. In fact, when you allow strategic planning to lead the way, major tasks and change efforts such as TQM, Value-Chain Management, service, empowerment, self-directed work teams, etc., are often among its most immediate, visible beneficiaries. The reason for this is that when you apply the five phases of a true systems thinking model, you can look at *any* project or program as a whole system within itself.

In other words, it is possible to initiate a successful major change project, even if it exists within an imperfect, analytic environment. Focusing on the entity you want to change, and then applying the system's A, B, C, D, E phases, can accelerate your desired changes, ultimately tying them into other major changes that should potentially be core strategies as well. The outcome is actually solid Strategic Quality Planning or Value-Chain Management, etc.

Example: Many of the Navy's Total Quality Leadership changes floundered, because they were treated as separate issues, unconnected to the system as a whole. My normal task is to help U.S. Navy commanders to tailor and integrate their Total Quality Leadership program into an overall strategic plan for the command. The same is true for a number of private firms that are focusing exclusively on process improvement. This is still an analytic approach to a systems problem. (Most change projects are piecemeal and only analytical, which is why they often fail to succeed as advertised.)

STRATEGIC LIFE PLANNING

Adapting the Systems Thinking Approach to planning your personal life is remarkably simple, and just as effective. In Strategic Life Planning, go back to the basic five questions that accompany each phase:

A. Where do I want to be (i.e., my ends, outcomes, purposes, goals, holistic vision)?
B. How will I know when I get there?
C. Where am I now: what are today's issues and problems in my life?
D. How do I get there (i.e., close the gap from Phase C to Phase A in a complete, holistic way)?
E. What is changing in my environment over the next 3 to 5 years? (Ask on an ongoing basis.)

The five-phase systems concept is exactly the same, only the focus of your outcomes and desired future will vary. Also, it's easier than other strategic planning, as fewer people are generally involved. However, you still need to identify and involve key stakeholders (i.e., spouse, family, others) to ensure you have someone play devil's advocate with your plans.

Another good point is that you probably do not need a full-time facilitator to assist you; just having periodic access to a strategic planning process expert will normally be enough. If the issues or personalities are particularly difficult, however, then having assistance in facilitating the process may be necessary.

To start Strategic Life Planning, find a relaxed time and space in which you can focus solely on the Personal Values exercise in Chapter #7, Ideal Future Vision.

Once you've begun with your personal values, to free up your mind to focus on the future, then proceed with the steps of the Reinventing Strategic Management model.

Of course, if you are doing this as a couple, it raises fundamental points of how you both see your desired future. For this reason, couples doing strategic planning should be aware of the risk that it poses. If you have different visions of the future in mind, it could pose substantial differences unless you're both willing to be flexible.

Example: I can speak definitively to the rewards of doing Strategic Life Planning. My wife, Jayne, and I created our 5-year life plan when we got married in 1991 and have been seeing concrete results and a very positive influence on our life together ever since. Writing this book was one of our goals, and we're ahead of schedule, adding finishing touches and gaining a very satisfying sense of accomplishment. Another goal was to work and travel extensively throughout the world, and we're well on our way to achieving that, even updating our plans annually in some exotic places (Great Barrier Reef, Bali, Big Sur, etc.).

Lastly, it has been very gratifying to see members of the Centre for Strategic Management (and lots of others) successfully develop and implement their own personal life plans, reaping fuller, more holistically-balanced lives than they'd previously experienced.

For those interested in this we also have published a book and workbook on Strategic Life Planning (Crisp Publications, 2000).

TEAM EFFECTIVENESS

Work gets done in organizations when groups of people work together as a team to accomplish the task. Most of these tasks require cross-functional teamwork and cooperation; hence the popularity of business process reengineering, and now, value-chain management. However, there is a big difference between a "group of people" and a team that is functioning effectively.

We have the only systems model within which to view teams and team effectiveness, despite the proliferation of team information and dynamics. A holistic look at a team and its multiple purposes is crucial if we are to maximize team effectiveness. See Figure 16.3 for our A, B, C, D, E model of a team.

Example: In order for a group of people to come together as a new planning team, they first must function effectively as a team. We rarely provide the training and understanding for them to function as a team, yet we expect them to instantly become a team. This is absurd! Even worse, although effective teams of six to eight people are best, and we've even doubled that for effective planning teams (15 max), one of our clients wanted to start with 20 people instead. We gave in against our better judgment, only to run into numerous team issues, preventing us from finishing the planning until we went back and covered this model along with the expected norms of behaviors. Once we started critiquing the team each planning day, we really picked up steam as a planning team. The final result is outstanding. It just took 3 extra days of planning to get there.

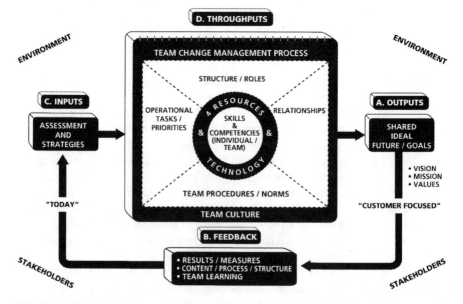

FIGURE 16.3 High performance team mode — the Systems Thinking Approach to creating high performance work teams. Courtesy of the Centre for Strategic Management, San Diego, CA, 1995 Revised. With permission.

PROJECT MANAGEMENT

Every project you can envision requires this same A, B, C, D, E systems framework. Project management experts who are reading this may say (and justifiably so) "what's new here? We've been using systems/outcome thinking for decades." They're right: project management seems to be the only profession in Western society where this systems thinking is the norm.

Example: Cardone Industries of Philadelphia learned this systems model through our work with them on strategic management. Subsequently, they had a project to figure out how to "tithe" their 10% of profits better than they had in the past. (If that last sentence blows your mind, it is because Cardone is a very unusual organization that tries to "glorify God in all they do.") As the largest remanufacturer of automobile parts, they are very successful. However, in order to accomplish this new project, Evan Curry, their Senior VP and project leader utilized our A, B, C, D, E systems model and very effectively planned and carried out this project, resulting in a whole new way for them to "glorify God." What a story!

PROBLEM SOLVING

All of us know the old problem-solving steps, taught since time immortal. However, the systems view is that we shouldn't be problem-solving yesterday's and today's issues as much as seeking systems solutions for the future. This isn't just word-smithing, but a whole different way to think. The biggest weakness in traditional problem solving is the conspicuous absence of Phases A, B, and E, as can be seen in Figure 16.4.

Example: (Opportunities vs. Problems). This is a way for you to stay opportunity-focused. One opportunity can change the course of business (Internet, anyone?), while solving all the problems just gets you back to zero. When Microsoft stops fighting with the U.S. government and focuses its entire attention on the marketplace and the customer, look out.

A FINAL NOTE: BEST PRACTICES RESEARCH

No matter which use of the Reinventing Strategic Management model you deem best for your organization — and no matter what type of organization you have — always keep in mind that knowing the best practices of competitive organizations can go a long way toward showing you what works and what doesn't. Remember, not all businesses are the same, but the best practices are. And the A, B, C, D, E Systems Thinking Approach model is a best practice because it models the way the world works.

A WORD ON PUBLIC VS. PRIVATE SECTOR PLANNING DISTINCTIONS

Though the private sector still has a long way to go in its approach to strategic planning and change management, it has at least begun the battle. The public sector,

"Put your discourse into some frame."
—William Shakespeare

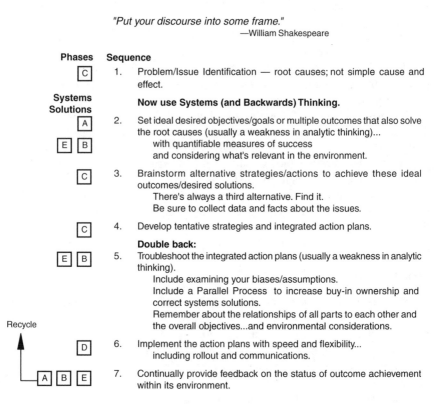

Phases **Sequence**

C 1. Problem/Issue Identification — root causes; not simple cause and effect.

Systems Solutions

Now use Systems (and Backwards) Thinking.

A 2. Set ideal desired objectives/goals or multiple outcomes that also solve the root causes (usually a weakness in analytic thinking)...

E B   with quantifiable measures of success
       and considering what's relevant in the environment.

C 3. Brainstorm alternative strategies/actions to achieve these ideal outcomes/desired solutions.
       There's always a third alternative. Find it.
       Be sure to collect data and facts about the issues.

C 4. Develop tentative strategies and integrated action plans.

Double back:

E B 5. Troubleshoot the integrated action plans (usually a weakness in analytic thinking).
       Include examining your biases/assumptions.
       Include a Parallel Process to increase buy-in ownership and correct systems solutions.
       Remember about the relationships of all parts to each other and the overall objectives...and environmental considerations.

Recycle

D 6. Implement the action plans with speed and flexibility...
       including rollout and communications.

A B E 7. Continually provide feedback on the status of outcome achievement within its environment.

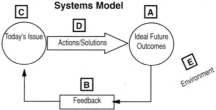

Systems Model

C — Today's Issue
D — Actions/Solutions
A — Ideal Future Outcomes
B — Feedback
E — Environment

FIGURE 16.4 System solutions vs. problem solving.

where it has taken any steps at all, has looked at planning as a "project" instead of a way of life. However, many organizations are now beginning to recognize that it is a serious undertaking that fundamentally changes how you run your business day to day.

One of the things that continually impresses me in my work with both public and private sectors, though, is how many similarities there are in the types of problems each encounters. One of the main differences within the public sector, however, seems to be in the degree of severity. Its problems are almost always similar to problems found within the private sector (particularly within staff support areas). However, it has a broader group of stakeholders, and is often burdened with confusing missions and the vicissitudes of the political arena.

More and more frequently, government leaders are pursuing such concepts as privatization and competition as their new core strategies. (See Chapter 10 for the 13 Principles of Reinventing Government.) The reasons behind this movement are many, but at their foundation is a desire for improved effectiveness in the face of dwindling and limited funds.

Example: Many, many public, government, and military organizations (such as the City of Indianapolis, Ministry of the Environment, British Columbia, San Diego Navy Public Works Center, Poway Unified School District, San Diego County Regional Occupational Programs, and Alberta, Canada Department of Agriculture, to name but a few) are working diligently toward a systems thinking approach to strategic management.

The following subsections discuss the most visible strategic issues the public sector must, in my opinion, resolve.

MANDATE VS. MISSION

Though every government organization has a legislative mandate, it's not the same as having a mission. Mandates tend to be broad (too broad, in fact) even up to eliminating self-initiative and creating dependency. Sometimes, a mandate is so broad it becomes necessary to zero in on just exactly what the organization's primary focus should be; after all, no organization, private *or* public, can be everything to everybody. That's nothing more than a blueprint for failure.

Trying to fulfill a mission that is outside the organization's roles and responsibilities (i.e., liberal do-gooders vs. self-help) is virtually impossible to achieve. I believe that:

> *Government control — "let the government take care of that" — has become a habit, removing challenges and opportunities ... and is actually eroding the general community.*

Example: British Columbia Buildings Corp. has a legal mandate stating that it could serve any public sector organization in the world. What has served them better, though, has been a mission that focuses primarily on serving the public sector in British Columbia — a far more manageable aim.

LACK OF A PROFIT MOTIVE

Because there is no specific profit motive in the public sector, organizations frequently interpret this to mean they don't need to be business-oriented; they read "business" as synonymous with "profit," when in fact these are two very different concepts.

Being "business oriented" means that an organization runs itself as a business; it's just that in the case of the public sector, the profit is zero. Running an organization as a business means using proven business concepts and tools for running any organization successfully. There is some science to running *all* organizations — so "why don't we use what we know" works, even in the public sector. The organization should also come out at the end of a year having spent the money that was budgeted or obtained by generating revenue, no more and hopefully less. Though it's definitely not profit oriented, a business-thinking mindset can substantially increase the public sector organization's responsibility and accountability, and even more importantly, its achievement of its mission.

Example: A good example of how a business-thinking mindset can change government's budgeting accountability is the county of Santa Clara in northern California. In streamlining its administrative work via a customer-focused approach and the establishment of an aggressive computer network, Santa Clara is in such good financial shape that it was able to build a long-term fund with a $30 million yearly budget.

POLITICIANS AS "BOARD OF DIRECTORS"

Public organizations don't have a board of directors; instead, they have politicians that act as stewards for the public/voters. Therefore, in order to successfully develop and implement a strategic plan, you must pay close attention to the electoral cycle. Otherwise, you run the risk of completing a 5-year, comprehensive strategic plan, and then discarding it for a "new-and-improved" plan brought in next year by the new reign. Time your strategic plan to the electoral cycle, but look beyond it to a vision that is shared by all.

LACK OF CUSTOMER FOCUS

With the lack of competition per se in the public sector, government organizations are often vague as to the identity of their customers. As a result, they often end up either trying to serve everybody — an impossible task — or just serving themselves. This lack of clarity (and lack of systems thinking) as to who their customer is leads to an unclear sense of purpose or mission as well. Often, these organizations fail to know, focus on, or even truly care about their clients and customers.

Not knowing who their customer is or what their mission is leads to a concentration on bureaucratic activities, rather than working with a clear sense of mission. Public sector employees need to view themselves as true public servants, instead of following a bureaucratic, hierarchical structure and system. They need to serve their specific clients in their mission statement, as well as the public that pays their salaries.

They also fail to distinguish between the services they provide, and the needed staff support areas — again, confusing ends and means.

MISSING MEASUREMENTS OF OUTCOME SUCCESS

As John Rollwagen, former CEO, Cray Research (and second-in-command to the late Commerce Secretary Ron Brown in the spring of 1993) once noted,

> Signs of that goalless condition are everywhere. There's a program in the Commerce Department. Every quarter it produces a document an inch thick. I discovered there

wasn't a single defined objective in it. Instead there was an amazing amount of activity information. That's what passes as progress toward a goal.

As this quote implies, focusing primarily on *activities* makes it very difficult for government organizations to develop concrete, visible outcomes and factors that can be used to measure progress and success.

That's where the Key Success Factors come in; for public sector organizations, it's a new paradigm for creating outcome performance measurements. Key Success Factors can provide an overall goal-setting process that will measure outcomes and success, including how well a public sector "customer" is truly served. Otherwise, the organizations will continue to confuse means and ends, resulting in poor direction and focus.

Parallel Process Means Public Consultation

In the public sector, there are many more stakeholders (other agencies, politicians, public "customers," special interest groups, etc.) than exist in the private sector. This makes the Parallel Process an even bigger need. The public sector needs to be more open in consulting with its clients — not just sharing information, but also getting and using their feedback.

Example: The three provinces in western Canada have what they call "open government." It's very proactive with their public "customers," funneling all information through a sort of open consultation/feedback forum. In fact, working with them on this was where we refined our own Parallel Process!

Low-Risk Leadership Styles

Strong leadership in change efforts (as well as accountability) has been missing in the public sector for far too long a time; look at almost any government around the globe today, and you'll see signs of severe distress and unrest in members of the public who should be government's beneficiaries. And, in fairness, it *is* more difficult to take strong stands as a public figure; it involves a huge risk of offending any number of constituency members.

Taking risks you must, however, as an increasingly informed and educated public demands it. Government organizations need strong, decisive leaders who are willing to be held accountable for their actions and opinions. More often, individuals at an administrative level in the public sector tend toward bureaucratic work flow. Rather than serving the public beneficiaries, they only serve "upward" to the politician's seat. So, don't ignore the upward pressure, but don't give up the leadership of your organization in serving your clients and customers, either.

Examples of Fine Public Servants

Dr. Robert Reeves, long-time Superintendent of Poway Unified School District, is a public servant who is one of the finest executives I've come across — public or private. As a result of his continuous innovation and creative leadership over the years, this school district is one of the most recognized and respected in the state.

The Premiere of Alberta, Canada, Ralph Klein, and U.S. Vice President Al Gore also deserve recognition for their attempts to fundamentally change and reinvent government.

Another unusually fine example of government leaders that I've observed in my work is Don Fast, Assistant Deputy Minister in the Ministry of the Environment in British Columbia. Individuals that are unafraid to make change, take chances in a savvy way, and manage their governmental organizations with a business-like approach are wonderful to work with.

Hats off to these leaders, and all those like them who understand the value of accountability, integrity, and business thinking — we need more like them.

PERCEIVED RESOURCE CONSTRAINTS

This is an area in which the public sector is very different from the private sector. Private sector organizations must first gather their resources, and then use them to get more (i.e., "it takes money to make money," as the old adage goes). Public sector organizations, however, often mentally start with a set number of resources as a given, and from there just spend it.

The very real problem with this is that it doesn't foster any real knowledge of how to get resources in the first place. Therefore, when government organizations have gone through their allotted supply, rather than move ahead and find more, they tend to stop all progress on the basis of resource constraints.

This creates a crutch mentality that goes nowhere. And, at the risk of redundancy, I'll ask again: if resource constraints truly are a genuine issue, then how did Germany and Japan rise from the ashes of a world war? Government organizations need, and in some cases are beginning to get administrators who have skills such as raising revenues through fund-raising and user fees, working out bureaucratic practices through business reengineering, privatizing government services, etc. They need to use resource allocation to set priorities based on their strategic plan and focus on the future — not yesterday.

Example: Private companies now regularly provide many of the municipal services in such large U.S. cities as Dallas, Houston, Kansas City, New York, Los Angeles, Phoenix, and Philadelphia. (See the monthly magazine, *Governing*, for continual examples of innovation in government — there's a lot more happening than most of us realize.)

LACK OF STAFF SUPPORT FOR STRATEGIC MANAGEMENT

The staff support services that are routinely available for strategic management in the private sector are usually absent in the public sector. Rarely will you find (1) someone that serves in a Planning Department, (2) effective Human Resource support, or (3) someone who has organizational development/facilitator skills. Add to this the fact that you'll almost never find (4) someone skilled in measuring outcomes, and it's easy to see why strategic management hits so many glitches in the public sector. There usually isn't an infrastructure in place to provide an organization with an internal support cadre necessary for success.

Example: Right now, the Alberta, Canada ministries and departments are struggling with their strategic management process. Though they've been successful in doing the right kind of strategic/business planning and budgeting, they don't have a strong internal support function to assist strategic change. As a result, this has proved to be a lingering problem, and has endangered the success of the entire process of change and of the major "reinventing government" initiative throughout Alberta.

The reverse is true for the City of San Diego, California, however, where they have had an entire organization effectiveness department to support city planning and change for over the past decade.

INEFFECTIVE CHANGE MANAGEMENT

I love this quote from David Osborne, co-author of *Reinventing Government:*

> The greatest obstacle to innovation in government is the **power of outdated ideas**. It's easy to dream up approaches to problems. The hard part is selling them to those who see the world through old lenses. The transformation from bureaucratic to entrepreneurial government isn't just change. It's a paradigm shift.

Paradigm shifts are without a doubt the greatest challenge to *all* strategic management and change, whether in the public or the private sectors. Through the private sector has more of a pattern of acceptance and growth through strategic change management, the public sector still has a far, far distance to travel. Just because President Clinton and Vice President Al Gore cut 250,000 people from the federal government's payroll in the 1990s doesn't mean there is a more effective, responsible government. Remember, both "cutting" and "building" strategies are necessary for future success — not just cutting alone.

QUESTIONS TO PONDER

- Has your strategic planning consistently followed the A, B, C, D, E phases of the systems model?
- Have you made sure to use these five phases, while tailoring your strategic management to your own unique specifications?
- Have you found which of the systems applications fit your current needs?
- If you are conducting strategic planning for a public sector organization, are you incorporating business-oriented and systems-thinking elements, such as those found in the private sector?

IN SUMMARY

We have discussed nine different and specific ways in which you can apply the five-phase, systems thinking approach to your strategic planning and change management needs. You may find other ways to apply this approach as you initiate your own strategic management process — that's fine.

The most important thing to remember about the Reinventing Strategic Management model is that its primary elements — the A, B, C, D, E systems phases — are the constant in this formula. No matter what configuration your planning/change effort may require, as long as you maintain and integrate these phases as its foundation, you'll be able to efficiently tailor a strategic planning and change process that works.

The flexibility and simplicity of this systems thinking model will empower you with the strength and persistence to deal with the dynamics of today's changing environment. It will enable you to create a strategic planning and change management process that is strong enough to consistently make the tough choices that can move you toward new, steady growth, and into the third millennium.

RECAP OF KEY CONTENT POINTS

- In the systems thinking approach, all strategic management is conducted within these five A, B, C, D, E phases of the systems model:
    Phase A (Future outcomes): Where do we want to be?
    Phase B (Feedback): How will we know when we get there?
    Phase C (Today's input): Where are we now and what strategies should guide us?
    Phase D (Throughput actions): How do we get there?
    Phase E (Environment): What is/will be changing in the environment? (Ask on an ongoing basis.)
- In systems thinking, you always, *always* focus on the outcomes — especially the key outcome of serving your customers and clients.
- There are many specific ways in which you can apply the five-phase, systems thinking approach to strategic management:
    1. Comprehensive strategic planning
    2. Strategic Planning Quick
    3. Microstrategic planning
    4. Three-year business unit planning/major support department planning
    5. Strategic change projects
    6. Strategic life planning
    7. Team effectiveness
    8. Problem solving
    9. Project management

- Public sector organizations are finding that they experience many of the same problems that face the private sector, and are beginning to use a business orientation and a systems approach to their planning.
- In applying a business-thinking approach, public sector firms face specific and contradictory issues in the following areas:
  Mandate vs. mission
  Lack of a profit motive
  Politicians as "board of directors"
  Lack of a customer focus
  Missing measurements of outcome success
  Parallel Process means public consultation
  Low risk leadership styles
  Perceived resource constraints
  Lack of staff support for strategic management
  Ineffective change management

"HOW-TO" ACTION CHECKLIST

Ten Absolutes for Reinventing Strategic Management (Planning and Change)

1. Have a clear vision/values of your ideal future with customer-focused outcome measures.
2. Develop focused and shared core strategies as the glue for all goal setting and action planning.
3. Develop and gain public commitments to Personal Leadership Plans by all top management leaders.
4. Redo your human resource management systems to support the new vision and values.
5. Set up an internal cadre support team with overall change management coordination that reports directly to the CEO/Executive Director.
6. Set up Strategy Sponsorship Teams of cross-functional leaders on each core strategy, if you are a larger organization.
7. Establish a Strategic Change Leadership Steering Committee to guide, lead, and manage all major changes.
8. Focus on and phase in the four Vital Few Leverage Points for Change over the next 2 to 5 years.
9. Institutionalize the Parallel Process with all key stakeholders, as the new way to run your business day to day.

10. Create a critical mass for change that becomes self-sustaining throughout the development of three-year business plans for all major divisions/departments.

17 Getting Started: Options

Just because we cannot see clearly the end of the road,
that is no reason for not setting out on the essential
journey. On the contrary, great change dominates the
world, and unless we move with change we will
become its victims

-John F. Kennedy

STARTING AT PHASES A, B, C – *OR* D AND E

The real key to a true systems model is not its A, B, C, D, E, phases or even its ten progressive steps. It is the circular nature of a system – and systems thinking – that is the key to its use in a very personal, practical, and flexible way. Another way to visualize it is as a yearly circle (Figure 17.1). Organizations need this *Systems Thinking Approach* to a Strategic Management System with a yearly cycle (not just a budgeting cycle) in order to become a high performing organization.

"We Now Need A Strategic Management System"

I need to stress at this point that an effective management system is more than just the sum of the parts…it is a set of integrated policies, practices and behaviors.

Sometimes having a good management system is confused with having high-quality employees. This is a mistake — the two are quite different in some important ways: having high-quality employees does not assure an organization of having a sustainable competitive advantage or even a short-term advantage.

-Edward J. Lawler III
The Ultimate Advantage:
Creating the High-Involvement Organization

The definition of a Strategic Management System is as follows:

- A comprehensive system to lead, manage, and change one's total organization in a conscious, well-planned, and integrated fashion based on our strategies — and using *proven research that works* — to develop and successfully achieve one's ideal future vision.

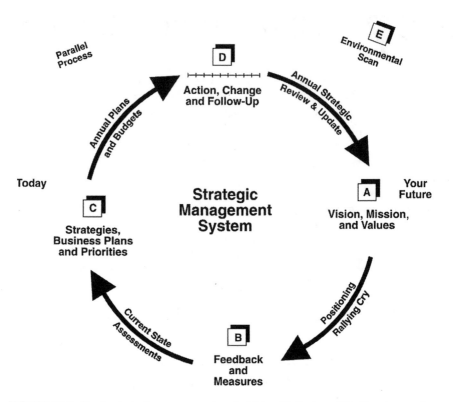

FIGURE 17.1 Yearly strategic management cycle: Using the Systems Thinking Approach —
thinking backwards to the future.

- *The new way to run the business* (i.e., "We manage our business in a
  systematic way based on our strategies).
- A method that is interactive and participative yet systematic.

The five-phase Systems Thinking Approach (and Reinventing Strategic Management model) enables you to easily tailor your application to your own needs and
current situation. With the systems approach, you can begin strategic planning and
change at any of its five A, B, C, D, E phases. In other words, if your organization
has already developed its vision, mission, and values statements (Phase A), you can
begin your planning process by shaping organizational Key Success Factors (Phase
B), and go on from there.

Or, if you have a complete Current State Assessment and have already developed
your strategies, you can start your full planning process at the three-year business
plan stage, or during annual planning and budgeting (end of Phase C).

The Systems Thinking Approach is not one of those processes where you have
to drop everything you've done and are doing and start from scratch. The major
benefit of the Systems Thinking Approach and model is its flexibility. Whether you're
a step ahead with certain portions of the planning process, have never done any of
the planning elements, or are in the midst of Value-Chain Management or other

large-scale change efforts, the Reinventing Strategic Management Model will adapt itself to your unique situation.

In general, there are five different options for beginning this curricular process. While we've described them all before, this chapter is meant to help you pull all this information together so you can get started on creating your customer-focused, high-performance learning organization via a strategic management system — no matter where you are today.

OPTION #1: PLAN-TO-PLAN

If you have never conducted a full-scale strategic planning and change process, this is the best starting point for you. The Plan-to-Plan step exists as a way to engineer success up front, before getting into the actual development of your strategic planning documents and their successful implementation.

Failed strategic planning can often be ascribed to the lack of advance or pre-planning. This is why our Reinventing Strategic Management model incorporates the Plan-to-Plan step: it is the educating, organizing, and tailoring step, involving prework on developing appropriate organizing tasks, and as such, it is vital to success. The nine potential key tasks in Plan-to-Plan (Step #1) are listed below.

Engineer Success Up Front
(The Bottom Line of How to Begin)

Instructions: How important is it to do the following before beginning planning? (High, medium, low.)

_____ 1. Conduct a Mini Organizational/High Performance Survey.

_____ 1a. Conduct a Strategic Business Design assessment and create a set of recommendations.

_____ 2. Establish and train your Internal Support Cadre in strategic management support/facilitation (process/structure).

_____ 3. Conduct Executive Leadership Skills Development so each executive has the capacity to lead strategic change (i.e., the Six Core Competencies of Centering Your Leadership presented in Chapter 5, such as
- Self-mastery — Level #1
- Interpersonal skills — Level #2
- Team skills — Level #3
- Across functions — Level #4

_____ 4. Conduct Executive Team Building to enhance your effectiveness to plan and work together to successfully implement your plan while dealing with the difficult issues of revolutionary change.

_____ 5. Conduct a Plan-to-Plan Day:
Morning: Executive Briefing on Strategic Planning or Strategic Change — The Educating Task
Afternoon: The Strategic Management Organizing Tasks

_____ 6.   Decide on middle management's Management Development Program as well.

_____ 7.   Conduct Strategic Life Planning (personal vision, values, etc.) before beginning (for either individuals, couples, teams, families, etc.).

_____ 8.   Conduct Market Research to better understand our customer's wants and needs vs. World-Class Star Results.

_____ 9.   Reexamine all your HR/People Management Practices to enhance "people as our competitive edge."

Then, and only then, begin strategic planning or strategic management (planning and change).

Option #2: Plan-to-Implement

If you have already completed your strategic plan, but need to bridge the gap between planning and implementation, this is the perfect starting point. It's where Goal #2 — ensuring successful implementation of your strategic plan — comes in.

The Plan-to-Implement step is about getting educated on the issues of change and completing a set of organizing and tailoring tasks, much like in the Plan-to-Plan step. The main difference between the two is that Plan-to-Implement is focused on the process of *educating and organizing* to manage the implementation of the strategic plan. (For further details on this step, refer to Chapter 13.)

Option #3: Some "In Process" Join-Up Points

As I mentioned earlier, when looking for the best place to begin building your strategic management system, it's always best to start wherever you are today. Thus, with a circular systems model, you just literally "join up" to the model right where you are, and carry on from there. The options open to you include the following:

- Conducting an Annual Strategic Review and Update as your starting point — then proceeding based on the recommendations/decisions from this audit.
- Conducting just the phase you need right now, such as visioning, measurements (Key Success Measures), or core strategy development — then putting in a Strategic Change Leadership Steering Committee to guide implementation.
- Conducting a pilot business planning process for a SBU or Major Support Department. Use it to learn and to develop an internal cadre.
- Conducting annual planning via your core strategies. Set the top three action priorities for each core strategy as the glue and organizing principles for all annual plans.

- Conducting large-group reviews on annual department plans, then conducting a strategic budgeting process.
- Beginning with a strategic budgeting process.
- Finishing your budgets, then setting up strategic change project teams on large, cross-functional issues. (Or, you can set up a full Strategic Change Leadership Steering Committee to guide the overall desired changes.)
- Setting up a Strategic Change Leadership Steering Committee to guide and coordinate large-scale change that is already in existence (i.e., TQM, business process reengineering, etc.).
- Setting up Strategy Sponsorship Teams for each core strategy, to guide and report on successful implementation.

Using the Systems Thinking Approach enables you to begin your implementation from your current situation, not some distant, rigid starting point. In a sense, it lets your situation decide *for* you. It takes you from wherever you are, and moves you into your desired changes without sacrificing your daily business operations. Over time, your strategic planning and desired changes will guide your day-to-day operations.

OPTION #4: SOME EDUCATIONAL WAYS TO BEGIN

In order to initiate an optimal strategic management system, you need some initial executive and staff training. Again, there is no set rule for the amount or type of training you'll need to do before beginning; it's up to you to tailor training in a way that best fits your organization's particular needs. If you do decide you need management training, there are a number of possibilities, including the following:

- Having internal staff trained and licensed to facilitate the systems thinking approach to the Reinventing Strategic Management process.
- Having internal staff trained and licensed on Reinventing Strategic Planning and Mastering Strategic Change.
- Conducting a Visionary Leadership Practices workshop to kick-start your strategic planning.
- Training senior and mid-level management in the Systems Thinking Approach concepts through a 2- or 3-day workshop, introducing the Reinventing Strategic Management model.
- Holding an annual management conference — keynoted with a presentation on strategic planning and change — using some key handouts and articles on "The ABCs of Strategic Management."

OPTION #5: LEARNING AND APPLYING STRATEGIC MANAGEMENT
CONCEPTS

The Centre's strategic planning framework and practice have been completely "reinvented" from a ground zero, research-based, blank sheet of paper. As a result, we require all of our strategic planning participants to read one of our books about this process and learn it in detail. This is the most effective way for each participant to internalize strategic management and for the organization to institutionalize its tailored Strategic Management System.

As part of this process, it is best to purchase this book for each participant. It covers every step of this system in detail. Then, you can (with the facilitator) set up a customized reading schedule matching your planning schedule using the chapter listing as a starting guide.

CRUCIAL SUPPORT NEEDED TO BE SUCCESSFUL

Obviously, the implementation of your strategic plan won't amount to a hill of beans if you don't plan realistically for just how much support, in terms of people, time, and money is required. Following is a checklist of all the elements you'll need as the support necessary to success.

SENIOR MANAGEMENT'S ACTIVE COMMITMENT

More than half of the strategic plans that fail do so because commitment from the top is either sporadic or half-hearted. If you desire a strategic planning and change process that is successful, you'll need a firm consensus and active commitment from your top management. Senior executives *must* play an interactive, visible role – not only in initiating the strategic plan, but also in following it through.

A TRAINED INTERNAL SUPPORT CADRE

After you've initiated your strategic planning and change process, is not the time to decide what kind (or how much) staff support you'll need. If you'll need clerical or administrative support, coordinators and liaison personnel for Key Success Factors, strategy implementation, Strategy Sponsorship Teams, and Strategic Change Leadership Steering Committees, it must be determined and assigned, beforehand.

EXTERNAL FACILITATOR

You'll need to determine whether you have qualified facilitators that can take your organization through the entire strategic planning and change process. This is an easy spot to quickly get into trouble; the scope of knowledge needed throughout this process is great enough to require training specific individuals to be global, organization-wide facilitators.

If you choose to go this way, the training time required is often substantial enough to negatively impact the original time frame of your strategic plan. For this reason, many organizations choose to use an external strategic planning and change management expert. Though you'll ultimately revert to internal facilitators, a professional consultant/facilitator can go a long way toward saving money and time and also helping you achieve results quicker.

BUDGETING AND RESOURCE ALLOCATION

In order to effectively manage any transition, you need resources; both people and money. Look at every activity required by your strategic planning and change process, including

- Strategic Change Leadership Steering Committee meetings
- Mastering Strategic Change workshops
- Key Success Measures/Goal tracking
- Communications and rollout
- Skills training (leadership/change management)
- Training of overall manager/coordinator/internal facilitator
- External facilitator/consultant
- Business unit planning processes
- Key stakeholder meetings
- Environmental scanning system
- Rallying cry project
- Cultural audit (organizational diagnosis)
- Yearly Follow-Up Strategic Management System Review
- Strategic change projects (Vital Few Leverage Points for Change)

Identify and allocate all the resources you'll need for these elements (including who is responsible to supply them), and budget how much you'll need for each one.

PROJECT PLANNING/YEARLY COMPREHENSIVE MAP

The best way to keep track of what activities you'll need in your change process is to create the yearly map (covered in Chapter 12): a specific, "by the numbers" implementation process that is visible and easy to track and follow. Developing this tangible list of those things you'll need to do in the next 12 months gives you a quick and easy checklist.

CREATING A CRITICAL MASS FOR CHANGE

Holding to the "people support what they help create" theory and creating this critical mass is probably the single most effective way to guarantee the success of your change process. It does, however, require a substantial, ongoing investment of time and energy, so be prepared to commit to it and anticipate it. (See Chapter 13 for full details.)

CAPACITY-BUILDING

Another, more subtle spin on creating a critical mass for change is something I call "capacity-building." This is about building a leadership within your organization that has the capacity to lead, guide, and complete the strategic planning and change process to the benefit of the organization. Having the range and depth of leadership that can see this type of long-term process through is crucial to your success and growth. Remember, it's the only true competitive advantage you have.

Lastly, when you've identified the resources and personnel needed to complete a successful strategic planning and change process, be sure to include them in your budgeting process. Neglecting this has a tendency to translate throughout the organization as a failure to view this process as an organizational priority.

PUTTING IT ALL TOGETHER: THE SYSTEMS THINKING APPROACH

Strategic planning and strategic change management
are really "strategic thinking." It's about
clarity and simplicity, meaning and purpose,
and focus and direction.

Throughout this book, you've often seen me comment on the contrast between analytical thinking vs. true systems thinking. Until relatively recent years, analytical thinking — that of breaking the problem or issue down into its individual parts, then problem-solving each part separately — held sway as the traditional approach to strategic planning. See the different mental maps shown in Figure 17.2.

The problem with this approach was that starting only with today's issues and problems, then breaking them down into their smallest components and solving each component separately, had no far-reaching vision or goal. Low interaction existed between departments; therefore, no critical mass for change existed, and change quickly deteriorated as a priority.

More recently, organizational development is beginning to combine these previously separate parts into solutions, moving toward what I call partial systems thinking. The partial systems approach is certainly an improvement over strictly analytical thinking, because it's at least the *beginning* of continuous improvement and integrating *X* with *Y*.

However, it tends to eclectically gather a piecemeal list of parts based on the latest planning and change fads, such as restructuring, decentralization, TQM, etc. The resultant problem with any of these fads is that they create a "what you see depends on where you sit" environment; you rarely end up trying to solve an overall, truly inclusive set of problems within the context of a shared collective vision.

Past, present, or future planning and change fads simply don't enter into true systems thinking. In the Systems Thinking Approach, the only element you focus on is the system that makes up your organization. From General Systems Theory, we know that a system cannot be understood by analysis, but only by synthesis, looking at it as a whole within its environment.

With this approach, you shape your organizational system into a customer-focused, market-driven organization, using the Organization as a System model to check every change for systems fit, alignment, attunement, and integrity. To truly manage strategically, you not only need a strategic plan, but you also must install a strategic change management system to guide its implementation.

Which is it for you?

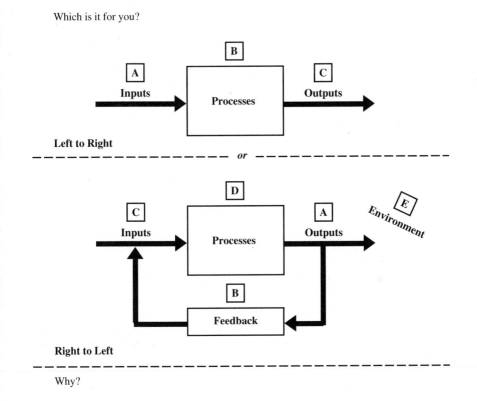

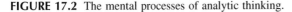

Right to Left

Why?

FIGURE 17.2 The mental processes of analytic thinking.

With its three Strategic Management goals —

1. Developing a strategic plan document
2. Ensuring its successful implementation and change
3. Building and sustaining high performance over the long term

— a Strategic Management System provides a practical, three-part/three-goal, systems thinking approach for changing the way you run your business day to day. It has the overall goal of creating (i.e., designing, building, and sustaining) your own customer-focused, high-performance learning organization of your own.

The key to succeeding is the ability to bridge the gap from Goal 1 to Goal 2. Typically, it is at this point where most plans fail. Within the Reinventing Strategic Management Model, however, this is achieved through the very crucial Step #8 (Plan-to-Implement) and the Mastering Strategic Change Workshop simulation. This is particularly unique to the Reinventing Strategic Management Model: no other planning models include such detailed systemic change implementation steps.

Another key to long-term success is the Annual Strategic Review and Update (Step #10). Rather than limiting your organization to just a yearly independent financial audit, you need to also conduct a yearly follow-up to diagnose the overall success of your strategic plan's implementation and change process. (Also, be sure to recycle your strategic plan and its annual priorities at this time.)

The final key to long-term success is increasing the range and depth of your leadership practices, including the skills of trainer/coach/facilitator (see the Visionary Leadership Practices workshop, among others). And remember, it's the only competitive business advantage for any organization over the long term.

The Reinventing Strategic Management Model is also unique in its three main premises, which incorporate both our three Seemingly Simple Elements and three Right Answers:

Premise #1: Planning and change management are a part of leadership and management.
(Right Answer #1: Install a strategic management system as a new way to run your business day to day.)

Premise #2: People support what they help create.
(Right Answer #2: Create professional management and leadership practices.)

Premise #3: Use systems thinking to focus on outcomes: serving the customer.
(Right Answer #3: Create a customer-focused, high-performance organization.)

With the Systems Thinking Approach, your planning encompasses the entire system that defines your organization. Using a systems approach in your planning and implementation enables you to think strategically and systematically about the overall changes you need and desire, without compromising those day-to-day activities you need to keep successful.

Systems thinking is based on the theory that a system is, in essence, circular. Using a systems approach in your strategic management, therefore, provides a circular implementing structure that can evolve, with continuously improving, self-checking, and learning capabilities (remember the feedback loop — the essence of the Learning Organization?).

In systems thinking, you no longer have to worry if you can't constantly be vigilant, watching over each and every step of the implementation process on a day-to-day basis. Simply put, if you've followed the systems-based Reinventing Strategic Management Model correctly, you already have a system of monitored activities in place, with ongoing, positive checks and balances. However, keep in mind that there are seven deadly sins of an ineffective strategic management system to avoid (Figure 17.3).

Lack of:

E	#1	Environmental Scanning (Step #1)

- Full Day Session
- SKEPTIC-Prework/System

B	#2	Feedback Loop/Success Measures (Step #3)

- Subgroup Work
- Measures for Customer/Employee/Business Units Success

C	#3	Current State Assessment (Step #4) Day

- Marketplace Information
- Organization Assessment and Design
- Creating the People Edge℠
- Middle Management SWOT

C	#4	Large Group Annual Department Plan Reviews (Step #7)

- One-Day Meeting
- Review All Plans Interactively

D	#5	Plan-to-Implement (Step #8)

- One-Day Session
- Complete All Tasks

D	#6	Follow-Up Tracking and Reporting Regularly

- Leadership Steering Committee
- Strategy Sponsorship Teams

C	#7	Three-Year Business Plans

- SBUs/MPAs
- Major Support Functions

FIGURE 17.3 The seven deadly sins of ineffective strategic management systems.

FOCUS–FOCUS–FOCUS

As in any ongoing activity, the key to successfully implementing your strategic plan will lie in whether you choose to focus on the "trivial many" or the "vital few." As described in earlier chapters, the following Vital Few Leverage Points came out of extensive best practices research:

Vital Few Leverage Points

- Successfully developing and deploying your strategic plan.
- Being a customer-focused/market-driven organization.
- Increasing your range/skills in leadership and management practices (including all key Human Resource Management practices).

- Eliminating waste through customer-focused TQM/business process reengineering/Value-Chain Management.
- Redesigning your organization's overall strategic business design to fit/complement the customer-focused desired positioning with watertight integrity.

Ask yourself how your organization compares to these best practices. The answer will quickly show you some success strategies for the next 3 to 5 years. You will have to work on some aspects of changing your organizational culture and capacity building to fit your ideal future. And you will definitely need both discipline and persistence. Yes, you will have to make tough choices to reach your vision, but it *can* happen.

In addition to discipline and persistence, however, you'll also need to focus, particularly when it comes to those tough choices. To successfully implement your organization's version of the Reinventing Strategic Management Model, you'll especially need to focus on each step along the A, B, C, D, E way, including the following:

- What is your mission? Who do you serve?
- What are your *core values?* (Limit these to those most dear to you.)
- Do you have ten (or fewer) *prioritized* Key Success Measures/Goals?
- Have you developed a small number of shared *core strategies,* with 3 annual priority actions attached to each? (Keep the number of core strategies small, with "from–to" clarity on anticipated changes.)
- Have your annual plans been formulated under the umbrella of your core shared strategies/action priorities as the glue and organizing principles?
- Do you have your budget in place, based on your Strategic Action Items (i.e., the top three priorities for each core strategy)?
- Do you have three-year business plans to focus each business unit/major support department (again, under the same umbrella)?
- Are your performance appraisals focused on evaluating everyone against your core strategies (results) and core values (behaviors)?
- Have you shaped priority agendas for (1) the regular Strategic Change Leadership Steering Committee and (2) the weekly Executive Staff Meetings, using the Key Success Measures as well as the core strategies (with their top three action priorities) as primary agenda items?

As the graphic in Figure 17.4 illustrates, with a sense of integrity and a commitment to focus, discipline, and persistence, you *can* design, build, and sustain a strategic management system. It can serve as the foundation that leads to the achievement of your customer-driven, high-performance organization. It may take 1 to 3 years or more to fully install, but it can be done, even in today's dynamic and revolutionary, globally changing environment.

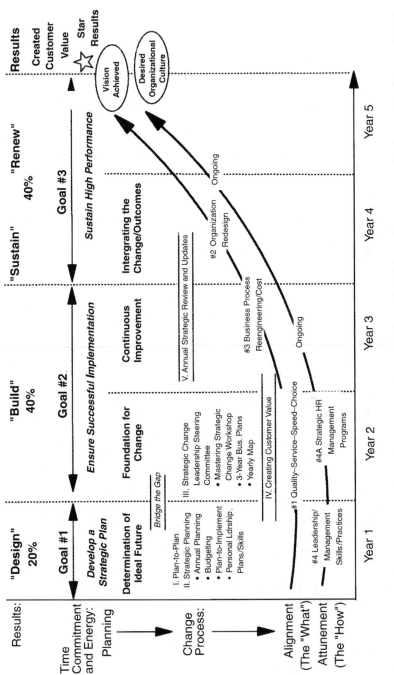

FIGURE 17.4 How to design, build, and sustain a customer-focused, value-added high-performance organization — The Systems Thinking Approach to creating customer value (a multiyear strategic management systems solution to creating your ideal future vision.

CHECKING STRATEGIC CONSISTENCY AND OPERATIONAL FLEXIBILITY

Today's turbulent environment can constitute a threat to even the most solid strategic plan. The Systems Thinking Approach outlined in this book contains a number of elements that will help you ensure the strategic consistency of your plan, while maintaining the operational flexibility needed to secure its commitment and its implementation.

Answer these questions to determine how proactive you are in strategic consistency:

- Have you developed a strategic plan to create your ideal future the way *you* want it to be (rather than others forcing a different future on you)?
- Is it now a shared vision?
- Are you using the strategic plan, with its Key Success Measures/Goals and core strategies to pursue your vision with strategic consistency, year after year?
- Have you put in place a Strategic Change Leadership Steering Committee to manage the overall changes necessary to achieve this vision?
- Are all major changes going on in the organization under its guiding umbrella, or do you "plan on the left and manage on the right?"
- Have you anticipated possible future changes or needs by installing an ongoing environmental scanning system and/or contingency plans?
- If, during your yearly review, you find your strategic plan to be no longer viable, are you prepared to redo it?

After you have answered the questions above, review the following points to determine the degree of your organization's operational flexibility:

- Have you put three-year business plans in place to ensure that: (1) your Strategic Business Units/Major Program Areas have their own specific plans based on your overall strategic plan, and that (2) your organization is planning closer to where competitive actions occur?
- Do you have annual department plans in place for all your units that are participatively developed, yet organized around your core strategies and top action priorities?
- Are you firmly committed to ongoing Strategic Change Leadership Steering Committee meetings? Have you discussed how the organization will handle any developments that result from these meetings?
- Are you also committed to Annual Strategic Reviews (and Updates), to keep the flexibility you'll need?
- Will you continuously focus on all the Vital Few Leverage Points for Change over the next few years, even if they're done more or less sequentially?
- Have you committed to improving your range and depth of leadership practices (from the top down)?

Once you've checked, prodded, and poked your Strategic Management System for its strategic consistency and operational flexibility, you've done everything you can. Now it's a matter of follow-through, persistence, and firm commitment to your organization's integrity in pursuing your Ideal Future Vision. While we do live in the real world, and acknowledge that we will not achieve perfection, I can guarantee you will come much closer to it by following your strategic management system. Always, *always* remember, though, that no matter how proficient you become in the processes of strategic planning and implementation, it won't go far without both discipline and persistence.

To summarize this entire book see the three keys to the "simple way" to success through Strategic Management below.

Strategic Management: It's Simple (Once You Use The Systems Thinking Approach)

The three keys:

1. Have a Shared Direction and Positioning
   A. Develop a strategic plan
      • Need a shared vision, values, and core strategies with clear future positioning.
      • Develop clear and focused organization-wide action priorities for the next year.
   B. Develop buy-in and stay-in to the plan
      • Communicate (stump speeches)
      • Involvement: participative management and WIIFM
2. Have a Strategic Business Design (with watertight integrity)
   A. Conduct a strategic business assessment and redesign
      • To ensure fit of all the policies and parts, people system and business processes of the organization
      • Using the overall direction, strategic plan, and positioning as the criteria
   B. Cascade down department work plans, budgets and accountability
      • Using the core strategies, action priorities, and redesign as the glue
      • Down and throughout the organization
3. Implement Strategic Change (successfully)
   A. Know and adhere to your roles
      • Leaders: to focus on content and consequences
      • Support cadre: for processes and infrastructure coordination
   B. Build follow-up structures and processes
      • To track, control, adjust, and achieve the plan and key success factor results
      • To reward, recognize, and celebrate progress and results

Summary

Systems thinking is beginning to help us all in a number of ways that can best be summed up by the following quotes.

I think, therefore I am.

-Rene Descartes

Simplicity and Complexity

I wouldn't give a fig for the simplicity this side of complexity, but I'd give my life for the simplicity on the far side of complexity.

-Justice Oliver Wendell Holmes

Simplicity and Genius

Any idiot can simplify by ignoring the complications. But, it takes real genius to simplify by including the complications.

-John E. Johnson, TEC Chair (The Executive Committee)

Simple Answers

For every complex problem there is a simple answer and...it is always wrong.

-H. L. Menkin

A Special Thanks

Ludwig Von Bertalanffy — the founder of General Systems Theory — is the "genius," major leader, and pioneer of the new 21st-century systems orientation and simplicity — through our holistic, synergistic, and integrated thinking called the Systems Thinking Approach.

Bottom Line

*What we think, or what we know, or what we believe, is in the end, of little consequence. The only consequence is what we **do**.*

References

Ackoff, R. (1970). *A Concept of Corporate Planning*. New York: John Wiley & Sons.

Ackoff, R. (1974). *Redesigning the Future*. New York: John Wiley & Sons.

Ackoff, R. (1981). *Creating the Corporate Future*. New York: John Wiley & Sons.

Ackoff, R. (1984). *Guide to Controlling Your Corporation's Future*. New York: John Wiley & Sons.

Ackoff, R. (1987). *Art of Problem Solving: Accompanied by Ackoff's Fables*. New York: John Wiley & Sons.

Ackoff, R. (1989). *Management in Small Doses*. New York: John Wiley & Sons.

Ackoff, R. (1991). *Ackoff's Fables: Irreverent Reflections on Business and Bureaucracy*. New York: John Wiley & Sons.

Ansoff, I. (1988). *New Corporate Strategy*. New York: John Wiley & Sons.

Band, W. (1991). *Creating Value for Customers: Designing and Implementing a Total Corporate Strategy*. New York: John Wiley & Sons.

Bardwick, J. (1998). *In Praise of Good Business: How Optimizing Risk Rewards Both Your Bottom Line and Your People*. New York: John Wiley & Sons.

Bean, W. C. (1993). *Strategic Planning That Makes Things Happen: Getting from Where You Are to Where You Want to Be*. Amherst, MA: HRD Press, Inc.

Below, P., Morrisey, G., Acomb, B. (1978). *Executive Guide to Strategic Planning*. San Francisco: Jossey Bass.

Bradford, W. (1987). *Managing for Excellence Guide to Developing High Performance in Contemporary Organizations*. New York: John Wiley & Sons.

Bryson, J. (1993). *Strategic Planning for Public and Nonprofit Organizations: A Guide to Strengthening and Sustaining Organizational Achievement*. San Francisco: Jossey Bass.

Buzzell, R., Gale, B. (1987). *The PIMS* Principles, Linking Strategy to Performance*. New York: The Free Press.

Carnevale, A. (1991). *America and the New Economy*. San Francisco: Jossey Bass.

Carver, J. (1990). *Boards That Make a Difference*. San Francisco: Jossey Bass.

Chandler, A., Jr. (1962). *Strategy and Structure: Chapters in the History of the American Industrial Enterprise*. Cambridge, MA: The MIT Press.

Clarke, C. J. (1993). *Shareholder Value: Key to Corporate Development*. Oxford: Elsevier Science.

Collins, J. C., Porras, J. I. (1997). *Built to Last: Successful Habits of Visionary Companies*. New York: Harper Collins Publishers, Inc.

Cope, R. G. (1989). *High Involvement Strategic Planning: When People and Their Ideas Really Matter*. Oxford, OH: Planning Forum (in association with Basil Blackwell).

Crosby, P. (1988). *The Eternally Successful Organization*. New York: McGraw-Hill.

Day, G. S. (1990). *Market Driven Strategy*. New York: The Free Press.

Donnelly, R. (1984). *Guidebook to Planning: Strategic Planning and Budgeting Basics for the Growing Firm*. New York: Van Nostrand Reinhold.

Douglas, R. (1993). *Unfinished Business*. Auckland, New Zealand: Random House.

Downes, L. (1998) *Unleashing the Killer App*. Boston: Harvard Business School Press.

Doz, Y. (1986). *Strategic Management in Multinational Companies*. Oxford: Elsevier Science.

Drucker, P. (1954). *The Practice of Management*. New York: Harper & Row.

Drucker, P. (1973). *Management: Tasks, Responsibilities, Practices*. New York: Harper & Row.

Drucker, P. (1989). *The New Realities*. New York: Harper & Row.

Dunham, A., and Marcus, B. (with Stevens, M., Barwise, P.) (1993). *Unique Value*. New York: MacMillan.

Ernst & Young. (1992). *Ernst and Young Executive's Guide to Total Cost Management*. New York: John Wiley & Sons.

Figgie, H., Jr. (1983). *The Reduction and Profit Improvement Handbook*. New York: Van Nostrand Reinhold.

Fogg, C. D. (1999). *Implementing Your Strategic Plan: How to Turn "Intent" into Effective Action for Sustainable Change*. New York: AMACOM.

Freedman, N. J. (1991). *Strategic Management in Major Multinational Companies*. Oxford: Elsevier Science.

Fuld, L. M. (1988). *Monitoring the Competition: Find Out What's Really Going On Over There*. New York: John Wiley & Sons.

Garten, J. E. (1997). *The Big Ten: The Big Emerging Markets and How They Will Change Our Lives*. New York: Basic Books.

George, C. (1968). *The History of Management Thought*. Englewood Cliffs, NJ: Prentice Hall.

Glueck, W. (1980). *Strategic Management and Business Policy*. New York: McGraw-Hill.

Goodstein, L. D., Nolan, T. M., Pfeiffer, J. W. (1992). *Applied Strategic Planning: A Comprehensive Guide*. San Diego: Pfeiffer & Co.

Goodstein, L. D., Nolan, T. M., Pfeiffer, J. W. (1992). *Applied Strategic Planning: An Introduction*. San Diego: Pfeiffer & Co.

Gorman, J., Calhoun, K. (contributor), Rozin, S. (1994). *The Name of the Game: The Business of Sports*. New York: John Wiley & Sons.

Haines, S. G. (1995). *Successful Strategic Planning*. Menlo Park, Crisp Publications.

Haines, S. G. (1995). *Sustaining High Performance*. Delray Beach, FL: St. Lucie Press.

Hax, A., Majluf, N. (1984). *Strategic Management: An Integrative Perspective*. Englewood Cliffs, NJ: Prentice Hall.

Hayden, C. (1986). *The Handbook of Strategic Expertise*. New York: The Free Press.

Hellebust, K., Krallinger, J. (1989). *Strategic Planning Workbook*. New York: John Wiley & Sons.

Hofer, C., Schendel, D. (1978). *Strategy Formulation: Analytical Concepts*. St. Paul, MN: West Publishing.

Hope, J., Hope, T. (1998). *Competing in the Third Wave*. Boston: Harvard Business School Press.

Hussey, D. E. (1994). *Strategic Management: Theory and Practice* (3rd ed.). Oxford: Elsevier Science.

James, B. (1984). *Business Wargames*. New York: Penguin Books.

Jantsch, E. (1980). *The Self-Organizing Universe*. Oxford: Elsevier Science.

Judson, A. (1990). *Making Strategy Happen: Transforming Plans into Reality*. Cambridge, MA: Basil Blackwell.

Kami, M. (1988). *Trigger Points: How to Make Decisions Three Times Faster, Innovate Smarter, and Beat Your Competition by Ten Percent (It Ain't Easy!)*. New York: McGraw-Hill.

Kaplan, R., Norton S., David. P. (1996). *The Balanced Scorecard*. Boston: Harvard Business School Press.

Karlof, B., Ostblom, S., Gilderson, A. J. (translator). (1994). *Benchmarking: A Signpost to Excellence in Quality and Productivity*. New York: John Wiley & Sons.

Klir, G. (1969). *An Approach to General Systems Theory*. New York: Van Nostrand.

Klir, G. (Ed.) (1972). *Trends in General Systems Theory*. New York: Wiley-Interscience.

Kono, T. (1992). *Strategic Management in Japanese Companies*. Oxford: Elsevier Science.

Kuhn, T. (1970). *The Structure of Scientific Revolutions* (2nd ed.). Chicago: University of Chicago Press.

Lewin, K. (1948). *Resolving Social Conflicts*. New York: Harper & Row.

MacMillan, I. (1978). *Strategy Formulation: Political Concepts*. St. Paul, MN: West Publishing.

Mann, J. (1998) *Tomorrow's Global Community*. Philadelphia, PA: BainBridge Books (Translator Book).

Mason, R., Mitroff, I. (1981). *Challenging Strategic Planning Assumptions Theory, Cases, and Techniques*. N Y: John Wiley & Sons.

McNamee, P. (1990). *Developing Strategies for Competitive Advantage*. Oxford: Elsevier Science.

McTaggart, J. M., Kontes, P. W. (contributor), Mankins, M. (contributor). (1994). *The Value Imperative: Managing for Superior Shareholder Returns*. New York: Free Press.

Mesarovic, M. (Ed.) (1967). *Views on General Systems Theory*. New York: John Wiley & Sons.

Meyer. (1993). *Fast Cycle Time: How to Align Purpose, Strategy, and Structure for Speed*. New York: The Free Press.

Migliore, H. (1986). *Strategic Long Range Planning*. Jenks, OK: RHM & Associates.

Migliore, H. (1988). *The Use of Strategic Planning for Churches and Ministries*. Tulsa, OK: Harrison House.

Mills, D. Q. (1992). *Rebirth of the Corporation*. New York: John Wiley & Sons.

Mintzberg, H. (1973). *The Nature of Managerial Work*. Englewood Cliffs, NJ: Prentice Hall.

Mintzberg, H. (1994). *The Rise and Fall of Strategic Planning*. New York: The Free Press.

Mintzberg, H., Quinn, J. B. (1992). *The Strategy Process Concepts and Contexts*. Englewood Cliffs, NJ: Prentice Hall.

Mintzberg, H., Ahlstrand B., Lampel, J. (1998). *Strategy Safari: A Guided Tour through the Wilds of Strategic Management*. New York: The Free Press.

Mirvis, P. H. (1993). *Building the Competitive Workforce: Investing in Human Capital for Corporate Success*. New York: John Wiley & Sons.

Mitroff, I. (1983). *Stakeholders of the Organizational Mind*. San Francisco: Jossey Bass.

Naisbitt, J. (1982). *Megatrends: Ten New Directions Transforming Our Lives*. New York: Warner.

Naisbitt, J., Aburdene, P. (1990). *Megatrends 2000: Ten New Directions For The 1990s*. New York: William Morrow.

Nolan, T. M., Goodstein, L. D., Pfeiffer, J. W. (1992). *Applied Strategic Planning: The Consultant's Kit*. San Diego, Pfeiffer & Co.

Nutt, P. C., Backoff, R. W. (1992). *Strategic Management of Public and Third Sector Organizations*. San Francisco: Jossey Bass.

O'Toole, J. (1985). *Vanguard Management: Redesigning the Corporate Future*. New York: Doubleday.

Osborne, D., Gaebler, T. (1992). *Reinventing Government: How the Entrepreneurial Spirit is Transforming the Public Sector*. Reading, MA: Addison-Wesley.

Pegels, C. C. (1998). *Handbook of Strategies and Tools for the Learning Company*. Portland, OR: Productivity Press.

Pfeiffer, J. W. (Ed.) (1991). *Strategic Planning: Selected Readings* (rev. ed.). San Diego: Pfeiffer & Co.

Pfeiffer, J. W., Goodstein, L. D., Nolan, T. M. (1989). *Shaping Strategic Planning: Frogs, Dragons, Bees and Turkey Tails*. San Diego, Pfeiffer & Co.

Pfeiffer, J. W., Goodstein, L. D., Nolan, T. M. (1986). *Applied Strategic Planning: A How To Do It Guide*. San Diego, Pfeiffer & Co.

Porter, M. (1980). *Competitive Strategy*. New York: The Free Press.

Porter, M. (1985). *Competitive Advantage: Creating and Sustaining Superior Performance*. New York: The Free Press.

Porter, M. (1990). *The Competitive Advantage of Nations*. New York: The Free Press.

Rappaport, A. (1986). *Creating Shareholder Value: The New Standard for Business Performance.* New York: The Free Press.

Robert, M. (1993). *Strategy Pure and Simple: How Winning CEOs Outthink Their Competition.* New York: McGraw-Hill, Inc.

Rolnicki, K. (1998). *Managing Channels of Distribution: The Marketing Executive's Complete Guide.* New York: American Management Association.

Ross, J., Kami, M. (1973). *Corporate Management in Crisis: Why the Mighty Fall.* Englewood Cliffs, NJ: Prentice-Hall.

Rothschild, W. (1984). *How to Gain (and Maintain) the Competitive Advantage in Business.* New York: McGraw-Hill.

Schonberger. (1990). *Building a Chain of Customers: Linking Business Functions to Create the World Class Company.* New York: The Free Press.

Shank, J. K., Govindarajan, V. (contributor). (1993). *Strategic Cost Management: The New Tool for Competitive Advantage.* New York: The Free Press.

Shanklin, W., Ryans, J., Jr. (1985). *Thinking Strategically: Planning for Your Company's Future.* New York: Random House.

Shapiro, E. C. (1991). *How Corporate Truths Become Competitive Traps.* New York: John Wiley & Sons.

Sibson, R. (1992). *Strategic Planning for Human Resources Management.* New York: AMACOM.

Snyder, N. H., Houghton, P. M. (contributor), Dowd, J. J. (contributor). (1993). *Vision, Values, and Courage: Leadership for Quality Management.* New York: MacMillan.

Stalk, G. Jr., Hout, T. M. (1990). *Competing against Time.* New York: The Free Press

Steiner, G. (1979). *Strategic Planning: What Every Manager Must Know.* New York: The Free Press.

Tourangeau, K. (1981). *Strategy Management: How to Plan, Execute and Control Strategic Plans for Your Business.* New York: McGraw Hill.

Tregoe, B., Zimmerman, J. (1980). *Top Management Strategy: What It Is and How to Make It Work.* New York: Simon & Schuster.

Trotter, W. (1984). *Strategic Planning Theory and Application.* Oxford, OH: Planning Executives Institute.

Ulrich, D., Lake, D. (contributor). (1990). *Organizational Capability: Competing from the Inside Out.* New York: John Wiley & Sons.

Unterman, I., Davis, R. (1984). *Strategic Management of Not-for-Profit Organizations: From Survival to Success.* New York: Praeger.

Vickers, G. (1970). *A Classification of Systems: Yearbook of the Society for General Systems Research.* Washington, DC.: Society for General Systems Research.

Von Bertalanffy, L. (1968). *General Systems Theory.* New York: Braziller.

Waddell, W. (1986). *The Outline of Strategy.* Oxford, OH: The Planning Forum.

Watson, G. H. (1993). *Strategic Benchmarking: How to Rate Your Company's Performance against the World's Best.* New York: John Wiley & Sons.

Weil, D. (1994). *Turning the Tide: Strategic Planning for Labor Unions.* New York: Lexington Books.

Weisbord, M. (1992). *Discovering Common Ground.* San Fransisco: Berrett Koehler.

Wheelwright, S. C., Clark, K. B. (contributor). (1992). *Revolutionizing Product Development: Quantum Leaps in Speed, Efficiency, and Quality.* New York: The Free Press.

Yankelovich, D. (1981). *New Rules.* New York: Random House.

Yavitz, R., Newman, W. (1982). *Strategy in Action: The Execution, Politics, and Payoff of Business Planning.* New York: The Free Press.

Index

Q

Quality measurement, 147
Quality network, 71–72
Quantity measurement, 147
Questionnaires, prebriefing, 73–74

R

Radical reengineering, 244–245
Rallying cry, 129–134, *see also* Ideal future vision
Reality check
 customer and key success measures, 145
 strategic management, 15–16, 231–234
Religion, 4
Request for Proposal (RFP), 241, 243
Resource
 allocation
  annual plans and strategic budgeting, 239
  business unit planning, 210
  support to be successful, 339
  ten ways to establish a budget, 241–248
 perceived constraints and private versus public
  sector planning, 328
 shared and matching strategic business units to
  mission statement, 212
Return on investment (ROI), 84, 177, 243
Review
 annual strategic and uptake
  annual review meetings, 308–309
  build and sustain a high-performance
   organization, 310–311
  time commitment, 310
  yearly assessment, 306–308
 Board of Director role, 24
 strategic management system
  institutionalizing, 15
  reinventing, 52
Revolutionary change, *see also* Change
 anticipated changes in next 10 years, 5–7
 implications for organizations of all types, 8–9
 the last 10 years, 3–5
 right answers, 9–11
Rewards programs, 245
Rewards/recognition team, 270, 279
RFP, *see* Request for Proposal
Ripple effect, 293, *see also* Rollercoaster of
 change
ROI, *see* Return on investment
Rollercoaster of change
 General Systems Theory, 37
 managing
  challenge, 262
  depression and anger, 260

 hope and adjustment, 261
 natural cycles, 262–267
 rebuilding, 261
 shock and denial, 259–260
 workshops on leading/mastering strategic
  change, 267–268
 principles and techniques, 293–297
 strategy development, 199, 202

S

SAIs, *see* Strategic action items
San Diego Department of Health, 119
San Diego Padres, 141–142
SaskEnergy Corporation, 227
Satellite systems, 6
Savings and Loans, 41–42
SBUs, *see* Strategic business units
Scattershot approach, 60
School districts, 52
SCLSC, *see* Strategic Change and Leadership
 Steering Committee
Scoreboard, 62
Screening, 146
Sears Corporation, 183
Self-funding, 145
Senior management, 4, 257–258, 284
SESS, *see* Strategic Environmental Scanning
 System
Shamrock organization, 289
Shared image, 213
Shock/denial, 259–260, 296, *see also*
 Rollercoaster of change
Simplicity, 192–193
Site-based management, 145–146
SKEPTIC, 79, 93, 94
Skeptics, 77
Skills, 256
SKYNET IV, 6
SMS, *see* Strategic management system
Socialism, 5
Speed, 190
Spillover effects, 212
SPOTS, *see* Strategic Plan On the Top Shelf
SPQ, *see* Strategic planning quick
SST, *see* Strategy sponsorship teams
Standard systems dynamics, 36
Strategic action items (SAIs), 201
Strategic budgets, *see* Budgets; Annual plans,
 strategic budgeting
Strategic business design, 158–160, 291–292,
 294–295